QUALITATIVE RESEARCH IN
INFORMATION SYSTEMS

D1376432

INTRODUCING QUALITATIVE METHODS provides a series of volumes which introduce qualitative research to the student and beginning researcher. The approach is interdisciplinary and international. A distinctive feature of these volumes is the helpful student exercises.

One stream of the series provides texts on the key methodologies used in qualitative research. The other stream contains books on qualitative research for different disciplines or occupations. Both streams cover the basic literature in a clear and accessible style, but also cover the 'cutting edge' issues in the area.

SERIES EDITOR
David Silverman (Goldsmiths College)

TITLES IN SERIES
Doing Conversational Analysis: A Practical Guide
Paul ten Have

Using Foucault's Methods
Gavin Kendall and Gary Wickham

The Quality of Qualitative Evaluation
Clive Seale

Qualitative Evaluation
Ian Shaw

Researching Life Stories and Family Histories
Robert L. Miller

*Categories in Text and Talk: A Practical Introduction
to Categorization Analysis*
Georgia Lepper

Focus Groups in Social Research
Michael Bloor, Jane Frankland, Michelle Thomas, Kate Robson

Qualitative Research Through Case Studies
Max Travers

QUALITATIVE RESEARCH IN INFORMATION SYSTEMS

A Reader

Michael D. Myers and David Avison

SAGE Publications
London • Thousand Oaks • New Delhi

SAGE Publications Ltd
6 Bonhill Street
London EC2A 4PU

SAGE Publications Inc.
2455 Teller Road
Thousand Oaks, California 91320

SAGE Publications India Pvt Ltd
32, M-Block Market
Greater Kailash - I
New Delhi 110 048

British Library Cataloguing in Publication data

A catalogue record for this book is available from the British Library

ISBN 0 7619 6632 3

Library of Congress Control Number is available

Printed and bound in Great Britain

Contents

Preface   vii

Acknowledgements   ix

Part I Overview of Qualitative Research

1   3
An Introduction to Qualitative Research in Information Systems
Michael D. Myers and David E. Avison

2   13
Choosing Appropriate Information Systems Research Methodologies
Robert D. Galliers and Frank F. Land

3   19
Power, Politics, and MIS Implementation
M. Lynne Markus

Part II Philosophical Perspectives

4
Studying Information Technology in Organizations: Research Approaches   51
     and Assumptions
Wanda J. Orlikowski and Jack J. Baroudi

5   79
The Case Research Strategy in Studies of Information Systems
Izak Benbasat, David K. Goldstein and Melissa Mead

6   101
Interpretive Case Studies in IS Research: Nature and Method
Geoff Walsham

7   115
The Critical Social Theory Approach to Information Systems: Problems
   and Challenges
Ojelanki K. Ngwenyama

Part III Qualitative Research Methods

8   129
A Critical Perspective on Action Research as a Method for Information
   Systems Research
Richard L. Baskerville and A. Trevor Wood-Harper

9   147
A Scientific Methodology for MIS Case Studies
Allen S. Lee

10
Scholarship and Practice: the Contribution of Ethnographic Research   169
   Methods to Bridging the Gap
Lynda J. Harvey and Michael D. Myers

11
CASE Tools as Organizational Change: Investigating Incremental and   181
   Radical Changes in Systems Development
Wanda J. Orlikowski

Part IV Modes of Analysing and Interpreting Qualitative Data

12   225
Information System Use as a Hermeneutic Process
Richard J. Boland, Jr

13
Symbolism and Information Systems Development: Myth, Metaphor and   241
   Magic
Rudy Hirschheim and Mike Newman

Bibliography   275

Author index   299

Subject index   307

Preface

Since the mid-1980s there has been increasing interest in qualitative research within the information systems research community. Today qualitative research is accepted as being able to provide important insights into information systems phenomena. Qualitative research involves the use of qualitative data, such as interviews, documents and participant observation, to understand and explain social phenomena. Qualitative researchers can be found in many disciplines and fields, using a variety of approaches, methods and techniques. In information systems research, there has been a general shift away from issues that are purely technological to issues that additionally include the managerial and organizational, hence an increasing interest in the application of qualitative research methods.

There have been three 'inspirations' for this book. The first stems from the success of Michael Myers' web resource entitled 'Qualitative Research in Information Systems' at www.auckland.ac.nz/msis/isworld/index.html, a joint publication of *MISQ Discovery* and *ISWorld*. This book is intended as a supplement to that work. Michael's work received the Value-Added Site Award for 1996-1997 sponsored by the Academy of Management's Organizational Communication and Information Systems Division and *ISWorld*. The above work is published in two forms. First, an archival version of the work was published in *MISQ Discovery* in 1997 (Myers, 1997a). *MISQ Discovery* is a department of *MIS Quarterly*, and is intended to engender new forms of knowledge dissemination. The journal is available in electronic form on the Internet at www.misq.org/discovery/index.html. Second, a living version of the work continues to be updated as part of both *MISQ Discovery* and *ISWorld Net* (Myers, living). *ISWorld Net* is an international information infrastructure for information systems researchers and educators throughout the world. Having a living version means that the work is dynamic and as an example of living scholarship is able to take full advantage of advances in computer and communications technologies.

The second 'inspiration' is the work of the International Federation of Information Processing (IFIP) Working Group 8.2 of which David Avison is chair. IFIP 8.2 has long campaigned for qualitative research in information systems and has held a series of conferences on qualitative research methods. The proceedings can be found in (Lee, Liebenau et al., 1997; Mumford, Hirschheim et al., 1985; Nissen, Klein et al., 1991). David has seen the atmosphere change at the three conferences from the tentative, almost apologetic, meeting in Manchester of people who argued that qualitative research had (possibly) a role to play in information systems to the most recent conference in Philadelphia by which time qualitative research in information systems (IS) had made a major impact. Many researchers wanted to hear more about our latest qualitative research work in IS.

The third inspiration is the perceived need for a book which brings together many of the best qualitative research articles in IS. Until now excellent articles on qualitative research in IS have appeared in many different places, for example in various journals and conference proceedings. In our international travels many colleagues have mentioned to us that a book which provided some of the 'classic' articles would be very useful, especially in the teaching of qualitative research methods and as a basic reader for PhD students in IS. The contribution of this book is to bring together many of these articles in one volume for the first time.

This book is therefore intended to satisfy the above needs and to complement the *MISQ Discovery/ISWorld* site. It provides many of the recommended readings in a readily accessible form. Following the introductory chapter, the book includes 12 chapters that discuss various approaches to qualitative research in IS. The authors are leading IS researchers from around the world.

The organization of this book is as follows: Part I provides a general overview of qualitative research in IS; Part II has chapters which introduce the reader to various philosophical perspectives; Part III includes chapters which discuss various qualitative research methods; and Part IV discusses modes of analysing and interpreting qualitative data.

We believe that providing a collection of articles such as this draws attention to the tremendous progress that has been made within the field of IS, particularly within the past decade. Our intention in bringing them together is to make them more accessible to IS scholars and students while at the same time making them available to qualitative researchers in other fields. We hope that this volume contributes to the further development of qualitative research in IS.

Michael D. Myers   David Avison
University of Auckland   ESSEC Business School, Paris
New Zealand   France

Acknowledgements

The authors and publishers wish to thank the following for permission to use copyright material.

Chapter 2: Association of Computing Machinery for Galliers, R. D., and Land, F. F. (1987) Choosing Appropriate Information Systems Research Methodologies, *Communications of the ACM*, 30, 11, 900-902

Chapter 3: Association of Computing Machinery for Markus, M. L. (1983) Power, Politics, and MIS Implementation, *Communications of the ACM*, 26, 6, 430-444

Chapter 4: Institute for Operations Research and the Management Sciences for Orlikowski, W. J., and Baroudi, J. J. (1991) Studying Information Technology in Organizations: Research Approaches and Assumptions, *Information Systems Research*, 2, 1, 1-28

Chapter 5: Society for Information Management and the Management Information Systems Research Center at the University of Minnesota for Benbasat, I., Goldstein, D. K., and Mead, M. (1987) The Case Research Strategy in Studies of Information Systems, *MIS Quarterly*, 11, 3, 369-386

Chapter 6: Macmillan Press and the Operational Research Society for Walsham, G. (1995) Interpretive case studies in IS research: nature and method, *European Journal of Information Systems*, 4, 2, 74-81

Chapter 7: International Federation of Information Processing Working Group 8.2 for Ngwenyama, O. K. (1991) The Critical Social Theory Approach to Information Systems: Problems and Challenges, in H.-E. Nissen, H. K. Klein, and R. A. Hirschheim (eds.), *Information Systems Research: Contemporary Approaches and Emergent Traditions*, North-Holland, Amsterdam, 267-280

Chapter 8: Association for Information Technology Trust for Baskerville, R. L., and Wood-Harper, A. T. (1996) A Critical Perspective on Action

Research as a Method for Information Systems Research, *Journal of Information Technology,* 11, 235-246.

Chapter 9: Society for Information Management and the Management Information Systems Research Center at the University of Minnesota for Lee, A. S. (1989) A Scientific Methodology for MIS Case Studies, *MIS Quarterly,* 13, 1, 33-52

Chapter 10: MCB University Press for Harvey, L., and Myers, M. D. (1995) Scholarship and research: the contribution of ethnography to bridging the gap, *Information, Technology & People,* 8, 3, 13-27

Chapter 11: Society for Information Management and the Management Information Systems Research Center at the University of Minnesota for Orlikowski, W. J. (1993) CASE tools as Organizational Change: Investigating Incremental and Radical Changes in Systems Development, *MIS Quarterly,* 17, 3, 309-340

Chapter 12: International Federation of Information Processing Working Group 8.2 for Boland, R. J. (1991) Information System Use as a Hermeneutic Process, in H.-E. Nissen, H. K. Klein, and R. A. Hirschheim (eds.), *Information Systems Research: Contemporary Approaches and Emergent Traditions,* North-Holland, Amsterdam, 439-464

Chapter 13: Institute for Operations Research and the Management Sciences for Hirschheim, R., and Newman, M. (1991) Symbolism and Information Systems Development: Myth, Metaphor and Magic, *Information Systems Research,* 2, 1, 29-62

Part I

Overview of Qualitative Research

1 An Introduction to Qualitative Research in Information Systems

Michael D. Myers and David E. Avison

Information technology and systems have now become ubiquitous in the developed world. Information systems are important to the private and public sectors, to individuals, organizations, nations and global institutions. Information systems pervade such diverse areas as agriculture, manufacturing, services, education, medicine, defence and government. Today, information systems affect almost everyone.

A number of fields, such as computer science and software engineering, concern themselves with information technology *per se*. However, the discipline which focuses on the development, use and impact of information technology in business and organizational settings is 'Information Systems' or IS for short. This area of study is quite new - it only emerged in the 1960s - however, the field has grown substantially. Most universities throughout the world now teach information systems, and the field has reputable scholarly journals, prestigious international conferences, and national and international associations.

Whereas much of the early research in the field had a technical focus (for example, on automating the back office or optimizing decisions), in the 1980s the focus shifted to the *management* of information systems. Then in the 1990s the focus broadened considerably, from the management of information systems to the relationship between IS and *organizations as a whole*. IS, as a field of study, has now expanded to include issues such as communication and collaboration between people and organizations, inter-organizational systems, electronic commerce and the Internet.

Given the tremendous scope of the field, it is perhaps not surprising that there is also great diversity in the research methods and approaches used to study IS phenomena. Both qualitative and quantitative research are welcomed in our top journals, as long as the research itself is of a high quality.

The purpose of this book is to bring together for the first time many of the best, indeed 'classic', articles illustrating the use of qualitative research in IS. The authors are leading IS researchers from around the world. A collection of articles such as this draws attention to the tremendous progress that has been made within the field of IS, particularly within the past decade.

This book is also intended to complement Michael Myers' web resource entitled 'Qualitative Research in Information Systems' (originally found in Myers, 1997a) (see also Myers, 1997b). The living version of this work can be found at www.auckland.ac.nz/msis/isworld (Myers, living). This book provides many of the recommended readings in a readily accessible form. Following this introductory chapter, the book includes 12 chapters that discuss various approaches to qualitative research in IS.

As an aside, these articles also evidence the richness of the topics in the IS domain and provide a good overview of the subject matter. We hope that you will use this book as only a starting point and that readers will wish to delve further, for example by looking into many of the references used (see bibliography). Our EndNote file of references in qualitative research can be downloaded from Myers (living).

The organization of this book follows the same structure as that of the web resource mentioned above. This structure is as follows: Part I provides a general overview of qualitative research in IS; Part II has chapters which introduce the reader to various philosophical perspectives; Part III includes chapters which discuss various qualitative research methods; and Part IV discusses modes of analysing and interpreting qualitative data. We have omitted a discussion of the use of qualitative techniques for data collection; this is because there are exemplars of their use readily available and their use is the same in IS research as it is in other disciplines. Good discussions of qualitative techniques for data collection can be found in Denzin and Lincoln (1994), Miles and Huberman (1984), Rubin and Rubin (1995) and Silverman (1993).

Overview of qualitative research

Research methods can be classified in various ways; however, one of the most common distinctions is between qualitative and quantitative research methods.

Quantitative research methods were originally developed in the natural sciences to study natural phenomena. Examples of quantitative methods now well accepted in the social sciences include survey methods, laboratory experiments, formal methods (for example, econometrics) and numerical methods such as mathematical modelling.

Qualitative research methods were developed in the social sciences to enable researchers to study social and cultural phenomena. They are designed to help us understand people and the social and cultural contexts within which they live. Examples of qualitative methods are action research, case study research and ethnography. Qualitative data sources include observation and participant observation (fieldwork), interviews and questionnaires, documents and texts, and the researcher's impressions and reactions.

Part I of the book contains three chapters that provide an overview to qualitative research. The article by Galliers and Land (Chapter 2) was one of the first articles in IS to argue for greater diversity in the use of research methods. Along with this present chapter, this sets the scene for the rest of the book. It is particularly interesting to read the technical correspondence that followed the article one year later (Galliers and Land, 1988; Jarvenpaa, 1988). We suspect that there would be more a meeting of minds today, with all authors agreeing IS researchers should choose research methodologies that are appropriate to the subject matter.

One of the classic (and most cited) empirical examples of qualitative research in IS is the article by Markus (Chapter 3). In a well-crafted article, she discusses how various theories help to explain power and politics in the implementation of Management Information Systems.

For a more in-depth look at the different methods being used by IS researchers, we recommend the following books edited by Galliers (1992), Mingers and Stowell (1997), Mumford, Hirschhiem et al. (1985), Nissen, Klein et al. (1991) and Lee, Liebenau et al. (1997). The latter three books were published under the auspices of the International Federation for Information Processing (IFIP) Working Group 8.2 (see http://istweb.syr.edu/~ifip/).

Philosophical perspectives

All research (whether quantitative or qualitative) is based on some underlying assumptions about what constitutes 'valid' research and which research methods are appropriate. In order to conduct and/or evaluate qualitative research, it is therefore important to know what these (sometimes hidden) assumptions are.

Part II of the book contains four articles looking at philosophical perspectives for qualitative research. For our purposes, the most pertinent philosophical assumptions are those that relate to the underlying epistemology which guides the research. Epistemology refers to the assumptions about knowledge and how it can be obtained (for a fuller discussion, see Hirschheim, 1992).

The article by Orlikowski and Baroudi (Chapter 4) develops some of the discussions of Chapters 1 and 2 and provides an excellent overview of the various research approaches and assumptions in IS research. Following Chua (1986), the authors suggest three distinct epistemological categories: positivist, interpretive and critical. This three-fold classification is the one that is adopted here. However, it needs to be said that, while these three research epistemologies are *philosophically* distinct (as ideal types), in the practice of social research these distinctions are not always so clear-cut. There is considerable disagreement as to whether these research 'paradigms' or underlying epistemologies are necessarily opposed and there is further debate about whether they can be accommodated within the one study.

It should be clear from the above that the word 'qualitative' is not a synonym for 'interpretive'. Qualitative research may or may not be interpretive, depending upon the underlying philosophical assumptions of the researcher. Qualitative research can be positivist, interpretive or critical (see Figure 1.1). It follows from this that the choice of a specific qualitative research method (such as the case study method) is independent of the underlying philosophical position adopted. For example, case study research can be positivist (Yin, 1994), interpretive

(Walsham, 1993) or critical, just as action research can be positivist (Clark, 1972), interpretive (Elden and Chisholm, 1993) or critical (Carr and Kemmis, 1986). These three philosophical perspectives are discussed below.

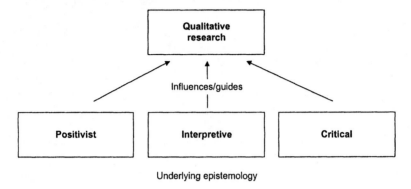

Figure 1.1 Underlying philosophical assumptions

Positivist research

Positivists generally assume that reality is objectively given and can be described by measurable properties, which are independent of the observer (researcher) and his or her instruments. Positivist studies generally attempt to test theory, in an attempt to increase the predictive understanding of phenomena. In line with this, Orlikowski and Baroudi (Chapter 4) classify IS research as positivist if there is evidence of formal propositions, quantifiable measures of variables, hypothesis testing, and the drawing of inferences about a phenomenon from the sample to a stated population.

The article by Benbasat, Goldstein and Mead (Chapter 5) is a good example of a positivist approach to doing case study research in IS.

Interpretive research

Interpretive researchers start out with the assumption that access to reality (given or socially constructed) is only through social constructions such as language, consciousness and shared meanings. Interpretive studies generally attempt to understand phenomena through the meanings that people assign to them and interpretive methods of research in IS are 'aimed at producing an understanding of the context of the information system, and the process whereby the information system influences and is influenced by the context' (Walsham, 1993, pp.4-5).

Examples of an interpretive approach to qualitative research include Boland (1991) and Walsham (1993). Klein and Myers (1999) suggest a set of principles for the conduct and evaluation of interpretive research.

The article by Walsham (Chapter 6) is a good example of an intepretive approach to doing case study research and therefore makes an interesting comparison with Chapter 5.

Critical research

Critical researchers assume that social reality is historically constituted and that it is produced and reproduced by people. Although people can consciously act to change their social and economic circumstances, critical researchers recognize that their ability to do so is constrained by various forms of social, cultural and political domination. The main task of critical research is seen as being one of social critique, whereby the restrictive and alienating conditions of the status quo are brought to light. Critical research focuses on the oppositions, conflicts and contradictions in contemporary society, and seeks to be emancipatory; that is, it should help to eliminate the causes of alienation and domination.

The article by Ngwenyama (Chapter 7) is a good example of a critical approach to IS research. Further examples are Ngwenyama and Lee (1997) and Hirschheim and Klein (1994).

Qualitative research methods

In Part III, we turn to qualitative research methods. Just as there are various philosophical perspectives that can inform qualitative research, so there are various qualitative research methods. A research method is a strategy of enquiry which moves from the underlying philosophical assumptions to research design and data collection. The choice of research method influences the way in which the researcher collects data. Specific research methods also imply different skills, assumptions and research practices. The four research methods that will be discussed here are action research, case study research, ethnography and grounded theory.

Action research

There are numerous definitions of action research; however, one of the most widely cited is that of Rapoport, who defines action research in the following way:

> Action research aims to contribute both to the practical concerns of people in an immediate problematic situation and to the goals of social science by joint collaboration within a mutually acceptable ethical framework (Rapoport, 1970, p. 499).

This definition draws attention to the collaborative aspect of action research and to possible ethical dilemmas that arise from its use. It also makes clear, as Clark (1972) emphasizes, that action research is concerned with enlarging the stock of knowledge of the social science community. It is this aspect of action research that distinguishes it from applied social science, where the goal is simply to apply social scientific knowledge but not to add to the body of knowledge.

Action research has been accepted as a valid research method in applied fields such as organization development and education. In IS, however, it is only within the last decade that action research has started to make an impact.

A brief overview of action research is the article by Susman and Evered (1978). Avison et al. (1999) and Baskerville and Wood-Harper (Chapter 8) provide an overview of the use of action research in IS.

Case study research

Case study research is the most common qualitative method used in IS (Alavi and Carlson, 1992; Orlikowski and Baroudi, 1991). Although there are numerous definitions, Yin (1994) defines the scope of a case study as follows:

> A case study is an empirical inquiry that:
> - Investigates a contemporary phenomenon within its real-life context, especially when
> - The boundaries between phenomenon and context are not clearly evident (p.13).

Clearly, the case study research method is particularly well suited to IS research, since the object of our discipline is the study of information systems in organizations, and 'interest has shifted to organizational rather than technical issues' (Benbasat et al., Chapter 5).

Case study research can be positivist, interpretive or critical, depending upon the underlying philosophical assumptions of the researcher.

A standard text for anyone wanting to do positivist case study research is the book by Yin (1994). Whereas Chapter 5 provides a good example of a positivist approach, the article by Lee (Chapter 9) suggests a scientific methodology for IS case studies. Lee argues that a case study is able to satisfy positivist criteria for scientific research. Interestingly, Lee cites Markus (Chapter 3) as being exemplar of positivist case study research.

For interpretive case studies, Walsham (Chapter 6) provides an excellent overview. Two good empirical examples of the interpretive case study method in IS are the articles by Myers (1994) and Walsham and Waema (1994). The article by Klein and Myers (1999) suggests a set of principles for the conduct and evaluation of interpretive case studies (and ethnographies) in IS.

Ethnographic research

Ethnographic research comes from the discipline of social and cultural anthropology where an ethnographer is required to spend a significant amount of time in the field. The ethnographer 'immerses himself in the life of people he studies' (Lewis, 1985, p.380) and seeks to place the phenomena studied in their social and cultural context.

After early groundbreaking work by Wynn (1979), Suchman (1987) and Zuboff (1988), ethnography has now become more widely used in the study of information systems in organizations, from the study of the development of information systems (Hughes, Randall et al., 1992; Orlikowski, 1991; Preston, 1991) to the study of aspects of information technology management (Davies, 1991; Davies and Nielsen, 1992). Ethnography has also been discussed as a method whereby multiple perspectives can be incorporated in systems design (Holzblatt and Beyer, 1993).

The article by Harvey and Myers (Chapter 10) provides an overview of the use and potential use of ethnography in IS research.

Grounded theory

Grounded theory is a research method that seeks to develop theory that is grounded in data systematically gathered and analysed. According to Martin and Turner (1986), grounded theory is 'an inductive, theory discovery methodology that allows the researcher to develop a theoretical account of the general features of a topic while simultaneously grounding the account in empirical observations or data'. The major difference between grounded theory and other methods is its specific approach to theory development. Grounded theory suggests that there should be a continuous interplay between data collection and analysis.

Grounded theory approaches are becoming increasingly common in the IS research literature because the method is extremely useful in developing context-based, process-oriented descriptions and explanations of the phenomenon.

The article by Orlikowski (Chapter 11) is a good example of the use of grounded theory in IS research.

Modes of analysis

Although a clear distinction between data gathering and data analysis is commonly made in quantitative research, such a distinction is problematic for many qualitative researchers. For example, from a hermeneutic perspective it is assumed that the researcher's presuppositions affect the gathering of the data - the questions posed to informants largely determine what you are going to find out. The analysis affects the data and the data affect the analysis in significant ways. Therefore it is perhaps more accurate to speak of 'modes of analysis' rather than 'data analysis' in qualitative research. These modes of analysis are different approaches to gathering, analysing and interpreting qualitative data. The common thread is that all qualitative modes of analysis are concerned primarily with textual analysis (whether verbal or written).

In Part IV, we look at modes of analysing and interpreting qualitative data. Although there are many different modes of analysis in qualitative research, just two approaches or modes of analysis will be discussed here: hermeneutics and approaches which focus on narrative and metaphor. Other approaches used in IS includes semiotics, and Klein and Truex (1995) provide a good example. It could be argued that grounded theory is also a mode of analysis, but since grounded theory has been discussed earlier, that discussion will not be repeated here.

Hermeneutics

Hermeneutics can be treated as both an underlying philosophy and a specific mode of analysis (Bleicher, 1980). As a philosophical approach to human understanding, it provides one philosophical grounding for interpretivism (see above). As a mode of analysis, it suggests a way of understanding textual data. The following discussion is concerned with using hermeneutics as a specific mode of analysis.

Hermeneutics is primarily concerned with the *meaning* of a text or text-analogue (an example of a text-analogue is an organization which the researcher comes to understand through oral or written text). The basic question in hermeneutics is: what is the meaning of this text (Radnitzky, 1970)? Taylor (1976) argues that:

> Interpretation, in the sense relevant to hermeneutics, is an attempt to make clear, to make sense of an object of study. This object must, therefore, be a text, or a text-analogue, which in some way is confused, incomplete, cloudy, and seemingly contradictory - in one way or another, unclear. The interpretation aims to bring to light an underlying coherence or sense (p.153).

The idea of a hermeneutic circle refers to the dialectic between the understanding of the text as a whole and the interpretation of its parts, in which descriptions are guided by anticipated explanations (Gadamer, 1976a). It follows from this that we have an expectation of meaning from the context of what has gone before. The movement of understanding 'is constantly from the whole to the part and back to the whole' (ibid.). As Gadamer explains, 'It is a circular relationship...the anticipation of meaning in which the whole is envisaged becomes explicit understanding in that the parts, that are determined by the whole, themselves also determine this whole.' Ricoeur suggests that 'Interpretation...is the work of thought which consists in deciphering the hidden meaning in the apparent meaning, in unfolding the levels of meaning implied in the literal meaning' (Ricoeur, 1974, p.xiv).

There are different forms of hermeneutic analysis, from 'pure' hermeneutics through to 'critical' hermeneutics; however, a discussion of these different forms is beyond the scope of this section. For a more in-depth discussion, see Bleicher (1980), Palmer (1969) and Thompson (1981).

If hermeneutic analysis is used in an IS study, the object of the interpretive effort becomes one of attempting to make sense of the organization as a text-analogue. In an organization, people (for example, different stakeholders) can have confused, incomplete, cloudy and contradictory views on many issues. The aim of the hermeneutic analysis becomes one of trying to make sense of the whole, and the relationship between people, the organization and information technology.

Boland's article (Chapter 12) is a good example of a research article in IS which explicitly uses hermeneutics. Other examples are those by Lee (1994) and Myers (1994).

Narrative and metaphor

Narrative is defined by the *Concise Oxford English Dictionary* as a 'tale, story, recital of facts, especially story told in the first person'. There are many kinds of narrative, from oral narrative through to historical narrative. Metaphor is the application of a name or descriptive term or phrase to an object or action to which it is not literally applicable (for example, a window in the Windows PC operating systems).

Narrative and metaphor have long been key terms in literary discussion and analysis. In recent years there has been increasing recognition of the role they play in all types of thinking and social practice. Scholars in many disciplines have looked at areas such as metaphor and symbolism in indigenous cultures, oral narrative, narrative and metaphor in organizations, metaphor and medicine, metaphor and psychiatry.

A good introduction to the use of metaphor in organizational theory is Morgan (1986). Polkinghorne's (1988) book on narrative has been extremely influential in the social sciences.

In IS, the focus has mostly been on understanding language, communication and meaning among systems developers and organizational members. In recent years narrative, metaphor and symbolic analysis have become regular themes in the International Federation of Information Processing (IFIP) 8.2 Working Group conferences.

The article by Hirschheim and Newman (Chapter 13) is an excellent example of the use of metaphor in information systems development.

Conclusion
We believe that providing a collection of articles such as this draws attention to the tremendous progress that has been made within the field of IS,

particularlyWe believe that providing a collection of articles such as this draws attention to the tremendous progress that has been made within the field of IS, particularly within the past decade. Our intention in bringing them together is to make them more accessible to IS scholars and students while at the same time making them available to qualitative researchers in other fields. We hope that this volume contributes to the further development of qualitative research in IS.

2 Choosing Appropriate Information Systems Research Methodologies

Robert D. Galliers and Frank F. Land

We believe we should draw attention to two disturbing tendencies in information systems research. The first relates to the primacy of traditional, empirical research more suited to the natural sciences at the expense of less conventional approaches that nevertheless provide important contributions to our search for improved knowledge. Although the experimental design of traditional IS research may well be academically acceptable and internally consistent, all too often it leads to inconclusive or inapplicable results. The second relates to the tendency of some of our most respected institutions to advocate a particular mode of IS research irrespective of the particular IS topic being studied. Evidence for both these contentions can be found in the results of a study undertaken by Vogel and Wetherbe (1984). For example, they suggest that as much as 85 percent of published IS research undertaken by leading U.S. institutions is of the traditional kind.

In order to gain some insight into what constitutes appropriate research in the field of IS, it is advisable first to consider the nature of information systems themselves and then to look at what we hope to gain from undertaking research in the area. Traditionally, the topic has often been viewed as residing, for the most part at least, within the province of technology. Increasingly, however, both IS academics and practitioners have begun to realize it is more appropriate to extend the focus of study to include behavioural and organizational considerations. This is explained by our wish to improve the effectiveness of IS implementations in organizations and to assess that impact on individuals or organizations.

This view of IS requires us to place computer-based information systems within the broader category of designed IS, which is itself just one component of our subject matter. Indeed, our field of study is much broader since it is concerned with IS and their relations with the organization and the people they serve (Land, 1986). This wider view brings with it added complexity, greater imprecision, the possibility of different interpretations of the same phenomena, and the need to take these issues into account when considering an appropriate research approach.

The problems inherent in IS research arising from this view of the subject matter and that call for new approaches are now well documented (McFarlan, 1984a; Mumford et al., 1985). Despite this, the focus remains for the most part on the scientific paradigm, the argument being that:

The empirical-analytical method is the only valid approach to improve human knowledge. What cannot be investigated using this approach, cannot be investigated at all scientifically. Such research must be banned from the domain of science as unresearchable' (Bleicher, 1982, p.141).

Rather than be banned 'from the domain of science' (or at least academic respectability!), the approach has been to treat IS research as a science, with as much as 50 percent of the effort being placed on laboratory-based experimentation or on field surveys (Vogel and Wetherbe, 1984). In both cases, heavy emphasis is placed on the use of statistical analysis, with the consequent need for exact measurement of the factors being studied; for example, x percent of a measured variance is due to factor y. Two major limitations of this style of research immediately surface:

1. There are only a limited number of factors that can be studied under laboratory conditions, and it is difficult to reproduce a 'real-world' environment in these circumstances. For example, a study of decision-making aids on the decision-making behaviour of a manager can only be properly studied in the real world decision-making environment (for example, one which is noisy, stressful and lacking in complete information). Studies that do not reproduce that environment may select as 'best' a technique that would be ineffective in the real world.
2. The need to apply values to variables often leads to the elimination of factors that, although they may have relevance, are difficult to value: thus applying to them zero value - which is probably the one value they do not have!

There are also grave dangers that arise from these limitations. The use of statistical tests implies a preciseness of measurement that is often not sustainable and could actually be misleading. The need to limit the number of factors studied could also lead to conclusions being drawn that again could mislead the unsuspecting. In this case, the problem is we are left not knowing whether different results could be obtained if other variables had been considered. Indeed, many researchers take pains to include caveats and disclaimers in papers arising from this kind of experimentation. And further research is invariably proposed with a view to discovering whether different results emerge from the study of different variables, thus compounding the fiasco.

Surely the measure of the success of research in an applied topic such as IS is whether our knowledge has been improved to the extent that this improved knowledge can be applied in practice. If, as a consequence of our experimentation, we mislead or produce conflicting or confusing results with little or no applicability, one is left wondering whether the experiment was worth undertaking in the first place and, more generally, whether much of this style of research is at all applicable to the IS field.

We would ask for greater diversity in the kind of IS research approach that is considered valid. IS is a meta-subject that spans many disciplines in the social sciences, in business, and, only occasionally, in the natural sciences.

Consequently, research that is appropriate in the latter is likely to be inappropriate in the IS field. IS, as we have defined the term, is also an applied discipline, not a pure science. It follows, therefore, that if the fruits of our research fail to be applicable in the real world, then our endeavours are relegated to the point of being irrelevant. Our research methods must take account of the nature of the subject matter and the complexity of the real world. The simple transference of research suited to the science laboratory to the study of IS is almost always doomed to fail.

A range of approaches is available to us, not simply the more traditional ones. Each has its own strengths and weaknesses (see Galliers, 1985) and will be more or less applicable in different circumstances. If greater thought is given to the choice of approach to take into account contextual factors, there is a far greater chance our endeavours will not be in vain. The research itself is likely to be more complex and difficult to pursue as a consequence, but the results are likely to make the effort worthwhile.

Unfortunately, due to the tendency to publish research of a more traditional kind, there are few published accounts of the successful application of the newer approaches. One well-documented exception to this rule relates to action research, for example in the application of so-called 'soft systems methodology' (Checkland, 1981).

To assist the IS researcher in making an appropriate choice, we propose a taxonomy of IS research methods (see Table 2.1). The taxonomy is based on those previously proposed by Galliers (1985) and Vogel and Wetherbe (1984). It differs from these earlier efforts, however, in that it does not suffer from the problem of overlapping categories by ensuring the *object* on which the research effort is focused and the *mode* by which the research is carried out are differentiated.

Most of the categories included in the proposed taxonomy require no introduction, given their common usage and the fact that detailed definitions have been provided in the literature already cited. However, two of the newer approaches, the subjective/argumentative and descriptive/interpretive categories, may require further explanation. The former is defined by Vogel and Wetherbe as capturing 'creative MIS research based more on opinion and speculation than observation' (Vogel and Wetherbe, 1984) and may therefore include some future research. The latter is illustrated by a number of papers in Mumford, Hirschheim et al. (1985), including one by Boland who classifies the approach as being in the tradition of phenomenology (that is, concerned with description). In addition, he recognizes the bias of the researcher in his/her observations, or rather interpretations, and hence the approach falls within the hermeneutical tradition as well. The simulation, or game/role-playing category, has been placed on the boundary of the traditional and newer approaches. This is to indicate that these kinds of approaches range from the positivistic (simulation) to the subjective (role playing).

Table 2.1 A taxonomy of IS reearch approaches

Object	Modes for traditional empirical approaches (observations)						Modes for newer approaches (interpretations)			
	Theorem proof	Laboratory experiment	Field experiment	Case Study	Survey	Forecasting[a]	Simulation[a] and Game/ role playing[a]	Subjective/ argumentative[a]	Descriptive/ interpretive	Action research
Society	No	No	Possibly	Possibly	Yes	Yes	Possibly	Yes	Yes	Possibly
Organisation group	No	Possibly (small groups)	Yes[b]	Yes[b]	Yes[b]	Yes	Yes	Yes	Yes[b]	Yes[b]
Individual	No	Yes	Yes	Possibly	Possibly	Possibly	Yes	Yes	Yes	Possibly
Technology	Yes	Yes	Yes	No	Possibly	Yes	Yes	Yes	Possibly	No
Methodology	No	No	Yes	Yes	Yes	No	Yes	Yes	Yes	Yes

[a]Includes future research
[b]Includes longitudinal field studies

The extended taxonomy for IS research hopefully illustrates the point that the scientific paradigm is not the only, nor indeed always the most appropriate basis for our research. Greater thought regarding the choice of research method is required as is a wider interpretation of what is seen as acceptable research. Hopefully, the proposed taxonomy assists on both counts.

3 Power, Politics, and MIS Implementation

M. Lynne Markus

No one knows how many computer-based applications, designed at great cost of time and money, are abandoned or expensively overhauled because they were unenthusiastically received by their intended users. Most people who have worked with information systems encounter at least mild resistance by those who are designated to input data or use the output to improve the way they do their jobs.

Many explanations have been advanced to account for people's resistance to change in general, to technological change in particular, and most specifically to management information systems (MIS) implementation efforts. Some of these explanations are informal rules of thumb that practitioners rely on in the heat of action; others are purportedly based on social scientific theories or research findings. Some are said to apply in every situation; others are contingent upon a variety of prevailing conditions. Some are mental models that form the basis for actions but are rarely articulated or explicitly examined for consistency and completeness; others are more formal models with clearly spelled-out connections. Familiar comments regarding resistance are:

1. To avoid resistance, get top management support and obtain user involvement in the design process (Lucas, 1974)
2. Technically sound systems are less likely to be resisted than those with frequent downtime and poor response time (Alter, 1975)
3. Users resist systems that are not 'user friendly' (assertions by IT equipment vendors)
4. All other things being equal, people will resist change (received wisdom)
5. People will resist an application when the costs outweigh the benefits (received wisdom).

Explanations of resistance are important because, however informal or implicit, they guide the behaviour and influence the actions taken by managers and systems analysts concerned with implementing computer-based applications. The premise of this chapter is that better theories of resistance will lead to better implementation strategies and, hopefully, to better outcomes for the organizations in which the computer applications are installed. This suggests the need to examine commonly used explanations and the assumptions underlying them in some detail.

Critical examination of implementers' theories regarding the causes of resistance is a process that, according to at least one view of resistance (cost versus benefits), implementers themselves may be expected to resist. Such examination is hard work, and the examiner runs the risk of discovering (a) that his or her mental models are just fine, in which case the effort appears wasted, or (b) that the explanations need changing, which is uncomfortable and requires more hard work. In addition, it is not likely that the commonly held heuristics mentioned earlier (for example, top management support) can be very far from wrong: in the first place, there is some academic research to support each one of them, and second, many analysts and managers have found that the heuristics have prevented them from making blunders in everyday situations. Consequently, many readers may decide that the uncertain benefits of examining their personal models of resistance are outweighed by the costs of doing so. This chapter is written either for those who compute the costs and benefits differently or for those whose behaviour is describable by a different explanation of resistance to change.

The argument of the chapter follows the following format: Three basic theories of resistance are presented and contrasted in terms of their underlying assumptions about information systems, organizations, and resistance itself. Several bases for evaluating the theories are enumerated, including the applicability of basic assumptions, the accuracy of predictions drawn from the theories, and the utility for implementers of the strategies and prescriptions derived from the theories. The chapter then proceeds to evaluate the theories using logic and the limited data of a single case. The chapter concludes with recommendations for implementers.

Types of theories

Kling (1980) has provided a very helpful starting point for examining theories of resistance. He identified six distinct theoretical perspectives: Rational, Structural, Human Relations, Interactionist, Organizational Politics, and Class Politics. Kling shows how these perspectives differ on a variety of dimensions, such as their view of technology and of the social setting into which it is introduced, their key organizing concepts, their ideologies of the workplace and of 'good' technology, and their implied theories of the dynamics of technical diffusion. For ease of comparison, he groups the first three perspectives into the category of Systems Rationalism and the latter three into Segmented Institutionalism.

This chapter builds upon Kling's work by exploring different theoretical perspectives as they relate to one small aspect of computing in organizational life - the introduction and implementation of computer-based information systems, and the human resistance that so often accompanies them. Since this chapter emphasizes the perspectives from the viewpoint of their implications for action, that is, for the implementation strategies of managers and systems analysts, rather than of their theoretical differences *per se*, this chapter may group Kling's perspectives differently while liberally drawing on his insights.

Three theories

An implementer trying to decide what to do about resistance of individuals or organizational subunits may hold one of three divergent theories about why that resistance occurred. First, the person or subunit may be believed to have resisted because of factors internal to the person or group. These factors may be common to all persons and groups or unique to the one being examined. Examples of explanations compatible with this theory are: people resist all change; and people with analytic cognitive styles accept systems, while intuitive thinkers resist them.

Second, the person or group may be believed to have resisted because of factors inherent in the application or system being implemented. Examples of compatible explanations are that people resist technically-deficient systems, systems that are not ergonomically designed, and systems that are not user friendly. A fair amount of research has been done to support the contention that technical and human factors problems are associated with resistance and system failure. For example, Ginzberg (1974) reviewed much of the (then) existing literature on OR/MS/MIS research and noted that several studies identified technical problems as a factor related to system failure (over 100 factors were mentioned at least once in the studies reviewed). Alter (1975) studied 56 systems and reported that technical problems were related to implementation problems in several cases.

These two theories are clearly divergent, because the first assumes that a person's (group's) behaviour is determined internally, and the second assumes that behaviour is determined externally by the environment or by technology. Nevertheless, implementers often implicitly hold both theories simultaneously, believing that behaviour is determined both from within and from without. An example of such a compound theory is: there is always a tendency for people to resist systems, but, other things being equal, they are less likely to resist ones that are well designed.

The third theory holds that people or groups resist systems because of an interaction between characteristics related to the people and characteristics related to the system. This theory is difficult to define, but easier to describe. The theory is *not* the same as a simultaneous belief in the two previously mentioned theories. The operant word in the definition is 'interaction'. Examples of explanations derived from the interaction theory are: systems that centralize control over data are resisted in organizations with decentralized authority structures, systems that alter the balance of power in organizations will be resisted by those who lose power and accepted by those who gain it, and resistance arises from the interaction of technical design features of systems with the social context in which the systems are used.

Several distinct variations of the interaction theory can be identified. One, which may be called the socio-technical variant, focuses on the distribution of responsibility for organizational tasks across various roles and on the work-related communication and coordination around this division of labour. New information systems may prescribe a division of roles and responsibilities at variance with existing ones; they may structure patterns of interaction that are at odds with the prevailing organizational culture. In this light, systems can be viewed as a vehicle for creating organizational change. The greater the implied change, the more likely the resistance. Similar articulations of a variant of the interaction theory can be found in Keen (1980), Ginzberg (1975), and Kling (1980).

It should be noted that this explanation identifies neither the system nor the organizational setting as the cause of resistance, but their interaction. The system-determined theory would predict that a given system be accepted or resisted in every setting because of its design features. The interaction theory can explain different outcomes for the same system in different settings. Similarly, the people-determined theory would predict the rejection of all systems in a setting in which any one system is resisted. The interaction theory can explain different responses by the same group of users to different settings. Compared with a concatenated people-plus-system-determined theory, the interaction theory allows for more precise explanation and predictions of resistance.

A second variant of the interaction theory can be called the political version. Here, resistance is explained as a product of the interaction of system design features with the intra-organizational distribution of power, defined objectively, in terms of horizontal or vertical power dimensions, or subjectively, in terms of symbolism. The appendix provides additional details on the political variant of the interaction theory and compares it briefly with other variants. The case analysis given in this chapter employs the political variant exclusively.

How are we to evaluate these theories? This is a difficult thing to do, if for no other reason than that there are several ways to do it, each of which may yield different results. Scientists are generally agreed that theories cannot be tested directly, which in our case means that it is impossible to say without doubt that people resist computer applications because of internal factors, external factors, or interaction effects. But the basic assumptions underlying the theories can be examined and compared with facts in the 'real world', predictions derived from theories can be tested against observed occurrences, and the implications for action derived from theories can be tested for their usefulness to implementers. This last test may be conducted independently of the first two, and implementers may prefer this. Because this chapter assumes that good implementation strategies derive from good theories, we attempt to address all three types of evaluations.

Basic assumptions of the theories

In order to perform the first type of evaluation, it is necessary to identify the assumptions that underlie the theories. Kling's list of theoretical perspectives yields two that are especially relevant for comparing theories of resistance with computer-based applications: assumptions about the nature of technology (in this case, information systems) and assumptions about the nature of the setting in which the applications are introduced. A third assumption can be added - beliefs about the nature of resistance. The first two dimensions, the people-determined and system-determined theories of resistance, are similar and easily contrasted with the interaction theory.

Assumptions about information systems

Information systems can be described and categorized in many ways: by type of processing technology - interactive or batch; by type of data (numbers, text, graphics, audio, video); by degree of centralization, distribution, or decentralization. One analytic scheme that proves especially fruitful for examining resistance is that of system 'purpose', which refers to the intentions of system designers. Purpose is a tricky thing to pin down, because systems can be viewed from many angles, and users may describe a system's purpose differently than designers. Rather than haggle about whose view is right, one can infer system purpose from system design features and other clues to the designer's goals, values, and intentions.

Generally speaking, system purposes can be lumped into two classes, depending upon whether the purposes are consistent with the Rational Theory of Management. Very briefly summarized, the Rational Theory of Management holds that organizations have goals and that they behave in ways that are consistent with achieving these goals. For many businesses, a major goal is to achieve a specified profit subject to certain constraints. System purposes that are consistent with the Rational Theory are: to rationalize work (achieve predictable outputs with consistent units of input - a goal of many operational systems), to enhance managerial decision-making and planning, to control and motivate the performance of employees toward agreed-upon goals, and to improve communication and coordination among people in the organization or between the organization and aspects of its environment (customers, suppliers, competitors, etc.).

Without denying the existence of these Rational purposes for systems, some researchers and theoreticians have pointed out that other purposes of systems can be identified. Kling (1978a) and Markus and Pfeffer (1981) have described systems whose purpose is to appear as though they were intended to rationalize work or to improve decision-making without having any real impact on organizational procedures or outcomes. Systems with this purpose can be useful in attracting outside funding or in discouraging external intervention. Another non-Rational purpose of systems is to change the balance of power inside a firm. The system described later in this chapter can be argued to have had the purpose of creating a power shift among organizational subunits, although great pains were taken to make the system appear as if the only motivations for it were Rational ones. Still another non-Rational purpose is to gain control over or reduce dependence on members of a different occupational group. Noble (1979) has described particular designs of numerically-controlled machine tools whose purpose, he argues, was for managers to wrest control over production from the hands of shop floor machinists. These purposes are not consistent with the Rational Theory, and hence are called non-Rational; there is considerable evidence to suggest that at least some systems are partly, if not totally, intended to achieve non-Rational purposes (Kling, 1980; Kling, 1982).

Assumptions about organizational contexts of use

The organizations in which information systems are used can be described by:

- *Structure:* functional, divisional, matrix, centralized, decentralized
- *Culture:* power-oriented, cooperative, Theory Z
- *Employment contracts:* professional, bureaucratic, semi-professional.

For purposes of understanding resistance, it is most useful to describe organizations in terms of the degree to which the people and subunits affected by the proposed information system are believed to have congruent goals and values or divergent ones.

The view of organizations that most frequently coexists with the Rational Theory of Management and with beliefs in the Rational purposes of information systems is that all organizational members share common goals for the organization and that, generally speaking, they will collaborate to achieve these objectives. In contrast, the non-Rational view assumes that different individuals or subgroups in the organization have different objectives depending upon their location in the hierarchy and that, in general, they can be expected to try to achieve these local goals rather than global organizational goals whenever differences exist. Some empirical work has described the existence of competing intra-organizational goal systems (Crozier 1964 and Dalton 1959 are classics), and analysts of the 'class politics' persuasion take chronic conflicts of interest between workers and managers as an article of faith (Braverman, 1974). Thus, there is reason to believe that, at least in some organizations at certain times, there are situations that do not conform to the Rational perspective.

Assumptions about the nature of resistance

Quite apart from one's view of the cause of resistance, people can hold different assumptions about the nature of resistance and the role it plays in organizations. As used in this chapter, resistance is defined as behaviours intended to prevent the implementation or use of a system or to prevent system designers from achieving their objectives. However, careful inspection of the trade press and even some MIS scientific literature will reveal that the term is also applied to behaviours that may not have these intentions. For example, the label 'resistance' is frequently applied to all cases of non-use of a system, even when non-use may reflect ignorance of the system's existence, inadequate training in system operation, or personal fear of the computer. This author would make the following distinction: where one individual's use of a system is not critical to the operation of a system, that individual's choice not to use the system cannot be considered resistance. Data entry is a use critical to the operation of a system; use of a decision support system to evaluate a stock portfolio by one analyst in a department of 20 is not. Resistance is easiest to identify when a person engages in behaviour that may result in the disruption or removal of a system that is interdependently used by others as well as by that person.

Social scientists are justifiably leery of any concept that requires an attribution of intention, for two reasons. First, behaviours can be observed, but intentions cannot. Second, the act of attributing intention often indicates more about the person doing the attributing than about the person to whom the intention is attributed. In other words, many people who identify behaviour as resistance are really saying, 'they are not doing things the way I want them to'. This implies that resistance is a relative rather than an absolute behaviour. It can only be defined in the context of two or more parties, each with desires and intentions. Party A intends to introduce a change of certain design; party B intends to prevent this from happening. Consequently, resistance can only be believed to be bad or undesirable if the intentions of the designer or implementer are accepted as good or desirable.

In the people-determined and the system-determined theories of resistance, the objectives and intentions of designers and implementers are never identified or analyzed. The implicit assumptions are either that designers' objectives are good, or that, whether good or bad, the intended users of a system do or should accept these objectives. Consequently, both of these theories tend to regard resistance as a negative result, which must be avoided or overcome.

In contrast, the interaction theory does not examine resistance out of the context of designer's intentions. The interests and intentions of both users and designers are identified and compared. When these interests are very similar, resistance rarely occurs. As the difference between their interests widens, the possibility of resistance increases. Resistance is viewed as neither good nor bad, unless you align yourself with the interests of either party. Resistance can be destructive, because it generates conflict and ill-will and consumes time and attention. But resistance can also be functional for organizations, by preventing the installation of systems whose use might have on-going negative consequences (for example, stress, turnover, reduced performance).

Table 3.1 summarizes the underlying assumptions about information systems, organizations, and resistance for each of the three theories. One basis for evaluating the theories is the degree to which data from real-world cases can be found to be consistent with the assumptions of the theories. If the assumptions are shown to be unrealistic or inoperative in natural settings, the theories may be rejected on this account. One case study from the author's research is presented to illustrate the application of the theories and to serve as a basis for preliminary evaluation.

Table 3.1 Theories of resistance: underlying assumptions

	People-determined	System-determined	Interaction theory
Cause of resistance	Factors internal to people and groups ------------------------- Cognitive style Personality traits Human nature	System factors, such as technical excellence and ergonomics ------------------------------- Lack of user friendliness Poor human factors Inadequate technical design or implementation	Interaction of system and context of use --- Socio-technical variant: Interaction of system with division of labour Political variant: Interaction of system with distribution of intra-organizational power
Assumptions about purposes of information systems	Purposes of systems are consistent with Rational Theory of management, can be excluded from further consideration	Purposes of systems are consistent with Rational Theory of Management, can be excluded from further consideration	Socio-technical variant: Systems may have the purpose to change organizational culture, not just workflow Political variant: Systems may be intended to change the balance of power
Assumptions about organizations	Organizational goals shared by all participants	Organizational goals shared by all participants	Socio-technical variant: Goals conditioned by history Political variant: Goals differ by organizational location; conflict is endemic
Assumptions about resistance	Resistance is attribute of the intended system user; undesirable behaviour	Resistance is attribute of intended system user; undesirable behaviour	Resistance is a product of the setting, users, and designers; neither desirable nor undesirable

Background of the FIS case study

The methodology employed in this case research study was historical reconstruction of the initiation, design process, design content, installation, and use of information systems in large manufacturing firms (Markus, 1979). Sources of data included interviews with over 30 designers and users of the systems and documentary evidence about the systems and the organizations. The documentary evidence included corporate annual reports (spanning, in the case of a financial information system (FIS), 15 years from 1964 to 1979), organizational charts, system training manuals, and design documents, and internal correspondence about the systems. Our account is organized as follows. The system is briefly described. Then the context of system use is examined to see whether the three theories apply. First, are there differences between resistors and non-resistors? Second, are there technical problems with the system? Third, what is the political context of system use? Subsequently, we evaluate the theories in the light of case data.

The FIS system

A financial information system collects and summarizes financial data for the Golden Triangle Corporation (GTC) (see Figure 3.1). The inputs to the system are transactions involving revenues and expenditures, assets and liabilities. The outputs are monthly profit and loss statements for each division and for the Corporation as a whole; balance sheets are produced by the system. The information managed by FIS is primarily used for external reporting purposes (to the SEC), although profit and loss information is relevant to managerial decision-making.

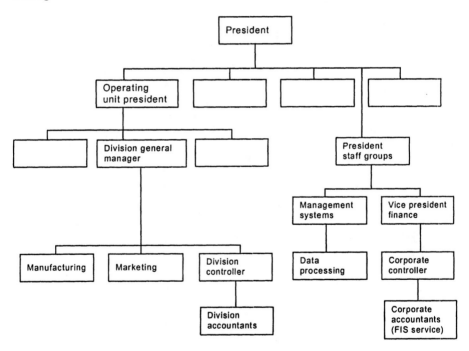

Figure 3.1 Golden Triangle Corporation, 1978

Obviously, financial reporting was not a new function at GTC, but FIS, installed in 1975, incorporated some innovative features. Prior to FIS, divisional accountants collected and stored transaction data however they saw fit, but reported summary data to corporate accountants in a standardized format (see Figure 3.2). With FIS, divisional accountants entered their transactions into the system (identified and retrievable by a 24-digit account code) which specified the type of transaction (asset - office furniture, expense - travel) and place of origin (group, division, plant). FIS automatically summarized these data into reports for corporate accountants and for the relevant division (see Figure 3.3).

In 1972, after the necessary investigations and approval, the task force arranged for the purchase of a financial accounting package from a software vendor (much to the chagrin of GTC's internal data processing department who would have preferred to build it themselves). The package purchased was designed so that it mirrored almost exactly the way in which financial accounting was then performed at GTC (see Figure 3.2), except that formerly manual databases were computerized, inconsistent summarization procedures were standardized, and consolidation was automated. Nevertheless, the FIS task force decided to modify the package, ostensibly to make use of modern database management techniques. In the process of modification, however, which took over 2½ years, the design team also replaced separate divisional databases with a single corporate database (see Figure 3.3).

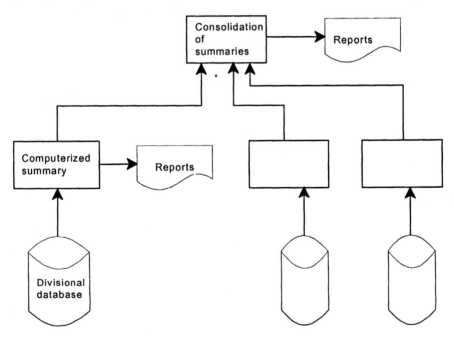

Figure 3.2 FIS purchased package design

The idea for FIS originated in the corporate accounting department around 1971. A task force was formed to evaluate the need for such a system and to estimate its costs and benefits. This task force was composed entirely of people from within the corporate accounting group, some of whom had considerable data processing experience.

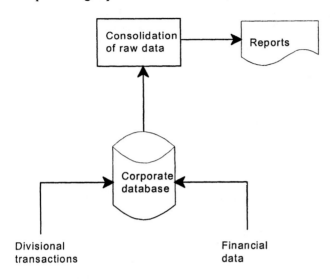

Figure 3.3 FIS final design

The task force members did not solicit information from divisional accountants about the design of FIS until 1974, when it was time to set up the database. Divisions were, however, invited to attend presentations describing the need for FIS and the benefits to be derived from it. Implementation of the system was to be done in phases. FIS task force members had decided to solicit a volunteer for the first division to 'go up' on FIS. After the initial division had found it workable, the other divisions would be required to use it. FIS was meant to be *the* corporate financial system.

Resistance to FIS

The largest division of GTC volunteered to pioneer FIS in January 1975. In October 1975, an accountant from this division wrote a memo complaining that

...Except for providing more detailed information, the FIS system has not been beneficial to us.

In response to complaints from this person and other individuals in several divisions, a study team was created to explore problems related to 'system inefficiency'. The study team met for several months and made technical recommendations to the data processing department. These changes proceeded slowly, and were set back in early 1977, when the data processing project leader quit.

In the meantime, other divisions had started up on the new system; all major divisions were using FIS by the end of 1975. This was surprising in light of the problems experienced by the initial FIS-using division, especially since participation in the system was supposed to be voluntary. Many accountants on the central corporate staff later pointed to this fact with pride as evidence of the success of FIS, but one person explained the incongruity as follows:

> Participation was voluntary on the surface, but there was a hidden inducement to participate. Those who wanted to wait to join FIS could do so, but they had to provide the same information manually. This would have been quite burdensome. So it really wasn't all that voluntary.

There is evidence that later divisional users were no happier about the new system than the original division. One division kept on using its old accounting methods after it started using FIS, even though this required twice the effort. There were frequent discrepancies between the two sets of books, and the staff of this division claimed that its system (thick manual ledger books!) was accurate and that FIS was at fault. The staff of this 'recalcitrant' division persisted in this behaviour for two years, until a member of the corporate accounting staff actually carried the old ledgers away. Some divisional accountants also admitted to slight 'data fudging' to circumvent the technical and human factors problems with the system.

> If it turned out that an account we needed had not already been defined to FIS, rather than wait for the special account creation run, we might change the plant code, just to get the data in. After all, we knew what the numbers really were!

At the same time, corporate accountants, who used the system for corporate consolidation, were delighted with it. FIS automatically performed tedious tasks of calculation and reporting that they had formerly done by hand. In addition, FIS provided several totally unanticipated benefits for them, such as automated tax accounting. Corporate accountants could not account for the resistance of the divisions' staff members. They bitterly denounced the 'troublemakers'. One said:

> I can't understand why the divisions don't like FIS. There are so many benefits.

But the divisional accounting staff apparently did not perceive these benefits, even after substantial experience with FIS. Here is an excerpt from another memo written by the accountant who first complained about the system in October 1975. This memo is dated August 1977.

> After being on FIS for several months, I expressed the opinion that the system was basically of little benefit. After two years and seven months, my opinion has

not changed. Even worse, it seems to have become a system that is running people rather than people utilizing the system.

When this author visited GTC, well over one year after that memo was written, many divisional accountants reported that they were still very unhappy with FIS.

Differences between resistors and non-resistors

From the preceding description, it can be seen that those who could be said by their behaviour to resist FIS were divisional accountants; those who accepted it and liked it were corporate accountants. According to the people-determined theory of resistance, resistors and acceptors should differ psychologically or cognitively in some significant way. In fact, several corporate accountants interviewed in 1979 subscribed to this notion: their stated explanation for the resistance was the personality characteristics of the resistors, who were 'troublemakers'. Although this author did not administer any psychological tests, there are some factors that lend credibility to the hypothesis that differences between the groups accounted for the resistance.

First, corporate accountants performed tasks that can be described as 'financial accounting'. They dealt with historical data, largely for purposes of external reporting. In contrast, divisional accountants, who reported to divisional general managers, can be described as 'managerial accountants'. They saw their role as one of providing future- and profit-oriented information to managers. Second, prior to 1975, there was little mobility between corporate and divisional accounting groups. Mobility would probably have encouraged more homogeneity in outlook; lack of it undoubtedly led to greater differences in outlook.

These differences, however, are not the inherent cognitive style differences usually studied by information systems theorists (Robey and Taggart, 1981). Rather, they are cognitive differences derived from status and functional location within a firm's hierarchy and division of labour.

Technical problems with FIS

According to the system-determined theory, resistance can be traced to human factors and technical design features. Evidence can be found in the FIS case to support the reasonableness of this contention.

Part of the reason for the complaints of early FIS users can be found in a series of technical and human factors problems with the system. The database management system chosen for this application did not work well with the computer's operating system, and there was insufficient main storage to meet the application's requirements. Consequently, downtime was frequent and reports were often late. At the same time, the schedules of monthly closings were not relaxed to accommodate the problems. In addition, the data entry procedures were cumbersome. For example, FIS represents accounts in 24-digit account codes; the system it replaced had 8-digit codes. New accounts had to be created almost daily, but to do so required a special computer run. In the special run, once weekly, the new account had to be related to the other accounts in the hierarchy. This was not quite as difficult as might be inferred from the 10^{24} possible accounts, but the rules for doing it were difficult to learn and not documented in a user manual. Transactions were entered into the system daily; those intended for an as-yet-undefined account wound up in a suspense account. Given the weekly periodicity of the account creation run, the suspense accounts often grew to staggering amounts.

Political context of FIS at GTC

According to the interaction theory, resistance can be attributed to an interaction between the design features of the system and features of its organization and social context of use. One aspect of this context is the intra-organizational politics and power dynamics between corporate and division accountants. Sufficient data exist in the FIS case to provide a basis for the plausibility of the interaction theory.

GTC is a major chemical and energy products manufacturing concern, with sales from its international operations exceeding $3 billion. It is currently decentralized into a staff group that includes corporate accounting and four operating groups with relative autonomy over marketing strategy and investment decisions for their product lines (see Figure 3.1). Within each operating group are several divisions, headed by general managers. Divisional accountants report directly to these general managers with only a 'dotted line relationship' to the corporate accounting group, whose role is to provide 'broad policy guidelines'.

This organizational structure dated back to about 1968. 1n 1967, Golden Chemical Company had merged with two energy product concerns to form GTC. In the restructuring, the old parent company was subjugated to a new corporate entity. This subjugation was reflected in the creation of a new staff group, corporation accounting, interposed between corporate management (which was disproportionately staffed with non-Chemical Company people) and the Chemical Divisions (see Figure 3.4). A Chemical Company manager (Howard) was chosen to head the corporate controller's office. Whether by accident or by design is unknown, but Howard was the rival of the head controller for the Chemical Company divisions (Spade). (Spade had hired Howard many years before.) Respondents described the relationship between the two men as 'strained at best', especially during 1972-1973, about the time that FIS was initiated and designed.

Howard found himself in an unenviable position. He had before him the task of creating an important and influential staff group where none had previously existed. Furthermore, his charter called for him to provide broad policy guidelines to all divisional accounting units, but he had no authority over them other than dotted-line relationships. Finally, because of his bad relationship with the Chemical Company controller, Howard was uncertain whether he had an accurate picture of reality: all data came to him through Spade.

Divisional Accountant. Corporate accountants felt the divisions were lying to them. And maybe there was some withholding of data on our side.

Corporation Accountant. Howard felt that the divisions were doing things behind his back, and that he needed a better way of ferreting out how the knaves were doing in the trenches. A large part of the reason for initiating FIS was to provide this information.

All three theories, then, appear at least plausible in the context of FIS since some data can be found to support their basic assumptions. It remains to demonstrate how well predictions drawn from each theory account for subsequent events in the case.

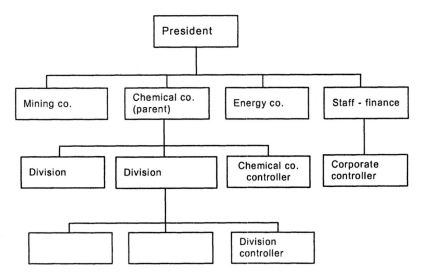

Figure 3.4 Golden Triangle Corporation, 1968

Predictions derived from the three theories

The people-determined theory leads to the prediction that replacing individual resistors or coopting them by allowing them to suggest improvements to the system might reduce or eliminate resistance. The system-determined theory predicts that if the technical features and human factors of a resisted system are changed, then resistance will disappear. The political variant of the interaction theory argues that neither of these changes will have much effect on the intensity of resistance if the resistance was generated by patterned interactions among competing groups. These predictions are summarized in Table 3.2.

Actual evidence from the FIS case supports the political variant of the interaction theory and gives no support to the other two. The test of a single case is not a strong proof, nor is it so intended here. But it can be a useful illustration. Consequently, the reader is invited to try out any version of the interaction theory on any familiar situation to test its ability to account for events. However, our exposition of the case does not stop with demonstrating the utility of the interaction theory in accounting for events: we now show the assumptions of the interaction theory to be useful in helping an implementer to predict, to gather data, to explain resistance, and to develop strategies for implementation.

Table 3.2 Theories of resistance: predictions

	People-determined	System-determined	Interaction theory (political variant)
Facts needed in real-world case for theory to be applicable	System is resisted, resistors differ from non-resistors on certain personal dimensions	System is resisted, system has technical problems	System is resisted, resistance occurs in the context of political struggles
Predictions derived from theories	Change the people involved, resistance will disappear	Fix technical problems and resistance will disappear	Changing individuals and/or fixing technical features will have little effect on resistance
	----------------	----------------	----------------
	Job rotation among resistors and non-resistors	Improve system efficiency Improve data entry	Resistance will persist in spite of time, rotation and technical improvements
			----------------
			Interaction theory can explain other relevant organizational phenomena in addition to resistance

Changing the people

The people-determined theory predicts, among other things, that if some acceptors were moved into positions occupied by the resistors, resistance among divisional accountants would diminish or vanish. While hardly a scientific test of this prediction, such an event did take place accidentally within GTC.

After 1975, GTC encouraged more mobility among corporate and divisional accountants for career development purposes. Under this policy, one of the corporate accountants who had participated in the design of FIS in the original design task force became the controller in one of the divisions. According to one informant, this accountant rapidly became convinced of the problems with FIS (at least as seen by divisional accountants) and became an active and critical member of the second efficiency task force formed in December 1977 to improve FIS.

Further, while it surely does not conclusively refute the people-determined theory, behavioural evidence and interview reports show that resistance continued. It persisted in 1979, four years after the introduction to FIS. Evidence to support this statement will be given shortly.

Fixing technical problems

The system-determined theory predicts that fixing technical problems eliminates resistance. The second FIS efficiency task force was formed in December 1977, composed of several 'resistors' (divisional accountants) in addition to data processing specialists. This task force made technical recommendations similar to those of the first task force, but also speculated about whether FIS should be scrapped and replaced. Before it could complete its deliberations on the latter issue, the second task force was disbanded in March 1978.

This date coincided with the completion of the technical recommendations from the two task forces. The Data Processing Department had purchased and installed a larger computer with a more powerful operating system. This technical change improved the efficiency of FIS. In addition, the processing mode of the system had been changed from a batch to a transaction (on-line) basis; together, these changes reduced downtime to an acceptable level. Changes were made to the method of data entry, from remote batch to on-line, and the method of creating new accounts was simplified.

In spite of all these improvements in technical features and human factors, divisional resistance to FIS did not disappear. In fact, when data were collected for this study, about one year after the last of these changes was installed, informants in the divisions still spoke resentfully of FIS. Many felt strongly that the system should be replaced because FIS was inadequate as a tool for managerial accounting, even though it (now) functioned adequately as a tool for performing financial accounting. (Managerial accounting was the chief concern of divisional accountants.) Corporate accountants, however, maintained that FIS was more than adequate for managerial accounting (not their specialty), and they were increasingly pressuring divisional accountants to use FIS for this additional purpose.

Organizational politics

The interaction theory predicts that neither changing people (by removing them, by educating them, or by attempting to coerce them), nor changing technical features of the system will reduce resistance as long as the conditions that gave rise to it persist. Resistance-generating conditions are mismatches between the patterns of interaction prescribed by a system and the patterns that already exist in the setting into which the system is introduced. According to the political version of the interaction theory (see the appendix), the existing political setting can be identified as follows.

Corporate accounting had little formal organizational power and no independent information on which to base its attempts to develop and administer broad policy guidelines. An obvious solution to this problem was to develop a system by means of which the necessary information would flow directly to Corporate Accounting without the intermediate step of manipulation by the divisions. This is precisely what FIS did, as can be seen in Figures 3.2 and 3.3.

The way in which FIS was designed implied a major gain of power for corporate accountants relative to their prior position vis-à-vis the divisional accountants. Prior to FIS, divisional accountants summarized raw data on the transactions in their divisions and sent the summaries to the corporate accountants for consolidation. Divisions retained control of their own data and exercised substantial discretion in summarizing it. This allowed them to 'account for' unusual situations before reports reached corporate accountants or divisional general managers. After FIS, however, all financial transactions were collected into a single database under the control of corporate accountants. The divisional accountants still had to enter data, but they no longer 'owned' it. FIS automatically performed the divisional summaries that both divisional and corporate accountants received. At any time, corporate accountants had the ability to 'look into' the database and analyze divisional performance.

Corporate accountants designed and used FIS to create a substantial change in the distribution of, or access to, financial data—a valued resource. It is not surprising that those who gained access (corporate accountants) were pleased with the system and that those who lost control (divisional accountants) resisted it by writing angry memos, maintaining parallel systems, engaging in behaviour that jeopardized the integrity of the database, and participating in a task force with the public objective of eliminating FIS and replacing it with another system.

Given the details of the design of FIS, it is likely that divisional accountants would have resisted it even if the loss of power implied for the divisions had been accidental. But there is some evidence that the corporate accountants acted deliberately in their design of the new financial accounting system. First, as mentioned above, they had sufficient motive to try to shift the power balance. Second, they clearly felt powerless in their dealings with the divisions. They staffed the FIS project team without any representatives from the divisions, who might voice objections to its design details. This group selected a package, which conformed in overall design principles to the existing information flows at GTC and modified it deliberately into a design that would alter the power balance between the two groups. Furthermore some observers with GTC were willing to ascribe the motivation behind FIS to political reasons. For example, the man who was Data Processing Manager in 1975 (long since gone to another company when interviewed in 1979) said:

> FIS was definitely established for political reasons... Howard wanted to take over the whole world... Therein started the wars between the Chemical Company and Corporate.

A design for FIS that entailed a power loss for one group and a power gain for the other could be expected to strongly affect power dynamics between the groups. Once the resistance of the divisional accountants is understood in this way, it is common sense as well as derivation from theory to hypothesize that changing human factors and even replacing a few key actors would do little to resolve the resistance. In fact, changing them did not eliminate the resistance.

Utility of the interaction theory to implementers

At this point, the superiority of the political variant of the interaction theory has been established based upon the ability of predictions drawn from it to account for the resistance to the system in one case. Rather than stop at this point, the case example can be extended a bit further to show what additional facts and data can be uncovered and explained by an analyst who uses this theory. These additional facts and data may be useful in designing an implementation effort. In the case of FIS, there are two additional relevant 'events': a reorganization of accounting within GTC that occurred in mid-1975, shortly after the start-up of FIS, and the on-going (in 1979) debate about what (else) should be done to or done about FIS.

In 1974, Spade retired. In the next year, his old position of Chemical Company Controller was first moved under the direct line control of corporate accounting and then eliminated the following year (see Figure 3.5). Similar changes were *not* made in the Energy Group of GTC. A member of the corporate controller's staff cited this as an example of what FIS was intended to accomplish:

> Corporate Accountant. If ... [the corporate reorganization in 1975 which eliminated Spade's job as Chemical Company Controller] ...had occurred several years previously, FIS might never have been instigated. The reorganization eliminated much of the need for FIS.

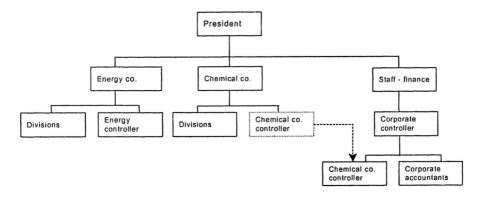

Figure 3.5 Golden Triangle Corporation, 1975

It may seem as though FIS caused this structural change. But it is probably more accurate to view the reorganization as an outgrowth of the same political situation that created the 'need' for FIS. The political variant of the interaction theory, then, helps an analyst understand this event and to explain the resistance it generated.

The political variant of the interaction theory also helps an analyst understand the dynamics of the intra-organization debate about FIS, which continued long after technical problems with the system were fixed. As interviews in 1979 disclosed, resistance to FIS had not disappeared but had changed its form: no longer were the divisions protesting the technical problems with the system (now solved); they were complaining that the corporate accountants were insisting they use FIS for tasks for which the system was inappropriate, namely, managerial accounting.

An administrator reporting to the President of one of GTC's operating groups summarized the feelings of many divisional accountants when he said:

> I think it's about time they realized that FIS is really an operational tool. It just can't do everything.

In this remark, he summarized the view that FIS had been grudgingly accepted by divisional accountants as a tool for performing financial accounting (balance sheets, taxes, and corporate consolidations), but that it was still being resisted as a managerial accounting tool. Divisional accountants argued strenuously that FIS was not useful for managerial accounting.

> FIS does not provide us with the data we need to prepare profit center reports. To prepare profit center reports we must maintain a separate system, the PGP system... They tell us we can use FIS for profit center reports! That's garbage! You *could* do it, but I've already told you how you have to enter data into FIS. To get a profit center report you have to enter each transaction by commodity code. There are a thousand commodity codes. This would be a horrendous job. Besides, PGP is our product gross profit report. We've had this system unchanged for almost ten years... Naturally, the profit figures from this and FIS should reconcile, but they never do, so we have to make the necessary adjustments...

But an analysis of interview notes, internal memos, and task forces minutes, covering the period from 1975 to 1979, indicates that the difficulty of using FIS was only a secondary complaint; proposed changes in the way managerial accounting would be done was the real issue, one that no amount of technical fixing would solve. Further, this real issue was one of potential loss of power for divisional (managerial) accountants. Consider the following evidence.

First, an early memo about FIS (outlining a presentation to GTC's top management) explained 'the direction we are heading' in the design of FIS. This direction represented a major shift in the way GTC did managerial accounting, that is, reporting to management about profit performance on specific products as opposed to the manipulation of aggregated, historical data. The intended shift in direction is clear in this excerpt from a 1972 memo:

> The last item of deficiencies that we list is the inability to analyze results on a total variance basis by business unit or corporate-wide. By that, we mean a lack of sales information by principal product and the lack of product line profitability. What was the volume of a given product? What was its price for a given period? What did that product contribute at the gross profit level? To me, the guts of our operation is what we do on a product line basis. In addition, we do not report on a given plant profitability. We feel that all this type of information, as was indicated, should all be part of a Financial Information System and available to management when needed.

Thus, corporate accountants had intended from the very beginning that FIS be used for managerial accounting, not just, as its name implies, for financial accounting.

Second, corporate accountants did not immediately reveal these intentions to the divisions. When the staff in the divisions first heard about it they were surprised. In an October 1975 memo complaining about FIS, the divisional writer noted:

> I think we have to take a good look at what we have right now and improve it before we take *any additional tasks* proposed for the FIS system.

The 'additional tasks proposed' referred to product profit (managerial) accounting,

Third, corporate accountants were quite well aware that the divisions did not see eye-to-eye with them on the issue of managerial accounting. The second FIS task force was created, it will be recalled, in December 1977 in response to another angry memo written by the accountant in the first FIS-using division. Responding to that memo, a highly placed corporate accountant referred to the heart of the resistance issue in this memo written in August 1977:

> I must say that I am not surprised that your attitude toward the FIS system has not changed... That same attitude is shared by the entire financial [sic] staff of your division, and hence, FIS will never be accepted nor will it be utilized fully as an analysis tool by your division.

'Analysis tool' here means a tool to be used in the analysis of managerial-oriented profit data. (Note the use of the term 'financial' to refer to the duties of divisional accountants.)

Finally, the divisional accountants themselves were quite explicit in distinguishing between operational and ease-of-use problems and use of the system for managerial accounting purposes. When the second task force was formed, it was partly 'to improve things from a public relations point of view as well as from a technical point of view', according to one corporate accountant.

But the divisional members of the committee did not intend to settle for symbolic gestures. 'It was never really stated as such but one question we were looking at was: 'should we look for a new system?' Task force minutes in December 1977 confirm this:

> During the sessions we have had thus far, one complex question already surfaced: is the system capable of being any more than a giant bookkeeping system, for example, can it ever effectively serve divisional needs for budgeting, reporting, allocations, etc? Therefore, we see two related issues we will attempt to offer recommendations on: (1) ways to deal with problems so the system can be counted on to operate effectively during month-end over the short-term, and (2) what, if anything, must be done to assure us that, for the long-term, we will have a system usable as more than a consolidator.

Since the task force was disbanded before they could tackle the second question, we will never know what they decided, but interview data suggests that the divisions remained very negative both toward FIS and toward the corporate accountants' proposed 'additional' uses for it.

Here is the situation in summary. From the perspective of the divisional accountants, financial accounting is the legitimate domain of corporate accountants. A system intended primarily for financial accounting would have no real impact on the divisions, provided, of course, that it was reasonably easy to use. The FIS system was not easy to use, but it was also not just a financial accounting system. It was intended to encroach upon the legitimate domain of the divisional accountants, that is, managerial accounting. Divisional accountants would resist the use of FIS for managerial accounting even if it were easy to use, and, in fact, their resistance continued beyond March 1978.

Who won? Did the corporate accountants succeed in the attempt to alter the balance of power between themselves and the divisions? The answer is not altogether clear. The corporate accountants did succeed in having the second task force disbanded (the axe man was the Vice-President of Finance) in March 1978, after the technical problems had been solved but before the committee could decide to replace FIS. The divisional accountants succeeded in redressing the more egregious faults of FIS, but failed in having it removed. In all likelihood, the net result was something of a draw: the corporate accountants had better information than before, an important power advantage in their dealings with the divisions, but not quite the total victory they had wished; the divisional accountants had regrouped and entrenched themselves to prevent any further losses.

Implications of the theories for implementation

The preceding analysis may have convinced an implementer that the interaction theory, at least in its political variation, has superior explanatory and predictive power. But the true test of the theories for the implementer will lie in their implications for implementation. Interaction theories are distinctly different from the people-determined, the system-determined and the people-plus-system-determined views of resistance in their implications for action. An implementer holding the people-determined theory of resistance, for example, would find certain tactics appropriate. Among these are: carefully selecting the people who will use a new system or allowing users to self-select after careful explanations about the system; training and educating users to change their cognitive styles or attitudes about computing, getting users to participate in the design process so that they will feel more committed to the outcome; gaining support of the users' bosses who will encourage or demand compliance of recalcitrant users; changing organizational structures or reward systems to conform to the features of the system.

An implementer who believes that systems determine people's behaviour will consider some different tactics and some of the same tactics for different reasons. Among these are: modifying packages to conform to the ways people think, work or do business; training system designers to improve technical efficiency, ergonomic excellence, and a smooth man-machine interface; involving users in the design process so that the design is better than that which would have been developed without user input.

Implementers who hold both people- and system-determined theories simultaneously will pick and choose among the tactics. To these people, user participation in design is the most desirable tactic, because it is consistent with both theories, albeit for different reasons. In the face of prolonged or intense resistance, however, they are often forced to choose between changing people or organizational structures and modifying the system; and in the process, they reveal their theory of last resort.

Implementers who hold the interaction theory of resistance find that no tactics are useful in *every* situation. User participation in the design process, for example, is clearly contraindicated in cases where powerful authorities have decided that a specific change, unpopular with users, *will* take place (see Markus, 1981). In such situations, users are likely to resent strongly a tactic that is meant to make them feel as though they have some say in the matter, when they obviously do not.

One major implication of the interaction theory is that computer-based systems alone cannot accomplish the task of radical organizational change. If radical change is desired, a thorough analysis of the existing situation should be conducted to identify factors that will facilitate or hinder the change. Examples of such factors can be inappropriate reporting relationships among individuals or groups, incentive schemes that do not reward the desired behaviour or punish undesired behaviour, unclear allocation of responsibility for certain tasks. Changes in these areas should be made before a system is implemented, and the system should be designed to be consistent with the revised organizational procedures. In cases like this, the organizational changes may generate resistance, but once they have been implemented, a system that supports them is unlikely to be the target of resistance itself.

Another implication of the interaction theory is that the specific designs of systems are in part a product of the relationships between users and designers. In the case of FIS, the designers were also systems users, as opposed to systems professionals. But similar cases of resistance have occurred where design objectives and specifics have been set by supposedly 'neutral' parties such as operations researchers and systems analysts. According to the interaction theory, no designers are ever completely neutral. Consequently, a great deal of thought and attention should be given to the tasks of structuring the relationships between users and designers and of developing methodologies for designing and implementing systems. For example, many organizations with centralized computing facilities have deliberately decentralized systems development to improve relationships between users and designers.

The most important implication of the interaction theory is that the best prescriptions for an implementation strategy and for the specific design content of a system will follow from a thorough diagnosis of the organizational setting in which the system will be used. At present, system builders are using methods such as structured systems analysis that allow them to describe and analyze only the technical features of a setting that is to be automated. To design systems that will not be resisted or to devise ways to modify resisted systems, this technical systems analysis must be augmented with a social or political analysis of the sort performed for FIS. Table 3.3 summarizes these conclusions.

Table 3.3 Theories of resistance: recommendations for implementation

People-determined	System-determined	Interaction theory
Educate users (training)	Educate designers (better technology)	Fix organizational problem before introducing systems
Coerce users (edicts, policies)	Improve human factors	Restructure incentives for users
Persuade users	Modify packages to conform to organizational procedures	Restructure relationships between users and designers
User participation (to obtain commitment)	User participation (to obtain better design)	User participation is not always appropriate

Conclusion

The final evaluation of the interaction theory (in whatever variation) is to show how it is useful to the implementer of systems. The theory leads to a model of organizational analysis and diagnosis that can be used to design systems that do not generate resistance or to devise strategies to deal with settings in which resistance has already occurred.

In the case of FIS, an analysis of this sort could have been performed prior to the system analysis and development effort to identify where resistance was likely to occur. Given the facts presented in this chapter, the analyst would probably have concluded that divisional accountants would certainly resist design features such as (a) the ability of the corporate accountants to retrieve and analyze raw (unsummarized) data, and (b) the necessity to do profit analysis at a level of aggregation that was meaningless to them. Knowing this and his/her own motives, the analyst could decide upon a course of action that may have included:

1. Altering the design of the system in ways that would be more palatable to divisional accountants;
2. Sacrificing some of the corporate accountants' objectives for the system;
3. Allowing divisional accountants to participate in selected aspects or all aspects of the system design process;
4. 'Buying' acceptance of the system by giving divisional accountants some other concessions valued by them;
5. Touting the system from the start as the ultimate 'managerial accounting information system';
6. Terminating the proposed project.

Once FIS was designed and resistance already apparent, an analysis could have been performed to determine precisely why the resistance occurred and what could be done about it. This analysis would also be useful in helping plan future system implementations involving one or more of the parties affected by the original system. In the case of FIS, one would conclude that for corporate accountants to persist in pressing their view of managerial accounting is probably organizational folly. Furthermore, relations between the two groups are now badly strained. Successful future implementations of financial systems will necessitate either improving these relationships or providing solutions to problems perceived by the divisional accounting group.

The interaction theory has the apparent disadvantage of providing no universal, noncontingent advice to systems analysts and management implementers of systems. But it is more useful than other theories for predicting resistance and for generating varied and creative strategies that will help both to prevent it and to deal with it when it arises. Two observations on the use of the theory are in order.

First, one key to the successful use of the interaction theory is that the implementer consider himself or herself as one of the parties in the analysis. Self-examination of interests, motives, payoffs, and power bases will lend much to the implementer's ability to understand other people's reactions to the systems the implementer is designing and installing.

Second, the analyst should recognize that the goal of the exercise is not to 'overcome' resistance, but to avoid it, if possible, and to confront it constructively, if not. In some cases, this indicates that the implementer may have to lose the battle and sacrifice a pet system project in order to win the war. Resistance is not a problem to be solved so that a system can be installed as intended: it is a useful clue to what went wrong and how the situation can be righted. If the implementer can divorce the need to see a system up and working from the need to achieve a particular result, many more degrees of freedom exist. In conclusion, although the process is difficult and time-consuming, the results produced from the application of the interaction theory of resistance are often substantially better than those produced from the application of the universal heuristics derived from other theories.

Appendix: Details of the political variation of the interaction theory

Several variations of interaction theories are possible; the basic constraint is the notion that resistance is caused by an interaction between organization and system. The specific organizational concepts an analyst uses may vary. The set used in this chapter are concepts of intra-organizational power and politics. Other sets of concepts are also consistent with the interaction theory. One example involves concepts of organizational learning and change (see Ginzberg, 1975; Keen, 1981; Kling, 1980).

The primary assumption of the political variant of the interaction theory is that information systems frequently embody a distribution of intra-organizational power among the key actors affected by its design. Intra-organizational power is an attribute of individuals or subgroups, such as departments, within the organization; it can be defined as the ability to get one's way in the face of opposition or resistance to those desires (Pfeffer, 1981). There are a number of ways by which an individual or subgroup can come to have power in an organization, including personal characteristics, such as being an expert or being charismatic, but position in the formal structure of the organization often provides greater access to specific power resources and the legitimacy required to use them. Pfeffer (1981) describes the major determinants of power: dependence of others on the power holder, ability of the power holder to provide resources, ability of the power holder to cope with uncertainty and irreplaceability, and ability to affect a decision-making process. All of these determinants of power are relevant to an understanding of MIS implementation, but the most frequently cited is ability to cope with uncertainty. The raison d'être of MIS is to provide managers with useful information, presumably so that they can cope better with variances arising from their production technologies and from the external units that supply inputs to and distribute outputs from the core technology.

The information required to cope effectively with uncertainty is distributed throughout organizations in a non-random way; some people/groups have more access to this than others, and this gives them power. Many management information systems are designed in ways that redistribute non-randomly the information required to cope with uncertainty; thus an MIS can alter bases of power. For example, a relatively stable balance of power will develop in the relationships between the purchasing, engineering, operations, and production control departments in any manufacturing organization. Sometimes engineering will call the shots, sometimes manufacturing. The introduction of a new logistics system may funnel all key information through the production control department, thus giving them an unaccustomed power edge in their dealings with other groups. The result might be a permanent redistribution in the balance of intra-organizational power, unless something happens to prevent it. The sufficiently powerful 'something' is resistance by those parties who stand to lose in the reallocation of power.

The political variant makes some precise predictions about where resistance is likely to occur around the implementation of information systems. Power, as it has been defined here, is a valuable resource. People and organizational subunits may differ in the extent to which they actively seek to gain power, but it is unlikely that they will voluntarily give it up. When the introduction of a computerized information system specifies a distribution of power that represents a loss to certain participants, these participants are likely to resist the system. Conversely, when the distribution of power implied in the design of an information system represents a gain in power to participants, these participants are likely to engage in behaviours that might signify acceptance of it: frequent use and/or positive statements about the system. In general, one would not expect people who are disadvantaged in their power position by a system to accept it (gracefully), nor would one expect people who gain power to resist.

Testing these propositions might involve comparing distributions of power bases before a system is installed with the distributions implied in a system's design, that is, identifying the winners and losers if the system were to be used exactly as designed. Clearly, however, there are some problems with this procedure. Necessary conditions for resistance (acceptance) in the hypotheses as stated are that people perceive the system to represent a power loss (gain) and that people's behaviour adequately represents their feelings. In some cases, people may misperceive the loss (gain) they receive as a result of the system. In other cases, people may feel it is not to their advantage to engage in behaviours that could be labelled resistance: criticizing the system, avoiding it, trying to bring out changes (Pfeffer, 1981). Most of these factors argue that, of the people or subunits that lose power in an objective comparison of new system with former conditions, only some of these are likely to resist, or to resist with any strength. Strength of resistance would appear to be strongly related to size of the loss and perceived importance.

Some of the specific conditions in the design of an MIS that will spell objective losses or gains in power can be spelled out. It is important to note that a single system can represent a power loss for several individuals or subunits, and at the same time, a power gain for several others. Access to information is probably less important as a basis of power than is the ability to control access to information or to define what information will be kept and manipulated in what ways (Kling, 1978a; Laudon, 1974; Pettigrew, 1972; Pfeffer, 1978). When a system centralizes control over data, the individual or subunit that gains the control is likely to accept the system readily, while those units losing control are likely to resist, even if they receive access to larger amounts of data in return. Similarly, decentralization of control over data is likely to be resisted by the formerly controlling unit and to be accepted by units gaining control.

If control over data (whether centralized or local) has prevented certain groups from obtaining needed or desired access to it, distribution of data, even unaccompanied by control over it, will provide those receiving it significant power gains. Their dependence on the controlling group will be reduced since they will have an alternative source of data. They are likely to accept a system which accomplishes this distribution. On the other hand, those whose data monopoly is threatened in the process are likely to resist. Distribution of data that makes the performance of a subunit more visible, hence subject to control attempts by other units, is likely to he resisted by the group whose performance is exposed (Lawler and Rhode, 1976) and accepted by those who would like to influence the others' performance.

The strength of resistance is also likely to be affected by the organizational position of the person or subunit to whom one loses power. If the 'winner' is located in a vertically superior position in the hierarchy, resistance is much less likely than if the winner is a peer. Formal authority relationships tend to make power differences between superiors and subordinates more legitimate than similar differences among groups at the same horizontal level in the organization.

At this point, the philosophical stance of the political variant toward resistance should be clear. Resistance is neither good nor bad in and of itself; whether or not it is so labelled usually depends on the vested interests of the person or group doing the labelling. Resistance can be an important, even organizationally healthy, phenomenon by signalling that an information system is altering the balance of power in ways that might cause major organizational dysfunctions. The political variant assumes that systems have no inevitable impacts on the organizations that employ them; ultimately, impacts will depend upon the choices made by people about how to use them. Some of these choices are exercised in the design process; others are expressed in the form of resistance, when previously unforeseen consequences that negatively affect a legitimate group of users come to light. Noble (1979) makes a similar point about the impact of technological change generally. Specifically, people can alter management information systems as they use them and thus prevent the realization of implied power distributions by sabotaging the system, providing inaccurate data, not using the system at all, keeping other sets of records, circumventing the intent of the system while obeying the letter, and many other ways. Mechanic (1962) describes some of the bases of power available even to people very low in the organizational hierarchy that could give the ability to affect the final outcomes of an MIS, and Strauss (1974) describes other tactics that have been used laterally between horizontally related subunits.

The degree of resistance generated by the introduction of a computerized information system is seen, then, in the political variant as a variable intervening between the degree of change in the intra-organization balance of power designed into a system and the degree of power shift actually realized in the organization. Obviously, resistance is not the only factor that could intervene here. Systems in practice rarely match perfectly the intentions of designers, partly because of imperfections in the translation and partly because use contributes to learning about how the system ought to have been designed in the first place. Even more important is the degree to which powerful organizational actors, who may directly benefit from others' loss in power and who may actually intend such loss, are motivated to try to overcome the resistance. The pre-existing balance of power and the relative adeptness of various groups at the use of political tactics for avoiding and overcoming resistance will largely affect the net outcome for the organization. These considerations are summarized diagrammatically in Figure 3.6.

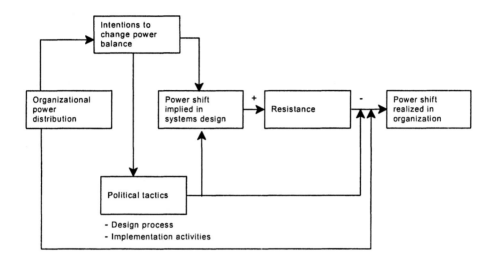

Figure 3.6 The political perspective

The fact that the political version of the interaction theory is only one of several raises the question, when is the political variant more likely than others to be appropriate for understanding MIS implementation? Pfeffer (1981) has discussed the circumstances under which organizational decision-making is likely to be accompanied by politics. While the process of designing systems is not the same as organizational decision-making, it is probably a special case; at least, some of the decision-making processes reported by Mintzberg, Raisinghard et al. (1976) bear a strong resemblance to the front-half of the information system life cycle. This implies that the political variant is most appropriate when conditions likely to produce political decision-making obtain: when there is disagreement about organizational goals and values; when uncertainty exists about the means required to produce the desired objectives; when resources are scarce; and when the decisions are important (Pfeffer, 1981).

Translating these factors into the information systems context suggests that the political variant is the most appropriate analytical framework when organizational participants disagree about the nature of the problem that a system is proposed to solve, when there exists uncertainty about whether a particular proposed system will solve the problem, and when the power bases allocated are highly valued and in short supply. These conditions are most likely to be met when the information system cuts horizontally across several diverse organizational subunits and has many different types of users. Thus the political variant may be more relevant to understanding the implementation of integrated operational information systems, whereas some other perspective, such as one based on concepts of organizational learning, may apply better to single-user decision support systems. However, although the political variant may not be most appropriate for every case, it considerably enhances the ability to explain and predict events surrounding the introduction of management information systems into complex organizations.

Acknowledgements

The author wishes to thank the many people who have made comments on the multiple incarnations of this chapter and the ideas contained in it, especially Rob Kling and Jeffrey Pfeffer.

Part II

Philosophical Perspectives

4 Studying Information Technology in Organizations: Research Approaches and Assumptions

Wanda J. Orlikowski and Jack J. Baroudi

The purpose of this chapter is to stimulate reflection on the implications of the research approaches we as researchers employ when we investigate information systems phenomena. Our intention is to motivate a more reasoned, reflective adoption of approaches from the diverse perspectives available to investigate the diverse arena of information technology development and use in organizations.

One of the most pronounced features of contemporary social research - and by this we mean those disciplines concerned with human phenomena (individual and collective) such as anthropology, psychology, sociology, and their applied fields of administrative science, education, industrial psychology and industrial sociology - is the great range of research perspectives that operate concurrently (Astley and Van de Ven, 1983; Burrell and Morgan, 1979; Morgan, 1980; Morgan, 1983; Pfeffer, 1982). These disciplines are marked by a plethora of 'schools of thought', each with its own meta-theoretical assumptions, research methodologies, and adherents. To the extent that one believes that the social phenomena studied within these fields are complex, the existence of a plurality of perspectives allows the exploration of phenomena from diverse frames of reference.

In information systems research, however, such a range of research traditions is not evident. In this chapter we present evidence of the lack of diversity in information systems research, by describing a survey in which we examined 155 information systems research articles published from 1983 to 1988. We found that although information systems research is not rooted in a single overarching theoretical perspective, it does exhibit a single set of philosophical assumptions regarding the underlying nature of phenomena being investigated, the appropriate research methods to be used, and the nature of valid evidence. Our intent in this chapter is to discuss the range of philosophical assumptions available to study IS phenomena, and to encourage greater debate and mindfulness around the assumptions we adopt when we embark on research investigations.

The chapter is structured as follows. In the first section we detail the results of a survey which provides evidence for a collective research tradition within the IS field, and discuss why we believe such a single philosophy toward studying IS phenomena can be limiting. In the following two sections we describe and illustrate two other philosophical research traditions which we consider to be valuable approaches to studying IS and their development and use in organizations. We conclude with some general recommendations for the information systems community.

A dominant perspective in information systems research

Much recent self-reflection in the IS discipline has involved discussion of the status of IS research vis-à-vis the norms of what constitutes a scientific discipline (Banville and Landry, 1989; Benbasat et al., 1987; Culnan, 1986; Culnan, 1987; Culnan and Swanson, 1986; Hamilton and Ives, 1982; Hirschheim and Klein, 1989; Keen, 1980; Klein and Welke, 1982; Lyytinen, 1987; Mumford et al., 1985; Weber, 1987). The purpose of these expositions has been to identify and articulate theoretical commonalities or topic syntheses. We argue however, following Chua (1986) and Webster and Starbuck (1988), that another indicator of a research tradition is the extent to which there exists a set of dominant philosophical assumptions or a worldview that informs the work of the researchers in a discipline. Chua (1986, p.602) suggests that a community of scientists share 'a constellation of beliefs, values and techniques' and these beliefs circumscribe definitions of 'worthwhile problems' and 'acceptable scientific evidence'. In the following section we show that information systems research has indeed been guided by a dominant worldview.

Evidence of a dominant perspective in information systems research

In an assessment of the published IS literature, Culnan's (1986) bibliographic citation analysis of IS research publications (1972 to 1982) established nine distinct (and disparate) research areas in the IS community. Further, Culnan (1987), again employing bibliographic citation analysis, identified five intellectual sub-fields within current IS research, suggesting 'that while MIS is still pre-paradigmatic, it has made progress, if one accepts the argument that MIS, like all social sciences, is a multiple paradigm discipline' (Culnan, 1987, p.347).

In this chapter we wish to argue that while there may be no theoretical or topic congruence among information systems researchers, there is a consistent philosophical world view that underlies much of the activity constituting IS research, and that binds IS researchers together. To explore this assertion we examined more than five years of published information systems literature - from between January 1983 and May 1988 - in four major IS outlets. These sources were *Communications of the ACM, Proceedings of the International Conference on Information Systems, Management Science,* and *MIS Quarterly.*

Table 4.1 displays the distribution of IS research published across these four sources. As we are concerned with research conduct, we excluded any conceptual or framework articles from consideration. A total of 155 empirical research articles were included in this analysis.

Table 4.1 Articles per journal

Journal	Frequency	Percent
Communications of the ACM	56	36.1
MIS Quarterly	49	31.6
Proceedings of ICIS	43	27.7
Management Science	7	4.6
TOTAL	155	100%

The research articles were categorized along several different dimensions. The first used Culnan's (1987) five topic-oriented research categories. These topic categories include research foundations, organizational approaches to IS, individual approaches to IS, IS management, and IS curriculum. Culnan's foundation and curriculum categories were excluded, as we were only concerned with approaches to research studies. The distribution of articles by Culnan's categories is presented in Table 4.2. This data confirms Culnan's (1986; 1987) conclusions in that, as in her studies, there does not appear to be one dominant theoretical topic area, but rather several different and distinct streams of research.

To explore the extent to which a dominant set of assumptions informs information systems research, we analyzed the sample in three different ways. The first is by research design, the second by time frame of the study, and the last by epistemology. A discussion of the implications of our findings is taken up in the following section. Table 4.3 presents the first breakdown showing the frequency of the various research designs. The three primary research designs that emerged from this analysis are case studies (13.5%), laboratory experiments (27.1%) and surveys (49.1%). These three designs account for almost 90% of the studies. Surveys, however, were clearly the dominant research method in this sample.

The data were then analyzed by time period of the study. Four different categories were sufficient to classify the data: one-shot cross-sectional, cross-sectional over multiple time periods, longitudinal, and process traces. Studies involving process techniques such as protocol analysis were classified separately, as they do not neatly fit into the other categories. They employ continuous data collection, but are not truly longitudinal, as the trace is typically conducted over a single discrete event - such as a meeting or problem-solving exercise - lasting a short period of time, such as a few hours. We distinguished between multiple-time-period, cross-sectional studies and longitudinal ones: the former employ some measure(s) administered at several time intervals, providing many discrete snap shots of the phenomenon; the latter are continuous studies, where the researcher engages with the phenomenon over an uninterrupted period of time, such as a few months or years. Longitudinal studies typically focus on issues of process. The breakdown of articles by time period is presented in Table 4.4. Static, one-shot, cross-sectional studies are clearly the predominant form of research in information systems. These studies account for 90.3% of the articles in our sample. Longitudinal and multiple time period studies account for only 4.5% and 3.9% of the sample, respectively.

Table 4.2 Articles classified by research category

Research category (Culnan 1987)	Frequency	Percent
Individual approaches to MIS design and use	85	54.8
MIS management	36	23.3
Organizational approaches to MIS design and use	34	21.9
TOTAL	155	100%

Table 4.3 Articles classified by research design

Research design	Frequency	Percent
Survey	76	49.1
Laboratory experiment	42	27.1
Case study	21	13.5
Mixed method	5	3.2
Field experiment	4	2.6
Instrument development	4	2.6
Protocol analysis	2	1.3
Action research	1	0.6
TOTAL	155	100%

Table 4.4 Articles classified by time period of study

Time period of study	Frequency	Percent
Cross-sectional: single snapshot	140	90.3
Longitudinal	7	4.5
Cross-sectional: multiple snapshot	6	3.9
Process traces	2	1.3
TOTAL	155	100%

Articles were finally examined for the underlying epistemology that guided the research. We followed Chua's (1986) classification of research epistemologies into positivist, interpretive, and critical studies. **Positivist** studies are premised on the existence of a priori fixed relationships within phenomena that are typically investigated with structured instrumentation. Such studies serve primarily to test theory, in an attempt to increase predictive understanding of phenomena. The criteria we adopted in classifying studies as positivist were evidence of formal propositions, quantifiable measures of variables, hypotheses testing, and the drawing of inferences about a phenomenon from the sample to a stated population. Exceptions to this are 'descriptive' studies. We found it useful to distinguish within the positivist category those studies where the researchers were working within a theoretical tradition, and those where the researchers' intentions were 'descriptive'. In 'descriptive' work, researchers attempted no theoretical grounding or interpretation of the phenomena; rather, they presented what they believed to be straightforward 'objective', 'factual', accounts of events to illustrate some issue of interest to the IS community. Our criterion for this 'descriptive' category was based on what the researchers thought they were up to in their exposition. That some might consider such 'objective' or 'factual' accounts problematic was seemingly not apparent to the researchers, or at least not evident in their discussion. 'Descriptive' articles typically included case studies, with or without simple descriptive statistics (frequencies and percentages).

Interpretive studies assume that people create and associate their own subjective and inter-subjective meanings as they interact with the world around them. Interpretive researchers thus attempt to understand phenomena through accessing the meanings that participants assign to them. In direct contrast to the 'descriptive' studies above, interpretive studies reject the possibility of an 'objective' or 'factual' account of events and situations, seeking instead a relativistic, albeit shared, understanding of phenomena. Generalization from the setting (usually only one or a handful of field sites) to a population is not sought; rather, the intent is to understand the deeper structure of a phenomenon, which it is believed can then be used to inform other settings. The criteria we adopted in classifying interpretive studies were evidence of a non-deterministic perspective where the intent of the research was to increase understanding of the phenomenon within cultural and contextual situations; where the phenomenon of interest was examined in its natural setting and from the perspective of the participants; and where researchers did not impose their outsiders' a priori understanding of the situation.

Critical studies aim to critique the status quo, through the exposure of what are believed to be deep-seated, structural contradictions within social systems, and thereby to transform these alienating and restrictive social conditions. The criteria we adopted in classifying critical studies were evidence of a critical stance towards taken-for-granted assumptions about organizations and information systems, and a dialectical analysis that attempted to reveal the historical, ideological, and contradictory nature of existing social practices.

Table 4.5 shows the breakdown of articles by epistemology. Positivism is clearly the dominant epistemology, accounting for 96.8% of the studies. 'Descriptive' articles make up a quarter of the positivist category, or 23.9% of the total sample. Interpretive studies represent only 3.2% of the total number of studies, and critical studies are not represented at all.

Table 4.5 Articles classified by epistemology

Epistemology	Frequency	Percent
Positivist	150	96.8
- 'descriptive'	*(37)*	*(23.9)*
- theoretically grounded	*(113)*	*(72.9)*
Interpretive	5	3.2
Critical	0	0
TOTAL	155	100%

The tables collectively show that while no one topic area or theory dominates IS research, there clearly is a prevailing set of assumptions about what constitutes acceptable IS research. This set of assumptions, that appears to influence much of the published IS research, is primarily survey or laboratory oriented, and investigates phenomena within a single cross-section or slice of time. It is not clear, however, that researchers consciously examine these assumptions; rather, it appears that they are largely taken for granted within the information systems research community.

Beyond a dominant research perspective in information systems research

Much of the IS research being conducted today is concerned with the ongoing relations among information technology, individuals, and organizations. For example, implementation studies (Alavi and Henderson, 1981; Franz and Robey, 1984; Ginzberg, 1981b; Lucas, 1981; Markus, 1983) are concerned with how information technology is successfully introduced into organizations. Systems development researchers (Bostrom and Heinen, 1977a and 1977b; Mumford and Weir, 1979) are concerned with building information systems that are efficient, effective, and that also increase users' job satisfaction. There is a large and growing interest in computer mediated support of communication, co-ordination, and group decision-making (Culnan and Markus, 1987; Kraemer and King, 1988; Malone et al., 1987; Poole and DeSanctis, 1989; Sproull and Kiesler, 1986). Information systems personnel researchers (Baroudi, 1985; Bartol, 1983; Ivancevich et al., 1983; Weiss, 1983) are concerned with understanding the processes that result in job dissatisfaction, turnover, and stress for systems builders. Other researchers have focused on the power shifts generated by technology and technological dependence (Lucas, 1984; Markus and Bjørn-Andersen, 1987; Saunders and Scamell, 1986). Many studies have been conducted into the effects of computerization on job skills and employment levels (see the review of studies by Attewell and Rule, 1984). The 'impacts school' of IS research examines the implications (individual, group, organizational and societal) of widespread use of information technology (Bjørn-Andersen and Pederson, 1980; Danziger et al., 1982; Kling, 1978b; Kling, 1980; Kling and Iacono, 1984; Laudon, 1974; Olson and Primps, 1984; Turner, 1984; Zuboff, 1988). These are only a sampling of topics that one can find under investigation; yet all share a common thread. All are concerned with the social processes surrounding the introduction, creation, use/misuse/disuse of information technology, as portrayed by Kling and Scacchi's (1982) metaphor of the ongoing 'web of computing.'

To date, as evidenced by the survey presented above, much IS research reflects a positivistic orientation, a research tradition that has its roots in the natural sciences. An exclusive view is, in our opinion, always only a partial view, and the dominance of positivism, by not acknowledging the legitimacy of other research traditions, has limited what aspects of IS phenomena we have studied, and how we have studied them. This has implications not only for the development of theory and our understanding of IS phenomena, but also for the practice of IS work. The findings of IS research filter into the practitioner community and are used as prescriptions for action. Restricted research, thus, has far-reaching consequences.

Through this chapter we wish to encourage a greater awareness and understanding of the diversity of assumptions that underlie various types of social research. In particular, we want to draw attention to the inadvertent restrictions we impose on our research when we unquestioningly accept the research assumptions of the dominant perspective. We suggest that there are a number of other philosophical perspectives that may be effective in helping us to study the phenomena of interest to information system researchers. In the following sections, we explore this claim in more detail by examining the various research perspectives with which social science researchers may approach their phenomena of interest. In discussing these various research approaches we draw on Chua's (1986) classification of the assumptions constituting the philosophical stances that researchers adopt towards the world and their work. Chua (1986, p.604) articulates three sets of beliefs that 'delineate a way of seeing and researching the world,' that is:

1.   Beliefs about the phenomenon or 'object' of study;
2.   Beliefs about the notion of knowledge; and
3.   Beliefs about the relationship between knowledge and the empirical world.

Various positions on these three sets of beliefs can be seen to constitute the distinctive research perspectives or worldviews that social science researchers have adopted towards their research (see Table 4.6).

Table 4.6 Beliefs underlying the conduct of research

Beliefs about	Explanation
Physical and social reality:	
Ontology	Whether social and physical worlds are objective and exist independently of humans, or subjective and exist only through human action
Human rationality	The intentionality ascribed to human action
Social relations	Whether social relations are intrinsically stable and orderly, or essentially dynamic and conflictive
Knowledge:	
Epistemology	Criteria for constructing and evaluating knowledge
Methodology	Which research methods are appropriate for generating valid evidence
Relationship between theory and practice	The purpose of knowledge in practice

Beliefs about physical and social reality.
Ontological beliefs have to do with the essence of phenomena under investigation; that is, whether the empirical world is assumed to be objective and hence independent of humans, or subjective and hence having existence only through the action of humans in creating and recreating it. Then there are beliefs about human rationality, which deal with the intentions ascribed by various researchers to the humans they study. For example, the discipline of economics is premised on beliefs about humans as utility maximizing, and as having limited access to information. Finally, there are beliefs about social relations, about how people interact in organizations, groups, and society. For example, researchers may believe social interactions to be stable and orderly in general, or they may believe them to be primarily dynamic and conflictive.

Beliefs about knowledge.
Epistemological assumptions concern the criteria by which valid knowledge about a phenomenon may be constructed and evaluated. For example, the positivist worldview asserts that a theory is true only if it is repeatedly not falsified by empirical events (Chua, 1986, p.604). Methodological assumptions indicate which research methods and techniques are considered appropriate for the gathering of valid empirical evidence. Which methods are considered appropriate clearly depend on how the veracity of a theory is established. Positivist researchers, for example, believe that large-scale sample surveys and

controlled laboratory experiments are suitable research methods, as they allow researchers a certain amount of control over data collection and analysis through manipulation of research design parameters and statistical procedures.

Beliefs about the relationship between knowledge and the empirical world.
These beliefs concern the role of theory in the world of practice, and reflect the values and intentions researchers bring to their work. That is, what do researchers believe is appropriate to accomplish with their research work, and what do they intend to achieve with a given research study. Some researchers pursue their research interests and certain kinds of theory to provide technical answers to specialized problems. Other researchers pursue theory which they hope will improve the social relations of organizations, or eliminate social inequities.

The following sections explore the underlying assumptions of three research philosophies that have been used to conduct social science research, including IS research: the positivist, interpretive, and critical philosophies. We will discuss each in turn, outlining the distinctive positions each assumes on the three sets of beliefs articulated in Table 4.6.

The positivist philosophy of information systems research

As indicated above, a positivist research perspective is dominant in information systems research - a status that reflects much of Western science. With roots in logical positivism, this perspective reflects the precepts informing the study of natural phenomena (Lincoln and Guba, 1985, p.36):

- The phenomenon of interest is single, tangible and fragmentable, and there is a unique, best description of any chosen aspect of the phenomenon.
- The researcher and the object of inquiry are independent, and there is a sharp demarcation between observation reports and theory statements.
- Nomothetic statements, that is, law-like generalizations independent of time or context, are possible, implying that scientific concepts are precise, having fixed and invariant meanings.
- There exist real, uni-directional cause-effect relationships that are capable of being identified and tested via hypothetic-deductive logic and analysis.
- Inquiry is value-free.

A number of commentators have indicated that the application of these precepts to research on social phenomena is problematic (Evered and Louis, 1981; Galliers and Land, 1987; Lincoln and Guba, 1985; Morgan, 1980; Morgan and Smircich, 1980; Weick, 1984). Indeed, many researchers practicing positivist research would agree that some of these precepts are ideals that are typically compromised in the exigencies of daily research activity. In the following we explore some of the assumptions underlying the positivist philosophy.

Positivist research philosophy: assumptions

Assumptions underlying the positivist research philosophy are examined in terms of Chua's (1986) three categories described above, as we will do for the other two philosophies in later sections.

Beliefs about physical and social reality.
Ontologically, positivist IS researchers assume an objective physical and social world that exists independent of humans, and whose nature can be relatively unproblematically apprehended, characterized, and measured. For example, organizations are understood to have a structure and reality beyond the actions of their members. The role of the researcher is to 'discover' the objective physical and social reality by crafting precise measures that will detect and gauge those dimensions of reality that interest the researcher. Understanding phenomena is thus primarily a problem of modelling and measurement, of constructing an appropriate set of constructs and an accurate set of instruments to capture the essence of the phenomenon. It is assumed, explicitly or implicitly, that there is a one-to-one correspondence between the constructs of a researcher's model and the events, objects, or features of interest in the world. The researcher herself is seen to play a passive, neutral role in this investigation, and does not intervene in the phenomenon of interest. For example, when researchers investigate the relationship between information technology and organizational structure, they assume structure to be objective and hence capable of being represented via a number of researcher-devised constructs and measures such as: span of control, division of labour, centralization, formalization, and hierarchical levels.

Most researchers subscribing to the positivist perspective assume that human action is intentional and rational, or at the least, boundedly rational. The assumption about social reality is that humans interact in relatively stable and orderly ways, and that conflict and contradiction are not endemic to organizations and society. When conflict does occur, its effect is seen to be dysfunctional to the social system (group, organization, or society) and hence it is something to be suppressed or overcome. Conflict is seen as serving to reveal some discrepancy in the system, as a symptom of a problem that can be corrected, hence preventing some potentially disruptive system breakdown.

Beliefs about knowledge.
With respect to knowledge, the epistemological belief of the positivist perspective is concerned with the empirical testability of theories, whether this requires theories to be 'verified' or 'falsified.' This belief, in what is known as the hypothetic-deductive account of scientific explanation, has two consequences (Chua, 1986, p.607):

* A search for universal laws or principles from which lower-level hypotheses may be deduced. Positivist researchers work in a deductive manner to discover unilateral, causal relationships that are the basis of generalized knowledge; that is, that can predict patterns of behaviour across situations (Putnam, 1983, p.41).

- A tight coupling among explanation, prediction, and control. If an event or action is only explained when it could be deduced from certain principles and premises, then knowing the principles and premises beforehand enables prediction and control of the event or action.

The search for general connections between information technology and changing environmental conditions or organizational forms - as evident, for example, in the contingency or transaction costs theories - assumes that the empirical world is largely characterized by knowable, constant relationships. To support such an epistemological belief, the positivist research perspective endorses a number of 'appropriate' research methodologies. The belief here is that following these sanctioned methodologies is the only way in which valid knowledge can be obtained - what Gibbons (1987, p.1) refers to as 'methodological monism.' He goes on to characterize the epistemological beliefs of this mode of inquiry as one in which units of data are assumed to be identifiable (for example, subjective attitudes) and assumed to exist independent of the method used to reveal or measure them. Sample surveys and controlled experiments are the primary data collection techniques, and inferential statistics is the data analysis method used to 'discover' causal laws. The validity and reliability of identifying and measuring instruments are crucial, as are researcher detachment from the research process, random assignment of subjects, and control over confounding influences. The concepts present in the language of the positivist research philosophy cannot reflect the everyday language usage of the study participants, as these are considered too ambiguous and subjective. Consequently, the concepts of positivist science 'must be redefined in order to eliminate the evaluative dimension and to ensure uniformity of measurement among researchers' (Gibbons, 1987, p.1).

An illustration of these practices can be found in Baroudi's (1985) work, where the author attempted to examine the relationship between boundary spanning activities of IS personnel, the ambiguity and conflict experienced as a consequence, and the impact this had on employee job satisfaction, organizational commitment, and turnover intentions. Each of the anticipated links was carefully stated a priori as an explicit hypothesis, and the direction of the relationship was pre-specified. The study paid close attention to employing standard instrumentation with established records of validity and reliability. Participants were required to express their experiences in terms of the researcher's constructs through questionnaire items, thus facilitating replication of this study and its findings by other researchers in other settings.

Beliefs about the relationship between theory and practice.
The relationship between theory and practice in the positivist philosophy is primarily technical. That is, as characterized by McCarthy (1978, p.139): 'If the appropriate general laws are known and the relevant initial conditions are manipulable, we can produce a desired state of affairs, natural or social.' Because positivists believe that scientific inquiry is 'value-free', what such a desired state of affairs is cannot be resolved scientifically. It is believed that as impartial observers, researchers can objectively evaluate or predict actions or processes, but that they cannot get involved in moral judgements or subjective

opinion. That is, researchers can comment on means, but not ends. This position is in direct contrast to that adopted by the interpretive and the critical philosophies, which argue that the very distinction between fact and value is itself a value judgement (Weber, 1947). The whole philosophical debate around the value-ladenness of assumptions, approaches, data, theories, and explanations is typically not engaged in by positivist researchers, who take for granted the value-neutrality of their position.

Another aspect of the value-neutral stance adopted by positivist researchers is the belief that they are detached from the phenomena of interest. Interpretive and critical researchers, in contrast, have argued that on a number of levels - conceptual, methodological, and substantive - all researchers are inherently implicated in the object of their research. In particular, this implication pertains to the role played by social research in practice. While it has been argued that there exists an independence between researcher and phenomenon of study in the natural sciences - though recent work in the history and philosophy of science has questioned even this assumption (Bernstein, 1985; Bhaskar, 1978; Kuhn, 1970b) - the same assertion cannot be made for the social sciences. While the results of natural science do not impinge on and change the nature of the phenomena studied, the results of social science do enter into the discourse of everyday human reality, and clearly can and do transform the nature of these phenomena. As Giddens (1987, p.19) notes, in the social sciences, unlike in natural science, there is no way of keeping the concepts, theories, and findings of the researchers 'free from appropriation by lay actors.' Clearly, IS research enters into the very constitution of the phenomena it studies. Indeed, a major goal of IS research is to have an impact on IS practice; that is, the findings of IS research are intended to inform and improve the development and use of information systems in organizations. Baroudi (1985), for example, concludes his study with recommendations for IS management. He states (p.353), 'The information systems manager may want to consider recruiting and selecting those individuals who have tolerances for both role ambiguity and role conflict, as these may be unavoidable conditions of the IS professionals' world.' To the extent that IS managers follow Baroudi's recommendations, they will change the relationships among the variables he observed. There clearly is a reciprocal and reflexive relationship between IS research and social reality; the two are not independent of each other. In the light of this, claims of objectivity and value-neutrality in information systems research may be misleading.

Positivist research philosophy: assessment

The positivist stream of research has institutionalized certain criteria of validity, rigour, and replicability in the conduct of scientific research. It has enforced standards of quality in empirical research, and has sought to build a tradition of cumulative knowledge across the various disciplines in which it is practised. Research models and results fill journals, and much has been learned about the development and use of information systems (Jarvenpaa, 1988). Difficulties arise, however, when proponents of this research perspective do not admit the validity of any other philosophical stance, precluding the possibility of different forms of knowledge and different assumptions about reality. From the perspective of many non-positivist researchers, such orthodoxy is unacceptably restrictive.

A number of commentators have discussed the limitations of the positivist research perspective (Burrell and Morgan, 1979; Chua, 1986; Lincoln and Guba, 1985; Morgan, 1983; Mumford et al., 1985; Putnam, 1983; Weick, 1984). We will just mention two here. The quest for universal laws leads to a disregard for historical and contextual conditions as possible triggers of events or influences on human action. The design and use of information technology in organizations, in particular, is intrinsically embedded in social contexts, marked by time, locale, politics, and culture. Neglecting these influences may reveal an incomplete picture of IS phenomena. Because the positivist research perspective tends to disregard the historical context of phenomena, positivist research studies are rooted in the status quo. For example, many of the IS research studies classified as positivist in the prior section were concerned with users' information system satisfaction levels. These studies, however, ignored the historical context within which systems are used which may affect satisfaction levels. Baroudi, Olson et al. (1986), for example, examined the link between user involvement, system usage, and user information satisfaction. While they found empirical evidence which suggested that user involvement was associated with information systems' satisfaction, they did not explore how the history and context of organizations may have influenced their data. The relationship between involvement and satisfaction may depend on the history of organizational practices regarding employee participation in decision-making. That is, where a firm has no tradition of worker involvement in organizational decision-making, the failure to consult users of technology may be less disruptive than in firms who have long-standing practices of involving their organizational members in workplace issues.

Likewise, the positivist aim to explain and predict external reality implies that people are not active makers of their physical and social reality. Positivistic research techniques encourage deterministic explanations of phenomena, in that these explanations emerge from interactions between the researcher and his subjects, where the researcher, by definition, dominates the relationship. In the search for causal relations, the positivist researcher focuses on the validity and control of the research procedures, and hence adopts a predefined and circumscribed stance towards the phenomenon being investigated. Such a posture is not conducive to the discovery and understanding of non-deterministic and reciprocal relationships. Laboratory subjects and survey respondents act and react mechanically to the research stimulus. Rowan (1973, p.210) notes: 'Research can only discover one-sided things if it insists on setting up one-sided relationships...You only get answers to those questions you are asking.' Only if we have strong reason to suspect that the relationships underlying our phenomena of interest, interaction among information technology and humans, are determinate and one-dimensionally causal, can we utilize such positivist techniques with confidence. As Markus and Robey (1988) elucidate, there is no reason to suspect that this is the case with information technology and human affairs.

In the following two sections, we examine two other research philosophies, the interpretive and the critical, which may offer powerful insight to our studies of IS phenomena.

The interpretive philosophy of information systems research

In this section we focus on the premises of the interpretive perspective, which is receiving increased attention and popularity in many social science fields (organizational studies, political science, sociology, marketing, education, and social psychology). A fundamental distinction between the interpretive and positivist worldviews is the former's primary presumption of social constructionism. Interpretivism asserts that reality, as well as our knowledge thereof, are social products and hence incapable of being understood independent of the social actors (including the researchers) that construct and make sense of that reality. The world is not conceived of as a fixed constitution of objects, but rather as 'an emergent social process - as an extension of human consciousness and subjective experience' (Burrell and Morgan, 1979, p. 253). The aim of all interpretive research is to understand how members of a social group, through their participation in social processes, enact their particular realities and endow them with meaning, and to show how these meanings, beliefs and intentions of the members help to constitute their social action. The interpretive perspective attempts 'to understand the inter-subjective meanings embedded in social life...[and hence] to explain why people act the way they do' (Gibbons, 1987, p.3).

Interpretive research philosophy: assumptions

Assumptions underlying the interpretive research philosophy are examined in terms of Chua's (1986) three categories described above.

Beliefs about physical and social reality.
Ontologically, the interpretive perspective emphasizes the importance of subjective meanings and social-political as well as symbolic action in the processes through which humans construct and reconstruct their reality (Morgan, 1983, p.396). For example, this tradition does not presume that organizational structure or social relations are objectively known and unproblematic, but attempts to understand how and why individuals, through their socialization into, interaction with, and participation in, a social world, give it a certain status and meaning. Meaning and intentional descriptions are important, not merely because they reveal subjects' states of mind which can be correlated with external behaviour, but because they are constitutive of those behaviours. Social reality is understood to be reproduced through ongoing interactions. Fay (1987, p.86) notes:

It is only because actors share certain basic conceptions that there can be certain types of social action. For example, the social practice of the market-place can occur given the shared constitutive meanings of (say) some conceptions of private property, the notion that in the exchange of goods and services some form of maximizing one's resources is the appropriate course of action, some idea of being an independent agent, etc.

Ontologically, interpretive IS research assumes that the social world (that is, social relations, organizations, division of labour) is not 'given.' Rather, the social world is produced and reinforced by humans through their action and interaction. Organizations, groups, social systems do not exist apart from humans, and hence cannot be apprehended, characterized, and measured in some objective or universal way. Unlike the premises of the positivist perspective where researchers are presumed to 'discover' an objective social reality, interpretive researchers believe that social reality can only be interpreted. While interpretive researchers share with the positivist philosophy a belief in relatively orderly interaction, this regularity is not attributed to functional needs of the social system, but to the shared norms and interests that bind humans together. While not positing conflict or contradiction as endemic to social systems - as does the critical philosophy (see the following section) - interpretive researchers recognize that as meanings are formed, transferred, and used, they are also negotiated, and hence that interpretations of reality may shift over time as circumstances, objectives, and constituencies change.

Beliefs about knowledge
The interpretive philosophy is premised on the epistemological belief that 'social process is not captured in hypothetical deductions, covariances, and degrees of freedom. Instead, understanding social process involves getting inside the world of those generating it' (Rosen, 1991). This philosophy challenges the positivist perspective's insistence of a disjuncture between everyday social practices and the language used to describe them. The interpretive position asserts that the language humans use to describe social practices constitutes those practices. Thus, understanding social reality requires understanding how practices and meanings are formed and informed by the language and tacit norms shared by humans working towards some shared goal. Interpretive researchers construct interpretations or explanations that account for the way that subjective meanings are created and sustained in a particular setting (Putnam, 1983, p.41). Such explanations are causal, but not in the positivists' uni-directional sense; neither are they sought for the same purpose. Interpretive researchers posit circular or reciprocally interacting models of causality, with the intention of understanding actors' views of their social world and their role in it.

The research methods appropriate to generating valid interpretive knowledge are field studies, as these examine humans within their social settings. Following on the ontological belief that reality is socially constructed, the interpretive researcher avoids imposing externally defined categories on a phenomenon. Instead of the researcher coming to the field with a well-defined set of constructs and instruments with which to measure the social reality, the interpretive researcher attempts to derive his or her constructs from the field by in-depth examination of and exposure to the phenomenon of interest. The categories and themes that emerge out of this approach are intended to closely couple those relevant to the study's participants.

The underlying premise of the interpretive researcher is that 'individuals act towards things on the basis of the meanings that things have for them, that meanings arise out of social interaction, and that meanings are developed and modified through an interpretive process' (Boland, 1979, p.260). In this attempt to understand meaning, positivist approaches are not useful. Rowan (1973, p.216) notes that in positivist research 'we are talking to "processed people" in the sense that they can only answer in terms of our questions and our categories.' In contrast, interpretive techniques allow participants to use their own words and images, and to draw on their own concepts and experiences. The primary endeavour is to describe, interpret, analyze, and understand the social world from the participants' perspective, and any rigid a priori researcher-imposed formulations of structure, function, purpose and attribution are resisted (Glaser and Strauss, 1967).

Beliefs about the relationship between theory and practice.
The interpretive research approach towards the relationship between theory and practice is that the researcher can never assume a value-neutral stance, and is always implicated in the phenomena being studied. Researchers' prior assumptions, beliefs, values, and interests always intervene to shape their investigations. The extent of researcher implication, however, is the cause of some debate within the interpretive tradition. Just as the positivist research perspective is not entirely homogeneous, with researchers differing on issues such as verifiability and researcher independence, the interpretive perspective is also differentiated. Two primary variants are recognizable, and they differ on the role of the researcher in investigating phenomena. Both variants recognize that human actors enact their physical and social reality, and that they come to share a set of meanings around this reality (Weick, 1979). In the 'weak' constructionist view, the researcher attempts, through various data collection techniques, to understand the existing meaning systems shared by the actors, and thereby interprets their action and events in her recounting. As Fay (1987, p.88) puts it: 'the social scientist is redescribing an act or experience by setting it into progressively larger contexts of purpose and intelligibility...[and] reveals what the agents are doing by seeing what they are up to and how and why they would be up to that.'

In the 'strong' constructionist view, however, the researcher is not merely presumed to describe a phenomenon in the words and categories of the actors, but is presumed to enact the social reality she is studying. Retelling the actors' story is never fully possible, as the interpretive schemes of the researcher always intervene, and hence the researcher in part creates the reality she is studying through the constructs used to view the world. Astley (1985, p.498) writes:

> The world of practice has its own 'objective' reality, but since as scientists, our only recourse to that world is through what we see and do, our knowledge is

unavoidably subjective in nature. The 'facts' constituting our knowledge, are necessarily theory-dependent, since we can perceive nothing except through the knowledge structure in which perception is embedded.... There is no direct access to reality unmediated by language and preconceptions.

This difference between weak and strong constructionist positions has implications for how interpretive research relates to research conducted in the positivist mode. From the viewpoint of weak constructionism, interpretive research is understood to complement positivist research, that is, by generating hypotheses for further investigation, and by filling in the knowledge gaps that positivist research cannot attend to, such as the contextual exigencies, the meaning systems, and the interaction of various components of a system. The researcher chooses between positivist and interpretive approaches based on the research question and the nature of the phenomenon of interest. This argument, postulated among others by Daft and Wiginton (1979), suggests that the positivist research approach (seen as encompassing 'low variety' techniques) is not complex enough to reflect all of the inherent complexity, ambiguity, and instability of organizational systems. Invoking the principle of requisite variety, Daft and Wiginton (1979, p.187) encourage the use of alternative 'high variety' methodologies. They note:

> If complex organizational behaviours are modelled as if they are simple, well understood, deterministic systems, or even as stochastic systems, then the resulting models will tend to be insignificant. We propose that languages of high variety are useful tools for developing models of organizations because they have sufficient scope and richness of meaning to describe organizational processes.

A similar case has been argued for IS research; that is, that the current positivist perspective has insufficient variety for the nature of the phenomena investigated by IS researchers (Benbasat et al., 1987; Kaplan and Duchon, 1988; Lee, 1991). And hence a call for triangulating the use of interpretive methods with positivistic ones has been issued.

For proponents of the strong constructionist view, however, no triangulation is possible, for there is no sense in which the interpretive perspective can accommodate positivistic beliefs. Interpretive research is seen to be based on philosophical assumptions that are essentially different from those of the positivist perspective. The role of interpretive research then, is not to complement positivist investigations, but to replace them. In this extreme view, a researcher cannot select his research perspective based on the nature of the phenomenon; for there is no way he can independently assess that nature without relying on his predispositions. Thus, in choosing a research approach, the researcher is in fact choosing which aspects of a phenomenon he wishes to focus on. The researcher constructs the form and nature of the phenomenon through the worldview he adopts to do the research. So the researcher's assumptions and values are deeply embroiled in the phenomenon - even in the very selection of a research approach. And if that is the case, then a researcher cannot really choose an 'appropriate' research method. One is reminded of Simons' allegorical tale recounted in Weick (1979, p.1) of the three baseball umpires disagreeing about the task of calling balls and strikes:

> The first one said, 'I calls them as they is.'
> The second one said, 'I calls them as I sees them.'
> The third and cleverest umpire said, 'They ain't nothing 'till I calls them.'

Interpretive research philosophy: empirical example.
In this section we will review a study exploring the interaction of technology in organizations which was executed using an interpretive research approach (Orlikowski 1989). This should help to illustrate the characteristics and assumptions of this approach.

Study description
In this study, Orlikowski (1989) studied how the deployment of information technology in primary business activities affected production workers. She was specifically interested in understanding how the use of information technology would change the division of labour and patterns of dependence among workers engaged in systems development work. The research site was a large consulting firm employing computer-aided software engineering (CASE) tools. Orlikowski studied several teams within the firm, making sure to include teams in all the various stages of the systems lifecycle. The study employed ethnographic techniques (Agar, 1980; Van Maanen, 1979; Van Maanen, 1988) such as observation of participants, researcher interaction with and study of CASE tools, documentation review, social contact, unstructured and structured interviews; and was executed over eight months, full-time within the firm and in those client sites where project teams were building application systems. Orlikowski employed a theoretical framework that focused her questions and observations; however, she used no structured instrumentation and conducted no statistical inference testing to analyze her data.

Orlikowski attempted to understand the implications of the CASE tools for the work and workers through understanding the norms and meanings the project team members shared around their work, how they interacted among themselves and with the CASE tools, and how these meanings and experiences changed with the deployment of the information technology. In her analysis she draws extensively on her field notes to illustrate and ground the findings. In addition to reporting the participants' experiences in their own words, Orlikowski attempts to interpret these experiences in terms of the theoretical model guiding the study. This theoretical interpretation allows her to restate the specific findings more generally, by deriving general interaction patterns that may be meaningful beyond the confines of the one research site.

Orlikowski found that the deployment of CASE tools had significant implications for the division of labour and relations of dependency among the project team members. In particular, she found that the use of information technology 'triggered structural changes within the project teams, which institutionalized the existing, formalized fragmentation into technical and functional groupings' and that such technological change 'undermines the homogeneity of the [firm's] "team" ideology by breeding subcultures and territorialism...[resulting] in tension and conflict on project teams.'

Study critique: strengths and weaknesses

This study has the distinctive flavour of interpretive research. Orlikowski clearly states her theoretical framework and assumptions up front, such that the readers may understand some of the biases she brings to the study. Second, she presents data directly from her field notes, hence allowing the readers to interpret the data and determine for themselves the adequacy of the interpretation. The study is careful to delineate the contextual conditions within which the research was conducted and the patterns of findings observed and analyzed. There is no underlying determinism, or search for universal laws. Orlikowski states:

> How this conflict is played out across various production arenas remains open to empirical elaboration...Different outcomes will be generated across different contexts and different outcomes may be generated over time within the same context. While such outcomes can never be predicted unequivocally, we can determine the likelihood of different patterns of response based on an understanding of contexts, actors, and resources.

The study draws heavily on participants' experiences and interpretations, and hence is very dependent on these interpretations. To the extent that individuals are confused, unaware, or deceptive, these findings will be misleading. A remedy would be to rely more on observation of participants or even participant observation on the part of the researcher, where intentions and impressions can be weighed against actual behaviours. Another limitation of this study is that while Orlikowski presents her field notes, we are only shown selected portions of the notes, and thus it is impossible to interpret this data within the context of the entire study and data collected. A possible, although potentially voluminous, solution would be to provide an appendix with some of the field notes presented in greater detail. Another potential shortcoming is the primary focus on CASE tools. We are left with little understanding of the organization or its members beyond their use of information technology. We have little understanding, for example, of how the recruitment practices of this firm may serve to reinforce its culture - perhaps more significantly than the information technology. Other potentially important structures, symbols, and practices of the firm are also not elucidated. However, the format within which these findings are reported - an article - are not conducive to lengthy descriptions of the site or explorations of the multifaceted nature of the workplace. Books have generally been the medium of choice for conveying interpretive research results, and the choice of an article in Orlikowski's case clearly limits her exposition options.

Interpretive research philosophy: assessment

The contribution of the interpretive research philosophy is that it reveals the underlying connections among different parts of social reality, by examining the social rules and meanings that make social practices possible (Gibbons, 1987, pp.7-8). This approach reminds us that the whole arena of social relations revolves around shared meanings, interpretations, and the production and reproduction of cultural and social realities by humans. It motivates investigations into how humans enact a shared, social reality through understanding human behaviour from the point of view and intentions of the human actors themselves. In particular, social process can be usefully studied with an interpretive perspective, which is explicitly designed to capture complex, dynamic, social phenomena that are both context and time dependent.

The interpretive research philosophy, however, has been subject to criticism (Bernstein, 1978; Bernstein, 1985; Burrell and Morgan, 1979; Fay, 1987; Gibbons, 1987). Fay (1987, p.92) suggests four different deficiencies. First, the interpretive perspective does not examine the conditions, often external, which give rise to certain meanings and experiences. Second, research in this perspective omits to explain the unintended consequences of action, which by definition cannot be explained by reference to the intentions of the humans concerned. These unintended consequences of action are often a significant force in shaping social reality. For example, Giddens (1979) suggests that an important and typically unintended consequence of human action is that which reinforces the actions, roles, beliefs, and relative power of members of a group, so as to sustain the structures and practices of that group as a whole over time. Third, the interpretive perspective does not address structural conflicts within society and organizations, and ignores contradictions, which may be endemic to social systems. This perspective cannot account for situations where participants' accounts of action and intentions are inconsistent with their actual behaviour, and hence it cannot discern or analyze the means by which actors may be blinkered in their self-understanding and limited in their social interactions. Finally, the interpretive perspective neglects to explain historical change; that is, how a particular social order came to be what it is, and how it is likely to vary over time. Fay (1987, p.96) notes that this perspective 'assumes an inherent continuity in a particular society, i.e., it systematically ignores the possible structures of conflict within a society, structures which would generate change.'

The critical philosophy of information systems research

An important distinction of the critical research philosophy is its evaluative dimension. More than either the positivist or the interpretive research perspectives, the critical researcher attempts to critically evaluate and transform the social reality under investigation. Where the other two research perspectives are content to predict or explain the status quo, the critical perspective is concerned with critiquing existing social systems and revealing any contradictions and conflicts that may inhere within their structures. Through fostering this type of self-consciousness and understanding of existing social conditions, critical researchers believe they can help to overcome oppressive social relations (Bernstein, 1978, p.181).

Critical research philosophy: assumptions

Assumptions underlying the critical research philosophy are examined in terms of Chua's (1986) three categories described above.

Beliefs about physical and social reality
The central idea within critical philosophy is the belief that social reality is historically constituted, and hence that human beings, organizations, and societies are not confined to existing in a particular state (Chua, 1986, p.619). Everything possesses an unfulfilled potentiality, and people, by recognizing these possibilities, can act to change their material and social circumstances. Despite this belief, the critical perspective recognizes that the capacity to enact change is constrained, because humans become alienated from their potential by prevailing systems of economic, political, and cultural authority. In the light of this alienation, an important objective of critical research is to create awareness and understanding of the various forms of social domination, so that people can act to eliminate them.

Another important idea in critical philosophy is that of totality, which implies that things can never be treated as isolated elements. A particular element exists only in the context of the totality of relationships of which it is a part, and the element and the whole are bound by an essential rather than a contingent interdependence. This dialectical relationship between elements and the totality is understood to be shaped by historical and contextual conditions. For example, a particular technology, such as a computer, is a productive force only in the context of those social relations in which it is used productively, such as a contemporary financial institution. In a different context of social relations, such as a pre-industrial society, that technology would no longer constitute a productive force. Or, following Chua (1986, p.619), consider system developers. They are not isolated elements that can be studied apart from their institutional and historical situation; rather, they exist only in the context of organizations producing and using information technology, and in the context and time of a society investing in information technology as a form of production and communication technology. Even as society and organizations give meaning to the roles, relationships, and actions of system developers, so system developers, by their action, help to shape and give meaning to the organizations and society of which they are members.

Social reality is understood to be produced and reproduced by humans, but also as possessing objective properties that tend to dominate human experience. Because of the dialectical understanding of elements and the whole, as well as the belief in human potentiality, the critical research philosophy emphasizes the processual development of phenomena. Social relations are not posited to be stable and orderly, but as constantly undergoing change. This instability is conceptualized in terms of fundamental contradictions that inhere in the social relationships and practices of societies and organizations (Benson, 1973; Edwards, 1979; Heydebrand, 1980; Ollman, 1976). The critical philosophy assumes that the contradictions inherent in existing social forms lead to inequalities and conflicts, from which new social forms will emerge.

Contradictions arise because of opposition among certain parts within the totality, and because of incompatible developments among the parts constituting the totality.

In their critique of advanced industrial societies, critical researchers examine the capitalist economies typical of these societies, and find a contradictory relationship between socialized labour and private appropriation of capital. Critical researchers thus posit that any organization that subscribes to the structural separation of labour and capital will embody antagonistic social relations, and that this inherent tension is the source of conflict as well as the basis of change. Further, because contradictory elements 'may be masked or concealed by a variety of devices - role segmentation, ideological formulations, segregation of participants, and others' (Benson, 1973, p.383), the role of critical research is to expose these hidden contradictions and thereby attempt to reframe the basic oppositions, potentially enacting a different social order. Contemporary critical researchers' view of contradiction is thus closely tied to their critique of class-based societies and capitalist forms of production. In this view, contradiction in social relations can only be removed by transforming the basis of society and the forms of organization and production - a state only attainable with the transcendence of capitalism.

Beliefs about knowledge

With respect to knowledge, the epistemological belief of the critical perspective is that knowledge is grounded in social and historical practices (Chua, 1986, p.620). There can be no theory-independent collection and interpretation of evidence to conclusively prove or disprove a theory. Because of the commitment to a processual view of phenomena, critical studies tend to be longitudinal (Benson, 1973, p.384). The research methods of choice are long-term historical studies and ethnographic studies of organizational processes and structures. Quantitative data collection and analysis are used, although to a lesser extent. The reliance on historical analyses is compatible with the belief that a phenomenon can only be understood historically, through an analysis of 'what it has been, what it is becoming, and what it is not' (Chua, 1986, p.621). This analysis leads to research outcomes that differ from positivist research. Benson notes (1973, p.391) that 'generalizations stemming from this approach would point to regularities of process rather than to cross-sectional differences,' and Burawoy (1985, p.18) comments that generalization in critical research 'seeks to illuminate the forces at work in society as a totality...[an] extension from the micro context to the totality that shapes it.'

These research outcomes differ from interpretive research on two counts. The first difference deals with the role of knowledge in human affairs; the second, with the relationship between theory and practice, which we deal with below. On the level of knowledge, critical researchers do not aim to only give a recounting or interpretation of how participants perceive, understand, and act towards various phenomena. As with interpretive researchers, critical researchers believe they need to understand the language of the humans they are studying, an understanding that is necessarily temporally and spatially bound. However, critical researchers depart from their interpretive colleagues, in that they believe interpretation of the social world is not enough. The material conditions of domination need also to be understood and critiqued, and these are typically not accessible by merely asking participants, who often are unable to perceive and penetrate the circumstances that shape and constrain them. Thus, researchers working in this tradition do not merely accept the self-understanding of participants, but also critically analyze it through the particular theoretical framework they adopt to conduct their work.

Beliefs about the relationship between theory and practice
The critical research philosophy towards the relationship between theory and practice is that the role of the researcher is to bring to consciousness the restrictive conditions of the status quo, thereby initiating change in the social relations and practices, and helping to eliminate the bases of alienation and domination. In this light, social research and social theory are understood as social critique. Steffy and Grimes (1996, p.326), writing about critical organizational research, note that its aim 'is to develop an organization science capable of changing organizational processes,' while Benson (1983, p.53) observes that critical theory must be 'reflexive, critical, and emancipatory, thus transcending alienated theorizing.' Burawoy (1985, p.18) writes that the nature and direction of this transcendence is suggested by the assumptions and theories that guide the research: 'A theoretical framework also leads us beyond what is, beyond verification, to what could be.'

   As with the other two perspectives we have discussed, researchers adopting the critical perspective differ in their beliefs about the role of the theorist in initiating social change. Benson (1983), for example, notes that the role of the critical researcher is always to go beyond mere studying and theorizing, to actively effect change in the phenomena being studied. Heydebrand (1983; 1985) extends this role even further by suggesting that critical research must also be reflexive, hence transformative not only of the object of investigation, but also of the investigator. Habermas (1963), on the other hand, distinguishes between the use of critical theories to initiate a process of self-reflection among human actors, and the actual selection of appropriate political action. While critical researchers are clearly responsible for the former, Habermas suggests that only participants in the community can carry out the latter task (Chua, 1986; McCarthy, 1978). He seems to assign a more analytic role to the researcher, although researchers, in their capacity as participants in organizations and societies, clearly could act to transform their social reality where appropriate. But neither this latter action, nor self-transformation, is seen as an essential component of his critical research agenda.

Critical research philosophy: empirical example

In this section we examine a study of the interaction between information technology and organizations that was executed using a critical research approach (Smith 1988). Reviewing such a study should help to highlight the unique characteristics of the critical perspective.

Study description

In this study, Smith (1988) was concerned with what impact the introduction of electronic point of sale (EPOS) systems in retail organizations would have on retail service workers. Working out of a critical perspective, he was interested in understanding how EPOS would influence the labour process, and in particular, the relationship between labour and management. Smith selected retail organizations based on the managerial control systems currently in place. He examined eight retail firms with established histories of Tayloristic work practices and much evidence of worker deskilling through management control systems (including technology). He contrasted these with eight other retail firms that had histories of craftwork practices and which had resisted management control systems that tend to deskill workers.

Smith conducted extensive interviews and observations in the sixteen different retail organizations. Beyond the upfront focus on labour process issues of control and deskilling, Smith reports no formal hypotheses and he employed no structured instruments or statistical inference testing. Smith draws on his field notes of interviews, observations, and documents to explain what he found, and to support the conclusions he drew. He suggests that the information technology represented by the EPOS systems did not change the control systems of the retail firms, but rather, that the retail organizations and, in particular, the institutionalized management control systems and history of work practices shaped the use and impacts of the EPOS systems. Smith reports that firms with established Tayloristic labour relations and work practices deployed EPOS to further deskill the workers, and used the information in the EPOS systems to centralize decision making in the hands of fewer and more senior managers of the organizations. In these efforts, not only the workers were affected; the local retail outlet managers found that their authority and decision-making discretion had been undermined. In striking contrast, Smith found that the use of EPOS in craft retail organizations, rather than being used to centralize buying decisions at senior levels and deskill workers, was used to provide information directly to the local managers, resulting in a greater decentralization of control and an increase in local autonomy. Smith (1988, p.159) concludes that the information technology represented by EPOS systems is 'malleable,' that is, capable of being deployed by managers in ways that reflect and sustain the existing social relations and management control systems.

Study critique: strengths and weaknesses

Smith's study can be seen to reflect a critical perspective, as the focus is on the social practices used by management to control the labour process. Underlying this focus is the assumption of conflict between labour and management, which it is believed is played out on the shop or office floor through the deployment of control systems and technologies. Additionally, Smith's work acknowledges the importance of history in shaping events. He examines the history of management control systems and work practices in the firms, and investigates the extent to which these institutionalized forms shape the current deployment of technology in the workplace. Finally, Smith explores subtle control mechanisms such as emotional labour that go beyond those evident in the EPOS systems and which have become so embedded in retail social practices over time that they are no longer observable or discernible by the workers and managers.

From a critical perspective, one of the primary weaknesses of this study is that while it describes how management practices influence the implementation and use of technology, this description does not aid the transformation of the status quo. An objective of critical research is to liberate those studied from the oppression and 'false consciousness' that constrain them. Smith's research does not attempt to do this; hence he has not tested his critical ideas in real organizational struggles. This could be remedied if Smith adopted a less passive stance towards social reality, and suggested how the workers could try and overcome their conditions. Another limitation of this study is its failure to address the nature and implications of contradictory social relations in the workplace. Contradiction is a key theme in the critical research tradition, and is not explored in great depth by Smith. He does not explicate how the tensions between labour and management are artefacts of a capitalist mode of production, or how they can be transformed. Finally, while Smith studies the history of labour practices within a few firms, he does not examine in any depth the role society has played in shaping these practices. A central tenet of critical research is its acknowledgment that organizational practices are shaped and constrained by larger social, economic and political forces. This could be remedied by grounding the analysis in the totality that informs relations in the workplace, such as competitive pressures on firms in the retail industry, government policies and trade union demands with respect to computerization, and the socialization of workers through institutions such as schools, communities, and the marketplace.

Critical research philosophy assessment

The critical research perspective offers a different view of the world than those of the positivist and interpretive perspectives. It alerts us to the reality of interdependence of parts with the whole, and that organizations cannot be studied in isolation from the industry, society, and nation within which they operate, and which they in part constitute. Likewise, we are exposed to the central influence of historical, economic, social, and political conditions on the nature and development of phenomena. And finally, this perspective reminds us of the constantly changing potential of humans who need not be confined by their immediate circumstances. The status quo is merely one moment along an evolving and emergent dynamic of social reality.

The critical approach also has some weaknesses; in part these are a function of the assumptions that guide critical researchers. For example, socio-economic class is seen as the primary determinant of antagonistic social relations. This almost exclusive focus on economic factors obscures the importance of other factors such as race and gender that have also led to dominating and repressive social relations. This selectivity in perspective is also reflected in critical researchers' recognition of the inherent opposition or contradiction in social relations. While an advance over the positivist and interpretive philosophies with their bias for functionalist theories, this view may overstate the extent to which contradiction is a function of class societies. Giddens (1979; 1981), for example, posits instead that contradiction is endemic to the human condition, and not exclusive to capitalist societies. He suggests that contradictory relations are apparent in people's connected/disconnected relationship with nature (existential contradiction) and the opposition of interests represented by the role of the state in individual affairs (structural contradiction) - conditions that permeate all societies. Critical researchers often are not critical enough of their own concepts and theoretical models. For example, some variants of critical research tend to be deterministic, assuming simplistically that all managers want more control and that labour is either docile or completely ignorant of this control, not allowing for the possibility that labour may have means to mitigate, subvert or transform the mechanisms that control them. Further, some commentators have suggested that critical researchers are not reflexive, not applying their notions of transcendence to themselves, and hence not accomplishing self-transformation or 'praxis' (Heydebrand, 1983). Finally, the form of theory and knowledge in this tradition is uncertain. As noted by Chua (1986, p.626): 'critical theorists do not share common philosophical standards for the evaluation of theories. What is acceptable theory or explanation is still debatable.' This ambiguity of evaluation may be difficult for proponents of the dominant research tradition to accept, given their experience with positivism's relatively unambiguous criteria for what constitutes valid knowledge.

Conclusion

We believe that all three of the research philosophies we have discussed above can offer insightful perspectives on the phenomena of interest in IS research. What is required is that researchers understand the implications of their research perspective, and act in ways that reflect that knowledge. Furthermore, researchers need to be aware of their research traditions and be open to the possibilities of other research practices, and not create an orthodoxy which precludes the use or publishing of different research. We must clearly state that it is not our intention to replace the positivist perspective with critical or interpretive ones. Rather, researchers should ensure that they adopt a perspective that is compatible with their own research interests and predispositions, while remaining open to the possibility of other assumptions and interests. They should understand and acknowledge the extent to which the perspective they adopt will focus their attention on some things and not others, and bias their views of the phenomena they study.

It is certainly true that the research approaches adopted by all researchers (not only IS researchers) are influenced to a greater or lesser extent by the various institutional contexts within which they are trained and work. An in-depth examination of the structural dimensions of conducting information systems re-search is beyond the scope of this chapter, and we will do no more than raise some issues for consideration (for more discussion see Podsakoff and Dalton, 1987). Research methods and assumptions are not learned and appropriated in a vacuum. They are heavily influenced by the doctoral program attended, the agendas of powerful and respected mentors, the hiring, promotion, and tenure criteria of employing institutions, the funding policies of agencies, the rules of access negotiated with research sites, and the publishing guidelines of academic journals. For researchers in relatively powerless positions, awareness of the influence of each of these elements in shaping their research philosophy, while not eliminating the constraints, may at least facilitate informed choice and risk taking. For researchers in more powerful positions, awareness of these elements may be a step towards trying to lessen the persistent bias towards positivist research studies.

The issue of self-reflection about research perspective applies to all researchers, whatever the perspective they adopt, whether interpretive, critical, or positivist. Morgan (1983, pp.389-391), drawing on Godel's theorem to emphasize that all theoretical formulations are necessarily incomplete (Godel, 1962), succinctly captures the message we have tried to convey here:

> [All] social phenomena may have many potential ways of revealing themselves and the way they are realized in practice depends on the mode of engagement adopted by the researcher...[I]n choosing a research strategy the scientist in large measure determines how the phenomenon being studied will be revealed, and indirectly, the consequences of the knowledge thus generated.

Acknowledgements

We would like to thank the associate editor, Dick Boland, and the three anonymous reviewers who provided many constructive comments and suggestions.

5 The Case Research Strategy in Studies of Information Systems

Izak Benbasat, David K. Goldstein and Melissa Mead

Dealing with research methodology, this chapter is of primary interest to academicians. However, to the extent that it may shift the mix of research done by the academicians, it will have significant implications for the practitioner. In particular, the chapter identifies the niche of case-oriented research work and suggests the types of problems where it can be most useful. It examines four research cases and suggests for each how the study could have been shaped to produce more useful insights. The chapter thus has twin objectives: to build the argument for case-oriented research and to identify how it can be done better. A hidden assumption on which the argument hinges is the willingness of the business community to participate candidly in well-designed, case-oriented research projects. Only through such involvement can this important avenue of research be mined; otherwise the researcher is driven to reliance on student experiments, questionnaires, etc., which, while useful for many domains of work, fail to illuminate others.

This article defines and discusses the case research strategy. Suggestions are provided for researchers who wish to undertake research employing this approach. Criteria for the evaluation of case research are established and several characteristics useful for categorizing the studies are identified. A sample of papers drawn from information systems journals is reviewed. The chapter concludes with examples of research areas that are particularly well suited to investigation using the case research approach.

There has been a growing interest in the use of qualitative techniques in the administrative sciences. For example, a full issue of *Administrative Science Quarterly* (Volume 24, 1979) has been devoted to qualitative methods. This interest has been sparked by a general dissatisfaction with the type of research information provided by quantitative techniques (Van Maanen, 1982). The dissatisfaction stems from several sources: the complexity of multivariate research methods, the distribution restrictions inherent in the use of these methods (for example, multivariate normality), the large sample sizes these methods dictate, and the difficulty of understanding and interpreting the results of studies in which complex quantitative methods are used.

Similarly, in the information systems field, Franz and Robey (1984) have suggested the use of idiographic rather than nomothetic research strategies. Idiographic research attempts to understand a phenomenon in its context. In such research, the investigator intensely examines a single entity or a particular event. Nomothetic methods, on the other hand, seek general laws and draw solely on procedures used in the exact sciences (Weick, 1984).

This article discusses the use of one qualitative technique, the case research strategy, in studies of information systems. It provides some suggestions about how to conduct and evaluate case study research. A sample of case-based research from selected IS journals is categorized according to a set of characteristics developed in this chapter. The articles in the sample are then evaluated.

We are not advocating an exclusive use of the case strategy. Many authors have commented that each research strategy has advantages and disadvantages; no strategy is more appropriate than all others for all research purposes. Benbasat (1984) showed that the goals of the researcher and the nature of the research topic influence the selection of a strategy. Case research is particularly appropriate for certain types of problems: those in which research and theory are at their early, formative stages (Roethlisberger, 1977), and 'sticky, practice-based problems where the experiences of the actors are important and the context of action is critical' (Franz and Robey, 1984).

The information systems area is characterized by constant technological change and innovation. IS researchers, therefore, often find themselves trailing behind practitioners in proposing changes or in evaluating methods for developing new systems. Researchers usually learn by studying the innovations put in place by practitioners, rather than by providing the initial wisdom for these novel ideas. For example, when companies experienced a growth in end-user computing in the late 1970s and early 1980s, academics were not able to offer a set of guidelines describing how an organization could effectively manage the introduction of end-user computing technology. Researchers first descriptively studied how organizations were managing end-user computing. These studies then formed the basis for the development of prescriptive management guidelines (for example, Rockart and Flannery, 1983).

We believe that the case research strategy is well suited to capturing the knowledge of practitioners and developing theories from it. Christenson (1976) points out that the trial-and-error process in which practitioners are engaged in is necessary for knowledge to accumulate. It is incumbent upon the scientists to formalize this knowledge and proceed to a testing stage. Before this formalization takes place, case studies could be employed to document the experiences of practice.

The IS field has also seen a shift from technological to managerial and organizational questions, and consequently more interest in how context and innovations interact. For example, airline reservation systems were very innovative technical achievements in the early 1960s. However, they became a key competitive factor in the changing airline industry within the last few years.

In order to understand this phenomenon, one must examine the structure of the industry, the role of deregulation, and the federal laws governing the industry.

To summarize, there are three reasons why case study research is a viable information systems research strategy. First, the researcher can study information systems in a natural setting, learn about the state of the art, and generate theories from practice. Second, the case method allows the researcher to answer 'how' and 'why' questions, that is, to understand the nature and complexity of the processes taking place. Questions such as, 'How does a manager effectively introduce new information technologies?' are critical ones for researchers to pursue. Third, a case approach is an appropriate way to research an area in which few previous studies have been carried out. With the rapid pace of change in the information systems field, many new topics emerge each year for which valuable insights can be gained through the use of case research.

Case research: definition

There is no standard definition of a case study. For our purposes, we will draw our definition from those presented by Benbasat (1984), Bonoma (1985), Kaplan (1985), Stone (1978), and Yin (1984). A case study examines a phenomenon in its natural setting, employing multiple methods of data collection to gather information from one or a few entities (people, groups, or organizations). The boundaries of the phenomenon are not clearly evident at the outset of the research and no experimental control or manipulation is used. Table 5.1 contains a list of eleven characteristics of case studies summarized from the papers mentioned above.

To place case studies in perspective, it is useful to contrast this approach with other methods commonly used by IS researchers. In laboratory experiments the researcher measures dependent variables while manipulating independent variables in a controlled environment. Similarly, field experiments involve the manipulation and measurement of clearly defined variables, but in a natural setting. Finally, in field studies researchers measure independent and dependent variables in their natural context; however, no control or manipulation is involved. A fundamental difference between case studies and these alternative methods is that the case study researcher may have less a priori knowledge of what the variables of interest are and how they will be measured.

In our survey of the literature, we identified three categories of qualitative research that appear to be considered as case studies. Our focus in this article, however, includes only one of these. For clarification we will define the two excluded categories - application descriptions and action research. Then we will describe key aspects of the execution of case research.

Application descriptions
Written by practitioners, application descriptions detail the author's experiences implementing a particular application, such as a database management system. The outcomes of these published projects are almost always successful and the

author concludes by providing a list of 'dos' and 'don'ts' for the implementation of similar systems. The author does not conduct a research study; instead, the objective is to successfully implement a specific system for a given assignment. Application descriptions are not included in our definition of case research.

Table 5.1 Key characteristics of case studies

1.	Phenomenon is examined in a natural setting.
2.	Data are collected by multiple means.
3.	One or few entities (person, group, or organization) are examined.
4.	The complexity of the unit is studied intensively.
5.	Case studies are more suitable for the exploration, classification and hypothesis development stages of the knowledge building process; the investigator should have a receptive attitude towards exploration.
6.	No experimental controls or manipulation are involved.
7.	The investigator may not specify the set of independent and dependent variables in advance.
8.	The results derived depend heavily on the integrative powers of the investigator.
9.	Changes in site selection and data collection methods could take place as the investigator develops new hypotheses.
10.	Case research is useful in the study of 'why' and 'how' questions because these deal with operational links to be traced over time rather than with frequency or incidence.
11.	The focus is on contemporary events.

Action research

We have also excluded action research. These are studies in which the author, usually a researcher, is a participant in the implementation of a system, but simultaneously wants to evaluate a certain intervention technique. An example might be the use of the socio-technical approach for system development. The articles in both this and the application descriptions categories are written by individuals who have an insider's view of the system in question. However, action research articles are authored by those whose original intent is to conduct research while effecting change (Susman and Evered, 1978). The action researcher is not an independent observer, but becomes a participant, and the process of change becomes the subject of research. Thus, the researcher has two objectives: to take action to solve a problem and to contribute to a set of system development concepts (Checkland, 1981).

The strength of these studies is the in-depth and first hand understanding the researcher obtains. Conversely, a weakness is the potential lack of objectivity stemming from the researcher's stake in effecting a successful outcome for the client organization. Further, generalizations to other situations where people less knowledgeable than the researcher apply the intervention technique may be difficult. Examples of action research in IS are found in Gibson (1975), Ginzberg (1981a), Mumford (1981) and Scott Morton (1971).

Case study research

In case studies the clear objective is the conduct of research. These are efforts where research questions are specified prior to the study by researchers who are observers/investigators rather than participants. We will discuss considerations that are important in selecting the case research approach and we will detail the mechanics of executing case research.

Conducting case research

Research themes and objectives - deciding on case research.

Given a specific research question, one must ask whether the case method is a useful approach. To judge the appropriateness of the case strategy, we can ask the following questions (drawn from Table 5.1):

1. Can the phenomenon of interest be studied outside its natural setting?
2. Must the study focus on contemporary events?
3. Is control or manipulation of subjects or events necessary?
4. Does the phenomenon of interest enjoy an established theoretical base?

Case methodology is clearly useful when a natural setting or a focus on contemporary events is needed. Similarly, research phenomena not supported by a strong theoretical base may be fruitfully pursued through case research. A rich natural setting can be fertile ground for generating theories. Conversely, when subjects or events must be controlled or manipulated in the course of a research project, the case approach is not suitable.

Quite often, however, the decision to use a case approach is not clear-cut. Both Yin (1984) and Bonoma (1985) discuss the usefulness of the case approach in various phases of research. Table 5.2 gives their terminology for the traditional exploration, hypothesis generation, and testing phases of knowledge accrual. Using qualitative methods may enhance research that is not strictly exploratory or descriptive. For example, Yin (1984) states that case studies could be used to explain phenomena. He considers Allison's (1971) study of the Cuban missile crisis an example of such studies. Allison proposed different theories to account for the same course of events, identified the one that provided the best explanation, and suggested how this theory could be useful to understand other situations. Bonoma suggests that the case strategy could play a role in both hypothesis generation and hypothesis testing. Bauer (as reported in Towl, 1969) refers to the use of the critical case (crucial experiment) to test a well-founded theory.

When the case approach is deemed appropriate, researchers may be uncertain about how to proceed. The remainder of this section offers practical aid to researchers for understanding and implementing case research.

Unit of analysis

Prior to searching for sites, the researcher should determine the unit of analysis most appropriate for the project. Will the study focus on individuals, groups (for example, a task force, profit centre, IS group) or an entire organization?

Alternatively, the unit of analysis may be a specific project or decision. In making this determination, the researcher should closely examine the research questions to be pursued. These often indicate an appropriate unit of analysis. Finally, the researcher should consider what generalizations are hoped for at the project's completion. Does the researcher hope to generalize to other organizations, individuals, or decisions, for instance?

When the research is highly exploratory, a single case may be useful as a pilot study. The goal will be to determine the appropriate unit and familiarize the researcher with the phenomenon in its context.

Table 5.2 Terminologies for stages

Traditional phases of knowledge accrual	Yin's (1984) framework	Bonoma's (1985) framework	Number of cases
Exploration	Description	Drift	Single or multiple case(s)
Hypothesis generation	Exploration	Design	Multiple cases
Hypothesis testing			
* Confirmation	Explanation	Prediction	Multiple cases
* Disconfirmation	Explanation	Disconfirmation	Single critical case

Single-case vs. multiple-case designs
Central to case research design is the decision to include one or several cases in the project. Most research efforts require multiple cases, but single cases are useful in specific instances. Yin suggests single-case studies are appropriate if:
1. It is a *revelatory* case, that is, it is a situation previously inaccessible to scientific investigation.
2. It represents a *critical* case for testing a well-formulated theory. According to Yin (1984, p.421), 'to confirm, challenge or extend a theory, there may exist a single case, meeting all the conditions for testing the theory.'
3. It is an *extreme* or *unique* case.

As Table 5.2 shows, single-case study projects are most useful at the outset of theory generation and late in theory testing. A single case used for exploration may be followed by a multiple-case study. This corresponds to Bonoma's drift stage in which researchers learn first hand the relevant jargon and context in which the phenomenon will be studied. A single case may also be used to test the boundaries of well-formed theory.

Multiple-case designs are desirable when the intent of the research is description, theory building, or theory testing. These three correspond to Bonoma's design, prediction, and disconfirmation stages, respectively. Multiple-case designs allow for cross-case analysis and the extension of theory. Of course, multiple cases yield more general research results.

Site selection
The factors that dictate a single-case design also determine site selection. When multiple cases are to be included in a study, however, choices must be made. It

is quite useful to consider a multiple-case project as analogous to the replication that is possible with multiple traditional experiments (Hersen and Barlow, 1976). Adopting this point of view, Yin (1984) proposes two criteria for selecting potential sites. First, sites where similar results are predicted may be used as 'literal' replications. Second, sites may be chosen for 'theoretical' replication. That is, chosen such that contradictory results are predicted. With careful site selection, the researcher can extend and revise the initial propositions of the study.

Site selection should be carefully thought out rather than being opportunistic. Researchers may begin site selection by considering the nature of their topic. Research on organization-level phenomena would require site selection based on the characteristics of firms. These may include the industry, company size, organizational structure, profit/not-for-profit status, public or private ownership, geographic coverage, degree of vertical or horizontal integration, and so on. Researchers interested in specific technologies, IS methodologies or organizational structures should consider these characteristics when selecting sites.

Once the limiting factors are determined, specific sites may be identified and approached. Regular scans of business newspapers and periodicals often turn up potential sites. Library research using indexes of industries, business literature, and marketing or financial research data may be helpful. Finally, talking with friends, colleagues, or acquaintances is a good way to identify potential research locations.

Approaching the potential site is a crucial point in orchestrating a case research project. Here again, the topic of study is key to determining whom to contact. The researcher must eventually contact the individual with enough authority to approve the project. Colleagues may be able to help with introductions. If not, prepare carefully before placing a cold call or writing to the organization. The researcher should clearly describe the project and who will be involved - researchers, assistants, or company employees. The contact should be told the amount of time, effort and expense required of the organization.

Two key points to be addressed in order to gain cooperation are confidentiality and benefits to the organization. The researcher must provide assurance that the organization will not be harmed by its participation. The organization and its employees must know that the researcher will not betray their confidence. On the other hand, the researcher should seek assurance that reasonable candour will be provided and that essential data will be made available.

The benefits to an organization participating in a research project are varied. They may include learning more about the organization, getting feedback and new insights from the researcher, and developing a relationship with the researcher. In addition, there is the opportunity to contribute to knowledge and business research. The organization may or may not wish to be identified when the research is published. If it does, there is the additional benefit of recognition and publicity.

Data collection methods

Multiple data collection methods are typically employed in case research studies. Ideally, evidence from two or more sources will converge to support the research findings. Yin (1984) identifies several sources of evidence that work well in case research (p.781).

1. Documentation - Written material ranging from memoranda to newspaper clippings to formal reports.
2. Archival records - Organization charts; service, personnel or financial records.
3. Interviews - These may be open-ended or focused (see Bouchard, 1976; Cook and Campbell, 1979).
4. Direct observation - Absorbing and noting details, actions, or subtleties of the field environment (see Webb et al., 1966 on unobtrusive measures).
5. Physical artefacts – Devices, outputs, tools.

   The goal is to obtain a rich set of data surrounding the specific research issue, as well as capturing the contextual complexity.

   Specific data to be collected will depend on the research questions and the unit of analysis. Prior to site visits, the researcher should outline, in detail, the data to be gathered. This may include a list of materials to be collected (documentation, archival records and physical artefacts) as well as questions for interviews and plans for direct observation. This formalization helps coordination when multiple investigators work together. It also provides some separation of data collection from data analysis. The goals of this planning should be to ensure good coverage of the research questions and excellent use of time spent on-site.

   This planning stage helps to structure projects that are inherently flexible. It gives the researcher a guide from which to work. As the project unfolds, the plan will be revised according to the researcher's judgement, unexpected observations, or limitations and opportunities.

   Finally, the researcher should be meticulous in record keeping. Precious data may be lost when entrusted to memory or not organized as soon after collection as possible. This is particularly important in multiple case designs where, as time passes, the details of various sites tend to run together. The researcher's goal should be to collect data in such a way that another researcher could pick it up and immediately understand it and work with it.

Data analysis and exposition

The analysis of case data depends heavily on the integrative powers of the researcher. Using multiple methods of data collection, however, offers the opportunity for triangulation and lends greater support to the researcher's conclusions. Working with a research partner may also provide invaluable assistance. Two researchers can capture greater richness of data and rely more confidently on the accuracy of the data.

   The key elements of data analysis are also critical to the written results of case research. As much as possible, the contextual and data richness of the study should be presented, and a clear chain of evidence should be established. The researcher's reasoning in establishing cause and effect or drawing out hypotheses should be clearly stated and defended. The research should move from objectives and questions, to assumptions and design choices, to specific data uncovered, and finally, to results and conclusions. Readers should be able to follow this path readily.

A critique of case-based research

To gain an understanding of the nature and quality of case research on IS, we surveyed the following journals and conference proceedings for the period January 1981 to December 1985: *Communications of the ACM*, the *Proceedings of the International Conference on Information Systems, Information and Management, MIS Quarterly* and *Systems, Objectives, Solutions*. In our estimation, these were the IS journals most likely to publish case-type articles. Our intention was to provide examples of case studies, not to do an exhaustive search.

After excluding the two categories of application descriptions and action research articles, we identified only five case papers in the *Communications of the ACM*, an average of one per year. There were few case papers in *Information and Management*; even if we include the action research and application description articles in this journal, case research makes up only 10% of all articles. The *Proceedings of the International Conference on Information Systems* included seven case papers, again about one per year. Finally, about 10% of the articles in the *MIS Quarterly* were case studies.

Compared to these journals, *Systems, Objectives, Solutions* had a substantial proportion of case research articles (about 25% of the articles published). This journal published case research articles in each issue and encouraged researchers to submit case studies. After four years as an independent publication, the journal merged with *Information and Management* in 1985.

Hamilton and Ives (1982), based on a sample of IS articles from 15 journals published between 1970-79, observed that 14% of these were case studies. Based on a similar sample between 1977-83, Vogel and Wetherbe (1984) report that about 17% of the published IS articles were case studies.

We approached the critique of the articles in our sample in two parts. First, we looked at four case studies in detail and evaluated their strengths and weaknesses. Then, we rated the whole sample of case studies based on our guidelines for conducting case studies.

Four case research studies

We chose the following four case studies because each took a different approach to investigation and they illustrate both the strengths and weaknesses in case study research.

Markus: IS Implementation

Markus (1981) examined the use of a 'production planning and profit analysis system' in two manufacturing plants within the same division of a company. The system was readily accepted in one plant, but was at first strongly rejected in the other (eventually it was put into use). Her case study attempted to find the reasons for the contradictory outcomes of implementation. Markus stated that an explanation based on user participation could only partially account for these findings. She observed that the plant that accepted the system exhibited a higher degree of user participation than the one that rejected the system initially. But how does one account for the later reversal?

Markus proposed a 'distribution of power' model to explain the different reactions to the system. That is, the lack of consonance between the distribution of power implied by the system and the distribution of power within the organization caused the failure of one plant to adopt the system. Based on this same model, Markus also explained why one system was rejected at first, but was eventually accepted when the organizational conditions that led to the initial rejection were changed.

Markus' research had to be carried out in a natural setting since it traced the evolution of the system's implementation from rejection to acceptance and the reasons for the switch. Markus was interested in answering a 'why' question: Why was the system used in one plant and not in another? The fact that both units were within a single company increased the internal validity of the case study. A large number of possible causes for the acceptance in one plant and not in the other could be eliminated since the sites shared the same organizational setting and company history. Thus, Markus took advantage of a unique opportunity to study an implementation issue. Since the opportunity was unique, Markus added to our knowledge about the implementation of systems, even though some previous research on the same topic existed.

The history of the implementation process, which spanned a period of six years, was described in detail. One flaw in the study, though, was the total lack of detail about the data collection methodology. The reader could only infer that interviews took place, since direct quotations from the people involved were used to support the author's arguments. Aside from this, it is not clear what, if any, additional data sources were used for triangulation and validation. This is of particular concern because the history of the project covered six years and the memories of the participants may have been inconsistent.

Dutton adoption of a fiscal impact model

Dutton's (1981) study of the City of Tulsa's adoption of a fiscal impact model and its eventual rejection was outstanding among case studies we looked at for the rich level of detail it provided about the implementation process. According to Dutton, the sequence of events was reconstructed based on newspaper accounts, government reports, documents, memos, over 20 lengthy unstructured interviews with participants having different perspectives on implementation, and telephone calls that preceded and followed site visits. As a final check for accuracy, a draft of the paper was sent to several respondents and important participants who had not previously been interviewed.

The purpose of the study was to examine the limitations of both the technical and organizational perspectives of the implementation process. Dutton stated that his study contributed to our understanding of the process of innovation rejection, a topic we know little about. Following a 16-page description of the events, the organizational and political environment, and the actors associated with the implementation process, Dutton explained how technical, organizational, and interpersonal factors influenced the implementation process. However, he concluded that the greatest determinant was the political environment; he described in detail how the organizational and technical factors were contingent on the political ones.

Dutton described events in such detail that readers could make their own, different interpretations if they wished. It is an exploratory paper that reveals an important factor in the implementation process.

One criticism of the study is that Dutton did not clearly define his original research objectives. Further, we do not know why he chose this particular site. Did he know about the outcome (failure of system) before he analyzed retrospectively the events that took place? If this is the case, then his original objective might have been to explore why a failure had occurred. Alternatively, was his intention to study the implementation of computer-based systems in city governments and describe the factors influencing the outcomes? In the latter case, the investigator was in the discovery stage; in the former case he was attempting to find the factors that caused a particular outcome. Since these concerns might affect the way the researcher approached data collection and thought about the issues in the case we believe that a clear statement of the initial objectives of the researcher should have been provided in the study description.

Pyburn: strategic IS planning

Pyburn (1983) investigated IS strategic planning processes that were underway in several companies, examined the business and technical context in which these plans were developed, and generated preliminary conclusions about the success or failure of the planning activity. He wanted to understand why a particular methodology worked well in some settings but not in others. The impetus for the study was the growing importance of such plans in the success of the overall IS effort, coupled with the lack of effectiveness of existing IS planning methodologies.

The method used was a comparative case study which, as described by Pyburn, 'relies on the fact that outcomes in the different sites were the results of identified differences in those factors measured for its conclusions' (Pyburn, 1983, pp.4-5). Therefore, he chose eight sites that were as similar as possible based on a number of characteristics, that is, a literal replication. Some of these characteristics, such as 'the company had formal business planning for five years' and 'top managers were willing to commit time to assist the research' made obvious sense. However, the reasons for other characteristics of the site selection, such as 'the companies were dominated by a founding family' and 'had corporate headquarters in relatively small cities,' were not immediately evident. It appeared that Pyburn was more concerned with choosing highly similar sites, rather than choosing a model group that was representative of companies involved in strategic IS planning.

In each site, Pyburn conducted in-depth interviews with the senior IS executive and the top management team (four to six individuals). He used a series of questions to gather data concerning the nature of the business, the factors critical to its success, the company's IS planning practices, and the extent to which IS was addressing the critical needs of the firm. In order to increase the reliability of the data collection process and to reduce interviewee bias, prior to the first interview, he administered a questionnaire that contained items similar to the questions subsequently posed in the interviews. The questionnaire data were analyzed using non-parametric statistical methods. For the interview data, a case description was written for each organization. For a given topic, a side-by-side presentation of all comments made by each interviewee for each topic was provided. (However, the case descriptions and comments were not included in the published paper and are presumably part of Pyburn's doctoral thesis on which the article was based.)

Based on the interview data and partially supported by questionnaire results, Pyburn identified three IS planning styles: personal/informal, personal/formal, and written/formal. He then determined the degree of success of IS strategic planning in each company. Since none of these planning approaches appeared to be uniformly successful in all the companies in which they were implemented, Pyburn pursued a contingency analysis. A number of factors, such as the perceived status of the IS manager and the complexity of the IS environment, were identified as important influences on the success or failure of the planning process. Finally, all of this information was tied together and the critical factors in the success of a particular planning style were identified. For example, a personal/informal style depended on both an informal general management style and high IS manager status.

Pyburn set forth clear research objectives prior to data collection. This led to a focused approach to the interviews and site selection, and the use of triangulation in data collection. He carefully explained each step of a logical process that eventually culminated in a preliminary typology of strategic MIS planning. The use of multiple sites allowed him to attempt a contingency analysis. This is a good example of an exploratory case study that proposed a classification scheme for MIS planning that could be further refined and tested in other studies.

A drawback of this work was that the type of detailed descriptions found in the Dutton and the Markus papers were not provided in this paper. Of course, the journal may have imposed length limitations that made it impossible to present the data collected from each of the eight sites. Books or monographs might be better vehicles to publish case study research. Nevertheless, the reader has to rely on the author's interpretation and cannot interpret the data independently.

Olson: centralization of the system development function

Olson (1981) examined the issue of whether the systems development function should be centralized or located in the user organization. Based on an analysis of the literature, Olson contended that there is no best way to organize the system development function; the decision depends on factors outside the IS function. She therefore conducted an in-depth study of two organizations in order to identify the factors that influence the organization of the system development function and the quality of the development process. She conducted extensive interviews with IS managers and key participants in the system design process, and administered questionnaires to users as well as those who were part of the design effort. Two computer-based systems (one an accounts receivable system, the other a benefits system) were selected from two large multidivisional companies. In one case, the systems development function was centralized; in the other it was decentralized to business divisions.

Olson's results showed that in the decentralized development group users had a higher level of information satisfaction, users participated less in the design of the system, and analysts were less satisfied with their jobs than in the centralized group. These results were based upon very small samples of users and analysts in each organization, a fact acknowledged by Olson. She suggested several conclusions about the effectiveness of user participation in the development process.

Olson chose her sample to bring out the differences associated with alternative organizations of the system development function. The views of the various participants in the development process were sought and data were collected by multiple means. Furthermore, recently completed systems were chosen to minimize the problems associated with retrospective data collection. A strength of the paper was the author's attempt to provide explanations for the outcomes based on what was observed from the cases. The IS departments of the two companies and their activities were described in reasonable detail, but little was offered to the reader about the companies themselves. Finally, since the outcomes were based only on a sample of two companies, this study could be considered only a basic exploratory case study.

The characteristics of the four case studies discussed above, as well as a sample of others identified in our survey, are outlined in Table 5.3. It is clear that the case studies have both similarities and differences. For example, the Pyburn and Dutton studies were both exploratory in nature, but differed in terms of sample selection and data gathering methods. One common feature of all four studies, which is not evident in the larger sample outlined in Table 5.3, was the detailed explanations that accompanied the findings. An investigator conducting a field study or experiment mainly relies on theory or a priori reasoning to deductively arrive at the outcomes. In these four studies, the investigators collected data, distilled the evidence, and inductively developed causal links to explain particular outcomes. While on the positive side the explanations were grounded in observed facts, our concern is that these facts were filtered through the subjective lenses of the investigators.

An overall evaluation of case studies

In this section, we will describe the nature and general quality of case research in IS. We'll evaluate the case studies in our survey based on our guidelines for conducting case research.

Research themes

The predominant theme in the case studies was implementation, that is, the possible causes of the success or failure of an information or decision support system (for example, Dickson and Janson, 1984). Since the process of implementation takes place over time, is a complex process involving multiple actors, and is influenced by events that happen unexpectedly, a case study methodology is well-suited to identifying key events and actors and to linking them in a causal chain. Examples of case study topics are: the impact of organizational strategy on the IS organization's structure (Schonberger, 1981), the impact of IS on organizational change (Robey, 1981; 1983), the impact of technology on organizational communications (Fulk and Dutton, 1984), the factors affecting the success of end-user developed applications (Rivard and Huff, 1984), and the role of user development (Mann and Watson, 1984).

Research objectives

In the published case research we surveyed, the objective of the study was seldom clearly specified. Among the exceptions were Pyburn (1983) and Hirschheim (1985b), who stated that their objectives were to describe and explore a phenomenon that was not well understood.

We would characterize most of case studies as exploratory in nature. They described the context in which an intervention occurred and the intervention itself. For example, Kraemer (1981) and Dutton (1981) described the implementation of model-based systems in the public sector. Almost all of these exploratory studies concluded with a list of suggestions to improve the success of future implementation efforts. It was difficult to determine if the researchers were at the same time attempting to generate hypotheses. An exception is the study by Ives and Olsen (1981) which basically described the nature of an IS manager's job.

Some case studies pursued an explanatory strategy by first describing the events that took place and then presenting multiple competing theories to explain the course of events (for example, Franz and Robey 1984, Kling and Iacono 1984, Markus 1983). Each of these studies used a sample of one case. For example, Markus (1983) evaluated three theories of resistance: people-determined, system-determined interaction-determined, and concluded that the interaction theory did a better job of explaining the causes of resistance to a system.

Some other studies also followed an explanatory strategy by testing hypotheses from a single theory (or a priori reasoning). White (1984) examined the influence of the cognitive style composition of a project team on its performance, and Schonberger (1981) tested the hypothesis that organization strategies will influence the structure of the IS organization. Although Schonberger clearly stated that he first observed two organizations with different IS department structures and then got interested in testing the influence of strategy on structure based on Chandler's (1962) theory, White appeared to be more ambiguous. It is not clear if she first observed two project teams with different cognitive styles and decided to test a hypothesis, or if she intended to test a hypothesis and then searched for an ideal sample of project teams with different compositions. However, we do not wish to single out her work for criticism since this was typical of the case studies in our sample.

In only one instance (Keen et al., 1982) were the authors' stated objectives both the exploration and testing of the explanatory power of theories. Two organizational change paradigms (the Lewin-Schein and Kolb-Frohman models) were used for theory testing. These provided a priori explanations of major factors that influence the success or failure of implementation efforts. Theory testing was done both by goodness of fit and by counter examples, that is, by the prediction and disconfirmation strategies suggested by Bonoma (1985).

In summary, we found that the IS case researchers we surveyed did not provide clear descriptions of where their topics fit in the knowledge building process. They thus did not justify their research purpose (drift, description, exploration and explanation) and did not allow readers to judge their work on a more informed basis.

Unit of analysis and site selection
The unit of analysis for a case study, and consequently for the selection of a particular site to study, was not provided in many of the published works. This is a problem consistent with the lack of clear research objectives discussed above, and probably an outcome of it. Several of the cases examined a single company or a subunit. Since these typically did not represent critical, unique or revelatory cases, they were presumably chosen based on availability and evidently the researchers' goals were to conduct exploratory case studies.

Markus' (1981) study previously described was a single-case sample containing two embedded units of analysis (two plants within the same division). It was rare because of the unique outcomes of the implementation process (one plant had a success, the other a failure with the same computerized system) and the unusual insights it offered.

Based on a large number of criteria, Keen, Bronsema et al. (1982) selected nine sites (countries) affiliated with an international bank. The criteria included IS development strategy, pace, focus, perceived ease of implementation, geographical dispersion, the size of the country, and the complexity of the operation. Two of the sites, which differed the most in terms of criteria, were selected for in-depth analysis. Even though this study appeared to be a single-case, embedded unit analysis, it could be considered a multiple-case design, due to the decentralized nature of the sites.

A study by Ein-Dor and Segev (1984) measured the relationship between the success of an IS and the perceived importance and investment in that system. They examined 10 subsystems supported by a logistics IS in a large organization in Israel. This was an embedded case study design in which the researchers conducted quantitative analysis of a large number of subunits. However, a problem of embedded designs that Yin (1984) mentioned and this study appeared to have, is that it makes the subunits the sole focus of the study and ignores the context, that is, characteristics of the organization as a whole. There was less focus on the context and more focus on a few aspects of the subunits. Thus, this study seemed to fall somewhere between a case and a field study, but had the strengths of neither.

The sites for some of the multiple-case research studies were chosen based on the study's research theme and objective. For example, to measure the effects of centralization, Olson (1981) chose two sites - one in which the system development function was centralized and one in which it was decentralized. To examine the influence of strategy on structure, Schonberger (1981) observed two organizations that had different IS department structures. The sites were chosen partly because they differed in terms of the outcome variable of interest, and partly on an opportunistic basis. Similarly, in their paper on factors affecting user involvement in DSS development, Mann and Watson (1984) presented three cases that demonstrated substantially different degrees of user involvement. However, the reader is not told whether the three cases were chosen from a larger sample because of their unique characteristics.

In other instances, the researcher sought a homogeneous sample with as many similar characteristics as possible (Pyburn, 1983). However, as we mentioned in our discussion of Pyburn's study, it was not obvious why these particular characteristics were chosen. In any case, the investigator did not know in advance what independent variables would prove to be important. The idea was to minimize the extraneous variables so that if significant factors were indeed found, there would be a high degree of confidence that only those factors caused the observed differences. In contrast to Pyburn's approach, Fulk and Dutton (1984), in their study of the impact of videoconferencing on organizational communications, chose two companies with different characteristics. One was a large aerospace company with offices on the east and west coasts that had recently started using videoconferencing. The second was a large western public utility with several years of routine utilization.

None of the multiple-case studies clearly stated the site selection objectives, that is, whether the investigator pursued a literal or a theoretical replication. Nevertheless, in most instances, the rationale for choosing a particular site combination was stated.

Sometimes the reasons for site selection were not easy to infer. For example, Robey (1983) studied eight companies located in different countries. Even though the samples appeared to be from differing organizations, the researcher did not explicitly state whether a literal or theoretical replication was the goal. In one study (Land et al., 1983) the three cases were chosen for a variety of disparate reasons. One company was chosen because one of the authors was involved in the implementation of a system there. In the second company, 2 out of 17 branches were selected because the implementation of a system went smoothly in one and was 'less successful' in the other. The third company was included in the sample because it had a recent, major shift from a manual system to a computerized system and it was self-contained. It thus appeared that the first case was chosen opportunistically, the second due to the observed outcomes, and the third based on a possible causal factor. In this particular study, it was difficult to infer whether the authors' goal was a literal or theoretical replication, or whether the cases were chosen for exploratory or illustrative reasons.

Authors in our sample did not indicate if their case studies were part of systematic/programmatic research plans. Most seemed to be stand-alone, one-shot studies. Only one case study was a triangulation in that it was a follow-up to a survey (Fulk and Dutton, 1984). Another case study was part of a large-scale effort to study various aspects of IS and their organizational impact, but the linkage to the larger study was not described in the paper (Robey, 1981).

Data collection
In about half of the case studies, the data were collected by multiple means; the other half relied solely on interviews. In two case studies, though, the data collection method was not specified at all. We believe that a clear description of data sources and the way they contribute to the findings of the research is an important aspect of the reliability and validity of the findings. Yin's (1984) suggestions about describing the case study protocol and having a case study database can serve as important guidelines.

Almost all of the studies used interviews for data collection. The interview questions were rarely specified and, when they were, it was in a very general form. Hirschheim (1985b), a notable exception, included the questions used in his semi-structured interview in an appendix. In some studies, researchers interviewed individuals who had different perspectives on a given process, for example, managers, users, and designers. Sometimes the researchers mentioned that they used documents and observations, but they did not provide any more detail about them.

A few studies of implementation in the public sector collected data from a large number of sources (King, 1983; Kraemer, 1981). These studies were similar to the Dutton (1981) study in the richness of their descriptions and data sources. The only study that used a longitudinal methodology is also an exemplary effort of data collection (Franz and Robey, 1984). To study user involvement in IS design, the investigators collected data over a two-year period. In order to achieve triangulation, data were gathered through questionnaires, critical incident files, unstructured interviews, documents and memoranda, observations at meetings and tape recordings. In this way, they attempted to get both an objective view of events and the subjective interpretations of participants.

Keen, Bronsema et al. (1982) used an outside expert with no knowledge of the system being implemented to interview participants with whom the research team (authors) had already talked and who were in conflict. This was done to reduce any bias arising from the expectations of the researchers. If other studies used such techniques to increase the objectivity of data collection, no mention was made of them.

Case data in the research surveyed was mostly qualitative. A few studies included quantitative observations, mostly in the form of questionnaire data (Dutton, 1981; Jick, 1979; Olson, 1981). In general, however, the degree of detail about data collection methods was not very revealing, a substantial problem with most of the case studies observed.

Concluding comments

Our intent in this article was to clarify the nature of the case research method, explain why it might be utilized in IS studies, survey its uses in IS research within the last five years, and offer some suggestions for improvement.

The case research strategy has mostly been used for exploration and hypothesis generation. This is a legitimate way of adding to the body of knowledge in the IS field. Exploration is, however, not the only reason for applying the case method. As discussed earlier, various authors have suggested the use of cases for providing explanation and for testing hypotheses.

No research strategy is better than all others. Unlike some of the contributors to Mumford, Hirschheim et al. (1985), we do not advocate exclusive reliance on case/action research methods. The selection of a research strategy depends on the current knowledge of a topic and the nature of the topic, among other factors. The case strategy is particularly well suited to IS research because the technology is relatively new and interest has shifted to organizational rather than technical issues. For example, case studies have been helpful in identifying the causal chain that led to the success or failure of an information system by revealing in chronological fashion the various actors and events that influenced the final outcome.

Several current topics within IS research are amenable to the case study approach. The use of an expert system for management support is one such area. Since expert systems are just beginning to be introduced into organizations, a case study of companies that are rather far along in the use of such a system would provide valuable insights. Sviokla (1986) has examined how an expert system that assists financial planners affects their jobs and the quality of the plans they produce. This revelatory use of the case method can provide hypotheses about the impact of expert systems technology on organizations. These hypotheses can then be tested using another research method, like a field experiment.

The relationship between information technology and corporate strategy is another area that could be explored further using a structured program of multiple case studies. From the case studies conducted to date, there is evidence that some companies use information technology more effectively as a strategic weapon than others (Parsons, 1983). A systematic study of several companies within one industry could provide important insights into why some companies use information technology more successfully than others.

One of the more difficult decisions that researchers must make is to determine when further case studies are needed in an emerging research area. For example, in the study of information technology and corporate strategy, Bakos and Treacy (1986, p.107) believe that:

> As this area of research matures, there is an increasing need to move beyond frameworks and toward explanatory models of the underlying phenomena. This type of research will allow us to build a cumulative tradition and to make normative statements to guide managerial actions.

In the IS area, there is some merit to both the view that more case research is needed and the view that quantitative techniques should be employed. Case studies can provide the organizational context for the study of the relationship between strategy and information technology. This is important even in this stage of the research. A formal model can provide significant insights into the more quantitative aspects of the issue, such as the economic impact of investing in information technology.

Recently there have been calls for a more detailed understanding of phenomena in the IS area. There is an interesting parallel between our call for higher quality case research and the argument presented by Todd and Benbasat (1987) for increased use of protocol analysis in the study of decision support systems. The use of protocol analysis in IS studies has increased within the last few years because many researchers believe that they have to open the 'black box.' They want to examine processes in order to better understand the effects of information technology on the people who work with it, and their influence on the technology. The intent is to carry out a detailed, in-depth examination of a small number of individuals. In a similar way, case research obtains detailed data about one or a few units.

The key difference between the case research method and protocol analysis is that, while both methods require little a priori specification of dependent variables and their measurement allow the investigator to use a high degree of discretion in structuring and interpreting the data, the case method also offers little control over the antecedent condition, for example, independent variables.

In this article we identified a number of problems that were common to most of the case research studies in the sample. Asking the authors to provide more information about their research objectives might alleviate some of these and research plans. However, it appears to us that, in many instances, the investigators had not considered some of the methodological issues. In general, the objectives of the researchers were not clearly specified. The reasons for selecting single-case versus multiple-case designs were not explained and the choice of particular sites was not tied to the design approach. In many cases the data collection method was ambiguous and details were not provided. The use of triangulation to increase reliability was rare.

Yin (1984) states that the reader of the case study should be able to follow the derivation of any evidence from initial research questions to the conclusions of the study. This chain of evidence will improve the reliability of the data. The point is that a case study should be more than an exercise in storytelling or an opinion piece; it should adhere to certain rules of procedure, as described in Yin

(1984) and discussed here. Although these procedures are not as detailed as one would find in a field study, survey or experiment, they are critical to allowing readers to assess the reliability and validity of the study's findings. In this way, IS researchers can better contribute to the knowledge building process and IS case research will come into its own.

Acknowledgements

Professor Benbasat was a Marvin Bower Fellow at the Harvard Business School while working on this chapter. He thanks the Fellowship program for its support during the 1985-86 academic year.

Table 5.3 An illustrative categorization of a sample of case studies

	Theme	Research thrust	Sample selection	Units of analysis	Data collection method	Level of description about units
Olson	Centralization/ decentralization of system development	Exploration	2 IS groups, differing on the degree of centralizaton of system development	Group	Interview and questionnaire	High
Markus	Implementation	Explanation	2 plants within same company differing on implementation success	Organizational subunit	Unspecified, inferred to be interviewed	High
Pyburn	IS strategic planning	Exploration	8 companies chosen based on similar characteristics	Organizations	Interview and questionnaire	Low
Dutton	Implementation of models in the public sector	Exploration and explanation	1 U.S. city	Organization	Multiple sources, high degree of triangulation	Very High
Hirschheim	Participative systems design	Exploration	20 individuals from 8 organizations with experience in participative design	Individuals and organizations	Interviews	Low
White	Cognitive styles of MIS project teams	Explanation	2 MIS teams in the same company differing in cognitive style composition of their members	Groups	Interviews	Low
Ives and Olson	Nature of IS manager's job	Exploration	6 IS managers chosen based on several common criteria	Individuals	Observations of each manager for 3-4 days	High, but at aggregate level
Keen et al.	Implementation of common systems in an international banking setting	Exploration and explanation	Banks in 9 countries (part of an international bank) selected on a number of criteria	Organizational subunits	Interviews	High
Fulk and Dutton	Effect of videoconferencing on organizational communication	Exploration	2 organizations, new user, one localized experienced user	Organization	Interview	High
Franz and Robey	User-led system design	Exploration and explanation	1 IS development team	Group	Longitudinal and multiple sources	High

6 Interpretive Case Studies in IS Research: Nature and Method

Geoff Walsham

The importance of social issues related to computer-based information systems has been recognized increasingly over the last decade, and this has led some IS researchers to adopt empirical approaches which focus particularly on human interpretations and meanings. The vehicle for such 'interpretive' investigations is often the in-depth case study, where research involves frequent visits to the field site over an extended period of time. This chapter focuses on such interpretive case studies in the IS field, and considers philosophical and theoretical issues concerning the nature of these studies, and methodological issues on how to carry out and report on studies in this tradition.

The development of the 'interpretive' empirical school in IS has not been free of controversy, and debate continues on the relative merits of interpretivist versus positivist approaches to IS (Orlikowski and Baroudi, 1991), or the possibilities for their combination (Gable, 1994; Lee, 1991). This chapter can be seen as one contribution to that debate, since it contrasts some elements of interpretivist and positivist approaches to case studies. However, despite these differences, there are many points of agreement between case study researchers working in these two traditions. For example, Yin (1984) adopts an implicitly positivist stance in describing case study research, but his view that case studies are the preferred research strategy to answer 'how' and 'why' questions would also be accepted by the interpretive school. Benbasat, Goldstein et al. (1987) also approach the issue of case studies from a positivist stance, but their argument that case study researchers need to be more explicit about their research goals and methods is also of relevance to interpretive IS researchers, and indeed is part of the rationale for this current chapter.

The IS literature contains reports and conclusions from a significant number of interpretive case studies, covering a range of topics and issues (for example, Boland and Day, 1989; Markus, 1983; Orlikowski, 1991; Suchman, 1987; Walsham, 1993; Zuboff, 1988). Most of this literature is concentrated on the substantive case studies themselves and the conclusions which can be drawn from them. This is clearly a desirable focus, but there are few published papers that provide a synthesized view of the nature and conduct of such case studies with specific reference to the field of computer-based IS; this leaves a gap in the literature where this chapter aims to contribute.

In the next section, the research tradition of interpretive case studies is described in more detail, and is contrasted with positivist approaches. This is followed by a section on the use of theory, which is a key issue in all research traditions. The remainder of the chapter is focused on methodological questions concerned with the conduct of empirical research, and on the issue of how to report and generalize results from such work. The final section draws some overall conclusions on interpretive case studies in IS research.

Philosophical basis of interpretive research

The ethnographic research tradition in anthropology is a valuable starting point for a consideration of the philosophical basis of interpretive case studies, since it has been widely drawn on by organizational researchers concerned with interpreting the patterns of symbolic action that create and maintain a sense of organization (see, for example, Smircich, 1983a). Geertz (1973) gives a concise view of the status of the data which are collected in an anthropological study:

> What we call our data are really our own constructions of other people's constructions of what they and their compatriots are up to. (p.9)

Van Maanen (1979), writing in the tradition of organizational ethnography, calls the interviewee's constructions first-order data and the constructions of the researcher second-order concepts. He warns that assuming an ethnographic stance is not a guarantee that researchers will collect valuable data no matter how long they stay in the field. Second-order concepts rely on good theory and insightful analysis, and mere collection of in-depth case study data does not provide these concepts in itself. Examples of second-order concepts in the IS literature, derived from interpretive case studies, include the 'informate' concept from the work of Zuboff (1988), and the concept of 'technological frames' in Orlikowski and Gash (1994).

A second feature of the anthropological tradition is its concern with 'thick description'. Geertz (1973) gives a fascinating example of this involving Jews, Berbers and the French in Morocco in 1912. The incident recounted involves 'sheep stealing' by one of the Jews, who Geertz calls Cohen, from some of the Berbers. However, on closer examination, the 'stealing' turns out to involve compensation for an earlier incident in which Cohen was robbed and nearly killed by members of the same Berber group. The French misunderstand this and put Cohen in prison for what they take to be simple theft on his part. Geertz uses the incident to point out that the ethnographer is faced with a multiplicity of complex conceptual structures, many of them superimposed upon or knotted into one another and which must be first grasped and then rendered intelligible to others.

The IS researcher entering an organization today is also faced with complex and intertwined conceptual structures which it is difficult to grasp and render intelligible as did Geertz in his anthropological work. The need for 'thick' description is just as important in trying to understand what is happening in connection with a complex computer-based information system, involving managers, users and designers, as it was in trying to interpret the interactions of Jews, Berbers and the French in Geertz's study. As a specific illustration of this, Boland and Day (1989) describe how a system designer reinterprets the behaviour of someone who at first she thought was trying to help with her design work, but on further reflection over a period of time she concludes that he was trying to isolate her from others for his own political interest. An IS researcher can only access these subtleties of changing interpretation by the use of approaches based on 'thick' description.

In discussing the purpose of his studies, Geertz argues that he is not trying to answer our deepest questions about other societies, but merely to make his interpretations of these societies available in the 'consultable record'. His goal is not to generate truth or social laws, and this interpretive approach can be clearly distinguished from the positivist tradition. This should not be taken to imply that interpretive work is not generalizable, although the nature of such generalizations is different in the two traditions. This point will be considered in some detail in the penultimate section of the chapter.

The differences between interpretive and positivist approaches can be addressed more formally by considering their epistemological and ontological stances. With respect to epistemology, concerned with the nature of knowledge claims, Archer (1988) defines positivism as the position that facts and values are distinct, and scientific knowledge consists only of facts. He contrasts this position with two alternatives: 'non-positivism' in which facts and values are intertwined and hard to disentangle, and both are involved in scientific knowledge; and 'normativism' which takes the view that scientific knowledge is ideological and inevitably conducive to particular sets of social ends. Either of the latter two positions is open for the interpretive researcher to adopt.

With respect to ontology, concerned with the nature of reality, Archer distinguishes between 'external realism' which considers reality as existing independently of our construction of it, 'internal realism' which views reality-for-us as an inter-subjective construction of the shared human cognitive apparatus, and 'subjective idealism' where each person is considered to construct his or her own reality. The usual ontological stance for an interpretive IS researcher would involve one of the latter two positions, particularly with regard to the human interpretations and meanings associated with computer systems.

The above brief discussion of epistemology and ontology is summarized in Table 6.1. It clearly distinguishes the positivist tradition, but it does not provide any definitive answers as to what precise philosophical stance should be adopted by the interpretive IS researcher. In the related field of 'systems', Mingers (1984) argued that there is considerable value in a careful examination of the philosophical basis of different types of interpretive approaches, and he identified the existence of at least four substantively different strands of thought:

phenomenology, ethnomethodology, the philosophy of language, and hermeneutics. He used this analysis to provide a thoughtful critique of the underlying philosophy of various key writers in the systems field, including Checkland (1981) on soft systems methodology. The different strands of thought identified by Mingers can be seen to underpin some of the research work on interpretive case studies in the IS field: for example, Zuboff (1988) drew on phenomenology, Suchman (1987) on ethnomethodology, and Boland and Day (1989) and Lee (1994) on hermeneutics. Further discussion of the nuances of these various interpretive positions is not possible here, but a principal conclusion from this section is that researchers need to reflect on their own philosophical stance, which should be stated explicitly when writing up their work.

Table 6.1 Alternative stances on knowledge and reality

Epistemology	Ontology
Positivism: Facts and values are distinct and scientific knowledge consists only of facts	*External realism:* Reality exists independently of our construction of it
Non-positivism: Facts and values are inter-twined; both are involved in scientific knowledge	*Internal realism:* Reality-for-us is an inter-subjective construction of the shared human cognitive apparatus
Normativism: Scientific knowledge is ideological and inevitably conductive to particular sets of social ends	*Subjective idealism:* Each person constructs his or her own reality

Use of theory in interpretive studies

A key question for researchers in any tradition, regardless of philosophical stance, concerns the role of theory in their research. Eisenhardt (1989) discusses this issue in the context of organizational research, and identifies three distinct uses of theory: as an initial guide to design and data collection; as part of an iterative process of data collection and analysis; and as a final product of the research. We now discuss each of these with respect to interpretive case studies. A summary of the examples in this discussion is given in Table 6.2.

Table 6.2 Examples of the use of theory in IS case studies

Use of theory	Interpretive IS case study
As an initial guide to design and data collection	Walsham (1993) drawing on Pettigrew
As part of an iterative process of data collection and analysis	Orlikowski (1993) using grounded theory
As a final product of the research	Orlikowski and Robey (1991)

The motivation for the use of theory in the earlier stages of interpretive case studies is to create an initial theoretical framework which takes account of previous knowledge, and which creates a sensible theoretical basis to inform the topics and approach of the early empirical work. For example, the theory of contextualism developed by Pettigrew (1987; 1990) suggested the need to study the content, context and process of organizational change when researching business strategy and its implementation in field studies. Walsham (1993) used this theory as a starting basis for the study of IS strategy and its implementation.

Although theory can provide a valuable initial guide as described above, there is a danger of the researcher only seeing what the theory suggests, and thus using the theory in a rigid way which stifles potential new issues and avenues of exploration. It is desirable in interpretive studies to preserve a considerable degree of openness to the field data, and a willingness to modify initial assumptions and theories. This results in an iterative process of data collection and analysis, with initial theories being expanded, revised, or abandoned altogether. A simple metaphor for this latter case is the use of scaffolding in putting up a building, where the scaffolding is removed once it has served its purpose.

With respect to theory as a final product of the research, Eisenhardt notes that the output from case study research may be concepts, a conceptual framework, propositions or mid-range theory. There is some irony in quoting Eisenhardt in the current chapter, since she explicitly states her epistemological position as positivism, and mid-range theory is something which should, according to her views, then be tested formally using positivist approaches. This position on the role of theory would not be acceptable to many interpretive researchers, although the view of theory as a desirable final product of case study research would be generally shared. For example, Orlikowski and Robey (1991) drew on structuration theory (Giddens, 1984) and their own empirical work in IS to construct a final product in the form of a theory in which the organizational consequences of information technology are viewed as the products of both material and social dimensions.

The three uses of theory in interpretive studies discussed above can be usefully compared with the 'grounded theory' approach of Glaser and Strauss (1967). These authors argued that the researcher should be primarily concerned with the discovery of theory directly from field data. Although they recognized the usefulness of existing theory, for example to provide conceptual categories for field research, they emphasized the primacy of constructing theory from the observed field data. In the specific domain of IS research, Orlikowski (1993) describes the use of grounded theory as the basis of her interpretive case studies on the adoption and use of CASE tools.

With reference to the three categories of theoretical use discussed earlier, Glaser and Strauss would play down the first use of theory as an initial guide to data collection, and would emphasize the latter two uses as part of the iterative research process and as a final product of the work. Indeed, Glaser and Strauss warned against the first use of theory in rather strong terms, and cautioned the researcher against doing too full a literature search before starting work:

> ... carefully to cover 'all' the literature before commencing research increases the probability of brutally destroying one's potentialities as a theorist. (p.253)

This author would not go so far. It is possible to access existing knowledge of theory in a particular subject domain without being trapped in the view that it represents final truth in that area. Glaser and Strauss's warnings are valuable for reflection, but they surely tend towards approaches which risk ignoring existing work.

An interesting discussion of the above issues is given in a book on new strategies in social research (Layder, 1993). Layder argues that researchers can, and must, draw on general theories and employ them in empirical research. He accepts the positive aspects of grounded theory and its emphasis on learning from field data, but argues that:

> ... the grounded theory approach must break away from its primary focus on micro phenomena. The very fixity of this concentration is a factor which prevents grounded theory from attending to historical matters of macro structure as a means cf enriching ... research on micro phenomena. (p.68)

An illustration of Layder's views translated to the IS domain is that research on micro phenomena of IS development and use can, and should, be informed by more general macro theories on the nature of organizations and social processes within them.

Conduct of empirical work

This section is focused on the conduct of empirical work for interpretive case studies, and three sets of issues have been selected for discussion, involving the role of the researcher, interviewing techniques, and reporting methods. This selection reflects the importance of these issues to the interpretive IS researcher. Mumford (1985) provides some useful advice to the IS researcher on other empirical issues such as the choice of research topic, collaboration with in-company personnel, and confidentiality.

Role of the researcher

Interpretive researchers are attempting the difficult task of accessing other people's interpretations, filtering them through their own conceptual apparatus, and feeding a version of events back to others, including in some cases both their interviewees and other audiences. In carrying out this work, it is important that interpretive researchers have a view of their own role in this complex human process. Two different roles can be identified, namely that of the outside observer and that of the involved researcher, through participant observation or action research. From an interpretive perspective, neither of these roles should be viewed as that of an objective reporter, since the collection and analysis of data involves the researcher's own subjectivity. In addition, and particularly with reference to in-depth case studies carried out over a period of time, researchers inevitably influence the interpretations of those people who are being researched, a process referred to as the 'double hermeneutic' by Giddens (1984). So, even if researchers view themselves as outside observers, they are in some sense conducting action research by influencing what is happening in the domain of action, if only by the sharing of concepts and interpretations with the personnel in the field site.

Despite the above qualification, the 'outside observer' role preserves more distance from the personnel in the field organizations. The latter will tend to view the researcher not as one of themselves, but as an outsider. The merit of this approach is that the researcher is seen as not having a direct personal stake in various interpretations and outcomes, and thus personnel will often be relatively frank in expressing their views, provided a rapport of trust can be established. The main disadvantage of this role is that the outside researcher will not be present on many occasions, and will not get a direct sense of the field organization from the inside. In addition, the researcher may sometimes be debarred from access to certain data and issues which are regarded as too confidential or sensitive to be shared with outsiders.

The role of participant observer or action researcher involves the researcher being a member of the field group or organization, or at least becoming a temporary member for some period of time. The merits of this are that the participant observer will get an inside view, and will not normally be debarred from confidential or sensitive issues. On the other hand, the involved researcher will be perceived as having a direct personal stake in various views and activities, and other personnel may be more guarded in their expressed interpretations as a consequence. In addition, unless participant observers or action researchers hide their research motives, which could be considered an unethical position (Mumford, 1985), they will still not be regarded as normal employees and thus not total insiders. A final problem with the role of involved researcher is the extreme difficulty of reporting the part one has played in the various matters under consideration. Self-reporting faces the twin dangers of overmodesty and self-aggrandizement, and it is particularly difficult to steer a middle path between these two extremes.

What advice can be given then on the choice of roles? In the view of this author, the researcher should consciously make the choice dependent on the assessment of the above merits and demerits in each particular case. For example, Nandhakumar (1993) argued that his study of the design and development processes of an executive information system was enhanced by his role as a participant observer, since it was possible for him to be involved in the day-to-day happenings of the design team from the viewpoint of an insider, in a way which would not have been possible for an outside observer. Whatever the

decision made by the individual researcher, it is essential that the choice is made
in an explicit and reflective way, and that the reasons are given when reporting
the results of the research.

Evidence from interviews

Yin (1984) argues that evidence for case studies may come from six sources:
documents, archival records, interviews, direct observation, participant
observation, and physical artefacts. However, with respect to interpretive case
studies as an outside observer, it can be argued that interviews are the primary
data source, since it is through this method that the researcher can best access the
interpretations that participants have regarding the actions and events which
have or are taking place, and the views and aspirations of themselves and other
participants. Even in the case of interpretive case studies being carried out as a
participant observer or action researcher, it can be argued that interviews are still
an important data source, since they enable researchers to step back and examine
the interpretations of their fellow participants in some detail.

With respect to interviewing style, this will vary between individuals,
depending on personality, but one key issue for all interviewers is the balance
which should be adopted by them between excessive passivity and
over-direction. If the interviewer directs the interview too closely, and refuses to
allow interviewees to express their own views except in response to questions
that are tightly controlled by the researcher, then the data obtained will lose
much of the richness of interpretation which is the raw material of sensitive
interpretive studies. However, a researcher can err too far the other way. If the
researcher is too passive, for example either by not prompting with questions
which follow some new direction taken by the interviewee or by not offering his
or her own ideas on some particular issue, a number of negative consequences
can result. The interviewees may conclude that the researchers are either not
interested in their views and/or that the researchers have no views of their own
on the subjects of investigation. This latter consequence can result in IS
interviewees, for example, doubting the professional competence of the
researchers in the IS domain, and future collaboration with the research project
becomes jeopardized.

A second important issue in interviewing concerns reporting media, since it is
vital in an interpretive study to 'capture' people's interpretations in as effective
way as possible, while at the same time conducting the normal social
interchanges of the interview. One approach is to tape-record all research
interviews. The advantage of this is that it provides a full description of what
was said, whereas note taking is necessarily partial. The main disadvantage is
that, in the case of confidential or sensitive material, the respondent may be
seriously inhibited by the presence of the machine. A second disadvantage of
tape recording as the sole medium is the time that needs to be spent in either
transcribing the tape recording or extracting a set of useful data from it. The
main alternative to tape recording is to make rough but extensive notes during
interviews, and to write them up in full as soon as possible after the interview.
Again, with respect to advice to the researcher, individual circumstances need to

be considered. Note taking supplemented by tape recording where appropriate is one sensible approach. Tape recording may be considered appropriate as a supplement in cases of relatively non-confidential material, particularly where the interview contains a large amount of relatively 'hard' data which it would be difficult to capture by note taking alone.

This sub-section has dealt with interviewing technique, but it is important to emphasize that good technique is a necessary but not a sufficient condition for good interviewing. Access to people's thoughts, views and aspirations requires good social skills and personal sensitivity on the part of the researcher, and these are less easily acquired than matters of technique. Zuboff (1988) described her interview approach as involving a 'non-judgemental form of listening'. Researchers should be constantly critical with respect to their own performance in this area, and one approach is to carry out interviews in pairs and subsequently to undertake a critique of each other's style and sensitivity.

Reporting methods

The issue of how to report fieldwork is important in all research, but it can be argued that it is particularly critical in interpretive case studies. Interpretive researchers are not saying to the reader that they are reporting facts; instead, they are reporting their interpretations of other people's interpretations. It is thus vital, in order to establish some credibility to the reader, that they describe in some detail how they have arrived at their 'results'. Reporting on 'soft' human issues is not an excuse for sloppiness.

So what should be reported in an interpretive case study? As a minimum, reporting on the collection of field data should include details of the research sites chosen, the reasons for this choice, the number of people who were interviewed, what hierarchical or professional positions they occupied, what other data sources were used, and over what period the research was conducted. With respect to data analysis, reporting should include how the field interviews and other data were recorded, how they were analyzed and how the iterative process between field data and theory took place and evolved over time. Orlikowski (1993) provides a good example of careful reporting on the above topics.

Before leaving the topic of reporting methods, one further caveat is worth mentioning. Van Maanen (1989) reminds us that establishing validity in the eyes of a reader is part of the art of persuasion, and is as much a matter of rhetorical style and flair as it is of accuracy and care in matters of theory and method. In other words, care in reporting is important, but is not sufficient, and Van Maanen suggests that the researcher must try to persuade by 'presenting a coherent point of view told with grace, wit and felicity' (p.32).

Generalizations from interpretive research

A critical issue for researchers concerns the generalizability of the results from their work, and Yin (1984) notes that this issue is often raised with respect to case studies:

'How can you generalize from a single case study' is a frequently heard question ... The short answer is that case studies ... are generalizable to theoretical propositions ... (p.21)

We will extend Yin's answer in this section to four types of generalization from interpretive case studies: the development of concepts, the generation of theory, the drawing of specific implications, and the contribution of rich insight. However, before discussing each of these generalizations in more detail, a short introduction is necessary on the nature of theorizing in the social sciences, viewed from an interpretive stance.

Bhaskar (1979) describes the scientific process in the natural sciences as involving three phases in which phenomena are identified, explanations for the phenomena are constructed and empirically tested, and the generative mechanisms at work are described. Bhaskar argues that the human or social sciences can be tackled using a similar methodology, but there are differences in that social structures do not exist independently of the actions and conceptions of the human agents in them, and the generative mechanisms of such structures are not space-time invariant. Thus, generative mechanisms identified for phenomena in the social sciences should be viewed as 'tendencies', which are valuable in explanations of past data but are not wholly predictive for future situations. The generalizations which we discuss below should, therefore, be seen as explanations of particular phenomena derived from empirical interpretive research in specific IS settings, which may be valuable in the future in other organizations and contexts.

We will now illustrate each of the four types of generalizations using specific examples, although it should be noted that the four types are not mutually exclusive categories. A summary of these examples is given in Table 6.3.

The first type of generalization concerns concepts. Zuboff (1988) used her interpretive case studies of IT use in US organizations to develop the 'informate' concept, which has been widely quoted in the IS literature and beyond. She introduced this concept as follows:

Thus, information technology, even when it is applied to automatically reproduce a finite activity, is not mute. It not only imposes information (in the form of programmed instructions) but also produces information ... information technology supersedes the traditional logic of automation. The word that I have coined to describe this unique capacity is informate. Activities, events, and objects are translated into and made visible by information when a technology informates as well as automates. (pp.9-10)

Table 6.3 Examples of generalizations from IS case studies

Type of generalization	Interpretive IS case study
Development of concepts	Informate – Zuboff (1988)
Generation of theory	Theory of organizational consequences of IT – Orlikowski and Robey (1991), Jones and Nandhakumar (1993)
Drawing of specific implications	Relationship between design and development and business strategy – Walsham and Waema (1994)
Contribution of rich insight	Limits of machine intelligence; differences between plans and practical actions; need for more thoughtful machine design – Suchman (1987)

A single concept such as 'informate' can be part of a broader network or an integrated clustering of concepts, propositions and world-views which form theories in social science (Layder, 1993). As an illustration in the IS field, it was noted earlier that Orlikowski and Robey (1991) drew on their empirical work in IS to construct a theoretical framework concerned with the organizational consequences of information technology. They argued that their framework could be used to guide studies in two main areas of information systems research, namely systems development and the organizational consequences of using IT. Jones and Nandhakumar (1993) describe the application of the framework to the analysis of an interpretive case study of the executive information system development process in a large manufacturing company. They conclude that the framework was valuable to their work, but go on to suggest some areas for further theoretical development. The two papers taken together provide a good illustration of theory generation and development based on interpretive IS case studies.

A third type of generalization from interpretive case studies involves specific implications in particular domains of action. Walsham and Waema (1994) draw a number of such implications based on an in-depth case study of the development of IS in a financial services company over an eight-year period. One implication concerns the relationship between the design and development process and business strategy:

> An ad hoc methodological approach to the development of computer-based information systems, accompanied by a clear business focus, can lead to rapid systems development, but the price paid for such an approach can be inflexibility and a lack of adequate integration. Design and development drawing heavily on formalized methods can be slow and geared to 'systems for today', if the development proceeds at a time when the business vision and related IS strategy remain unclear. (p.171)

The quotation above uses verbs such as 'can' rather than 'will' in line with the earlier discussion of generalizations as tendencies rather than predictions. The implication provided a good description of a 'generative mechanism' in the case study which was investigated, and it may prove a useful insight for related work in other organizations and contexts.

The final category of generalization which we will consider here is that of 'rich insight' from interpretive case studies. This phrase is designed to capture insights from the reading of reports and results from case studies that are not easily categorized as concepts, theories, or specific implications. For example, the book by Suchman (1987) discusses the problem of human-machine communication based on an interpretive case study of the use of a particular copying machine. She develops concepts such as 'plans' and 'situated actions', various theories regarding human-machine interaction, and specific implications in domains such as artificial intelligence. However, this reader gained more from the book than is captured by these categories, since Suchman provided rich insight on a wide range of topics, including the limits of machine intelligence, the inherent differences between plans and practical actions, and the need for more thoughtful machine design.

A further illustration of the above point follows from noting that the selection of the 'informate' concept from Zuboff's book does not do justice to the richness of the insights which many readers have gained from her work. This can be judged by the way it has been widely quoted on topics such as the changing nature of work in contemporary society, and the need to empower workers in the information age in order to make fuller use of their human capabilities. We should not be misled into too narrow a view of the generalizations which readers can gain from studying the reports and results from interpretive case studies, and the category of 'rich insight' attempts to describe these broader and more diffuse implications.

Conclusion

A number of writers in the IS field have already demonstrated that interpretive case studies, if carried out and written up carefully, can make a valuable contribution to both IS theory and practice. However, the volume and range of such studies are relatively limited at the present time. It can be argued that there is a need for much more work from an interpretive stance in the future, since human interpretations concerning computer-based information systems are of central importance to the practice of IS, and thus to the investigations carried out by IS researchers.

This chapter has aimed to contribute to the future development of the interpretive school of IS research by providing discussion and guidance on a range of issues. These were concerned both with the philosophical and theoretical nature of interpretive studies in the IS field, and with methods of conducting and reporting such work. The chapter has aimed to provide a useful reference point on these issues, and more generally to encourage IS case study researchers to reflect on the basis, conduct and reporting of their work.

7 The Critical Social Theory Approach to Information Systems: Problems and Challenges

Ojelanki K. Ngwenyama

For some time now critical social theory has been put forward as an alternative to traditional approaches to information systems research and practice. It has however remained a mystery to 'outside' observers, because of the language of its discourse, and radically different position on scientific enterprise. This chapter attempts to open the discourse on critical social theory by presenting a review of basic concepts and discussing some of the theoretical problems and challenges which must be addressed if progress is to be made in applying it to the practical issues of information systems.

The past decade has seen much discussion about the theoretical foundations of the various information systems research programmes and the future of information systems as a discipline (McFarlan, 1984a; Mumford et al., 1985). These discussions have been useful in that they have exposed many of our theoretical assumptions to debate and critical reflection. More recently, Hirschheim and Klein (1989) have presented an analysis and classification of the general theoretical assumptions of various approaches to information systems research into four paradigms: Functionalism, Social Relativism, Radical Structuralism, and Neohumanism. Although much research has been carried out within each of the paradigms, some approaches have not received adequate attention. One such approach, critical social theory, which falls within the neohumanist paradigm, has been primarily limited to theoretical issues. However, the potential contribution of critical social theory to new knowledge about information systems development and usage has been discussed by several researchers.

Mingers (1981) was one of the first to point out its relevance to applied systems thinking. He specifically pointed to the work of Habermas as a fruitful starting point. As he explained:

More recently Habermas has produced a critique of science and technology which includes an attack on systems theory and particularly systems analysis. It might appear, at first sight, that the two should be dedicatedly opposed and yet, although there are important disagreements, the striking similarities make it seem possible that the two approaches may both benefit from a dialogue.

More recently Klein (1984) and Lyytinen and Klein (1985) have made the argument that critical social theory could inform the theoretical assumption of several traditional approaches to information systems and perhaps free the discipline from what they call the 'poverty of scientism'. Much work needs to be done, however, in order to clarify the critical social theory perspective and research programme. It is the objective of this chapter to help demystify the critical social theory approach, and open it up for debate and critical analysis by both critical and traditional theorists. The focus of the chapter is on outlining: (a) the main concerns of critical social theory, specifically Habermas's critical social theory; (b) the theoretical assumptions of critical social theory as they might apply to information systems research and practice; (c) to offer a critique of the current application of critical social theory to information systems research; and (d) to outline a methodology for practice oriented research.

Fundamental assumptions of critical social theory

Critical social theory is a school of thought which has as its primary objective the improvement of the human condition. Its focus, according to its founders (Horkheimer, Adorno, Fromm, and Marcuse) is on general theoretical problems, as well as specific investigations of concrete problems of contemporary social organization. The approach was to break with traditional hypothetical deductive methods, which are oriented towards the preservation and gradual reformation of the status quo. Critical social theory was intended to be a radically different approach which would take into account the human construction of social forms of life and the possibility of their recreation. At the inaugural address of the opening of the Institute for Social Research in 1937, Horkheimer outlined the goals of critical social theory as follows:

> The critical theory of society on the contrary (... to the positivist view of social science) has as its objects men as the producers of their total historical forms of life. The conditions of reality from which science starts out, appear to it not as given to be established and calculated purely on the basis of laws of probability. What is in each case given, depends not solely upon nature but also upon what men wish to make of it. The objects and the manner of perception, the statement of the problem and the interpretation of the answers are created from human activity and the degree of its power (Frisby, 1972, p.107).

The primary difference between traditional social theory and critical social theory is the researcher's attitude toward his/her world and work. Fundamentally, traditional social theory is premised on the analysis and understanding of the status quo. By implicit acceptance of 'what is', traditional social theory does not challenge, but contributes to the preservation of the status quo. Further, because of its rejection of value issues, it is easily transformed into reified ideology. Critical social theory on the other hand, is concerned with finding alternatives to existing social conditions which more adequately address human desires. Its research focuses on the emancipation of individuals and the human species in general. Critical social theory rejects the separation of value and inquiry, knowledge and action, and challenges the unity of the scientific method with regard to social affairs.

The critical social theory programme for social research and practice is grounded on five fundamental assumptions:

1. People are the creators of their social world, and as such, can change it if they wish.
2. All scientific knowledge about the social world is socially constructed, and as such, cannot avoid being infused with 'value orientations', because all social constructions are value laden. Value orientations can be identified in both implicit and explicit forms of ideology held by the researchers.
3. Reason and critique are inseparable. As Marcuse (1968) explains: reason means the capacity to understand the existing social world, to criticize it, and to search for and present alternatives to it. Reason here is to be understood in the Hegelian sense, as the critical faculty which reconciles knowledge with change toward the goal of human freedom. It is through critical reason that the inherent distortions of the social affairs can be reconstructed and understood.
4. Theory and practice ought to be inextricably interconnected, because the task of critical social theory is seen as that of reconciling knowledge with the satisfaction of the human need for self-improvement.
5. Critical social theory must be reflexive: that is, it must concern itself with the validity conditions of knowledge and change which it produces. Therefore, researchers following this approach must collaborate with those who will be affected by it, opening it up to public debate and critical reflection.

A summary of the fundamental assumptions follows:

1. People have the power to change their world.
2. Knowledge of the social world is value laden.
3. Reason and critique are inseparable.
4. Theory and practice must be interconnected.
5. Reason and critique must be reflexive in practice.

Habermas's contribution to critical social theory

In line with the stated fundamental assumptions, Habermas has set out to broaden the discourse on critical social theory to include various strands of contemporary thought. In the early 1960's, he entered the Popper-Adorno debate over the philosophical foundations of social science, attacking the narrowness of 'instrumental reason' and 'the technological imperative' of modern science. He felt that scientific and technological thought had become too dogmatic, extending its instrumental rationality into all spheres of life, reducing political and social issues into matters of technical rationality. He believed that a critical approach with a broader notion of rationality was needed to ensure that society maximizes the benefits of technological advancements while minimizing the disadvantages. In an attempt to extend beyond instrumental rationality, Habermas adopts from Kant's critical philosophy, the notion of *practical reason*, *critique*, and *reflective judgement*, incorporating them in his principles for critical inquiry. He has also provided significant criticisms of modern theories of management and social control, such as functional systems and organizational theory, cybernetics, game theory, and decision theories, which are the current core not only of information systems research, but also of management and other applied behavioural sciences.

In studying extensively the methodological problems of knowledge acquisition of the social sciences, Habermas set out to construct a conceptual framework upon which a critical scientific methodology suitable to critical social theory research could be based. In *Knowledge and Human Interest* (Habermas, 1968) he outlines a program for the development of this methodology. He starts by identifying at the transcendental level, three types of knowledge interest which he believes drive all human inquiry: (1) technical; (2) practical; and (3) emancipatory (see Table 7.1). Technical knowledge interest has as its concern the human need for prediction and control of the natural and social world. It is rooted in instrumental rationality and focuses on defining means for achieving given ends. Consequently, its major products are technology: for example, management procedures, problem solving methods and so on. Technical knowledge interest is validated with regard to its effectiveness. Practical knowledge interest, on the other hand, is concerned with our quest for self-understanding. The focus of practical knowledge interest is on understanding social forms of life, traditions, social behaviour and relations, and offers as its products improved social consciousness and humanity. It uses communicative rationality and is validated with regard to truth and clarity. Emancipatory knowledge interest is related to our concern for freedom from physical and mental restrictions and social distortions. It uses dialectic rationality for critical reflection and analysis of instrumental rationality, and its products, with regard to their 'rightness'. Emancipatory knowledge interest also focuses on the establishment of norms for justice and enhancement of human freedoms. Each type of knowledge interest is believed to represent a frame of reference (or mental mode) through which researchers apprehend and make sense of the world as they seek to obtain knowledge about it.

Habermas sees science and its project of improving the human condition as a collaborative effort where people (scientists and non-scientists) work together to achieve its ends. Such being the case, communication is central to the performance of a collaborative science. The question then becomes; how do the participants guard against systematic distortions and violations of free and unencumbered scientific discourse? Habermas has defined two classes of criteria for analyzing and validating discourses: (a) content, and (b) relationship. The content criteria deal with the truth and clarity of every communicative action, while the relationship criteria deal with the appropriateness and sincerity of those actions. For Habermas the act of entering scientific discourse means that the participants are committed to finding a solution by force of better argument, and must adhere to domination-free cooperation and communication. Facts may not be misrepresented, and jargon may not be used to mystify, as this would violate the principle of ideal discourse.

Table 7.1 Fundamental human knowledge interests

Knowledge interest	Object of interest	Orientation	Knowledge products
Technical	Natural world Social structures	Prediction/Control	Scientific knowledge Technology
Practical	Social relations	Mutual understanding	Social consciousness
	Tradition		Humanity
Emancipatory	Technology Social relations	Social criticism	Norms for justice Freedom

Conceptual foundations for critical social theory methodology

The universe of inquiry of critical social theory spans the objective-subjective spectrum of social reality. It emphasizes open collaboration by giving primacy to the actors' participation in the creation of a social world with meaning appropriate to them. Physical and organizational structures, social relations, symbolic interactions as well as each actor's interpretation of these are the universe of inquiry for critical social theory research. In order to make sense of this 'messy' world, the inquirer must focus on both process and context from an individual as well as an institutional perspective. To deal with this task, critical social theory adopts pluralistic inquiry methods that are heavily oriented towards interpreting and mapping the meaning and social construction of the universe of inquiry. This allows the researcher to be sensitive to the life-worlds of participants which are central to understanding the way social actions are constructed and executed. The approach is one of active participation, observation and analysis of contextual data. This strategy enables the analysis of social contexts in which social actions are embedded.

Critical social theory aims to integrate the three fundamental knowledge interests into a holistic approach to inquiry and intervention (see Table 7.2). In support of technical knowledge interest, it admits the inquiry methods of empirical sciences as appropriate to problems of technical control and prediction in engineering research. Technical control and prediction are not limited to nature - people are included as well (for example, human systems engineering, such as marketing research and behaviour control). Critical social theory recognizes the other knowledge interests as mitigating influences to the possible excesses of instrumental rationality and balances these with the communicative rationality of practical knowledge interest and the dialectic rationality emancipatory knowledge interest. Critical social theory also recognizes *the difference between observing nature and observing people* in scientific research. People are not inanimate objects serving only as passive objects of observation for the researcher. Under observation, they may adopt different behaviours depending on their perception of the role of the researcher, thus invalidating the principle of asymmetric observation. Further, *critical social theory does not accept that science is value free; it makes explicit its value position*, which is the improvement of the human condition. Improvement of the human condition here means freeing people from social and psychological distortions and barriers to social progress.

Table 7.2 Conceptual foundations of critical social theory methodology

Knowledge interest	Universe of inquiry	Inquiry methods	Rationality	Validity claim
Technical	Objective world	Empirical	Instrumental	Effectiveness
Practical	Shared Subjective	Descriptive Interpretive	Communicative	Truth Clarity
Emancipatory	Inner-subjective	Critical Interpretive	Dialectic	Justice

Research problems and challenges

It would be instructive at this point, to classify current critical social theory - information systems research in order to clearly identify the nature of it, and its possible future directions. The concepts of Figure 7.1 are used as the schema for analysis (see Table 7.3), as they offer a simple and straightforward classification which adheres to the basic assumptions of critical social theory. On the theoretical level, two types of research are identified: (a) Decisionistic - work which provides criteria, principles, or guidelines for dealing with a specific class of problems. Few papers report this type of research (see Table 7.3); and (b) Reflective - work which focuses on critique. By far, most of the research falls within this category (see Table 7.3), with the focus being on the foundations of information systems. On the practical level we have: (c) Interventionist - action oriented work which intervenes or provides methods for intervention into information systems research and practices with the clear objective of improving it; and (d) Experiential - participant observation work on information systems research and practice to collect data for theory building and critical reflection. So far, very little research has been reported at the level of practice.

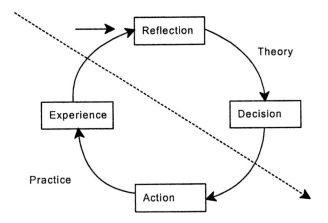

Figure 7.1 The critical social theory inquiry-change process

Much of the work listed above can be criticized on two important aspects: (1) Communicative competence - their use of jargon serves to create barriers to free and open participation in the debate; (2) Reductionism - by separating theory from practice, and narrowing the focus to issues of theoretical interest, a grave sin has been committed against the philosophy of critical social theory. More attention needs to be given to work which integrates the four quadrants of the schema. Although the use of the schema in this analysis could be characterized as reductionist, the aim is to point out how the existing research has been segmented in focus. Another important problem that the critical social theory programme must face is the question of an appropriate methodology. The next section presents a brief discussion on how action science might contribute to a solution of this problem.

Table 7.3 Critical social theory schema for classifying research

	Decisionistic	Reflective
Theoretical	Klein and Hirschheim (1985) Lyytinen (1986b)	Hirschheim and Klein (1989) Klein (1984) Klein (1986b) Klein (1986a) Klein and Hirschheim (1983) Klein and Hirschheim (1988) Klein and Lyytinen (1985) Lyytinen (1986b) Lyytinen (1986a) Lyytinen and Klein (1985) Ngwenyama (1987)
Practical	Ngwenyama (1990)	Ngwenyama (1990)

Toward an action science research strategy

Action science is a methodology for practice oriented social research developed by Argyris (1970a) and Argyris, Putnam et al. (1985). It is considered an exemplar of critical social theory because it shares similar core assumptions: (1) critique of the status quo and a search for alternatives to it; (2) collaborative action for learning and fundamental change; (3) free and open participation by individuals in the creation of their social world; (4) critical self-reflection as a methodology for improving self-awareness and transformation. Like critical social theory, action science is concerned with bridging the gap between science and intervention (that is, theory and practice, knowledge and action). As a science, it focuses on producing 'knowledge of action', which informs social practice. It assumes a definition of 'knowledge of action' that goes beyond that of mainstream applied science. While the latter is concerned with the technical problem of choosing the best means to achieve specified ends, and defines knowledge of action as knowledge about the relationship between means and ends, action science extends the definition to include a normative component which concerns the choosing ends. It holds that value judgements are not simply 'emotive utterances' but social facts which have consequences in the social world. Action science is concerned not only with technical effectiveness but also with the validity of norms for guiding open and informed choices and responsible action. Both action science and critical social theory take the position that technical knowledge in the absence of intelligent and responsible choice of ends is impractical and often dysfunctional. Although it would be useful to enter a discussion on action science, space does not permit. For a comprehensive overview see Argyris, Putnam et al. (1985). The following is a summary of the basic principles of action science:

1. It seeks to enact reflective inquiry as a fundamental aspect of social practice. The ground of its knowledge claims is the community of social practice, which is the ultimate judge of its validity.

2. It seeks to produce generalized knowledge of action through reflective inquiry of social practice which is guided by norms of public testing, falsifiability, intersubjective agreement on data and explicit inference.

3. It is concerned with the interpenetration of empirical, interpretive, and normative claims, insofar as they relate to the meaning and logic of action.

4. It seeks to create alternatives to the status quo and to promote learning and change at the level of norms and values, by focusing on double loop learning and frame breaking.

Action science methodology

The action science methodology intends to produce knowledge which can be characterized by two main criteria: (a) immediate usefulness in action situations; and (b) unconformable propositions and theory, falsifiable by practitioners in real-life action situations. It follows then that the universe of inquiry is practice. The approach is a collaborative process in which scientist and participants of the *action situation of interest* enquire into problems of social practice in a learning context. The learning context is designed to foster learning about the constraints of practice and about alternative ways of constructing it. The process of action learning is a cycle of public critical reflection and experimentation-in-action in which taken-for-granted routines are challenged, alternatives developed and tested, and new competences learned (see Figure 7.2). Communicative action is the primary source of data for inquiry and analysis. It is an important form of social action which provides a window for inquiry into the *logic of action,* that is, the rules and tacit theories which inform the actor's routines (Argyris, Putnam et al., 1985; Gronn, 1983; Habermas, 1979; Habermas, 1981; Habermas, 1984; Wynn, 1979).

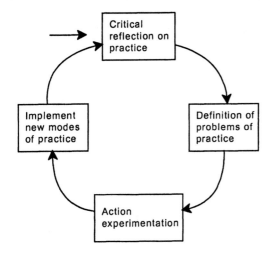

Figure 7.2 The action learning cycle

The action-experimentation process

Action-experimentation is a process in which participants in real-life action situations collaborate with action scientists to identify and solve problems of social practice. The process seeks to foster open and free participation in which individuals are encouraged to: (a) select problems for study which are relevant to them; (b) take responsibility for data collection; and (c) participate in data analysis. The rules of action science inquiry, although designed to push back constraints of real-life conditions for collecting and analyzing data, and testing hypotheses, are nevertheless generalizable in everyday practice.

The aim of action science is to help individuals learn the rules and shared norms of inquiry so that they can implement these as aspects of regular practice. Data collection and analysis are not separated in action science research as they are in other research programmes. There are, however, preferred approaches to conducting action science research which share well defined strategies for collecting data, conducting action-experiments, and ensuring internal validity and consistency. A range of methods is employed to ensure reliable data collection: (1) participant observation; (2) audio and video taping; (3) interviews; (4) action experiments; and (5) participant written cases. In action science research several of these methods are used together to accommodate cross-checking and minimize data pollution. Two types of data are elicited: (a) what individuals say and do as they perform their routines; and (b) their self-reports of what they were thinking and feeling at the time of action. Since action science promotes collaborative inquiry, the participants are encouraged to select problems for study which are relevant to them.

Three conceptual tools are used for data analysis: (a) theory-in-use models; (b) the ladder of inference; and (c) cognitive maps. The first are a set of abstract explanatory and normative models, or ideal types, that guide the researchers in doing data analysis. They were developed by Argyris and Schön (1974) to help action scientists decide which data and causal sequences of actions are important to their problem solving.

The ladder of inference serves three functions. First it is used to derive maps of action from collected data. These models are then tested in the action context. Second it is used to help connect generalized knowledge to specific cases during the design of new action strategies. Finally, it is a tool for retracing and making public the inferences that actors make when carrying out their action strategies.

The third tool, mapping, gives recognition to the fact that participants edit their organizational experience into scripts of personal knowledge. A cognitive map consists of the concepts and relationships an actor uses to understand action situations. When these maps are limited to defining causal relationships, they are called cause maps. Maps can be either graphic or narrative representations of action-strategies. They describe the tacit and propositional logic which are embedded in the action-strategies along with their effects on the behavioural world of the actors.

Hypothesis testing

Hypotheses are derived from maps and tested in real-life action-experiments. Although the action context is a formidable domain for ensuring the validity tests, it is the only setting that provides the multitude of interacting variables which actors face in practice. Testing is a repetitive cycle of mapping action-situations, deriving hypotheses, designing action-experiments, and implementing them in practice (see Figure 7.3). The objective of this activity is to develop generalizable maps suitable for problem analysis and solving across a wide variety of case situations.

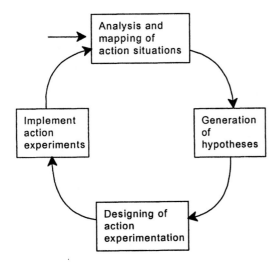

Figure 7.3 The action-experimentation cycle

Conclusion

This chapter has presented a review of the basic assumptions of critical social theory, and its principles for collaborative practice-oriented research. The analysis of current research suggests that it is time to re-orient toward more practical concerns. The critical social theory approach was never intended to be an abstract philosophy. It was to bring about real change in the human condition. Although it may be argued that rushing from theory to practice results from the fear of speculation, and from shallowness of action and knowledge (Von Schelling, 1958), it must be remembered that *Theoros* (the Greek god with whom theory is associated) was sent out to contemplate the cosmos only on holidays; *praxis* dominated the workdays.

Much fieldwork is needed to understand better how information systems research and practice can be improved by critical social theory. The latter sections of the chapter have attempted to deal with the methodology problem which has impeded progress on practice oriented research. While work continues on adapting and implementing an action science methodology, other methods need to be identified and tested for suitability to this type of research. Further, the discourse needs to be more accommodating of other forms of social research and practice if a dialectic is ever to be achieved. The critical theory information systems research programme could learn a great deal from dialogues with the *soft systems approach* and *trade union perspective*.

Acknowledgements

The author wishes to thank Prof. Gareth Morgan, Faculty of Administrative Studies, York University, and the referees for their valuable comments.

Part III

Qualitative Research Methods

8 A Critical Perspective on Action Research as a Method for Information Systems Research

Richard L. Baskerville and A. Trevor Wood-Harper

The purpose of this chapter is to review critically the origins, techniques and roles associated with a growing information systems research method known as 'action research'. This method is widely cited as an exemplar of a post-positivist social scientific research method, ideally suited to the study of technology in its human context. We seek to illuminate both the attractions and the detractions that this method holds for IS researchers.

The discipline of IS seems to be a very appropriate field for the use of action research methods. IS is a highly applied field, almost vocational in nature (Banville and Landry, 1989). Action research methods are highly clinical in nature, and place IS researchers in a 'helping-role' within the organizations that are being studied (see Schein, 1987). It should not be surprising that action research is the 'touchstone of most good organizational development practice' and remains the primary methodology for the practice of organizational development' (Van Eynde and Bledsoe, 1990, p.27). Action research merges research and praxis thus producing exceedingly relevant research findings. Such relevance is an important measure of the significance of IS research (Keen, 1991). However, the action research method has proved very unpopular with North American IS research. Action research articles in major North American research publications are extremely rare. Orlikowski and Baroudi (1991) discovered only one action research article among the 155 major research publications between January 1983 and May 1988. Action research contributed only 0.6% of this research literature. Despite its overwhelming acceptance in organizational development, it is virtually non-existent among North American IS research.

Outside North America, action research has made more contributions to the literature of the IS research community. In particular, Checkland's soft systems methodology (Checkland and Scholes, 1990; Checkland, 1981) has influenced IS research by linking action research and systems development. This has increased the presence of action research in British, Scandinavian and Australian IS literature. However, action research is not a predominant IS research method even in those geographic areas. Given the conducive relationship between the vocational nature of the IS field and the clinical nature of action research, why is action research contributing so little to the IS research literature (particularly in North America)? Perhaps we are missing an understanding of the relationship between IS research domains and the features of action research.

This chapter is organized as follows: first a philosophical viewpoint (is established) for the study. Following this introduction, the origins of the method are considered. The chapter continues by briefly describing the method and then discussing its role in IS research. In conclusion the features of action research that present the IS researcher with problems and opportunities are clarified.

Critical reviewers have revealed serious doubts about the appropriateness of research into IS. Jarvenpaa, Dickson et al. (1985) found that experimental IS research was lacking in task and measurement validity. Ives and Olson (1984) found that IS survey research suffered from poor instruments and lack of control. Baroudi and Orlikowski (1989) found a general lack of statistical power in IS research. Benbasat, Goldstein et al. (1987) noted that IS case study investigators had a history of ignoring methodological issues, and a failing to specify clear objectives. Cooper (1988) pointed to underlying problems in the natural sciences paradigm currently associated with IS research and suggested the adoption of methodological pluralism.

As the critical revelations of IS research problems continue, interest grows in alternative methods of discovery. No doubt interest will rise in post-positivist research methods such as grounded theory (Glaser and Strauss, 1967), deconstruction (Rosenau, 1992) and action research. This latter method has a longer history and has attracted perhaps the largest following in certain geographic regions (such as Northern Europe, England and Australia). Since the action research method involves the close collaboration of both researchers and practitioners, a thorough understanding of its techniques and implications may be essential to everyone in the field of IS during the final decade of the 1990s.

The philosophical issue

No accurate description of action research can avoid consideration of its philosophy. This is because its usage entails some assumptions about scientific knowledge that are not widely institutionalized. This is important for the scientists who apply the method, since some of their colleagues may earnestly question the findings on very fundamental grounds.

This difficulty is diminishing, however, as the field of IS enters a new stage in its maturity. Many scientists who have interests in the field are becoming more concerned with the social and psychological aspects of the introduction of technology into the human work place, rather than concentrating only on the technical aspects (Blackler, 1988). Some IS research is becoming more sophisticated (or perhaps esoteric) in its social science, and this is confronting IS scientists with the disparate philosophies of science that have haunted the social sciences for decades (Klein et al., 1991).

The present social scientific institutions are broadly based on the empirical tradition, and parallel the current philosophy of the natural sciences. In this, IS science is not an exception. The IS foundations in computer science and engineering imply an appreciation of mathematics and physics. Scientists can conduct research on this basis and be assured that the findings will be accepted by the widest majority of their colleagues. This means that IS research scientists presently can contribute meaningful research without understanding or participating in the philosophical turmoil at the sociological periphery of IS science.

These alternative philosophies endorse research methods that may not appear to be scientific to the scientist schooled only in the statistical tradition of Pearson, the nomothetic logical positivism of Hempel or the falsifiability of Popper (see Hirschheim, 1985a). The consequences of this limited perspective are threefold: dismiss the findings of such methods as unscientific, accept such findings on good faith or the reputation of the author, or lodge a considerable investment in grappling with the philosophical literature. The latter course is not a short side trip for the busy scientist; it also will not be a totally happy experience. The threatening discovery that some views of science discredit the findings of traditional methods is reached quickly (commonly called 'positivist-bashing'). The more recent post-modern views of social science have altogether dismissed the idea of grand unifying scientific paradigms as an impedance (Rosenau, 1992).

Action research is a method that could be described as a paragon of the post-positivist research methods. It is empirical, yet interpretive. It is experimental, yet multivariate. It is observational, yet interventionist. Enticingly, the research subjects are often quite willing to pay the costs of being studied, especially since they may influence the outcomes of the project. To an arch positivist it should seem very unscientific. To the post-positivist, it seems ideal.

Origins of action research

The action research method developed when the calamities of World War II precipitated massive social changes in the research arena of the social sciences. Lewin (1951) is credited with developing the method at the Research Center for Group Dynamics (University of Michigan) in order to study social psychology within the framework of field theory. However, another group working independently at the Tavistock Clinic (later the Tavistock Institute) developed a similar method as a sort of psychosocial equivalent of operational research (Trist, 1976).

The Tavistock Institute dealt with psychological and social disorders caused by battlefields and prisoner-of-war camps. Previous to this war, these psychological syndromes had not been identified in such a large population of patients. Scientists did not understand enough about the complex causes of such social illnesses to formulate confidence in any universal treatments. Each case appeared somehow 'different'. Hence, the idea of social action arose. Scientists intervened in each experimental case by changing some aspect of the patients' being or surroundings. Since scientist and therapist were one, the scientists were participants in their own research. The effects of the actions were recorded and studied. In this manner, a body of knowledge was developed about successful therapy for the illnesses (see Rapoport, 1970).

Lewin's work (1951) sought a general theory of how social change could be facilitated. His original model of action research included iteration of six phased stages, rather than the five now commonly assumed. The six stages were (1) analysis, (2) fact-finding, (3) conceptualization, (4) planning, (5) implementation of action, and (6) evaluation. While the level of abstraction is slightly different, the essential method is very similar to the later version described below.

Action research has been linked closely to systems theory from its inception, although Susman and Evered (1978) (and later Susman, 1983) made the most seminal connections. These ideas recognize that human activities are systematic, and that action researchers are intervening in social systems. Warmington (1980) explicitly described the implications of action research for the field of systems analysis.

At Lancaster University, Checkland's (1981) extensive use of action research in the methodology of systems development is a landmark for the technique in IS research. Checkland's view of human activity systems drew considerable IS attention to action research. Checkland not only used the approach extensively in developing the soft systems methodology, but action research concepts for gaining professional knowledge permeated the soft systems approach itself.

Despite the attention currently focused on action research in the IS research community, we must recognize that the technique never succeeded in procuring strong status in the mainstream of social psychology or social science research (Sanford, 1976). Outside IS, widely published action research arises mostly in applied health fields (for example, Israel et al., 1989; Jowett, 1988; Webb, 1989) and management research (for example, Lukka, 1987). It seems to have been forced to the periphery of legitimate scientific methodologies today, perhaps because its post-positivist foundations frequently bring epistemological contention into the discussions of the research findings.

Clark (1972) cast action research as a methodological 'orphan' in post World War II science. He attributed the failure of action research to 'get off the ground' in the 1950s and 1960s to the funding structure of social science research. He reasoned that research was being increasingly sponsored by public money. In response, leading researchers tended to seek projects that relied on 'hard' quantitative data: projects that sported the computer analysis that attracted government attention. This post-war emphasis on 'professionalism' and precise data collection methods led to a general decline in qualitative research skills.

Another factor is the relationship between action research and consulting. This should not be surprising, since the mainstream of consulting literature can be traced back through Lippit and Lippit (1978) to Schein's Process Consultation (1969). Schein based process consultation on Lewin's action cycle and Gordon Lippit was Lewin's PhD student. The consulting literature and action research literature emerged among separate streams of thought from Lewin, and rarely reference each other. Still, observers may easily confuse these two intellectual cousins, requiring action researchers to defend their method against the challenge that 'this is nothing but consultancy!' (Jönsson, 1991, p.393).

We see that IS research scientists considering the adoption of the action research method must recognize its tenuous stature as a scientific method. This is not a mainstream social science technique being applied in the new field of IS. Rather it is an obscure, contentious method found on the periphery of mainstream social science being transported into the IS field. Perhaps, as its proponents imply, this is the field within which it will finally flourish. However, it may alternatively continue to dwell on the periphery of IS research as it has in other branches of social science.

Description of the method

Action research is an interventionist approach to the acquisition of scientific knowledge that has sound foundations in the post-positivist tradition. Blum (1955) explained the essence of action research as a simple two stage process. First, the diagnostic stage involves a collaborative analysis of the social situation by the researcher and the subjects of the research. Hypotheses are formulated concerning the nature of the research domain. Second, the therapeutic stage involves collaborative change experiments. In this stage changes are introduced and the effects are studied.

However, in order to achieve scientific rigour, additional structure is usually imposed on action research. The most prevalent description (Susman and Evered, 1978) details a five phase, cyclical process which can be described as an 'ideal' exemplar of the original formulation of action research. In practice such methods often vary depending on the application. This ideal approach first requires the establishment of a client-system infrastructure or research environment. Then, five identifiable phases are iterated: (1) diagnosing, (2) action planning, (3) action taking, (4) evaluating and (5) specifying learning. Figure 8.1 shows this action research structural cycle.

The client-system infrastructure is the specification and agreement that constitutes the research environment. It provides the authority, or sanctions, under which the researchers and host practitioners may specify actions and provides the legitimation of those actions as beneficial to the client or host organization. Considerations include the boundaries of the research domain, and the entry and exit of the scientists. It must also patently recognize the latitude of the researchers to disseminate the learning gained in the research. This infrastructure must define the responsibilities of the client and the researchers to each other. For example, the infrastructure will probably assume that the researchers will not purposely specify actions that are harmful to the organization.

A key aspect of the infrastructure is the collaborative nature of the undertaking. The research scientists work closely with practitioners located within the client-system. These individuals provide the subject system knowledge and insight necessary to understand the anomalies being studied. Clark (1972, p.65) described these practitioners:

For convenience it is useful to think of the practitioner as part of a set of actors who are oriented to solution of practical problems, who are essentially organizational scientists rather than academic scientists.

Diagnosing corresponds to the identification of the primary problems that are the underlying causes of the organization's desire for change. This involves self-interpretation of the complex organizational problem, not through reduction and simplification, but rather in a holistic fashion. This diagnosis will develop certain theoretical assumptions (that is, a working hypothesis) about the nature of the organization and its problem domain.

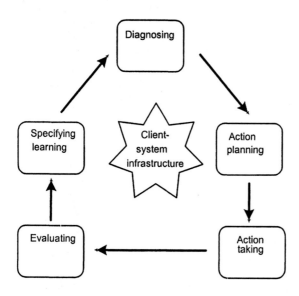

Figure 8.1 The action research cycle (Susman, 1983)

Researchers and practitioners then collaborate in the next activity, action planning. This specifies organizational actions that should relieve or improve these primary problems. The discovery of the planned actions is guided by the theoretical framework, which indicates both some desired future state for the organization, and the changes that would achieve such a state. The plan establishes the target for change and the approach to change.

The action-taking phase then implements the planned action. The researchers and practitioners collaborate in the active intervention into the client organization, causing certain changes to be made. Several forms of intervention strategy can be adopted. For example, the intervention might be directive, in which the research 'directs' the change, or non-directive, in which the change is sought indirectly. Intervention tactics can also be adopted, such as the recruiting of intelligent lay persons as change catalysts and pacemakers.

After the actions are completed, the collaborative researchers and practitioners undertake the evaluating of the outcomes. This includes a determination of whether the theoretical effects of the action were realized, and whether these effects relieved the problems. Where the change is successful, the evaluation must critically question whether the undertaken action, among the myriad routine and non-routine organizational actions, was the sole cause of success. Where the change is unsuccessful, some framework for the next iteration of the action research cycle (including the adjustment of the hypotheses) should be established.

While the activity of specifying learning is formally undertaken last, it is usually an ongoing process. The knowledge gained in the action research (whether the action was successful or unsuccessful) can be directed to three audiences. First, what Argyris and Schön (1978) called 'double-loop learning', the restructuring of organizational norms to reflect the new knowledge gained by the organization during the research. Second, where the change was unsuccessful, the additional knowledge may provide foundations for diagnosing in preparation for further action research intervention. Finally, the success or failure of the theoretical framework will provide important knowledge to the scientific community faced with future research settings.

The action research cycle can continue, whether the action proved successful or not, to develop further knowledge about the organization and the validity of relevant theoretical assumptions. As a result of the studies, the organization thus learns more about its nature and environment, and the constellation of theoretical elements of the scientific community continues to benefit and evolve.

Hult and Lennung (1980) summarized this process with their meticulously developed definition of action research:

> Action research simultaneously assists in practical problem-solving and expands scientific knowledge, as well as enhancing the competencies of the respective actors, being performed collaboratively in an immediate situation using data feedback in a cyclical process aiming at an increased understanding of a given social situation, primarily applicable for the understanding of change processes in social systems and undertaken within a mutually acceptable ethical framework.

Action research therefore attempts to link theory and practice, thinking and doing, achieving both practical and research objectives (Susman, 1983). The gaining of knowledge is seen as an active process, such that our beliefs are redefined in the light of the outcomes. A means for dealing with reality is more desirable than a representation of reality. Action research is a pragmatic approach which desires to 'come to terms' with the world.

Role of the method

Like any research method, action research is most valid within a domain of ideal research questions. Some research questions can be more effectively answered by other methods. Some research questions cannot be effectively answered by any other method. This section begins with the features of the known domain of ideal research questions within the IS field. Following this the features of this method that present the researcher with problems or opportunities are explored.

Domain of ideal use

The type of learning created by action research represents enhanced understanding of a complex problem. The researcher obtains information about a particular situation and a particular environment. This then gives a contingent value to the truth learned. The researcher expects, however, to generate knowledge which will further enhance the development of models and theories. The aim is the understanding of the complex human process rather than a universal prescriptive truth.

Also, the mutually accepted ethical framework discussed above may cause some concerns. If the goals of the researcher and client differ drastically there is tension. The researcher has lost sight of the fact that he is to be of value to those whom he researches. Therefore, parties must negotiate their goals. Some method for satisfying all of their goals must be found (Warmington, 1980).

Finally, in the process of learning, an explicit, clear conceptual framework must exist which the researcher imposes on the situation. This must be acceptable to the researcher and the organizational actors in the action research study (Warmington 1980). This is needed so that the explicit lessons will emerge from the research cycle.

The ideal domain of the action research method is therefore revealed in three distinctive characteristics of the method:

1. The researcher is actively involved, with expected benefits for both researcher and organization.
2. The knowledge obtained can be immediately applied. There is not the sense of the detached observer, but that of an active participant wishing to utilize any new knowledge based on an explicit, clear conceptual framework.
3. The research is a cyclical process linking theory and practice.

Checkland (1985) based the intellectual context on a simple model of the elements of any piece of research (see Figure 8.2). He referred to this as the 'organized use of rational thought'. The essential elements of this model are F, an intellectual framework of linked ideas - a theory; M, a methodology for using this framework; and A the area of application - research question. The ideal domain of a research method is one where M provides the richest scientific knowledge about F in the context of A. Considering action research within this model, Figure 8.3 depicts how this method cycles the research themes of F and M through A to generate reflection, action and ultimately scientific findings (Checkland, 1991). From Checkland's perspective, action research is a cycle of continuous inquiry where theory interacts with practice. This continuous interaction of theory and practice is the major characteristic of the ideal domain of the action research method.

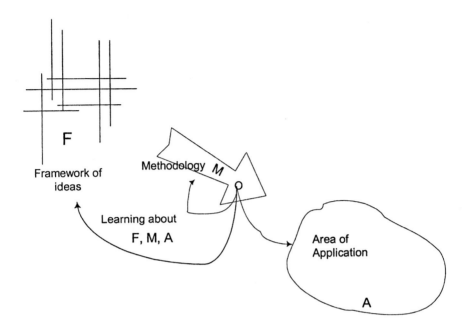

Figure 8.2 Organized use of rational thought (Checkland, 1985)

To claim that theory and practice interact where research is most closely focused on the techniques and principles of a vocation is tautological. Yet, if the field of study in IS is 'vocational in character', as Banville and Landry (1989, p.58) suggest, then the ideal domain of action research (as characterized above) includes the very broadest range of IS research questions.

Within this domain, we can further identify at least one area of research which may be outside its ideal of the more common approaches. This area deals with new or changed systems development methodologies. Galliers and Land (1987) identified six general application areas in IS research: society, organization, small group, individuals, technology and methodology. They found that, out of the available research methods, mathematical modelling and laboratory experiments were inappropriate for research into methodologies. The complex, multivariate settings of systems development methodologies inevitably open a validity question for any method that assumes abstracted causality. Case studies, under the characteristic constraint of non-intervention (Jenkins, 1985) are incapable of studying new or changed methodologies, since the introduction of such changes is necessarily interventionist. We cannot study a newly invented technique without intervening in some way to inject the new technique into the practitioner environment, that is, 'go into the world and try them out' (Land, quoted in Wood-Harper, 1989). This leads us to conclude that action research is one of the few valid research approaches that researchers can legitimately employ to study the effects of specific alterations in systems development methodologies. It is both rigorous and relevant.

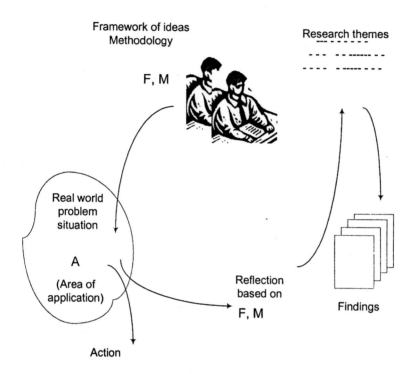

Figure 8.3 Cycle of action research (Checkland, 1991)

Rigorous intervention

It is impossible to study changes to a systems development method within a rigorous case study research approach. This is because the introduction of the methodical changes necessarily requires intervention. The researchers must alter the subjects insofar as the researchers must suggest the changes in method and provide training or training materials, that is, the method as a structure for behaviour must be changed in the research subject domain.

Relevance

Alternative research methods (to action research) must struggle to maintain relevance to the real world. Laboratory experiments and statistical models are necessarily abstracted from the richly multivariate circumstances in the real world. The empirics of action research require that it takes place fully within such multivariate real-world environments. Relevance is less of a problem.

The relevance of action research to systems development methodology has not been forcefully stated in the past. We suggest that action research, as a research method in the study of human methods, is the most scientifically legitimate approach available. Indeed, where a specific new methodology or an improvement to a methodology is being studied, the action research method may be the only relevant research method presently available.

Problems and opportunities

Researchers who wish to apply action research will have several problems of concern. However these problems are more likely to be general difficulties with research in social science rather than problems peculiar to action research. For example:

1. The lack of impartiality of the researcher has led to rejection of the action research method by a number of researchers. However this is not necessarily a problem singular to the action research method. It is rooted in the philosophical supremacy of the researchers. Philosophical supremacy refers to the refusal of scientists to accept any knowledge founded in any alternative philosophy of science other than their own (Baskerville, 1991). The same problem would confront a researcher who chooses to study new methods using opinion questionnaire survey methods. The lack of relevance would lead to the rejection of this knowledge by a number of researchers.

2. Some of the action research offered to the scientific community lacks rigour. This makes it difficult for the work to be assessed for the award of research degrees and for publication in academic journals. It also undermines credibility of the method with research funding agencies. Here we distinguish rigorous action research from liberal action research. Rigour relates to fitting the research methods to the problem in order to produce valid scientific explanations, and the use of multiple methods to produce valid research constructs (Straub, 1991). Liberal action research results when the researchers become so involved in the immediate practical effects of the research they neglect the scientific discipline. This loss can be a natural consequence of the researchers' concern for their subjects. Rapoport (1970) recognized this as the goal dilemma of action research. On the contrary, rigorous action research clings tenaciously to its disciplined constructs of cyclical theoretical infrastructure, data collection and evaluation: there is a clear cycle of activity; there is a premise; a pronounced theory (under test); there is empirical data collection (for example, diaries). We note that the lack of scientific discipline is a reasonable complaint about liberal action research, but we also recognize there are similar complaints about other research methods (for example, survey methods, see Baroudi and Orlikowski, 1989).

3. Action research is sometimes branded as 'consulting masquerading as research'. The historical reasons for this were discussed earlier. At least four factors clearly differentiate action research and consulting (see Gummesson,

1988): (i) researchers require more rigorous documentary records than consultants; (ii) researchers require theoretical justifications and consultants require empirical justifications; (iii) consultants operate under tighter time and budget constraints; (iv) the consultation is usually linear - engage, analyze, action, disengage - while the action research process is cyclical. These differentiations are not widely known and even seasoned action researchers sometimes have trouble delineating action research from consulting (Jönsson, 1991). Rapoport called this the role dilemma of action research. Perhaps this too arises from sloppy action research, action research that loses its scientific threat and finally converts entirely into consulting. The researcher using this method often must remain particularly strong and loyal to their research rigour, since client interests tend to subjugate scientific necessities (Seashore, 1976).

4. Action research is context-bound, and not context-free. Therefore it is difficult to determine the cause of a particular effect that could be due to the environment, researcher or methodology. This means that action research produces narrow learning in its context because each situation is unique and cannot be repeated. Certainly action research is more deeply engulfed in any multivariate social experimental approach. But this is the nature of an idiographic method. It still has an underlying theory that is tested and either falsified or sustained. Because the theory arises from particular needs, action research is a fine theory discovery method. This is a very important characteristic of action research, since the theoretical progress of IS research is alarmingly slow (Alavi et al., 1989). Like other scientific methods, further testing and even cross-method triangulation must generalize by confirming or falsifying any causal links suggested by action research theories. In this regard an action research study is no less effective and credible than most cross-sectional statistical survey methods.

These problems are actually general problems of social science research. In reality action research shares these problems with the other methods. Perhaps the distinguishing difficulties with action research are those of degree rather than taxonomy. Rapoport (1970) identified three dilemmas in action research: ethics - personal over-involvement with the research; goals - the two taskmasters in social research (subject and science); and initiatives - the practical pressures that interfere with the conduct of 'a disinterested pursuit of knowledge'. Scientists who employ other methods, even survey research, also know these three dilemmas. These are not peculiar to action research.

These dilemmas are much stronger in action research projects. Perhaps many, if not most, action researchers are trapped by these pitfalls. When they attempt to present their findings, the shortcomings of the projects are rightly discovered. If this is the case, then the difficulty with action research is not one of poor understanding of the method by those who review the research, but poor understanding of the method by those who conduct the research. The solution is better training for action researchers. Such training will help prepare action researchers for negotiating the dilemmas.

Characteristic strategies

In the preceding paragraphs, action research is shown to be no less credible as a social science research method than any of its alternatives. The action researcher, however, faces more challenges in maintaining rigour in the research. The social science research community has entertained enough liberal action research to confuse reviewers and examiners about the exact characteristics of proper action research. In this section some characteristic strategies are offered for researchers who demand scientific rigour while conducting action research. These quality guidelines will also be useful to those who must examine action research for graduate degrees, and those who must review action research for publications or grants.

Consideration for the paradigm shift

Action research does not occur in the traditional positivist philosophy of science and has its own domain of ideal research questions. Is action research appropriate for the question (for example, immediately relevant methodology or theory-formulation)? Also, who composes the main body of scientists concerned with this research question? If this body chiefly contains scientists whose reference disciplines do not recognize methodological pluralism, then the action researchers must substantiate carefully the interpretive scientific foundations of their project in order to achieve credibility. Without credibility, the research will not spawn future follow-up work.

Establishment of a formal research agreement

The ethics of human subjects research discourage research without the 'informed consent' of the subject. This implies that conducting action research under the disguise of consulting would be unethical. Further, clients may welcome the research content of action research - pleased to learn that their problems are worthy of scientific interest. They may fund peripheral costs of the research such as data compilation and preparation of working papers. Further, the client may wish to review publications for public relations purposes. In return, the researcher may charge no fee, or discount consulting fees in return for an action research agreement.

The consent and disclosure agreement is only part of the client-system infrastructure. The researcher should prepare the subjects for the 'warrants' that will authorize the research team to initiate action within the organization. Researchers should clearly brief subjects concerning the experimental nature of the action-taking and the iterative nature of the learning cycle.

Provision of a theoretical problem statement

One of the most important differences between the diagnosis stage of an action research project and the advice stage of a consulting project is the careful theoretical foundation of diagnoses. The theoretical foundation must be present as a premise if the experiment (the intervention action) is to remain valid as research. Therefore the diagnosis document should include a scholarly statement of the theoretical underpinnings of the diagnosis. Understandably, iterations of the research cycle may lead to learning that adjusts the theory to keep it consistent with the observations. The mutations of this theory should be recorded carefully in the research notebooks.

Planned measurement methods

Action research is certainly empirical, although the collected data may be very unstructured. Rigorous action researchers plan methodical data collection methods. This is critical for credibility since it is ultimately impossible for the researchers to sustain claims of validity in their data analysis if the data cannot be produced for examination.

Argyris, Putnam et al. (1985, p.239) viewed 'Talk as data: a window onto the logic of action'. They suggested a range of reliable data collection techniques such as audiotaped observations, interviews, action experiments and participant-written cases. Action experiments entailed discussions with subjects 'on the spot' during action taking, while participant-written cases were the written recollections of the subject following action taking.

Outside the context of action research, Naur (1983) suggested the use of diaries as research data collections. Researchers may collect data by keeping diaries - and requiring their subjects to keep diaries. Teams can keep group diaries to reduce the volume and subjectivity of the data. Such diary activity alone is a serious intervention since there is evidence that diary-keeping can improve the management of IS development projects (Jepsen et al., 1989). Formal, detailed diaries pose serious difficulties for data analysis, considering the volume and unstructured nature of the data. The researchers can impose some organized structure to the diaries that will aid in data analysis.

Data validity is a problem with these techniques, partially because of the interpretive nature of the data but also because of the intersubjectivity of data capture. The researchers inevitably influence their subjects and vice-versa. The presence of a disassociated 'watcher', a monitor, may improve validity somewhat. The monitor is an independent, knowledgeable individual who seeks to validate the research. The monitor attends interviews, reviews diaries or other data collections, and proof-reads working papers. The role of the monitor is to discover inadvertently misguided research assumptions caused by the close personal involvement of the primary researcher. Regardless of the data collection method, rigorous action researchers design and specify the measurement techniques clearly when setting up research infrastructure. Above all, rigorous researchers clearly pronounce the measurement approach before undertaking the intervention.

Maintain collaboration and subject learning

Another characteristic strategy of rigorous action research is the careful nurturing of collaboration with subjects. The subjects may well have key knowledge that is critical to the discovery of important aspects of the theory under test. Rigorous action researchers avoid dominating the diagnosis and action planning phases (that is, assuming the authoritative role of the external consultant).

The cycle of subject learning is also critical for developing the knowledge necessary to claim any idiographic usefulness for the theory under test in the action research project. During the learning cycle, the subjects acquire learning about the immediate problem situation. This leads to imperative modification of action-taking and sustains the action research cycle. Without subject learning, the action research cycle ends prematurely.

Promote iterations

Action research is also characteristically cyclical. The research data should record the repetitive planning, taking and evaluating of organizational actions. In this environment action failures (in terms of the immediate problem situation) are as important as action successes. Rigorous action research cannot disguise negative effects of some actions, as these may provide richer learning than the positive effects. The cycles will continue until the immediate problem situation is relieved. Unfortunately this sometimes occurs before adequate data is collected to resolve conflicts within the theory. That is, in some cases, an action research project may not generate enough data to support adequate analysis of a generated theory - even idiographically.

Restrained generalization

Action research, being naturally idiographic, presents researchers with a serious conflict regarding any generalization from the project findings. As mentioned earlier, only the most tentative causal links can be claimed owing to the multivariate nature of the study. Yet for a vocationally-oriented field like IS, it is the promise of generalizability that interests the majority of scientists. It is generalization that makes theories relevant. Some scientists believe such relevance is as important as rigour in the achievement of important IS research (Keen, 1991).

For the action research, the traditional foundation of generalization, diachronic reliability, is problematic. This is the traditional repeatability criterion underlying many positivist methods. An action research project, by nature of its intervention into a unique organizational setting, can never be repeated. Kirk and Miller (1986) suggested that synchronic reliability was more useful in qualitative research. This form of reliability is based on the consistency of observations within the same time period. These observations represent alternate forms of data (for example, two researchers) relating to the same phenomenon. These data would never be identical but should be consistent with the theory under test.

Some authorities dismiss reliability altogether as a necessary premise of generalizability. Gummesson (1988) argued that validity (the degree to which the research accomplished its intended goals within its scientific paradigm) was a sounder criterion for generalization. Generalization based on the validity of action research, although lacking any substantial proof of reliability, is no less acceptable than generalization from statistical samples based on reliability but lacking substantial proof of validity.

> It no longer seems so 'obvious' that a limited number of observations cannot be used as a basis for generalization. Nor does it appear to be 'obvious' any longer that properly devised statistical studies based on large numbers of observations will lead to meaningful generalizations (Gummesson, 1988 p.78).

Action researchers can legitimately generalize their findings on the basis of the validity of their research. In addition, action researchers can design synchronic reliability into the structure of their research project. However they must exercise restraint in their conclusions since these must be reported from a limited number of observations. This, of course, implies another characteristic of rigorous action research: circulation of the results to the scientific community. Thus the theory will evolve under the pressure of further study and correction.

Conclusion

Action research is regarded by many as the ideal post-positivist social scientific research method for IS research. The present scientific institutions in IS, however, broadly favour the current philosophy of the natural sciences. Further, action research rose from problems experienced in the field of social psychology, yet never succeeded in procuring major status in the mainstream of social psychology or social science research. This suggests that action researchers in IS assume certain risks that their findings will be rejected on philosophical grounds.

The features and characteristics of the approach define a domain of ideal use for the method. Within this domain, perhaps the study of IS development methodology is most critical to our field. A number of problems confront the action researcher such as lack of impartiality, lack of discipline, confusion with consulting and its context-bound nature. However these problems confront researchers using alternative methods as well. The difficulty with action research may be a matter of degree, and the easy loss of scientific rigour.

Action researchers can achieve scientific rigour through a number of characteristic strategies. First they must establish an ethical client-system infrastructure and research environment. They must plan their data collection carefully. They must observe iterative phases that formulate theory, plan action, take action, and evaluate the action. Through this process they must promote collaboration by the subjects and support their subjects' learning cycles. Despite the idiographic nature of the study, the researcher may imply certain generalizations based on the theory and learning. Reports of the research must disseminate the scientific knowledge achieved by the study to allow future work that can confirm or refute any causal suggestions or claims of generalized theory.

The origins and techniques of action research have yet to draw a large following in the mainstream of social science. Altogether, the features of the domain of ideal use, the features of the method that create problems and opportunities, and the strategies for applying the method represent the major characteristics of the role of this method for IS researchers. A critical review of these reveals that this research approach could appropriately assume a growing role in mainstream IS research and practice.

Acknowledgements

The authors have adopted a certain specific phraseology suggested by an unknown reviewer's comments which we found to be much clearer than our own. Our thanks to this reviewer.

9   A Scientific Methodology for MIS Case Studies

Allen S. Lee

There is a strong case-study tradition in the academic field of management information systems (Benbasat et al., 1987; Fulk and Dutton, 1984; Kling, 1978b; Kling and Iacono, 1984; Kling and Scacchi, 1982; Kraemer et al., 1987; Laudon, 1974; Leonard-Barton, 1987; Markus, 1983; Markus, 1986). At the same time, case researchers in general are still attempting to clarify the methodological basis upon which to conduct case studies (Benbasat et al., 1987; Datta, 1982; Dukes, 1965; George and McKeown, 1985; Herriot, 1982; Hersen and Barlow, 1976; Huberman and Crandall, 1982; Louis, 1982; Luthans and Davis, 1982; Miles, 1979; 1982; Yin, 1981a; 1981b; 1982a; 1982b; 1984). The objective of this chapter is to present a scientific methodology with which to conduct case studies of management information systems (MIS). In doing so, the chapter applies and builds upon concepts that pertain to case study methodology and that the author developed in his previous research (Lee, 1985; 1986; 1987a; 1989). In order to provide a practical demonstration of how these methodological concepts are usable in case studies of management information systems, the chapter illustrates them with extensive material taken from an actual published MIS case study - Markus (1983) 'Power, Politics and MIS Implementation'.

In particular, this chapter: (1) provides an overview of the methodological problems involved in the study of a single case, (2) offers a description of scientific method, (3) elucidates how the MIS case study by Markus fits this description, (4) responds to the problems involved in the study of a single case, and (5) summarizes what the article's scientific methodology for MIS case studies does, and does not, involve.

What is science?

The formulation of a particular scientific methodology for conducting MIS case studies and identifying the methodological problems associated with this type of research depends on what is meant by 'science' in the first place. In determining this meaning, there are numerous models of science from which to select. Indeed, philosophers of science - the scholars who make it their job to observe scientists and to explain what it is that scientists do - have not yet settled, among themselves, on a single model of what science is:

> Is scientific advance registered by increasing probability (Carnap), by discrete verifications (the logical positivists) or falsifications (Popper), by revolutions (Kuhn), by growing consensus (Polanyi), by progressive versus degenerating research programs, conducted over long periods (Lakatos), or what? The debate goes on (Tice and Slavens, 1983, p.418).

The model used in this chapter is what social scientists call the 'natural science model' of social science (Behling, 1980, p.483; Burrell and Morgan, 1979, p.4; Daft, 1983, p.539; Schön et al., 1984, p.9; Susman and Evered, 1978, pp.582-583). According to this model, natural science is the ideal on which social science should model itself. There are three reasons for selecting this particular model of science.

First, among management researchers, the natural science model is a well-known and widely accepted model for conducting studies in social science. Behling (1980) advocates the natural science model:

> Research methods similar to those used in the natural sciences have long been the norm in organizational behavior and organization theory...Clearly, the authors of mainstream texts in organizational behavior and organization theory accept the natural science model of good research. Those who include research methods chapters...clearly follow this approach and generally appear to owe an intellectual debt to Kerlinger, a strong proponent of the natural science model (p.483).

As such, the natural science model suggests itself as a useful device for introducing scholars, unfamiliar with case studies, to this type of research.

Second, many of the criticisms directed against case studies are voiced from the perspective of the natural science model. It is the critics of case studies, not scholars already working in the case study tradition, who need to be convinced of the legitimacy of case studies. Recognizing this, the chapter demonstrates the legitimacy of case studies by using the standards of the critics themselves.

On the one hand, the natural science model of social science represents a view of science taken by many (if not most) social scientists (Behling, 1980; Burrell and Morgan, 1979, p.4; Daft, 1983, p.539; Schön et al., 1984, p.9; Susman and Evered, 1978, pp.582-583). On the other hand, the philosophy of science would recognize the natural science model to be a descendant of logical positivism - a view of science that philosophers of science themselves had originated, but subsequently abandoned (Bernstein, 1978; Bernstein, 1983; Schön, 1983, pp.37-49). Whereas it is the chapter's responsibility to point out the disparity in viewpoints of these two communities of scholars (philosophers of science on the one hand, and many (if not most) social scientists on the other), it is beyond the chapter's scope to investigate the ramifications of the disparity, much less to resolve it. (For a detailed examination of this matter, see Lee, 1987a; 1989.)

Practically speaking, the audience for this chapter – management scholars critical of, or unfamiliar with, case studies – largely subscribe to the natural science model. For this reason, an effective strategy for approaching this audience would be to proceed with a framework they already find familiar and acceptable – namely, the framework of the natural science model.

Third, the chapter recognizes that a scientific methodology, which applies the natural science model, actually complements and supports the methods traditionally associated with case studies. The natural science model is primarily a model for testing theories, not formulating theories in the first place. Methods traditionally used by case researchers to formulate theories (Benbasat et al., 1987; Filstead, 1970; Garfinkel, 1967; Geertz, 1973; Kirk and Miller, 1986; Lee, 1989; Louis, 1982; Sanday, 1979; Taylor, 1979; Van Maanen, 1979; Yin, 1981a; 1981b; 1982b; 1984) may therefore still be applied *in addition to* the methods specified by the natural science model. Thus, this chapter respects and preserves the traditional function of case studies in suggesting hunches and generating theories for later testing - a function recognized by scholars of all persuasions. Specifically, the methodology formulated in this chapter: (1) allows MIS case researchers to continue using the tools they have traditionally used, and (2) enables MIS case researchers to conduct case studies that test theories by using the natural science model.

Methodological problems raised by the study of a single case

In this chapter an MIS case study refers to the examination of a real-world MIS, as it actually exists in its natural, real-world setting. In holding MIS research to the standard of the natural science model, four problems can be identified in MIS research that is conducted in the form of case studies. These problems are discussed in the next four sections.

Problem 1: Making controlled observations

The first problem concerns *how to make controlled observations*. In testing for relationships theorized to exist among different factors, natural scientists routinely observe the influence of one factor on another factor, where the potentially confounding influences of all other factors are somehow removed or 'controlled for'. Laboratory experiments in the natural sciences accomplish this through the use of control groups and treatment groups. In statistical experiments, it is accomplished with the help of statistical controls, such as those available through a multivariate regression analysis. Unfortunately for the MIS case researcher, (1) the study of a real-world MIS in its real-world setting precludes, by its very nature, the laboratory controls of laboratory experiments, and (2) the study of a single case commonly yields more variables than data points - a situation that renders inapplicable the statistical controls of statistical experiments (Yin, 1981a)

Problem 2: Making controlled deductions

The second problem concerns *how to make controlled deductions*. Making controlled or logical deductions with mathematical propositions as is commonly done in the natural sciences is a standard, non-controversial practice. However, since it is rare (though certainly not undesirable) for a case study to be quantitative, the MIS case researcher is typically denied the methodological convenience of working with numerical data and mathematically stated propositions. Instead, the case researcher must somehow manage with qualitative data and verbally stated propositions. Making controlled deductions with verbal propositions (that is, qualitative analysis), while certainly possible, is more problematic: 'For quantitative data, there are clear conventions the researcher can use', such as the widely accepted and well-known rules of algebra through which the validity of mathematical deductions is known, 'but the analyst faced with a bank of qualitative data has very few guidelines for protection against self-delusion...How can we be sure that [a qualitatively deduced] finding is not, in fact, *wrong*?' (Miles, 1979, p.590).

Problem 3: Allowing for replicability.

The third problem concerns *how to allow for replicability*. Research in the natural sciences is routinely replicated as a means of assuring the objectivity of the research. However, the MIS case researcher is unlikely to observe the same set of events - namely, the same configuration of individuals, groups, social structure, hardware, and software - unfold again in the same way. The non-replicability of the same observations would clearly hinder subsequent attempts by independent investigators wishing to verify the findings of a particular case study.

Problem 4: Allowing for generalizability

The fourth and last problem concerns *how to allow for generalizability*. An often-admired quality of theories in the natural sciences is their applicability to a range of settings. (In this sense, theories in the natural sciences are said to be 'nomothetic', as opposed to 'idiographic'.) However, the fact that the study of a single case is marked by unique and non-replicable events would make the study vulnerable to charges that its findings cannot be extended to other settings.

The following section describes a scientific methodology for MIS case studies - a methodology that follows from the natural science model. Use of this methodology allows the final section of this chapter to address the problems (identified above) associated with case studies.

A description of scientific method

In modelling MIS case studies on natural science, we must ask: How does inquiry in natural science proceed? Specifically, what is meant by the natural science model?

In his classic text, *Introduction to Logic*, Copi (1986) provides a lucid description of the logic of reasoning used in the natural sciences. 'Few propositions of science', he explains, 'are directly verifiable as true. In fact, none of the important ones are. For the most part they concern unobservable entities, such as molecules and atoms, electrons and protons, chromosomes and genes' (p.483). As a result, the manner of verification in the natural sciences is indirect rather than direct. 'The pattern of indirect testing or indirect verification consists of two parts. First one deduces from the proposition to be tested [the proposition being the theory] one or more other propositions capable of being tested directly [these latter propositions being the predictions]' (p.486). In the terminology of logic, a theory's predictions are its conclusions. 'Then these conclusions are tested and are found to be either true or false. The researcher then compares what the theory predicts and what is actually observed. If the conclusions are false, any proposition that implies them [namely the theory] must be false also. On the other hand, if the conclusions are true, that provides evidence for the truth of the proposition being tested, which is thus confirmed indirectly' (p.486).

Karl Popper (1968) describes the same procedure in *The Logic of Scientific Discovery,* where he calls it the deductive testing of theories (pp.32-33, p.60, pp.109-111). It is deductive in the following sense. The natural scientist applies a theory (for example, 'All men are mortal') to a set of facts or initial conditions ('Socrates is a man'), from which a conclusion or prediction is deduced ('Socrates is mortal'). It is the prediction - as a deduced statement - that is then tested against an observation statement (for example, 'Socrates dies').

In this procedure, an observation that contradicts a prediction would be sufficient to cast doubt on (perhaps to the point of falsifying) the theory from which the prediction follows. On the other hand, an observation that confirms a prediction is never regarded as conclusively establishing the theory's truth. The reason is that a different set of empirical circumstances, or initial conditions, to which the same theory may be applied, would result in yet another prediction (for example, 'Plato is mortal' or 'Superman is mortal'), which in turn would open up the same theory to yet another opportunity for its falsification. Thus, the ever-present possibility for contradictory evidence to surface in a subsequent test requires that a theory always be regarded as falsifiable. Indeed, falsifiability is the demarcation criterion that Popper uses to distinguish science from non-science (pp.40-42).

Scientific method, in the form of the deductive testing of theories, is widely known. Kuhn (1970a), whose school of thought is a rival to Popper's, expresses that 'no field is potentially a science' unless its theories are cast according to 'Sir Karl's demarcation criterion' (p.245). The now common characterization of theories, in both natural science and social science, as falsifiable, refutable, testable, or disconfirmable, is an indication of the widespread extent to which the deductive testing of theories is practised.

Falsifiability is just one requirement that a theory must satisfy in order to be scientific. There are three additional requirements, which are all associated with the concept of the deductive testing of theories (Popper, 1968, pp.32-33). One of these requirements is logical consistency: as long as the different predictions that may be deduced from the theory are not mutually contradictory, the theory can be said to be logically consistent. Another requirement is that the theory must be at least as explanatory, or predictive, as any competing theory. The last requirement is that the theory, while falsifiable, must survive the actual attempts made at its falsification.

In the way that scientific method appears in the natural science model, the notion of controlled observation comes into play in the last step (namely, the step where the researcher makes a comparison between what is predicted and what is observed). In this step, the researcher must be able to show that the observed effect can be attributed to the factor being tested and that the potentially confounding effects of other factors have been removed or 'controlled for' (Campbell and Stanley, 1963). This chapter has already mentioned laboratory controls and statistical controls as examples of how observations can be made in a controlled way.

An exemplar for scientific MIS case studies

Markus' (1983) 'Power, Politics, and MIS Implementation' captures the major features of scientific method that Copi and Popper describe. As such, the MIS case study by Markus may be regarded as an exemplar for scientific MIS case studies in general, where the meaning of 'scientific' is the one embodied in the natural science model.

Markus' research is the intensive study of a single case, involving the entire configuration of individuals, groups, social structure, hardware, and software in the setting of an organization that she calls Golden Triangle Corporation (GTC). Through interviews and documents, Markus observes events in the way they unfolded in their natural setting at GTC.

By conducting her research in this way, Markus invokes the severe methodological problems mentioned earlier. They are the problems of: (1) how to make controlled observations, (2) how to make controlled deductions, (3) how to allow for replicability, and (4) how to allow for generalizability.

Despite these problems, the MIS case study by Markus still succeeds in crafting a theory about MIS implementation that conforms to the requirements of falsifiability, logical consistency, predictive power exceeding that of competing theories, and survival of the empirical tests aimed at falsifying it.

Markus presents three alternative theories on an equal footing and then compares the deductions (the predictions) of each against observations made in the setting at GTC. All are theories about resistance to MIS implementation efforts. The case itself involved people's resistance to GTC's newly computerized Financial Information System (FIS).

The people-determined theory involves 'factors internal to the person' (p.431). When people factors such as human nature, cognitive styles, or personality traits are incompatible with the requirements of a computerized information system, the system's intended users, according to the people-determined theory, will resist its utilization.

The system-determined theory involves 'factors inherent in the application or system being implemented' (p.431). Markus cites the following as examples of system factors that incur resistance: lack of user-friendliness, technically deficient systems, and poor ergonomic design (p.431). According to the system-determined theory, when such factors are present, the system's intended users will resist its utilization.

The interaction theory, the most sophisticated of the three theories, involves people factors as well as system factors. However, Markus says, 'This explanation identifies neither the system nor the organizational setting as the cause of resistance, but their interaction' (p.431). She describes the interaction theory in the following ways:

> ...resistance is explained as a product of the interaction of system design features with the intraorganizational distribution of power, defined either objectively, in terms of horizontal or vertical power dimensions, or subjectively, in terms of symbolism (p.432).
>
> ...Resistance-generating conditions are mismatches between the patterns of interaction prescribed by a system and the patterns that already exist in the setting into which the system is introduced (p.438).
>
> ...The primary assumption...is that information systems frequently embody a distribution of intraorganizational power among the key actors affected by its design. Intraorganizational power is an attribute of individuals and subgroups....
>
> ...When the introduction of a computerized information system specifies a distribution of power which represents a loss to certain participants, these participants are likely to resist the system. Conversely, when the distribution of power implied in the design of an information system represents a gain in power to participants, these participants are likely to engage in behaviors that might signify acceptance of it....
>
> ...[A necessary condition for resistance to the implementation of a system is that] people perceive the system to represent a power loss...(p.442).

All three theories refer extensively to the existence of phenomena that are neither directly observable nor easily discernible: human nature, cognitive styles, personality traits, factors internal to the person, user friendliness, technical deficiency in a system, ergonomics, horizontal and vertical dimensions of intra-organizational power, power in terms of symbolism, and (perhaps most important and most directly unobservable of all) the distribution of power implied in the design of an information system. None of the three theories is therefore directly verifiable as true.

In this context, Copi's remarks on scientific method, already quoted above, are worth repeating: 'Few propositions of science are directly verifiable as true. In fact, none of the important ones are. For the most part they concern unobservable entities, such as molecules and atoms, electrons and protons, chromosomes and genes.' Hence, because direct verification is not feasible, theoretical propositions are tested indirectly instead. This manner of testing involves what Popper calls the deductive testing of theories, the details of which were described earlier in the chapter.

As it turns out, Markus provides an exemplary demonstration of how an MIS case study is capable of carrying out the deductive testing of theories. She tests for the truth of the three theories (and for the presence of the unobservable phenomena) in the following way. Whereas the three theories refer to phenomena that are not directly observable, they nonetheless yield predictions of events that (if the given theory is true) would be observable. Thus Markus' strategy is to use the contrary theories to make contrary predictions about what would happen in the same setting. The theory that emerges unfalsified in this competition would be judged scientific.

'The people-determined theory leads to the prediction that replacing individual resistors or co-opting them by allowing them to suggest improvements to the system might reduce or eliminate resistance' (p.437). However, resistance to the new information system persisted despite GTC's practice of job rotation and mobility. Markus gives the example of an accountant, one of the designers and advocates of the system, who had originally been working in corporate accounting and then became the controller in one of the divisions that had resisted the system all along. He subsequently came to resist the system himself. This observation falsifies the people-determined theory.

'The system-determined theory predicts that fixing technical problems eliminates resistance' (p.437). However, the resistance continued despite corrective actions taken to address a number of major technical problems. Significantly, the problems were identified by a task force whose members were (as characterized by Markus) 'resistors'. The corrective actions were the installation of a larger computer with a more powerful operating system, a change in processing mode from batch to online, and a simplified method in the software by which managers could create new accounts. Markus (1983) writes, 'when data were collected for this study, about one year after the last of these changes was installed, informants in the [resisting] divisions still spoke of FIS [Financial Information System]. Many felt strongly that the system should be replaced...' (p.438). Markus reports no mitigation in the resistance - a mitigation that the system-determined theory predicts. These observations falsify the system-determined theory.

> The interaction theory predicts that neither changing the people (by removing them, by educating them, or by attempting to coerce them), nor changing technical features of the system will reduce resistance as long as the conditions which gave rise to it persist. [The prediction is that there will be resistance as long as there are] mismatches between the patterns of interactions prescribed by a system and the patterns that already exist in the setting into which the system is introduced (Markus, 1983, p.438).

Markus describes the interaction pattern that was already in place at GTC as consisting of autonomy experienced by the divisional accountants and dependence experienced by the corporate accountants. The divisional accountants controlled their own data (often in thick, manually maintained ledger books) and could therefore reconcile unusual situations before releasing reports. The corporate accountants had to go through the divisional accountants to obtain financial data, which was 'a valued resource' (p.438). This conflicted with the interaction pattern prescribed by FIS, under which 'all financial transactions were collected into a single [computerized] database under the control of corporate accountants...At any time, corporate accountants had the ability to 'look into' the database and analyze divisional performance' (p.438). Markus' observation showed resistance to FIS, just as predicted by the interaction theory.

The interaction theory satisfies the four requirements that Popper observes to be satisfied by all scientific theories. First, it is falsifiable (for example, the interaction theory would have been falsified if Markus had observed acceptance of FIS despite the difference between the interaction pattern that was in place and the one that FIS prescribed). Second, its logical consistency is known through the mutual compatibility of the different predictions that Markus considers (pp.437-438). Third, it is confirmed, not falsified, by the observations in the GTC case study. Fourth, and most important, its predictions succeed, whereas the predictions of its rival theories - the people-determined theory and the system-determined theory - fail. In crafting the interaction theory so that it satisfies the four requirements, Markus not only attains her specific research goal of explaining resistance to MIS implementation efforts, *but also demonstrates how an MIS case study is able to capture the major features of scientific method* in the way that scientific method is embodied in the natural science model.

It must be emphasized that the conclusions drawn by Markus in her case study are only tentative at best. After all: (1) there may exist (or come into existence) some corporate accountants at GTC who, when transferred into one of the divisions, will continue to accept, and never come to resist, FIS; (2) the improvements in the technical features of the system may not yet have reached the threshold at which the resistance would diminish observably; and (3) the resistance may persist even when the interaction pattern, required by FIS, comes to be more like the interaction pattern already in place. These possibilities, however, do not weaken Markus' case study, but actually strengthen it by emphasizing the extent of the interaction theory's falsifiability and allowing the case researcher to improve the theory by pointing out where later surprises may occur. No scientific explanation - whether Markus' interaction theory or a theory of physics - may ever be conclusively proven true. According to the logic of the deductive testing of theories, a theory can only be shown to be false, or not (yet) false. In scientific research, further tests are always in order.

Response to the problems involved in the study of a single case

This section discusses the four severe methodological problems associated with case research in the way they are manifested in the case study by Markus. The discussion establishes the context in which the chapter, in its final section, will articulate what a scientific methodology for MIS case studies does, and does not, involve.

How to make controlled observations

A critic of case research may point out, correctly, that Markus fails to utilize either laboratory controls or statistical controls when making observations to test the three theories. However, Markus solves the problem of how to make controlled observations by utilizing *natural controls*.

A simple but clear example of this (referred to earlier) is Markus' test of the people-determined theory, in which a particular accountant, upon moving from his position in corporate accounting to controller in one of the divisions, changes from being an advocate of FIS to one of its resistors. This particular test 'controls for' or 'holds constant' the people factors by focusing on just one person (the accountant), and 'varies' or 'treats' the situation external to the person by observing his move from corporate accounting to a division. Thus, Markus is able to cleanly attribute the accountant's new behaviour (resistance to FIS) to the 'treatment' (the change in the situation external to the accountant) rather than to the 'control' (the people factors - the factors internal to the accountant). Indeed, by making this controlled observation, Markus falsifies the people-determined theory, which predicts no change in behaviour where there is no change in people factors.

In utilizing natural controls and treatments to test predictions, the case researcher must do more than wait passively for desired controls and treatments to materialize. Rather, the case researcher must actively apply his or her ingenuity in order to derive predictions that take advantage of natural controls and treatments either already in place or likely to occur. For example, in Markus' prediction concerning the people-determined theory, the control (the holding constant of people factors) is already in place by virtue of focusing on just one person, and the treatment (the variation in the environment) takes advantage of the person's move from one part of the organization to another. In general, it is incumbent upon the case researcher to scan the empirical material for the presence of natural controls and treatments that may be incorporated into the formulation of a prediction. (This is no different from the activity of the statistician who, in utilizing a multiple regression analysis to analyze 1980 census data, scans the data to identify what factors might serve as the appropriate independent variables and, hence, as the statistical controls.)

MIS case researchers who wish to utilize natural controls will find themselves in good company. Investigators in some of the natural sciences, such as astronomy, geology, and human biology, are also unable to conduct laboratory experiments for obvious reasons and are therefore also prevented from utilizing laboratory controls in order to make controlled observations. Instead, these investigators routinely conduct natural experiments in which they utilize natural controls, through which they have been able to achieve impressive results (Nagel, 1979, p.452). MIS case researchers who invoke natural controls would therefore be employing a research strategy no different from, and no less scientific than, what is employed by these natural scientists. In using natural controls, MIS case researchers would therefore be keeping within the natural science model. To pursue this line of thinking would take us beyond the scope of this chapter, but would lead to the conclusion that case studies can be conducted as a form of natural experiment, which is already a conventional form of research practiced in the 'hard' sciences (Lee, 1989).

How to make controlled deductions

In qualitative analysis, as performed by Markus in her case study, how can deductions be made in a controlled (that is, logical) way? In mathematical analysis, turning to the rules of algebra can readily check the validity of deductions involving mathematical propositions. In qualitative analysis, there is no corresponding body of rules as succinct or easily applied as the rules of algebra for verifying the validity of deductions involving verbal propositions.

To respond to this problem, it must first be emphasized that mathematics is a subset of formal logic, not vice versa. Logical deductions in the general case do not require mathematics. *An MIS case study that performs its deductions with verbal propositions (that is, qualitative analysis) therefore only deprives itself of the convenience of the rules of algebra; it does not deprive itself of the rules of formal logic, to which it may therefore still turn when carrying out the task of making controlled deductions.*

Indeed, Markus herself provides examples of controlled deductions involving verbal propositions. (Namely, she deduces several different, verbally expressed predictions from the three different, verbally expressed theories as applied to the verbally expressed facts of the situation at GTC.) With regard to logical form, Markus' deductions involving verbal propositions are identical to and no less valid than, the deduction of the verbal proposition, 'Socrates is mortal' (the prediction) from the two other verbal propositions, 'All men are mortal' (the theory) and 'Socrates is a man' (the facts or initial conditions).

Like the situation pertaining to the utilization of natural controls, MIS case researchers will find themselves in good company with regard to analysis that utilizes the medium of verbal propositions, as opposed to mathematical propositions. Consider biology and the theory of evolution. For Darwin, the medium of logical deduction was words and sentences, not numbers and mathematics (Kaplan, 1964, pp.245-246).

How to allow for replicability

How might an independent investigator go about replicating the findings of the MIS case study by Markus?

One way - perhaps the most conceptually straightforward way - would be to attempt to replicate the case study in exactly the way that Markus performs it. For the independent investigator, this would involve the attempt to apply the same three theories to the same set of initial conditions in order to deduce the same predictions as Markus, and then test these predictions against the same observations made by Markus. The obvious difficulty with this procedure is that, in an MIS case study, any observed configuration of individuals, groups, social structure, hardware, and software in a real-world setting is highly unlikely to recur and be observed again. Thus, an independent investigator could not verify the findings of the MIS case study by Markus, at least not through this conceptually straightforward procedure.

Fortunately, there is at least one alternative procedure. The independent investigator could apply the same theories as tested in the original case study to a different set of initial conditions (for example, the facts of the situation at AAA Corporation or XXX Corporation), thereby resulting in different predictions (for example, if the people-determined theory is true, then individuals who share the same people factors at XXX Corporation will display no difference in their level of resistance to, or acceptance of, the computerized information system at XXX, regardless of the rank and location of their position in the organization). In other words, the investigator would be working with a new prediction, 'Plato is mortal', as opposed to the original prediction, 'Socrates is mortal'; even though the prediction would be different, it would still be the same theory being tested. Such new predictions would call for observations different from the ones made by Markus and would therefore relieve the independent investigator of the impossible task of attempting to replicate the observations made in the original case study. Consequently, even though the observations in a particular MIS case study are non-replicable, the case study's findings (that a particular theory is confirmed or disconfirmed) would be replicable.

How to allow for generalizability

The fact that Markus' case study of GTC is marked by unique and non-replicable events renders it vulnerable to the charge that its findings cannot be extended to other settings. However, such a criticism, applied to the study of a single case, would be misplaced. A comparison to experiments conducted in the natural sciences clarifies the issue.

Consider a natural science theory that has so far been confirmed in just a single experiment (whether a laboratory, statistical, or natural experiment). Of course, the theory would not be generalizable on the basis of the single experiment, since the experiment would have tested the theory against just a single set of empirical circumstances. Instead, the theory would be generalizable to other sets of empirical circumstances only on the basis of actually being confirmed by additional experiments that test it against those other sets of empirical circumstances. The same point holds true for case studies. No theory concerning MIS would be generalizable on the basis of a single case study, since the single case study would have tested the theory against the empirical circumstances of just a single setting. Instead, the theory concerning MIS would be generalizable to other settings only on the basis of actually being confirmed by additional case studies that test it against the empirical circumstances of those other settings.

In other words, generalizability is a quality describing a theory that has been tested and confirmed in a variety of situations, whether such testing is conducted through case research, laboratory experiments, statistical experiments, or natural experiments. As such, generalizability poses no more, and no less, of a problem for MIS case research than it does for the studies conducted in the natural sciences. In taking this position, the MIS case researcher would, again, be in step with the natural science model.

What a scientific methodology for MIS case studies does, and does not, involve

In suggesting how MIS case studies might be carried out, this chapter has offered a scientific methodology that involves: (1) the deductive testing of theories, where (2) the theory must be (a) falsifiable, (b) logically consistent, (c) more predictive than other theories, and (d) not falsified by the tests it experiences. As such, this scientific methodology is no different from, and therefore no less rigorous than, scientific methodology as it is practised in the natural sciences.

At the same time, this chapter takes the position that the scientific methodology of the natural science model does not involve, as objectives, the utilization of any of the following, even though they may often be regarded (in this chapter's view, improperly) as necessary elements in scientific research: laboratory controls, statistical controls, mathematical propositions, and replicable observations. Instead, each one of these happens to be a means to an objective in scientific research rather than the objective itself. MIS case studies are capable of achieving the same scientific objectives through different means.

Laboratory controls and statistical controls, for example, constitute a means to controlled observation - an objective that MIS case studies are able to achieve through natural controls. Likewise, mathematical propositions constitute a means to controlled or logical deduction - an objective MIS case studies are able to achieve through verbal propositions that apply the rules of formal logic, of which the rules of mathematics are but a subset. Finally, replicable observations constitute a means to the replication of a theory's confirmation or disconfirmations – an objective MIS case studies are able to achieve by testing the same theory through new predictions, thereby calling for new observations rather than replications of old ones.

The chapter has also taken the position that scientific methodology does not involve generalizability based on the result of a single test, whether it is a single test taking place in an MIS case study or a single test taking place in a laboratory experiment of the natural sciences. Instead, generalizability is a product of successive testing across a range of settings, not a single test in a single setting.

It is worth emphasizing how the particular scientific framework described in this chapter allows us to identify some case studies as having more analytical rigour than others. There are two ways in which analytical rigour may be assessed.

First, there is simply the matter of whether a given case study explicitly addresses each of the four requirements. As a check for falsifiability, does the case study consider any predictions through which the theory of interest could be proven wrong? As a check for logical consistency, are all the predictions considered consistent with one another? As a check for empirical validity, does the case study confirm the theory through empirical testing? Finally, as a check for relative predictive power, does the case study rule out rival theories? These questions presume, of course, that the theory of interest is stated explicitly in the first place and that predictions following from the theory are also explicitly stated. MIS case studies that satisfy all four requirements explicitly and successfully are more rigorous than MIS case studies that satisfy any of the four requirements implicitly or unsuccessfully.

Table 9.1 compares a number of MIS case studies with respect to the four requirements. Of course, none of the cited case studies was conducted with the avowed purpose of fitting this chapter's scientific framework, so any value judgements pertaining to the quality of these studies would be inappropriate. Instead, the table is intended simply as a guide for the reader who wishes to pursue additional examples of MIS case studies that illustrate, to varying extents, the scientific methodology this chapter has described.

The second matter pertaining to analytical rigour is one of degree. Some case studies may satisfy the four requirements better than other case studies. For instance, first, consider the requirement that the theory of interest be confirmed through empirical testing. Confirming the theory by successfully testing it through just one of its predictions would not be as rigorous as successfully testing it through several of its predictions. Likewise, confirming the theory in just one organizational setting would not be as rigorous as confirming it in two or more organizational settings. As the number of explicitly derived predictions or the number of organizational settings is increased, the theory's degree of confirmation may also be increased.

Second, the requirement that the theory of interest be more predictive than any rival theory may, of course, be satisfied more rigorously by increasing the number of rival theories against which its predictive performance is compared. As the number of rival theories considered is increased, the theory's degree of relative predictive power may also be increased. Incidentally, with respect to the research strategy of using a single case study to distinguish among competing theoretical explanations, Allison (1971) established the primary scholarly model used by Markus (1983), Kling and Iacono (1984), and others.

Third, the requirement that the theory of interest be logically consistent may be more rigorously satisfied by increasing the number of predictions derived from it, then making sure that none of the predicted events contradicts or precludes one another. In contrast, deriving just two predictions from the theory, and checking that they do not contradict each other, would provide minimal rigour. Thus, as the number of explicitly derived predictions is increased, the theory's degree of logical consistency may also be increased.

Table 9.1 Checking MIS case studies against the four requirements

Case study author(s)	Main theory of interest	The Four Requirements			
		Does the case study consider any predictions through which the theory could be proven wrong?	Are all the predictions consistent with one another?	Does the case study confirm the theory through empirical testing?	Does the case study rule out rival theories?
Markus (1983)	'Interaction' theory	Yes[a]	Yes[b]	Yes[c]	Yes[d]
Kraemer, Dickhoven, et al. (1987)	Theory of successful model implementation in federal agencies	Yes[e]	Yes	No[f]	No[g]
Kling and Iacono (1984)	'Organizational politics metaphor'	Yes[h]	Possibly[i]	Yes[j]	Yes[k]
Laudon (1974)	Theory of resistance to centralized computing in state and local governments	Yes[m]	Yes	No[n]	No[g]
Kling (1978b)	Theory of interplay between technical features and social setting	Yes[p]	Possibly[i]	Yes[q]	Yes[r]
Kling and Scacchi (1982)	'Web models'	Yes[s]	Yes	Yes[t]	No[u]
Leonard-Barton (1987)	Theory of factors influencing user acceptance	Yes[v]	Possibly[i]	Partially[w]	No[g]
Fulk and Dutton (1984)	Theory of organizational uses of video-teleconferencing	Not applicable[x]	Not applicable[x]	No[x]	No[x]

Finally, the requirement that the theory of interest be falsifiable may be more rigorously satisfied by increasing the number of predictions derived from it and through which the theory could be proven wrong. In other words, as the number of explicitly derived predictions is increased, the theory's degree of falsifiability may also be increased.

Campbell (1975), too, has referred to the situation of the case researcher who pursues analytical rigour in the ways just suggested. 'In some sense, he has tested the theory with degrees of freedom coming from the multiple implications of any one theory' (p.182). In other words, Campbell is extending the concept of 'degrees of freedom' beyond its traditional statistical meaning. There are three ways Campbell's extended notion of 'degrees of freedom' can be applied to describe the analytical rigour of a case study. Since increasing the number of predictions also increases the number of different ways in which the case study's finding (for example, that the theory of interest is confirmed) could be subsequently replicated, the degree of replicability can also be increased.

First, there are the degrees of freedom in the number of predictions the case study considers. As the degrees of freedom are increased in this category, the theory's degree of falsifiability, degree of logical consistency, and degree of confirmation can all be correspondingly increased. Increasing the degrees of freedom in this category therefore allows the case study to strengthen the extent to which it satisfies three of the four requirements.

Incidentally, because increasing the number of predictions also increases the number of different ways in which the case study's finding (for example, that the theory of interest is confirmed) could be subsequently replicated, the degree of replicability can also be increased.

Second, there are the degrees of freedom in the number of cases or organizational settings in which a given theory is tested. As the degrees of freedom are increased in this category, the theory's degree of confirmation can be correspondingly increased. Increasing the degrees of freedom in this second category therefore allows the case study to strengthen the extent to which it satisfies one of the four requirements.

Incidentally, increasing the number of cases or organizational settings also allows the degree of generalizability to be correspondingly increased. It should be noted that increasing the number of cases or organizational settings is not necessarily the same thing as increasing the number of data points in a statistical study. The latter is often done simply to increase the 'level of confidence' associated with a single, statistically inferred observation (for example, the observation that 'the true mean is different from zero'), whereas the former involves increasing the total number of observations. In other words, increasing the number of data points will increase the 'degrees of freedom' only in the conventional statistical sense of this term, not in the additional senses this chapter is explaining.

Third and last, there are the degrees of freedom in the number of rival theories against which the theory of interest is compared. As the degrees of freedom are increased in this category, the theory's degree of relative predictive power can be correspondingly increased. Increasing the degrees of freedom in this third category therefore allows the case study to strengthen the extent to which it satisfies one of the four requirements.

Table 9.2 compares the same MIS case studies considered in Table 9.1 with respect to the three categories of degrees of freedom. As the table shows, the greater a case study's degrees of freedom in each category, the greater the case study's analytical rigour. A particular case study's 'analytical strategy' might therefore be described in terms of the number of degrees of freedom it pursues in each category.

Table 9.2 Checking the degrees of freedom of MIS case studies in three categories

Case study author(s)	Main theory of interest	Three Categories of Degrees of Freedom		
		Number of predictions considered	Number of cases or organizational settings considered	Number of rival theories considered
Markus (1983)	'Interaction' theory	Several[a]	1	2[d]
Kraemer, Dickhoven, et al. (1987)	Theory of successful model implementation in federal agencies	30[e]	2[y]	0
Kling and Iacono (1984)	'Organizational politics metaphor'	Several[h]	1	3[k]
Laudon (1974)	Theory of resistance to centralized computing in state and local governments	4[m]	4[z]	0
Kling (1978b)	Theory of interplay between technical features and social setting	Several[p]	1	1[r]
Kling and Scacchi (1982)	'Web models'	5	2[aa]	1[u]
Leonard-Barton (1987)	Theory of factors influencing user acceptance	Several[v]	1	0
Fulk and Dutton (1984)	Theory of organizational uses of video-teleconferencing	0[x]	1	0

Notes for Table 9.1 and Table 9.2

(a) One prediction is explicitly stated (in Table II, p.437): 'Changing individuals and/or fixing technical features will have little effect on resistance.' Other predictions pertaining to the interaction theory are considered implicitly in the discussion (pp.437-438).

(b) This refers to predictions that the case study treats explicitly as well as implicitly.

(c) See p.438.

(d) The case study rules out the 'people-determined' theory and the 'system-determined' theory (p.438).

(e) The case study states 30 predictions (these are the 'propositions' on pp.256-287). Each prediction makes it possible to refute the theorized impact of a specific variable. (See Figure A1, p.257, for a list of the 30 variables.)

cont.

(f)   The case study's objective is theory formulation, not theory testing. Still, the theory and predictions are consistent with the facts of the two cases considered (the 'TRIM/MATH' computer model and the 'DRI' computer model).

(g)   Only one theory is formulated and considered.

(h)   All predictions treated are implicit. For example, the case study states (p.1225): 'The CBIS did not simply evolve along a natural path nor did it drift, rather it was pushed in a specific direction which would increase the power and control of key actors within the organization'. Thus the reader may infer the prediction that, if the organizational politics metaphor is true, then we should observe neither evolution along a natural path, nor drift, but observe development in a direction that would increase (not decrease or keep constant) the power and control of key actors within the organization.

(i)   The case study provides sufficient material for the reader to infer predictions (as the prediction in note h was inferred) that may then be compared.

(j)   For example, the prediction mentioned in note h is confirmed.

(k)   The case study rules out the technological evolution metaphor, the economic rationality metaphor, and the organizational drift metaphor (pp.1222-1223). The reader may infer additional predictions, pertaining to these three theories that are implicit in this portion of the case study.

(m)   The theory contains the variables of 'homogeneity', 'interdependence', and 'internal integration' (pp.67-75). The case study states four predictions explicitly: (1) 'We hypothesize that ceteris paribus, the more organizations are homogeneous with respect to tasks - the production of similar products or services - the more likely they share similar environmental and internal problems, the more likely it is that they will interact with each other in dealing with shared problems and the more likely they are to pursue collective solutions to those problems [such as sharing and using a centralized, computerized database system]' (p.69); (2) 'Here we hypothesize that high and increasing levels of interdependence among social units are conducive to higher levels of social integration among those units, and supportive of efforts attempting to increase integration [such as sharing and using a centralized, computerized database system]' (p.71); (3) 'Therefore, we hypothesize a trade-off between homogeneity and interdependence in relation to integration of a social system. If both qualities are high in a system, increases in integration would be supported. If both are low, further integration would be most difficult. If of opposite sign, one low and the other high, the effects should tend to cancel out' (p.72); and (4) 'For these reasons we hypothesize that under conditions of high internal unit integration, resistance to system integrating efforts will be very high, and/or the terms under which such units are included into larger systems will be very favourable. Furthermore, we suggest that if resistance remains high, and if the demands of highly integrated units are very high, the integrating effort will cease or force will be resorted to' (p.73).

(n)   The study qualifies itself by taking the position that the theory 'is not itself proved by the [four] case studies [but] is intended to serve as a guide to the cases' (p.91). However, this qualification may be read as a sign of modesty, since the study (in Table 3, p.75) offers what appear to be the favourable results of empirically testing the predictions mentioned in note m. Moreover, the study even describes specific sets of empirical conditions pertaining to the bureaucratic reform process and states the level of resistance predicted for each. These sets of empirical conditions are presented under the headings of the 'pluralist model'; the 'collegial model'; the 'notables model' and the 'reputational elite model' (pp.80-90).

(p)   All predictions treated are implicit, but the case study provides sufficient discussion for the reader to infer them. The theory of interest is that a computerized information system's impacts are a joint product of its technical features and its social setting. One prediction the reader may infer is that, if the theory is true, then deficient technical features alone will not bring about a lack of impact or a negative impact. Whereas this prediction is clearly refutable, it is confirmed by the facts the case study reports.

(q)   See p.492.

cont.

(r)   The case study rules out the theory that either the technical features alone or the social setting alone, can determine the impacts of a computerized information system.

(s)   The case study states five predictions (these are the propositions on p.26).

(t)   See pp.55-63.

(u)   The case study compares 'web' models to 'discrete-entity' models, but states (p.70): 'We have not organized this article to test the relative explanatory power of the discrete-entity and web models.'

(v)   One prediction is explicit (p.10): 'It seems reasonable to hypothesize that the first adopters of SSA might be younger, more highly educated in the computer field, and more skilled in computer languages than their colleagues who are not yet using, and may never use, SSA.' Other predictions treated are implicit.

(w)   The prediction (mentioned in note v) was refuted (p.14): 'Age, type of education, and skill in Fortran and PL1 showed no relationship to SSA use'. Other predictions were confirmed.

(x)   This case study avows (p.106): 'Our purpose was not to provide a controlled experimental comparison...but rather to gather exploratory and descriptive data.' This case study is included as a reminder that case studies may also be legitimately used for the purposes of exploratory analysis and theory generation, not just theory testing. With respect to theory generation, this particular case study may be regarded as a useful contribution toward the development of a theory of the organizational uses of video teleconferencing.

(y)   See pp.21-22.

(z)   See pp.12-14.

(aa) See pp. 40-53.

The central concern of this chapter has been to address certain methodological issues pertaining to MIS case studies. However, the chapter's analysis and conclusions may have ramifications that go beyond matters of MIS case studies alone. These ramifications might prove interesting to scholars and practitioners alike.

For MIS scholars, the chapter's discussion of scientific method might prove interesting for its relevance to MIS research in general, not just MIS case studies. Research methodology in the study of management information systems has been gaining attention as a problem, in itself, that deserves investigation. In the spirit typical of methodological inquiry, MIS academics are making their own research methodology their object of study. (For example, see Ein-Dor, 1986; Jenkins, 1986; Kauber, 1986; Klein, 1986; Naumann, 1986; Wand and Weber, 1986. These papers were presented at the MIS Researcher's Workshop, held at the November 1986 annual meeting of the Decision Sciences Institute.) This methodological inquiry addresses not only what it means for our research to be 'scientific', but also such matters as the role of frameworks, epistemology, and paradigms in MIS research. In this regard, the chapter's view of scientific method could help secure the emerging position of qualitative research in MIS and perhaps, at the same time, reconcile the perceived differences between quantitative and qualitative approaches in MIS research. For a provocative view of the qualitative methods that are emerging in MIS research see Bjørn-Andersen (1986), Goldstein (1986), Markus (1986), Rosen (1986). These papers were presented at the panel on the 'Use of Qualitative Methods in MIS Research', held at the 1986 annual meeting of the International Conference on Information Systems. For an introduction to the use of qualitative methods in general see

Filstead (1970), Kirk (1986), Yin (1984), as well as the December 1979 issue of *Administrative Science Quarterly.*

In this larger methodological context, it is interesting to observe that this chapter's schema for assessing analytical rigour (illustrated in Tables 9.1 and 9.2) recognizes no differences between quantitative and qualitative approaches. (Indeed, the case study by Leonard-Barton (1987) involves statistical inference.) The degrees of freedom in each category (which follow from the four requirements of the natural science model) can be greater or smaller, whether the theory of interest is stated in the form of mathematical propositions or verbal propositions. In other words, a qualitative case study can possess more analytical rigour than a statistical study using LISREL, just as the reverse may be true. In this sense, any distinctions between quantitative and qualitative approaches are artificial and inconsequential. Neither type of research is inherently more rigorous than the other. In other fields of academic research, the perceived differences between quantitative and qualitative approaches have, unfortunately, become institutionalized into opposing camps.

In the field of organizational studies, the existence of opposing camps is clearly evident.   Morey & Luthans (1984), in their review of the organizational literature, describe the opposition between the two camps as objective versus subjective (Burrell and Morgan, 1979), nomothetic and idiographic (Luthans and Davis, 1982), quantitative versus qualitative (Van Maanen, 1979), outsider versus insider (Evered and Louis, 1981), and etic versus emic.   This has generated concern over what Morey and Luthans call the 'widening gap between the two major orientations to organizational research' (p.29) – a gap so wide that some researchers have called for a rapprochement between the two approaches (Evered and Louis, 1981; Luthans and Davis, 1982; Morey and Luthans, 1984).

In the field of operations research, the interdisciplinary quantitative/qualitative approach, which characterized the field shortly after its founding during World War II, eventually gave way to the dominance of quantitative approaches. Only recently has the non-mathematical camp re-emerged to challenge, or complement, the mathematical camp. See Ackoff (1979) for a historical review of the events in the development of the field of operations research.

Some of the methodological concepts in this chapter may prove helpful in avoiding a similar schism in the academic field of MIS.

For MIS practitioners, the chapter's discussion of scientific method might prove interesting for demystifying the aura of MIS research that claims to pursue scientific rigour, whether it involves the qualitative study of a single case or the utilization of a sophisticated statistical tool such as LISREL. The discussion of scientific method - especially the four requirements that a scientific theory must satisfy - may empower MIS practitioners themselves to identify the point at which scientific rigour is achieved in an MIS research effort, and beyond which further rigour, especially if pursued at the expense of professional relevance, can be called into question.

Finally, it is important to point out that, in the actual formulation of scientific knowledge, neither natural scientists nor social scientists necessarily think in terms of the formalized procedures of any model of science, including the natural science model. Lee (1987b) states: 'These procedures do not address the private, mental process by which a scientist formulates scientific knowledge, but rather the public process by which the scientist will on occasion retrospectively test the truth of the already formulated knowledge for acceptance by his or her peers' (p.577). Kaplan (1964) refers to the former process as the actual 'logic in use' by a scientist, and the latter as a 'reconstructed logic' (p.8). In recognizing the natural science model as one among many possible reconstructed logics of science, the chapter also recognizes the need for future research to investigate the ramifications that alternative models of science could have for MIS case study methodology.

10 Scholarship and Practice: The Contribution of Ethnographic Research Methods to Bridging the Gap

Lynda J. Harvey and Michael D. Myers

Research methods are the means by which knowledge is acquired and constructed within a discipline. Research methods need to be both relevant and rigorous in order to be accepted as legitimate within a particular field of knowledge. Information systems (IS) is a field which has multiple stakeholders in its knowledge development, operating in contexts which have to deal with multiplicity, cross-linkage, diversity and continually emerging changes, demanding integration as a key perspective. The diversity needs to be applauded rather than denied, even in the customarily slow-to-change world of research.

The stakeholders in IS research include scholars, practitioners, educationists, users, politicians, economists and citizens (present and future). In this chapter, the authors concentrate on the conflicts of objectives between scholars and practitioners as stakeholder groups in IS research, looking at how the differences exposed can show areas of potential integration and can point the way to choosing both relevant and rigorous research methods. It is an assumption of this chapter that there is a gap between the process of knowledge generation conducted by researchers and that conducted by practitioners. The authors seek to show how ethnography provides the principles to support both groups, hence bridging the gap. The purpose of the chapter is to show how ethnographic research methods can generate knowledge, which is useful to both practice and scholarship.

Scholarly and practical knowledge

Lyotard argues that the knowledge game is a social process whereby discourses develop to segregate legitimate and non-legitimate frameworks for action (Lyotard, 1984; Lyotard and Thebaud, 1985). Within any discipline there are likely to be a variety of such discourses, displaying conflicts between the expressed languages of the discourses even though the content may seem very similar. These differences are a critical way of strengthening alternative views, but they can create problems in reconciling the surface differences against the deeper consensus of beliefs and meanings (Lyotard, 1988). According to Lyotard, the surface differences can create barriers to shared actions between groups holding different discourses even though they may share deeper common concerns, leading to social reality differences which negate collaboration. Anyone taking a critical perspective to knowledge contribution needs to expose the surface differences, in a self-critical manner, so that any shared common concerns can emerge and a new consensual discourse can be allowed to develop.

In the knowledge field called information systems research, the surface discourses of the stakeholder groups of scholars and practitioners appear to be disparate. Scholars are expected to be concerned with the development of knowledge which is generalizable (that is, knowledge which is, in principle, a-contextual and a-historical), while practitioners are concerned with the development of knowledge which is immediately usable in specific problem contexts. However, analysis of the practical discourses of both stakeholder groups shows more similarities than differences.

Scholars are primarily concerned with developing knowledge that can be defended as 'true' knowledge; scholarly research needs to be able to justify the validity of accepted approaches to data collection and analysis. Validity is really a word for the standardization of quality across a particular interest group; it is a key sign in the legitimation of knowledge practices. In practitioners' discourses, validity is also a major concern but it is not named as such, rather it is named 'quality control'. Although practitioners are not a unified body (since the term includes a broad range of job descriptions), all IS practitioners need to be confident that information generated is based on sound knowledge. In order to accomplish this, principles are applied to the procedures whereby information is gathered and the knowledge bases are challenged. Just as any scholar neglects the challenge of validity at her/his peril, any IS practitioner who supplies a client with invalid data or with information from a poor quality knowledge source is likely to suffer.

Scholars in the IS field are characteristic in that they must be concerned to generate valid knowledge which can, at least in principle, be informative to practice. Scholars in IS are expected to substantiate their contributions to practical knowledge by showing which contextual areas can benefit. Likewise, any practitioner is expected to justify their knowledge-seeking and generation activities against measures of the practicability of outputs.

In the field of IS, the areas of research concern are delineated in such a way as to reflect practical areas of development. For example, information systems analysis is separated as a research area from IS applications. Information systems design is separated into software design practices, database design and development practices, human computer interface design areas, and systems configuration areas of concern. Information systems development looks more towards the use of tools and methodologies for controlling IS development practices and the building of information systems hardware and software objects, considering the importance of creating a 'fit' with their social and cultural institutional contexts. Clearly, the actual definition of IS research areas reflects the applied, practical nature of the discipline. There is little research which looks at the nature of systems of information per se; IS research is almost always justified in terms of the way in which it helps to aid the understanding of IS practice.

As a research field, then, IS research displays a fundamental moral order relating to IS practice. Such a moral order affects the legitimation act of naming and accepting particular research approaches (Foucault, 1972), where IS researchers have to show where their research fits and how their research has practical implications. Paradoxically, however, the actual discourse practised is not obviously akin to that shared by practitioners. The discourse of IS researchers concentrates more on research methods which lean towards the language of positivism (Orlikowski and Baroudi, 1991), thus rendering the voice of the practitioner less legitimate and making more invisible the knowledge generated by the practitioners. (Foucault 1970 provides a discussion of invisibility and legitimation).

The indications are that the scholars of the IS discipline are in conflict with their own moral order in their adoption of the language of positivism when dealing with the issues pursued in their research, issues shared with the practitioners in IS. The language of positivism is applied to the scrutinization of research practices, through the domain of research methods and their application to research questions. This chapter argues that a more appropriate consideration of research methods can dispel some of the conflicts in the moral order of IS researchers, allowing for the development of knowledge generation approaches which are appropriate to both scholars and practitioners.

The chapter proceeds as follows. The next section looks at current IS research practices in their historical context, showing how the argument for methodological pluralism has come to the fore. Qualitative research approaches are then discussed, looking at the approaches as creators of an alternative discourse, alternative to but not contradictory to that shared by the classically scientific research approaches. The following section looks at ethnography as a particular form of qualitative research. The critical hermeneutic approach to ethnography is discussed in relation to its usefulness for both scholars and practitioners as a means by which they can realistically justify their knowledge outputs. Next, the contribution of ethnography to IS research is discussed, both as an actual and as a potential method. Finally, the limitations of the ethnographic research method are outlined, concluding with consideration of the need to bridge the gap between scholarly knowledge and practical knowledge in IS research.

IS research practices

IS research practices need to be viewed in the light of their historical context. What was important as a concern in IS research a decade ago is now seen as less so, being overridden by other concerns. The output from IS research has consistently shown that it is the social and organizational contexts of information systems design, development and application which lead to the greatest practical problems. (Examples are provided by Hirschheim and Newman, 1991; Newman and Robey, 1992; Walsham, 1993). The area has been consistently refined down through information systems research and this has led to the realization that all aspects of any information system have a highly complex, and constantly changing, social context. The complexity resulting from this realization has led to the need to develop richer theories of information systems as social objects but, as Hirschheim and Newman point out, many of the existing theories attempting to deal with this are 'unfortunately, at an elementary stage of development' (Hirschheim and Newman, 1991, p.30).

In their literature analysis of the historical preferences for research methods in information systems research practices, Orlikowski and Baroudi (1991) found a clear preference for positivist research. This is a form of research discourse, which depicts an a-historical and a-contextual view of information systems. As argued earlier, this is not easily mappable on to the practical knowledge development procedures of practitioners, which have a tendency to regard context and history as crucially important.

Despite the clear historical preference for information systems researchers to adopt a positivist view of knowledge generation, there is a growing recognition made of the need to temper the quasi-experimental forms of research with those which are more concerned with contextual analysis. For example, the area of decision support systems (DSS) has long been a central research topic in the information systems field. From the group decision support systems (GDSS) area, the computer-supported co-operative work (CSCW) area has developed and this area has openly embraced more contextual forms of research methods, alongside the quasi-experimental approaches.

For example, at the ACM 1992 Conference on CSCW (Turner and Kraut, 1992), there were many indicators of more qualitative research methods being adopted (for example, Bentley et al., 1992; Hughes et al., 1992; Orlikowski, 1992). Similarly, for five years the International Conference on Information Systems (ICIS) has run panels or workshops dealing with qualitative techniques. It would seem that information systems researchers are becoming more accepting of the need to adopt techniques that consider the historical and contextual aspects of information systems. This has the potential for moving the discourses between knowledge workers who are scholars and knowledge workers who are practitioners closer together.

Ethnography

Arguments, which put forward the need to consider context in research, tend to support qualitative techniques (Lee, 1991; Orlikowski, 1991). However, there is an extremely broad range of qualitative techniques, ranging from anything that does not directly deal with numbers to the most in-depth and self-reflective interpretive techniques. Also, many qualitative techniques do make reference to numerical representations of the contextual elements under observation. There are many ways that the distinction between qualitative and quantitative can be contrived (Lee, 1991) and the referential differences tend to be seen more as epistemological shifts, often paradigmatic in nature (Galliers, 1985). But there is still one major difference which is of relevance to this chapter and that is the different ways in which context is treated.

In more traditional quantitative techniques, context is treated as either a set of interfering variables that need controlling, known as noise in the data, or other controlled variables which are experimentally set up in order to seek for cause and effect relationships. In the more traditional qualitative approaches, context is treated as the socially constructed reality of a named group, or groups, of social agents and the key task of observation and analysis is to unpack the webs of meaning transformed in the social process whereby reality is constructed. In quantitative techniques, cause and effect are the main objects being searched for, while, in qualitative techniques, meaning in context is the most important framework being sought.

Because context is crucial to qualitative observations and analyses, techniques that explore contextual webs of meaning are important. The main body of techniques fall under the domain of an approach called ethnography, which developed out of the social science called anthropology. After early ground-breaking work (Suchman, 1987; Wynn, 1979; Zuboff, 1988), ethnography has now become more widely used in the study of information systems in organizations, from the study of the development of information systems (Hughes et al., 1992; Orlikowski, 1991; Orlikowski and Robey, 1991; Preston, 1991) to the study of the use of information technology forms (Yates and Orlikowski, 1992) also including the study of aspects of information technology management (Davies, 1991; Davies and Nielsen, 1992). Ethnography has also been discussed as a method whereby multiple perspectives can be incorporated in systems design (Holzblatt and Beyer, 1993) and as a general approach to the wide range of possible studies relating to the investigation of information systems (Pettigrew, 1985). In the next two sections, the origins of ethnography in anthropology are briefly presented and then a particular form of ethnography, which uses critical hermeneutics, is discussed.

The origins of ethnography

The first anthropologist to adopt the ethnographic research method was Bronislaw Malinowski, who in 1922 published his now famous book Argonauts of the Western Pacific. This book was based on Malinowski's fieldwork among the Trobriand Islanders. It is useful to understand why Malinowski adopted this approach (for more detail see Darnell, 1974; Kuper, 1973).

Before Malinowski, anthropologists had collected volumes of material from non-Western cultures and societies all around the world. However, despite this vast collection of material, very little of it made any sense to Western observers. The social and cultural practices in other cultures seemed strange and 'primitive', if not frightening. An anthropologist would typically document a particular cultural practice (for example sorcery), and then try to explain it by comparison with other practices of the same kind in other cultures. Thus, Frazer's The Golden Bough, first published in 1890, was an encyclopaedic collection of various cultural practices from around the globe (Frazer, 1890). Where Malinowski departed from previous researchers was in suggesting that cultural practices from other societies could only be understood by studying the context in which they took place. All previous research had simply taken various cultural practices out of context – and that is why they appeared strange. By learning the local language and living in a society for at least one or more years, by trying to understand the meaning of particular cultural practices in context, only then would other cultures and societies start to make sense to Western observers.

After Malinowski's lead, the ethnographic research method involving intensive fieldwork became established in anthropology as the dominant form of research. Anthropologists coined the term 'ethnocentrism' to refer to the tendency of people in most cultures to think of their own culture as the best and most sensible. A good ethnography, however, was one that 'sensitized' the reader to the beliefs, values, and practices of the natives in another society. If, after reading the ethnography, actions which were previously seen as absurd, strange or irrational 'made sense', then that ethnography had achieved its purpose.

Today there is critical debate within anthropology concerning the ethnographic research method (Van Maanen, 1988). There are many different schools or views within anthropology about ethnographic interpretation. These views are relevant to the ethnographic study of information systems as they show the variety of approaches already being adopted within the source discipline. Although we are unable to discuss this critical debate within anthropology in depth, one of the landmark publications in this debate is Clifford and Marcus's (1986) work (see also Clifford, 1988; Marcus, 1992).

Sanday (1979) divides ethnography into the holistic, semiotic and behaviouristic schools of thought, and she further divides the semiotic school into thick description and ethnoscience. Each school of thought has a different approach to doing an ethnography. For example, most ethnographers of the holistic school say that empathy and identification with the social grouping being observed is needed; they insist that an anthropologist should 'go native' and live just like the local people (for example, Cohen, 1985; Evans-Pritchard, 1950). The assumption is that the anthropologist has to become like a blank slate in order understand local social and cultural practices fully. The anthropologist acts like a sponge, soaking up the language and culture of the people under study.

On the other hand, Clifford Geertz, the foremost exponent of the 'thick description' (semiotic) school, says that anthropologists do not need to have empathy with their subjects (Geertz, 1973; Geertz, 1983; Geertz, 1988). Rather, the ethnographer has to search out and analyze symbolic forms – words, images, institutions, behaviours – with respect to one another and to the whole that they comprise. Geertz argues that it is possible for an anthropologist to describe and analyze another culture without having to empathize with the people. He says that anthropologists need to understand the 'webs of significance', which people weave within the cultural context, and these webs of significance can only be communicated to others by thickly describing the situation and its context. An alternative to the above is the adoption of a critical perspective on ethnographic research. For example, Forester (1992) used the critical social theory of Habermas in the development of an approach called critical ethnography. Forester used critical ethnography to examine the facetious figures of speech used by city planning staff to negotiate the problem of data acquisition. Myers (1987) used critical hermeneutics to illuminate the ethnographic research process in his study of the independence movement in the Melanesian nation of Vanuatu (see also Marcus and Fischer, 1986). The critical hermeneutic approach to ethnography, which we advocate, is discussed below.

Critical hermeneutics

Hermeneutics is the science of interpretation, concerned with analysis of the meaning of a text or text-analogue. The basic question in hermeneutics is 'What is the meaning of a text?' (Radnitzky, 1970, p.20). Taylor says that:

> Interpretation, in the sense relevant to hermeneutics, is an attempt to make clear, to make sense of an object of study. This object must, therefore, be a text, or a text-analogue, which in some way is confused, incomplete, cloudy, seemingly contradictory – in one way or another, unclear. The interpretation aims to bring to light an underlying coherence or sense (Taylor, 1976, p.153).

The idea of a hermeneutic circle refers to the dialectic between the understanding of the text as a whole and the interpretation of its parts, in which descriptions are guided by anticipated explanations (Gadamer, 1976a, p.117). As Gadamer explains, 'It is a circular relationship...The anticipation of meaning in which the whole is envisaged becomes explicit understanding in that the parts, that are determined by the whole, themselves also determine this whole'.

It follows from this that we have an expectation of meaning from the context of what has gone before. The movement of understanding 'is constantly from the whole to the part and back to the whole' (Gadamer, 1976a, p.117). Ricoeur points out that 'Interpretation...is the work of thought which consists in deciphering the hidden meaning in the apparent meaning, in unfolding the levels of meaning implied in the literal meaning' (Ricoeur, 1974, p.xiv).

Hermeneutics is used to explore the socially constructed contexts of institutions and organizations (Berger and Luckman, 1967) and, as an approach to meaning analysis, it has been used in many disciplines, including education, medicine, anthropology, sociology and architecture (Vattimo, 1988). It has also been taken up by researchers in the information systems area (for example, Boland, 1991; Lee, 1991; Winograd and Flores, 1987). The principles of hermeneutics have been applied to the analyses of the metaphorical nature of theories of information (Boland, 1987) and of systems development (Hirschheim and Newman, 1991). Hermeneutics is a recognized framework for the analysis of organizations (Bryman, 1989), in particular when looking at organizational culture (Frost et al., 1985), and has been applied to the analysis of socio-technical interactions

(Barley, 1986). This makes it a potentially important approach to the analysis of information systems in organizations.

There are different forms of hermeneutics, all concerned with the textual treatment of social settings, but not all concern themselves with reflective critique of the meaning of interpretations derived from textual analyses. The early hermeneuts such as Dilthey advocated a 'pure hermeneutics', which stressed empathic understanding and the understanding of human action from the 'inside'. As Radnitzky points out, however, pure hermeneutics is uncritical in that it takes statements or ideologies at face value (Radnitzky, 1970, p.20). He cites Gadamer as saying that 'we don't have to imagine oneself in the place of some other person; rather, we have to understand what these thoughts or the sentences expressing them are about' (Radnitzky, 1970, p.27).

More recently, critical hermeneutics has emerged following the debates between Habermas and Gadamer (Gadamer, 1976b; Myers, 1995; Ricoeur, 1976; Thompson, 1981). There is a potential tendency to view interpretation as a closed and exact form, but critical hermeneutics recognizes that the interpretive act is one which can never be closed as there is always a possible alternative interpretation (Taylor, 1976). In critical hermeneutics the interpreter constructs the context as another form of text, which can then, of itself, be critically analyzed so that the meaning construction can be understood as an interpretive act. In this way, the hermeneutic interpreter is simply creating another text on a text, and this recursive creation is potentially infinite. Every meaning is constructed, even through the very constructive act of seeking to deconstruct, and the process whereby that textual interpretation occurs must be self-critically reflected on (Ricoeur, 1974).

Critical hermeneutics takes seriously the reflective critique of the interpretation applied by the researcher and so offers insights about how understanding takes place. As Myers (1994) points out, critical hermeneutics requires the researcher to become aware of his or her own historicality. This awareness of the dialectic between the text and the interpreter has been brought to the fore in contemporary hermeneutics. Classical or 'pure' hermeneutics ignored this dialectic in the attempt to understand a text in terms of itself.

Adoption of the critical hermeneutic perspective leads to criticism of non-dialectical views of ethnographic research, such as those of the holistic school. Ethnographers of the holistic school, in their attempt to 'go native' and understand other cultures 'in their own terms', in effect deny the glossing of those views by the interpretive act of the analyst. The end result is tantamount to a recourse to objectivity due to a taking for granted of the need for the critical analysis of the dialectics of the interpretive process. The role of the observer is treated as context-free, ignoring the fact that every interpretive exploration leads to a new understanding, thus rendering history as the most vital attribute of ethnographic analysis, the history of the material and the history of the interpretation. Zuboff's study of computer-mediated work (Zuboff, 1988) took the dialectical process of historical critique as fundamental to the ethnographic work being carried out. She argued that 'history would offer only a brief window of time during which such data could be gathered' (Zuboff, 1988, p.xiv).

The critical hermeneutic perspective leads to the recognition that any ethnography is a form of historiography. The critical ethnographer is essentially situated in history, the history of the situation and of the interpretation, and is also part of a wider set of social, economic and political relationships. One of the key tasks of a critical ethnographer is to be aware of the historical context in which research takes place and to reflect this critically on to the research process itself. In arguing for a reflexive anthropology, Kahn points out that the interpretation of culture(s) 'is in fact part of a process of construction' and says that anthropologists themselves 'are similarly part of a broader socio-historical process' (Kahn, 1989, p.22) (see also Scholte, 1972).

The hermeneutic-dialectic perspective openly recognizes that understanding of an institutional context is not gained by the researcher suspending her or his prejudices. Rather, the ethnographer is encouraged to become critically aware of them, making them explicit in the process of learning about cultural differences, a process not unlike the behaviour of practitioners who have to traverse a variety of sub-cultures within organizations (Orlikowski and Baroudi, 1991).

This cultural bridging process is typically one attributed to systems analysts and business analysts in the information systems field, where they have to mediate between the users in the various business units and the more technically-oriented IS staff. This implies that the critical hermeneutic approach to ethnography also has great potential for helping this group of practitioners to conduct their work in an informed and rigorous manner (although a discussion of how critical ethnography could be used by IS and business analysts is beyond the scope of this chapter).

In the next two sections, the major contributions and limitations of this approach to information systems research are briefly explored.

Contributions

Ethnography offers a rigorous approach to the analysis of the institutional contexts of information systems practices, with the notion of context being one of the social construction of meaning frameworks. Ethnography, as a research method, is well suited to providing information systems researchers with rich insights into the human, social and organizational aspects of information systems development and application. When the form of ethnography known as critical hermeneutics is used (although this is not the only one), the findings can be rigorously scrutinized to allow for a thorough analysis of the processes of information systems practices, thus supplementing the more traditional approaches which tend to concentrate on content rather than process.

Because ethnography deals with actual practices in real world situations, it allows for relevant issues to be explored and frameworks to be developed which can be used by both practitioners and researchers. It also means that researchers can deal with real situations instead of having to contrive artificial situations for the purpose of quasi-experimental investigations.

Knowledge of what happens in the field can provide vital information to challenge and explore some of the assumptions gained from a mainly experimental-based body of knowledge. For example, Suchman and Wynn (1984) found that office conversations are tied to evolving customs and practices, which are not easily documented (see also Wynn, 1991). Hughes, Randall et al. (1992) showed how their ethnographic studies led them to question some widely-held assumptions about systems design. They found that the information provided by the ethnography provided a deeper understanding of the problem domain and that conventional principles normally thought of as a 'good design' could be inappropriate for co-operative systems.

Contrary to the theoretical position of much of the IS research literature which assumes that information technology will transform existing bureaucratic organizational forms and social relations, Orlikowski's (1991) ethnographic research showed how the use of new information technology led to the existing forms of control being intensified and fused. Orlikowski's work highlights the complex and often contradictory ways in which such technologies can be used. Overall, ethnographic research such as Orlikowski's points our attention to the non-instrumental appropriation of IT systems, and their ultimate embeddedness in local workplace cultures.

Another reason for using ethnography to study actual practices in real world situations is that it enables a researcher to study organizations as the complex social, cultural and political systems that they are. A critical ethnographic analysis requires a researcher to consider many different perspectives: to look at the views of the various stakeholders in an organization and the real value conflicts that there may be, and to look at the objective social impacts which may result from the implementation of new information systems. Ethnographies can also show differences in how information technologies tend to be used in different contexts.

The use of ethnographic research methods means that opportunities which arise from contextual situations can be built on, instead of avoided. As Zuboff (1988) argues, a 'window of opportunity' can be found to explore particular issues, for example where 'people who are working with technology for the first time were ripe with questions and insights regarding the distinct qualities of their experience' (Zuboff, 1988, p.13). By applying a critical hermeneutic approach to the analysis of such situations, a rigorous body of knowledge can be developed, which contributes directly to the support of the practical knowledge developed by practitioners. This can only enhance information systems research, allowing for practically relevant, rigorous research to be conducted in an effective way.

Limitations

One common criticism of ethnographic research is that it leads to in-depth knowledge only of particular contexts and situations. Until a large body of knowledge of many situations is developed, it is difficult to develop more general models of the meaningful contexts of various aspects of information systems development and application. However, generalizable knowledge is often neither relevant nor meaningful, in which case we are better off understanding specific contexts. Also, the lack of generalizability is more of a limitation due to the novelty of the approach in the field of information systems research than it is a limitation per se. Time should overcome this problem and lead to a much more widely informed body of knowledge. Also, it is possible to generalize from one ethnography to theory, just as it is possible to generalize from one case study to theory (Walsham, 1993; Yin, 1994).

The second major limitation is the time factor. Doing an ethnography takes a great deal of time, due as much to the time needed to prepare the members of the organization for acceptance of such an in-depth and scrutinizing approach as to the time needed to gather data and carry out many levels of interpretive analysis. The process of ethnography can be overwhelming for new researchers. They cannot enter situations with fixed frameworks and prepared questions, but can only offer those with whom they are working the view that they will be observing and collecting a great deal of data, none of which can be predicted beforehand. This can be most disconcerting for managers in the institutional contexts who wish to have some idea of the outcome of the research before they expose themselves and their institution to the research process. After having tackled this access issue, the ethnographer is often faced with the embarrassing situation of discovering many of the 'warts and all' aspects of the context; a great deal of tact and care is needed which is best handled through the development of honest and thoughtful relationships with those in the situation. There are many ethical research issues associated with ethnography because of the in-depth and holistic nature of the discoveries which emerge. These have to be tackled thoughtfully and self-reflectively by the researcher. Having dealt with all these issues, the researcher is then left with a mountain of textual and documentary material which demands analysis. The analytical process has to be holistic, following threads of discourse in order to build up scenarios which are then challenged by other meaning frameworks. The process is daunting and difficult, demanding that a great deal of intellectual and emotional capability be brought to bear on the process of analysis. However, despite the difficult and time-consuming nature of ethnographic research, we believe that these considerations are outweighed by the fact that ethnographic research is a very 'productive' research method considering the amount and likely substance of the research findings.

Finally, perhaps the worst part of the outcome is in dealing with the publication of results. The common format of the positivistic, hypothetico-deductive approach cannot be adopted. Rather, a more story-telling approach is needed, which can be greeted with disdain by unsympathetic reviewers who may misinterpret the style as non-rigorous. This problem is compounded by the holistic nature of the research process making the delineation of the results into an average length journal chapter (20 pages) a very difficult task. The net result appears too often to be just a presentation of what happened in a situation, making ethnographic work appear to be some weak form of a case study approach, which it is not. Writers of ethnographies have many epistemological and theoretical questions of interpretation to cope with (Van Maanen, 1988) but these issues are compounded in the information systems research area where the expectation is that singular findings will be presented in individual articles, in a distinctive and segmented manner, and the net result will be an accumulation of the many small findings into a large body of knowledge. With ethnographic research, the approach and the resultant nature of the knowledge is more holistic so that each article is really a microcosm of the total knowledge, making the knowledge generated recursive rather than cumulative, a distinction which is obscure and often not appreciated by those who operate through more traditional approaches. This issue can only be solved by having more discussion on ethnographic research approaches so that greater appreciation can be gained.

Conclusion

Information systems research is different from traditional scientific research in that it has to develop a body of knowledge which enhances the practical knowledge of workers in the institutional contexts under investigation. This leads to problems for researchers who may choose to give up rigour for relevance or the reverse of sacrificing relevance for rigour. Ethnography offers a research opportunity to conduct rigorous research which is of direct practical relevance. When supported by perspectives such as critical hermeneutics, the rigour is strengthened and more is discovered of the situation, leading to more knowledge with high potential for relevance to practitioners. This makes the ethnographic approach a worthy contender for bridging the gap between scholarly knowledge and practical knowledge, thus allowing for scholarship and practice to develop in collaborative coexistence.

11 CASE Tools as Organizational Change: Investigating Incremental and Radical Changes in Systems Development

Wanda J. Orlikowski

This chapter presents the findings of an empirical study into two organizations' experiences with the adoption and use of computer-aided software engineering (CASE) tools over time. Using a grounded theory research approach, the study characterizes the organizations' experiences in terms of processes of incremental or radical organizational change. These findings are used to develop a theoretical framework for conceptualizing the organizational issues around the adoption and use of these tools - issues that have been largely missing from contemporary discussions of CASE tools. The chapter thus has important implications for research and practice. Specifically, the framework and findings suggest that in order to account for the experiences and outcomes associated with CASE tools, researchers should consider the social context of systems development, the intentions and actions of key players, and the implementation process followed by the organization. Similarly, the chapter suggests that practitioners will be better able to manage their organizations' experiences with CASE tools if they understand that such implementations involve a process of organizational change over time and not merely the installation of a new technology.

CASE tools have generated much interest among researchers and practitioners as potential means for easing the software development and maintenance burden threatening to overwhelm information systems departments. While interest and investment in CASE tools have been rising steadily, actual experiences with tools have exhibited more ambiguity. For example, while some studies report improvements in productivity from the use of CASE tools (Banker and Kauffman, 1991; Necco et al., 1989; Norman and Nunamaker, 1988; Swanson et al., 1991), others find that the expected productivity gains are elusive (Card et al., 1987; Yellen, 1990) or eclipsed by lack of adequate training and experience, developer resistance, and increased design and testing time (Norman et al., 1989; Orlikowski, 1988a; Orlikowski, 1989; Vessey et al., 1992).

While these contradictory experiences with CASE tools appear puzzling and difficult to interpret, the research presented in this chapter suggests that by shifting the focus away from specific outcome expectations, we may be able to make some sense of the apparently inconsistent findings. This chapter argues that the adoption and use of CASE tools should be conceptualized as a form of organizational change and that such a perspective allows us to anticipate, explain, and evaluate different experiences and consequences following the introduction of CASE tools in organizations.

To date, there has been no systematic examination or formulation of the organizational changes surrounding CASE tools. Much of the literature on CASE tools has tended to focus on discrete outcomes, such as productivity, systems quality, and development costs, while neglecting the intentions and actions of key players, the process by which CASE tools are adopted and used, and the organizational context within which such events occur. Issues of intentions, actions, process, and context around information technology are not new to the IS field. For example, implementation research has looked at the process through which technology is introduced (Ginzberg, 1981b; Rogers, 1983). Also, the interactionist approach (Markus, 1983) and the reinforcement politics approach (George and King, 1991) have examined the role of social context in shaping the introduction and use of technology, while the structuration perspective (DeSanctis and Poole, 1994; Orlikowski and Robey, 1991) has emphasized the centrality of players' deliberate, knowledgeable, and reflective action in shaping and appropriating technology. Yet contemporary discussions around CASE tools in research, education, and practice tend to gloss over these issues.

In this chapter, the implementation of CASE tools is understood as a specific case of technology-based organizational change. As such, the core research question is: what are the critical elements that shape the organizational changes associated with the adoption and use of CASE tools? In answering this question, the chapter is organized as follows. First is a description of the empirical findings that emerged from a grounded theory study of two organizations that implemented CASE tools in their systems development operations. Next is the development of a theoretical framework that conceptualizes the findings in terms of three central categories: strategic conduct, institutional context, and change process.

The grounded theory approach was useful here because it allows a focus on contextual and processual elements as well as the action of key players associated with organizational change elements that are often omitted in IS studies that rely on variance models and cross-sectional, quantitative data (Markus and Robey, 1988; Orlikowski and Baroudi, 1991). While the findings of this grounded theory study are detailed and particularistic, a more general explanation can also be produced from the results (Dutton and Dukerich, 1991; Eisenhardt, 1989; Leonard-Barton, 1990). Yin (1989) refers to this technique as 'analytic generalization' to distinguish it from the more typical statistical generalization that generalizes from a sample to a population. Here the generalization is of theoretical concepts and patterns. This generalization is further extended in this chapter by combining the inductive concepts generated by the field study with insights from existing formal theory, in this case from the innovation literature (a strategy recommended by Glaser and Strauss, 1967). The outcome is a general conceptualization of the organizational changes associated with adopting and using CASE tools that should both contribute to our research knowledge and inform IS practice.

The chapter makes three principal contributions. First, drawing on the rich data of two organizations' experiences, the chapter generates a grounded understanding of the changes associated with implementing CASE tools in systems development. This grounded theory is valid empirically 'because the theory-building process is so intimately tied with evidence that it is very likely that the resultant theory will be consistent with empirical observation' (Eisenhardt, 1989, p.547). While many believe that building theory from a limited number of cases is susceptible to researchers' preconceptions, Eisenhardt (1989) argues persuasively that the opposite is true. The iterative comparison across sites, methods, evidence, and literature that characterizes such research leads to a 'constant juxtaposition of conflicting realities [that] tends to "unfreeze" thinking, and so the process has the potential to generate theory with less researcher bias than theory built from incremental studies or armchair, axiomatic deduction' (p.546). Second, the grounded theory developed in this chapter adds substantive content to our understanding of the central role played by individual actors, their institutional context, and the processes they enact in adopting and using CASE tools. Such an understanding has been absent from the research and practice discourses on CASE tools. The approach followed here focuses specifically on developing such an understanding, thus bringing a fresh set of issues to the already researched topic of CASE tools (Eisenhardt, 1989). Third, the chapter integrates a specific grounded theory with the more formal insights available from the innovation literature, developing a more general framework that will allow researchers and practitioners to explain, anticipate, and evaluate various organizational changes associated with the adoption and use of CASE tools.

The chapter is structured as follows. The first section describes the research methodology and the two research sites. The next section presents the research findings, describing the experiences of each organization in turn. The discussion section follows, integrating the specific concepts and findings of the field research with insights from the innovation literature into an analytic framework for conceptualizing CASE tools adoption and use in organizations. The conclusion then assesses the contribution of the research framework and findings, both for future research and for the management of CASE tools in organizations.

Research methodology

The research methodology followed is that of grounded theory (Glaser and Strauss, 1967; Martin and Turner, 1986; Turner, 1983), with an aim of generating a descriptive and explanatory theory of the organizational changes associated with CASE tools rooted in the experiences of specific systems development operations. This approach has been effectively used in organizational research (Ancona, 1990; Eisbach and Sutton, 1992; Isabella,

1990; Kahn, 1990; Pettigrew, 1990; Sutton, 1987) and is adopted here for three primary reasons.

First, grounded theory 'is an inductive, theory discovery methodology that allows the researcher to develop a theoretical account of the general features of a topic while simultaneously grounding the account in empirical observations or data' (Martin and Turner, 1986, p.141). This generative approach seemed particularly useful here given that no change theory of CASE tools adoption and use has been established to date. While models of information technology implementation do exist (Ginzberg, 1981b; Lucas, 1978; Markus, 1983) these deal largely with the development stages of IS implementation and focus extensively on user involvement and user relations. As a result, they are less applicable to the issue of organizational change in general and to the case of CASE tools adoption and use in particular.

Second, a major premise of grounded theory is that to produce accurate and useful results, the complexities of the organizational context have to be incorporated into an understanding of the phenomenon, rather than be simplified or ignored (Martin and Turner, 1986; Pettigrew, 1990). As indicated above, a number of theoretical approaches emphasize the criticality of organizational context in shaping technology use in organizations. Such a conviction also informs the research in this chapter, and the use of a grounded theory methodology allows the inclusion and investigation of this key organizational element.

Third, grounded theory facilitates 'the generation of theories of process, sequence, and change pertaining to organizations, positions, and social interaction' (Glaser and Strauss, 1967, p.114). As indicated above, the change an organization undergoes in adopting and assimilating CASE tools, as well as the processes of appropriation and use that system developers engage in to incorporate the tools in their work lives, has tended to be neglected in the CASE tools literature. A research approach that specifically includes elements of process and change was thus particularly appropriate here.

These three characteristics of grounded theory - inductive, contextual, and processual - fit with the interpretive rather than positivist orientation of this research. The focus here is on developing a context-based, process-oriented description and explanation of the phenomenon, rather than an objective, static description expressed strictly in terms of causality (Boland, 1979; Boland, 1985; Chua, 1986; Orlikowski and Baroudi, 1991). In the language of Markus and Robey (1988) and Mohr (1982), the chapter develops a process, not a variance theory. Such a theory describes and explains the process of adopting and using CASE tools in terms of an interaction of contextual conditions, actions, and consequences, rather than explains variance using independent and dependent variables (Eisbach and Sutton, 1992). This orientation 'gives primacy to realism of context and theoretical and conceptual development as research goals' (Pettigrew, 1989, p.283).

The methodology of grounded theory is iterative, requiring a steady movement between concept and data, as well as comparative, requiring a constant comparison across types of evidence to control the conceptual level and scope of the emerging theory. As Pettigrew (1989) notes, this 'provides an opportunity to examine continuous processes in context in order to draw out the significance of various levels of analysis and thereby reveal the multiple sources of loops of causation and connectivity so crucial to identifying and explaining patterns in the process of change' (p.14). To facilitate this iteration and comparison, two field sites were studied and analyzed in turn, a strategy also adopted by Kahn (1990). The initial concepts thus emerged in one organizational context and were then contrasted, elaborated, and qualified in the other.

Site selection

Following Glaser and Strauss' (1967) technique of theoretical sampling, the two organizations were selected for their similarities as well as their differences. Theoretical sampling requires paying attention to theoretical relevance and purpose. With respect to relevance, this selection process ensures that the substantive area addressed - here the adoption and use of CASE tools - is kept similar, or as Eisenhardt (1989) notes, 'is likely to replicate or extend the emergent theory' (p.537). Thus, both organizations chosen for this study had within the past few years implemented CASE tools into their systems development operations and mandated their use on all new systems development work. In addition, the CASE tools themselves, while not identical, were compatible across the two organizations in that both were life-cycle tools that integrate the phases of analysis, design, coding, and testing. Both sets of tools provide similar capabilities, such as design aids (for example, data flow diagrams), data modelling facilities (for example, entity-relationship modelling), screen and report design utilities, data repositories, code generators, test data generation, and version control. While the one set of CASE tools is based on the structured systems design approach (Yourdon and Constantine, 1978), the other is based on information engineering (Martin, 1990a; Martin, 1990b; Martin, 1990c). Thus, the two sets of CASE tools are philosophically similar, drawing on the same basic software engineering tenets of functional decomposition, separation of process and data, and sequential development phases.

Because the purpose of the research was to generate theory applicable to various organizational contexts and distinguish different change processes, differences were sought in organizational conditions, such as the nature and scope of systems development activity and the method of CASE tools acquisition. As a result, the two companies selected also differ on other organizational dimensions, such as industry, location, size, structure, and culture. The consulting firm (SCC) [the names of the two organizations have been disguised] is in the software business, developing information systems for external clients. In 1987, it employed 13,000 consultants and earned $600 million in revenues. SCC acquired its CASE tools by developing them in-house. The petro-chemical firm (PCC) is in the petroleum products business, having earned $6.3 billion in revenues in 1987. It has an internal information systems division, which employs 320 people and develops and maintains information systems for internal business units. PCC acquired its CASE tools by purchasing them from an outside vendor. These differences in organizational conditions allowed useful contrasts to be made during data analysis, which challenged and elaborated the emerging concepts.

Data sources

In both research sites, data were collected through a variety of methods: unstructured and semi-structured interviewing, documentation review, and observation. This triangulation across various techniques of data collection is particularly beneficial in theory generation because it provides multiple perspectives on an issue, supplies more information on emerging concepts, allows for cross-checking, and yields stronger substantiation of constructs (Eisenhardt, 1989; Glaser and Strauss, 1967; Pettigrew, 1990).

Data collection focused on the topics of context, technology, key players, and change process. It sought information on, among other things: the environment, mission, structure, and culture of the firm and IS department; the size, location, and composition of the IS department; the history of systems development in the firm (including configurations, standards, policies, and procedures); the rationale for the tools' acquisition; the nature and methodology of the tools acquired; the CASE tools' implementation strategy and schedule; managerial commitment; user involvement; training; individual and team experiences with the CASE tool and changes associated with use of CASE tools in such areas as skills, knowledge, work, performance, and interaction with peers, superiors, and users.

Data collection, coding, and analysis proceeded iteratively (Glaser and Strauss, 1967) with the early stages of the research being more open-ended, and later stages being directed by the emerging concepts, and hence involving more strategic selection of informants and more structured interview protocols [copies of the more structured interview protocols are available from the author on request]. Overlapping data analysis with data collection, as Eisenhardt (1989) notes, provides a number of advantages: 'it not only gives the researcher a head start in analysis, but more importantly allows researchers to take advantage, of flexible data collection. Indeed, a key feature of theory-building case research is the freedom to make adjustments during the data collection process' (p.539).

The first field study was conducted within a large, multinational software consulting firm (SCC), which builds customized software applications for client firms across various industries, such as financial services, manufacturing, retail, and government. The data were collected as part of a larger research study that consisted of an in-depth field study conducted over eight months in three SCC offices (Orlikowski, 1988b). This larger study examined the social process of developing, implementing, and using process technology in a software production environment.

Five different application projects were studied, having been strategically selected to allow exposure to the use of CASE tools in all major phases of the systems development process (requirements analysis, conceptual design, detailed design, programming, testing, and implementation). An average of four weeks was spent on each project, observing and interviewing team members in their daily systems development work and in their interaction with each other and the CASE tools. One hundred and nineteen interviews were conducted, each lasting an average of one and a half hours. Participants in the study spanned SCC's hierarchic levels, from junior analysts to senior project managers, and included some client users who were participating in the projects (see Table 11.1).

Table 11.1 Type and amount of interviews conducted at SCC

Position	Applications Development	CASE Tools Support	Total
Partner (Senior Manager)	5	5	10
Manager (Project Manager)	27	15	42
Senior Consultant (Senior Analyst)	13	18	31
Staff Consultant (Junior Analyst)	11	4	15
Client (User)	11	10	21
TOTAL	67	52	119

The second field study was conducted within an information services division, located at the headquarters of a large petroleum products company (PCC). Nine different application projects were examined, representing the total number of PCC projects utilizing CASE tools. Forty interviews were conducted, each lasting an average of one hour. Participants in the study included members at multiple levels of PCC's information services division, from junior analysts to the division manager, including technical support specialists and a few of the users assigned to the projects (see Table 11.2). Informal discussions were also conducted with the consultants and vendor specialists that were facilitating PCC's adoption and use of the CASE tools.

Table 11.2 Type and amount of interviews conducted at PCC

Position	Applications Development	CASE Tools Support	Total
Partner (Senior Manager)	8	4	12
Manager (Project Manager)	5	2	7
Senior Consultant (Senior Analyst)	11	4	15
Staff Consultant (Junior Analyst)	4	-	4
Client (User)	2	-	2
TOTAL	30	10	40

In each site, documentation about the company, the IS projects, and the CASE tools were examined. Use of the particular tools at each site was observed, both in 'observe-only' mode and in a mode that had the system developers 'talk through' their various systems development tasks. While the primary unit of analysis was the organization or organizational department undergoing changes associated with CASE tools, the grounded theory approach encourages the collection of inter-related data at other levels of analysis (Pettigrew, 1990; Yin, 1984; Yin, 1989). In this case, the experiences of individual developers, technical specialists, managers, and users, as well as the larger institutional context, were also examined. As Leonard-Barton (1990) notes about her studies of technological transfer, 'in order to understand all the interacting factors...it was necessary that the research methodology slice vertically through the organization, obtaining data from multiple levels and perspectives' (p.249).

Data analysis

The data were analyzed within each site, as well as across the two sites, to detect similarities and compare differences. Within SCC (the first site), the iterative approach of data collection, coding, and analysis was more open-ended and generative than in PCC, which focused on the development of concepts, properties, and relations, and on following the descriptions of how to generate grounded theory set out by Glaser and Strauss (1967) and Eisenhardt (1989). Because the study of SCC was part of a larger research project, the detailed write-up of the site and all the data generated by interviews, observations, and documentation were examined and coded by focusing on the change experiences associated with the CASE tools. This technique uses a form of content analysis where the data are read and categorized into concepts that are suggested by the data rather than imposed from outside (Agar, 1980). This is known as open coding (Strauss and Corbin, 1990), and it relies on an analytic technique for identifying possible categories and their properties and dimensions. Once all the data were examined, the concepts were organized by recurring theme. These themes became prime candidates for a set of stable and common categories, which linked a number of associated concepts. This is known as axial coding (Strauss and Corbin, 1990), and it relies on a synthetic technique of making connections between sub-categories to construct a more comprehensive scheme. The SCC data were then re-examined and re-coded using this proposed scheme, the goal being to determine the set of categories and concepts that covered as much of the data as possible. This iterative examination yielded a set of broad categories and associated concepts that described the salient conditions, events, experiences, and consequences associated with the adoption and use of CASE tools in SCC.

These initial concepts guided the second field study conducted in PCC, allowing the process of data collection, coding, and analysis to be more targeted. Following the constant comparative analysis method (Glaser and Strauss, 1967), PCC's experiences were systematically compared and contrasted with those of SCC. This analysis also used Miles and Huberman's (1984) technique for across-site pattern comparison and clustering, which involves matrix displays to compare key events, triggers, and outcomes (as evident, for example, in the contrasts of Table 11.3).

Table 11.3 Organizational change around CASE tools - concepts and findings

Categories	Concepts	Data (from SCC)	Data (from PCC)
Environ-mental context	Customers	• Fortune 500 companies commission SCC to custom build typically large, transaction-oriented applications software	• External customers purchase petro-chemical products: they care about speed, cost, and quality with which these are produced
	Competitors	• Large software development houses building complex systems • Some even providing hardware and maintenance support	• Other major oil companies investing heavily in information technology for competitive advantage
	Technologies	• Increasing number of hardware/software environments • CASE tools recently appeared on the market	• Increasing number of hardware/software environments • CASE tools recently appeared on the market
Organization-al context	Corporate strategies	• Increase profitability for firm and partners • Decrease time and costs of software development • Leverage technical and managerial skills on project teams	• Grow market share in petro-chemical business • Decrease costs and streamline operations • Use information technology for competitive advantage
	Structure and culture of firm	• Matrix structure: controlled via hierarchy: teams operate from local offices • Competitive culture reinforced by 'up or out' career path: from staff consultant, through senior and manager, to partner	• Divisional form, with business units having significant autonomy • Hierarchical operating structure; entry level into firm typically through IS • PCC promotes 'career development' and 'lifetime employment'
IS context	Role of IS in firm	• Software development is SCC's core business since 1960s • Application systems developed on a project-by-project basis for external clients from diverse industries in a custom-built, stand-alone mode	• IS division recently centralized after being dispersed among the various spearate business units • Stand-alone applications commissioned/funded by business units
	IS structure and operations	• Ad hoc project teams formed to work on client engagements • Projects conducted at client sites, range from a few months to years, and include tens to hundreds of developers • Project teams managed by partner and senior manager	• IS division organized to mirror the structure of the company: one application group for each business unit • Stand-alone systems for business units developed and maintained by application group dedicated to supporting that business unit

cont.

	IS policies and practices	• In-house standardized firm methodology, mandated on all projects, and in use for decades • All new recruits trained in SCC's development methodology	• No standardized firm methodology in place; each team adopts own approach • Need to support the '200 plus' technologies makes a uniform set of policies and practices difficult
	IS staff	• 13,000 systems developers at all levels throughout firm • Recruits hired at entry-level from college, typically liberal arts, sciences, business, and engineering	• 320 full-time staff at all levels in the IS division • All recruiting staff at all levels in the IS division employees can choose among application development, technical specialist, or line career paths
Conditions for adopting and using CASE tools	Articulating IS problems	• Increased competition from other software development firms • Increased demand from clients for larger, integrated applications • Increased risks as firm depends on specialized technical knowledge of system developers who have high turnover	• Lack of system integration; incompatible technologies in firm • Data quality problems: massive redundancy and inconsistency • Increased recognition that the information systems 'gridlock' and 'mess' are hurting PCC's competitive position
	Formulating CASE intentions	• Increased productivity • Decreased time and costs of systems development • Increased leverage of technical and managerial skills	• Competitive advantage • Development of an information architecture with shared data and shared applications
Adopting and using CASE tools	Acquiring CASE tools	• In-house development of integrated CASE tools based on existing firm practices and methodology • Dissemination of CASE tools to all offices in the firm	• Committee recommends strategic plan and development of integrated information architecture • IEM obtained, and then IEF CASE tools to enforce use of IEM
	Changing IS policies and practices	• Use of CASE tools mandated on all projects • CASE tools taught to all system developers • Adjustments to systems development policies and practices to accommodate the CASE tools	• Use of CASE tools mandated on all new development work • CASE tools taught to all system developers • New systems development policies (e.g. standards for shared data) and new development practices (e.g. cross-functional teams) established
	Changing the IS structure and operations	• No significant change in the organization of work, except that tool support specialists are included in projects • CASE tool skills augment existing systems development skills • Systems developers rely heavily on CASE tools	• New groups formed in IS division to build shared applications, support tools, and maintain shared data resource • Existing systems development skills replaced by IEM and IEF • System developers rely heavily on CASE tools

cont.

	Changing the IS role vis-à-vis clients	• Products delivered to clients remain custom-built, stand-alone systems, built and funded on a project-by-project basis • Incremental changes to systems delivered to clients are evident in the size and complexity of applications developed	• Applications no longer commissioned and owned by business units; applications and databases are built according to the IE strategic plan and 'logical build sequence' • 'Data ownership' is eliminated; data is accessible to everyone
Consequences of adopting and using CASE tools	System developers' reactions	• Technically oriented system developers resent CASE tools, fearing loss of status, expertise, and marketability • Business-oriented system developers welcome CASE tools, favouring removal of tedious work and ability to spend more time on analysis	• Most system developers welcome CASE tools, influenced by their frustration with 'systems mess', limited systems development status quo, and the belief that CASE will enhance skills, jobs, status, and marketability
	IS managers' reactions	• Perceive improved productivity and profitability • Believe CASE tools have leveraged technical and managerial skills	• Frustrated by reaction of business units • Attempt to deal with resistance and inertia; inability to get middle and lower levels of business committed to IEM, IEF, and architecture
	Clients' reaction	• Minor (although they bear its cost) • Some are impressed by the technological sophistication of tools	• Resistance to redefinition of IS role and new policies around data sharing and sequence in which systems can be built • Conflict over apparent loss of power with respect to IS

Data from PCC were first sorted into the initial concepts generated by SCC's data. It soon became clear, however, that the initial concepts generated by the first site did not accommodate some of the findings emerging from the second site. Accommodating PCC's experiences led to some important elaborations and clarifications in the emerging theoretical framework and forced a reconsideration of some of SCC's experiences. For example, the category 'consequences of adopting and using CASE tools' did not include a concept having to do with client reactions to the CASE tools because this was not salient at SCC. PCC's experiences, however, indicated that client relations were indeed very relevant in shaping the interpretations and use of CASE tools and substantially influenced their effectiveness in the organization. Redefining the initial concepts to incorporate considerations of PCC's experiences required returning to the SCC data and re-sorting and re-analyzing them to take account of the richer concepts and more complex relations now constituting the framework. This ability to incorporate unique insights during the course of the study is one of the benefits of a grounded theory research approach, an example of what Eisenhardt (1989) labels 'controlled opportunism', where 'researchers take advantage of the uniqueness of a specific case and the emergence of new themes to improve resultant theory' (p.539).

The iteration between data and concepts ended when enough categories and associated concepts had been defined to explain what had been observed at both sites and when no additional data were being collected at PCC or found at SCC to develop or add to the set of concepts and categories, a situation Glaser and Strauss (1967) refer to as 'theoretical saturation'. The resultant framework is empirically valid because it can account for the unique data of each site and can generalize patterns across the sites (Eisenhardt, 1989). The categories and concepts thus developed are shown in Table 11.3.

Precautions were taken to corroborate the interpretations made (Miles and Huberman, 1984; Yin, 1984). Emerging concepts were checked for representativeness by examining them across participants and with multiple methods. For example, participants' reports of the criteria they used to evaluate which CASE technology to implement were checked against the documentation available from feasibility studies, while the purported youthfulness of PCC's information services department was checked by referring to personnel records. Triangulation across data sources (multiple informants at different levels of the firm, from different functional affiliations, and across sites) and across data collection methods (interviews, documentation, and observation), further served to strengthen the emerging concepts. The constant comparative method also requires the searching out and checking of contrasts and negative evidence, thus forcing the confrontation of emerging explanations with possible alternative ones. Finally, the participants in the study (particularly those at PCC) provided commentary, correction, and elaboration on drafts of the findings and framework.

Research results

The process of organizational change around CASE tools, developed from the two organizations' experiences, is depicted in Figure 11.1. The figure shows the categories and concepts that emerged as salient from the data analysis, as well as how they interact with each other. This process is proposed as an initial formulation of the key concepts and interactions that portray CASE tools as a process of organizational change. No claim is made that the concepts and interactions presented here are exhaustive. Further organizational change studies around CASE tools should add to or modify the ideas presented here - this is how we build on each other's work.

The organizational change process is influenced by the structurational premise that human action and institutional contexts interact over time (Orlikowski and Robey, 1991). Starting on the left side of Figure 11.1, we can walk through this process. Initially, IS managers, influenced by their environmental, organizational, and IS contexts (arrow 1) recognize and articulate some problem with the systems development process and/or the kind of systems produced. In response to this interpretation, the managers choose to invest in CASE tools as a way of dealing with the perceived problem, formulating certain intentions for what

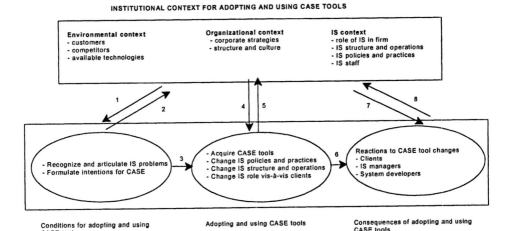

Figure 11.1 Process of organizational change around CASE tools (key concepts and interactions generated by SCC and PCC)

changes they hope the CASE tools will occasion. In drawing on their contexts to articulate these interpretations and intentions, the managers also, and typically unintentionally, reinforce those contexts (arrow 2). The managers' actions - articulating a problem and formulating a solution - (labelled conditions for adopting and using CASE tools) lead managers to acquire a particular set of CASE tools and put them to use in systems development (arrow 3). In addition to being influenced by articulated interpretations and intentions, the IS managers' actions are influenced by the institutional context within which the tools are acquired and deployed (arrow 4) (for example, external context, such as available products on the market at the time, and internal context, such as corporate strategies). Having acquired CASE tools, IS managers may take action (labelled adopting and using CASE tools) such as changing IS policies, practices, operations, and relations with clients. In doing so, they affect the institutional context, changing it to a greater or lesser extent (arrow 5). Actions regarding adoption and use, in turn, result in various experiences and outcomes (arrow 6) as the key players - IS managers, system developers, and clients - act on and react to the changes (labelled consequences of adopting and using CASE tools). These actions do not occur in a vacuum but are influenced by the institutional context in which they occur (arrow 7). Similarly, action taken here by the managers, developers, and users will influence the institutional context (arrow 8), either reinforcing or changing it (Orlikowski and Robey, 1991). In the following section, these concepts and their interaction over time are discussed in detail for each of the two field sites. Because the constant comparative method of analysis was adopted here, all concepts will be discussed for both organizations. Even if a concept emerged as relevant in only one site, it is nevertheless useful to consider its role in the other site so as to contrast the experiences of the organizations.

SCC

Institutional context

As depicted in Figure 11.1, the categories of environmental, organizational, and IS context were found to be relevant in influencing the adoption and use of CASE tools in SCC. The concepts constituting these categories are discussed in turn.

Customers

Because SCC is in the software business, IS services constitute the core business. SCC's customers, typically large Fortune 500 firms, purchase custom-built applications systems. Each SCC systems development project is a stand-alone engagement, with the system developers building an information system to meet specific functional requirements specified by the paying client. All work conducted on a client engagement is charged to the client, so the effort is concentrated on the specific system to be built. Occasionally, SCC obtains a follow-on contract with a satisfied client, which may be related to the previous system built.

Competitors

SCC competes with large software development houses as well as in-house development shops. It attempts to differentiate itself by building large, complex systems and has earned a reputation for successful systems development in various industries. While facing some competition, SCC is firmly established as one of the leaders in the software development market.

Technologies

The information technologies of the 1980s were represented by a plethora of hardware and software environments. SCC has been forced to keep up to date with these new technologies because it has to work with them at client sites. It was also during the early 1980s when the notion of CASE tools began to gain credibility, and interest in using such tools to assist systems development grew quickly within SCC.

Corporate strategies
SCC is committed to increasing revenues and profitability, which directly benefits the senior managers (owners) of the firm. In addition, there is interest in decreasing the costs of the core production process - systems development - as well as leveraging the existing technical and managerial skills in the firm.

Structure and culture
SCC is organized as a matrix, with control of the systems development practice exercised hierarchically from the firm's headquarters, while the development work is conducted via ad hoc project teams operating out of local offices. The firm has a particularly competitive culture, which is reinforced by the strict, single career path that every employee follows. Employees advance in lock-step pattern from staff consultant through senior consultant and manager to senior manager over a period of about 10 years. The 'up or out' nature of this career path ensures a high turnover within SCC, at a rate purported to be higher than normal for the IS industry.

Role of IS
SCC has been developing computer-based information systems for its clients across various industries since the 1970s. Although SCC also does some strategic planning and organizational development consulting, software development is its primary product and service. SCC is usually contracted to design and develop specific applications, with the installation, support, and maintenance of these applications being left to the clients. The applications are typically large stand-alone transaction processing systems used to support major administrative activities.

IS structure and operations
SCC's production process is organized by project, with most of the systems development work being conducted at clients' sites. Ad hoc project teams, varying from around 10 to over 100 personnel, are formed at the beginning of each client engagement. The projects extend from a few months to a number of years in duration and cost from a hundred thousand to a few million dollars. Each project is headed by a senior manager who oversees its general pace and direction and is administered by a project manager who exercises day-to-day control over project activities.

IS policies and practices
For over a decade, SCC's work practices have relied on the firm's own standardized systems development methodology, which combines the techniques of Yourdon structured systems design, Warnier-Orr program design, and Chen's entity-relationship data modelling. SCC's policy is that all employees should be trained in the methodology and that all systems development work should be based on it. The methodology is thus well entrenched within the company, in use on all SCC projects, and thoroughly documented in many large paperbound volumes, as well as in computer form. Given the firm's practice of only hiring at

entry level, this methodology comprises the primary production knowledge of SCC system developers. Senior managers attribute much of their company's success to the consistent use of the methodology across the firm. For example, a brochure published by SCC cites a senior manager as saying that the firm's methodology 'reflects over 30 years of experience by SCC in developing and maintaining information systems in virtually every industry throughout the world...[it] is truly a proven approach'.

IS staff
Because systems development is SCC's core business, it pays careful attention to how it hires and trains its system developers. It hires almost exclusively at entry level by recruiting at major colleges around the country. Most recruits have liberal arts, business, and engineering backgrounds, while a few have specialized in computer science. SCC spends considerable time and money training its recruits how to develop application systems using SCC's own systems development methodology. At the time of the study, there were approximately 13,000 system developers employed at various levels throughout SCC.

Conditions for adopting and using and adapting CASE tools

Two types of managerial action created the conditions that led to the adoption and use of CASE tools: (1) recognizing and articulating IS problems and (2) formulating intentions for CASE tools.

Recognizing and articulating IS problems
During the 1980s, SCC's senior managers began to perceive increased competition from a number of other large software developers, as well as a growing demand from prospective clients for more integrated application software. They interpreted these pressures as threats to their competitive position and their profitability ratio.

Formulating CASE intentions
In response to this perceived threat, SCC's senior managers focused on increasing productivity and decreasing the time it took to build application systems. They reasoned that this could be accomplished through greater managerial leverage (that is, by increasing the number of consultants per senior manager and expanding span of control) and reduced dependence on technical skills. In the past, SCC had to ensure that system developers knew a range of programming languages, database management systems, teleprocessing software, and operating systems so they would be sufficiently versatile to operate in the multiple computer environments operated by their clients. Teaching the developers this knowledge took time and effort and required regular updating because such skills were technical and specific, quickly becoming obsolete as new computer products appeared on the market. SCC thus saw CASE tools as a

way of decreasing costs, improving leverage, and increasing productivity. A senior manager noted:

> The cost of building information systems is getting out of hand now. So we have to look at people cost, which is the most important component. SCC has to be tool-oriented given the sorts of fees we charge and the kinds of people we hire. We need to increase our productivity, as there is a scarcity of DP people, and people turn around a lot. So SCC takes a high risk by investing knowledge in individuals who may leave soon. We need to leverage that risk. We have to be able to divorce knowledge from programmers. That's why we invest in tools.

Likewise, another manager explained their intentions this way:

> The skills issue is another motivator for us [to] use tools. It is expensive to educate people, particularly in the technical details. If we can embody the knowledge of technical experts in the tools, then a less experienced person can work with the tools and become an expert. So we factor out the complexities of systems development and embed these in the tools. Then we can forget about them because the tools insulate us from the technical environment.

Adopting and using CASE tools

Following the decision to invest in CASE tools, managers introduced these tools into SCC by taking four types of action: (1) acquiring CASE tools; (2) changing IS policies and practices; (3) changing the IS structure and operations; and (4) changing the IS role vis-à-vis clients.

Acquiring CASE tools

In response to their understanding of the key business issues facing the firm and their strategy for addressing them, SCC's senior managers initiated the adoption of CASE tools and disseminated their use throughout the firm. Instead of purchasing a set of CASE tools developed by an outside vendor, SCC managers decided to build their own tools because they had the requisite resources in-house to undertake such a task, and such a strategy would allow SCC to capitalize on the established expertise and experience with its systems development methodology.

Because SCC had a heavy investment in its existing methodology - with all the firm's work practices and knowledge predicated on it - SCC senior managers were concerned not to lose this asset as they began to use CASE tools. Consequently, they commissioned SCC's in-house technical support group to develop a set of integrated CASE tools that were based on the firm's standardized methodology and years of accumulated practice knowledge.

Changing IS policies and practices

Once the CASE tools were built, SCC senior managers established a new policy that mandated their use on all large projects. As one manager pointed out, the firm policy quickly became 'tools, tools, and tools'. Complementing this policy was the requirement that all system developers be trained on the tools. This was fulfilled either as part of the developers' annual continuing education courses or - where system developers needed to use the tools sooner - on the job at client sites, with technical specialists conducting ad hoc CASE training classes. Despite the new policy, the work practices of SCC developers were not significantly changed by the implementation of CASE tools because these tools had been deliberately constructed to support SCC's established systems development methodology and existing work practices. A senior systems analyst at SCC observed:

> There have been no real changes with the tools, except that we have more efficiency, more consistency, and more standardization...This is not strange though, as the tools have the same fundamental premises as the non-tooled environment did - procedural code, sequential development, structured design. And we built tools for these things without trying to fundamentally change things.

Thus, beyond being mediated by the CASE tools, systems development in SCC was not changed significantly through the adoption of the CASE tools. Indeed, the tools, because they reflected SCC's existing systems development methodology, reinforced the firm's established work practices and norms. As one manager noted, 'The methodology has not been affected by the tools, as we are not fundamentally changing the direction or discipline of our work.'

Changing the IS structure and operations

No major structural changes to accommodate the CASE tools were deemed necessary, and none were implemented, although some operational adjustments were made on the projects. Procedures and checklists were incorporated into project schedules to ensure that the tools were applied correctly, while technical specialists were included on project teams to ensure that the CASE tools were available, reliable, and suitably customized to clients' environments. Responsibilities around systems development had shifted somewhat, with technical and supervisory skills leveraged when the tools facilitated the abstraction of systems development knowledge from the underlying hardware and software environment. This served to monitor and coordinate systems development work. The system developers began to spend more time with users doing business analysis and more time in front of workstations interacting with the tools. For many developers in SCC, particularly those who had had no other experience with systems development, this reduced their need to acquire technical knowledge while it increased their dependence on the CASE tools. While knowledge of and experience with the CASE tools became a prerequisite for advancement in the firm, no new career paths were introduced.

Changing the IS role vis-à-vis clients

After the adoption of CASE tools, there was little attempt on the part of senior managers to change SCC's interactions with its clients. Jobs were still sold on a project-by-project basis; systems that were built were still largely stand-alone, and clients still paid for all the systems development work performed by SCC employees. What did change, however, was that the CASE tools became part of the price of the project. Thus, added to the total project cost were the cost of installing hardware at the client site to run the tools, the cost of full-time technical specialists to support the tools, and the cost of training developers and client-users participating in the project on the use of the tools. Client relations, thus, remained essentially the same, and the use of CASE tools served to reaffirm rather than redefine SCC's role with respect to its clients.

Consequences of adopting and using CASE tools

Various consequences followed SCC's adoption and use of CASE tools, and these are expressed in terms of the reactions of three key players: clients, IS managers, and system developers.

Client reactions to CASE changes

Because there appeared to be little change in client relations following the dissemination of CASE tools within SCC, it is not surprising there was no marked client reaction to changes. SCC system developers continued to deliver custom-built, stand-alone information systems to the clients, just as they had always done.

The nature of the application systems being delivered to clients was largely unaffected by the tools, although a few project managers noted that the applications being built with CASE tools tended to be larger or more complex than would have been feasible had CASE tools not been used. It seems that knowing that CASE tools would be available during systems development raised expectations about the possibility of building large systems with more features and greater functionality. Beyond these product enhancements, however, the CASE tools did not significantly influence client experiences and actions.

IS manager reactions to CASE changes

SCC managers believed that use of the tools had led to greater productivity (although this was based more on intuition than any formal measurement) and an increased ability to leverage senior and technical personnel on projects. One senior manager said:

> With tools we can make money leveraging people, that is, having many bodies even at lower rates can be profitable with tools...[The] tools allow us to leverage inexperienced people on our project. So we can take a kid out of school, let's say with a major in English, and in a very short time he can achieve high productivity, that is, achieve the productivity level of a client programmer with 10 years' experience. It's not that we are making him more effective at his job, but we are

dumping him into a production environment that has 10 years of programming experience built into it.

From the viewpoint of managers, tools decreased the firm or project's dependence on specific individuals, whose particular knowledge of specific software and hardware configurations were difficult if not impossible to replace. With tools embodying complex technical expertise as well as knowledge of specific application systems, system developers became more replaceable and interchangeable. As a result, the risks and costs of large-scale systems development were seen to have been reduced.

System developer reactions to CASE

The reaction of SCC system developers to the changes accompanying the CASE tools centered on individual issues of skills, work experiences, and learning opportunities. They were less concerned with the impacts of CASE tools on the overall productivity of the firm, or the effectiveness of particular projects. Rather, they were interested in realizing their own individual aspirations, both in the short term (for example, acquiring particular knowledge or specific experience), and the long term (for example, attaining career goals, either within SCC or in the larger business community). Two different reactions to the CASE tools are evident at SCC; one rooted in a technical and the other in a business orientation toward systems development.

Technical orientation

Many of the system developers who planned a career in IS (for example, as system designers, analysts, or managers) perceived CASE tools as a threat to their hard-earned skills (for example, knowledge of operating systems and programming languages) and experiences with specific hardware and software systems. Concerned with job security and career mobility, these developers believed that their marketability was depreciated by the proliferation of CASE tools. They feared that demand for technical expertise (traditionally high for IS personnel) would decline as a result. Some of these system developers also felt less personally involved in their work, mediated as it now was through the tools. One junior analyst resigned in protest over having to use tools, noting, 'I just couldn't take this generated code stuff, and not having any input into the programming...Also the things I was learning are not marketable.'

Having automated users' tasks for years, system developers were beginning to experience the abstracting influences of automation in their own work. A senior analyst observed that CASE tools limited the possibility of acquiring and using technical knowledge in systems development because using tools amounted to a 'form-filling exercise'. He felt this had long-term implications for those developers who 'don't know the underlying reasons for things. They don't know why they do things in a certain way. So we find that they are almost helpless without the tooled environment. They are only able to find canned solutions to standard problems'.

There was also a perception among many of the technically oriented developers that tools had decreased their opportunities to learn new technologies. On one of the projects, a new database management system was introduced, and system developers eagerly anticipated learning a new, sophisticated product that they perceived would be intellectually challenging and would enhance their skills portfolio. Their excitement was short-lived, however, for they soon realized that the database system would only be accessible by the CASE tools and that they would have no direct contact with the new product. A sense of lost opportunity was sharply felt and resented.

Business orientation
Most of the system developers whose career goals were oriented toward business or general management had a different reaction to CASE tools. These individuals did not perceive their careers in terms of systems design or IS management and did not see tools as threatening their skills or marketability. For such system developers, the tools provided welcome relief from the tedium and complexity associated with the technical details of large application systems.

These developers believed the CASE tools expedited their work, allowing them to spend more time on the tasks they enjoyed (such as business analysis), and that the tools helped them appear more productive and hence more valuable to their projects and SCC. One analyst noted, 'tools do prevent us from learning technical details. And that's good, as no one comes to SCC to be a programmer.' And a senior analyst observed, 'I don't want to turn out delightful code or make the coding activity creative. I must get the job done simply, and tools make things simple.' Because these developers attached little value to the technical expertise now embedded in CASE tools, they perceived the tools as facilitating their work rather than as jeopardizing their expertise or status.

A discussion of the general patterns and implications of SCC's CASE experiences is taken up in the discussion section.

PCC

Institutional context

As with SCC, the environmental, organizational, and IS contexts of PCC provided important information about its experiences with CASE tools. Because PCC's IS division is internal, its environmental context includes aspects of the environment outside PCC, as well as that inside PCC but external to the IS division.

Customers
PCC customers purchase petroleum and chemical products, unlike the software products purchased by SCC customers. While information technology is not a critical component in the products purchased by PCC customers, it does influence the speed, cost and quality with which products are produced and

delivered (for example, electronic billing at gas service stations). The IS division's customers are other business units within PCC, which use information services to meet their units' particular functional requirements.

Competitors
Major oil companies make up the bulk of PCC's competitors, and PCC's senior managers believe these competitors are investing heavily in information technology across both upstream and downstream value chains. This has put pressure on the IS division to provide more competitive technology to the various business units. As a senior manager commented, 'Information technology is one of the few levers that we must pull to gain competitive advantage.'

Technologies
Like SCC, PCC faces an increasingly diverse array of hardware and software environments, and given the range of its operations (for example, oil pipelines, chemical processing, inventory and customer support), the IS division has to keep on top of many developments in various technological areas. The development and marketing of CASE tools in the 1980s generated interest among some IS managers, who wondered if these tools could help PCC's systems development challenges.

Corporate strategies
At the time of the study, PCC was interested in both growing its existing business (increasing market share) and streamlining its operations by cutting costs and redesigning business processes. There was a heightened recognition among senior managers that information systems were critical to running their business and that these should be more effective. Using information technology to gain competitive advantage thus became a general corporate strategy.

Structure and culture of firm
PCC is organized divisionally with business units representing the major areas of the business (for example, research, refining, sales, human resources, etc.) The firm is mature and well established within its industry. Its culture was described by one manager as 'paternalistic', and this is evident in its conservatism and strong emphasis on quality of work life and career development programs. PCC has no mandatory 'up or out' career policy. On the contrary, it is widely known, as one senior analyst commented, to 'hire people for life'.

Role of IS
PCC's IS division was formed in the late 1980s, representing a centralization of resources from dispersed business units into a separate division under the vice president of technology, who reported to the company's president. Before consolidation, systems development work in PCC was handled by distributed IS groups located within separate business units. Information systems built under this arrangement were local in scope and funding and were used solely by individual business units. After consolidation, IS still developed specific

information systems for the functional requirements of individual business units. These systems (and their data) were commissioned on an 'as needed' basis by the business units and then subsequently paid for and 'owned' by these business units.

IS structure and operations

While IS had been consolidated functionally, its structure and operations still reflected its distributed origins. The division was organized into separate application groups whose members represented and serviced the separate business units they had supported in the past. Indeed, some of the system developers even retained their physical location within the various business units 'to remain close to the users'. There was little coordination across the application groups, with each group essentially being funded by and focused on its own internal clients. There was thus little incentive to consider the corporate implications of application systems.

IS policies and practices

While the IS function had been consolidated, its distributed history left a legacy of incompatible technologies and non-uniform IS practices and policies. These divergent approaches to systems development were continued after consolidation; each application group continued to service its specific clients as it had done before. No standardized systems development methodology or common set of standards and procedures was enacted. As a result of this eclecticism and the '200 plus technologies' deployed within PCC, system developers' knowledge and practices were broad and diverse, reflecting the traditional dispersion and decentralized focus at PCC.

IS staff

Like SCC, PCC also hired its system developers at entry level from college, although it typically drew from computer science or engineering programs. Within the IS division, employees could choose to follow one of three career paths: two in IS - application development and technical specialization - and one into the business out of the IS division. Indeed, as a senior IS manager noted, 'we're the entry point into the rest of the firm. PCC believes that some technology training is valuable to everyone. So people spend three to five years here before moving into the professional side of business.' At the time of the study, there was a total of 320 full-time members of the IS division. These included managers and individuals engaged in application development, maintenance, and technical support activities.

Conditions for adopting and using CASE tools

Two types of action created the conditions that led to the adoption and use of CASE tools: (1) recognizing and articulating IS problems and (2) formulating intentions for CASE tools.

Recognizing and articulating IS problems

With the IS consolidation, the managers of the newly formed IS division assessed the role and status of information technology within PCC. They found what one senior analyst described as a 'complex mosaic of bridges, data redundancy, and data integrity problems' and a set of information systems that a manager characterized as 'spaghetti junction'. Centralization had bestowed upon the IS division a wide diversity of hardware and software with little or no integration, and an extensive duplication of corporate data. The company was reputed to have as many as 20 product files and - as one technical specialist graphically put it, 'as many customer databases as Kellogg's has cornflakes'. Senior IS managers interpreted this chaotic state of information systems to be hurting PCC competitively. Three of them commented:

> We had automated in isolation due to the natural evolution of systems in response to business demand and current technology. So we have islands of automation.

> Data were dispersed throughout the company, coding schemes were inconsistent and different, and people were drawing incorrect conclusions from poor data.

> We came to the realization that IS was not serving the business as it should.

Formulating CASE intentions

Given their articulation of the state of information systems at PCC, IS managers believed that to gain competitive advantage through information technology they would have to significantly improve the quality of PCC's data and integrate its disparate systems. Two IS managers explained:

> Senior business people were dissatisfied with the systems. They were a bunch of spaghetti. They wanted a shared environment to get good information.

> Systems long outlive the business that sponsored them, and they fit an organization at a point in time. We need systems that are more generic and can span business area and time. The value added now is cross-functional coordination.

Based on their assessment, senior IS managers commissioned an IS strategy committee to examine alternative ways to deal with the 'systems gridlock.' After six months of deliberations, the committee proposed a long-term IS strategy for PCC, which called for the construction of a corporate-wide information architecture. This proposal was premised on the belief that a shared corporate data environment, providing timely data to appropriate users, would generate changes in business practices and lead to improved firm performance. To realize this architecture, the committee recommended the adoption of a standard systems development methodology and CASE tools.

Adopting and using CASE tools

Four types of actions were relevant in understanding the move toward CASE tools in PCC: (1) acquiring CASE tools; (2) changing IS policies and practices; (3) changing the IS structure and operations; and (4) changing the IS role vis-à-vis clients.

Acquiring CASE tools

To implement the committee's broad vision, the IS division acquired the information engineering methodology (IEM), an approach to systems planning, analysis, and design based on shared data (Martin, 1990a; 1990b and 1990c). At the corporate level, IEM provides both an integrated systems plan and an enterprise-wide view of data from which the corporate data infrastructure - known as the information architecture - is constructed. At the project level, IEM provides a detailed project view of data and specific development techniques with which to design and construct specific systems within the infrastructure. An IS manager explained the committee's conviction that the information architecture, methodology, and tools were all indispensable: 'We need a shared architecture to guide us as we develop new systems, and we need a methodology and CASE tools to help this development, [or] else we'll retreat to our prior bad habits'. The IS strategy committee had recommended that PCC adopt a set of integrated CASE tools that were compatible with the selected methodology. While two products on the market were compatible with IEM - information engineering workbench (IEW) from Knowledgeware and Texas Instrument's information engineering facility (IEF) - only the latter was deemed sufficiently integrated for PCC's requirements. A few months after standardizing on IEM, PCC acquired the IEF CASE tools. Significantly, the IS managers stressed that their adoption of CASE tools was not targeted at increasing productivity. One manager commented, 'we went to [CASE tools] to implement the architecture rather than for efficiency gains'.

Changing IS policies and practices

The adoption of the IE methodology and IEF CASE tools created, for the first time within PCC, a single, standardized approach to systems development. IS managers mandated the use of the standardized approach on all new systems development projects. They arranged for extensive training programs for IS personnel involved in new systems development, and they hired consultants to help establish new IE-based systems development standards and procedures, as well as policies for sharing the data and applications comprising the corporate information architecture.

Changing the IS structure and operations

IS managers signalled their commitment to the new methodology and tools by making a number of structural and operational changes. The IS division was reorganized and three new groups were created: (1) an architecture group (to develop the corporate-wide architecture); (2) a shared applications group (to develop and maintain cross-functional applications); and (3) a data and technology group (to manage the firm's shared data resource and to support the CASE tools). The separate IS groups that had serviced individual business units were retained to maintain existing stand-alone systems and to assist local end-user computing.

Many systems development jobs had changed as a result of the structural changes in the IS division - some developers moved to the shared applications development group, while others joined the technical support group to maintain the new shared databases and CASE tools. Most of the IS employees experienced major changes in their responsibilities, skill sets, and work norms. For example, they had to learn the new concepts and techniques of IEM and IEF, as these had become the only sanctioned approach to systems development. Further, development of shared applications required considerable negotiation with users and members of other project teams to resolve issues around the interpretation, definition and handling of shared data.

System developers and users were not accustomed to thinking of systems or data beyond the boundaries of separate functional units because such a practice previously had been unnecessary and inconceivable. Making this change at PCC required new training courses within the IS division that imparted skills of negotiation, relationship-building, and conflict resolution - competencies that, as one IS manager indicated, had never before been considered part of the narrow technical role played by IS. A senior IS manager commented on the changes experienced by his division: 'There has been significant cultural change in the systems group due to tools'.

Changing the IS role vis-à-vis clients

PCC's IS managers hoped that the use of CASE tools - in conjunction with their implementation of the IE methodology and corporate architecture - would facilitate the redesign of business processes in the business units as well as in IS. This attempt to influence the business represented a significant departure from the reactive relationship that IS had traditionally maintained with its internal business clients. Instead of developing stand-alone functional systems for internal business units as commissioned, the IS division now took a proactive stand toward information systems within PCC.

IS designed an information architecture and identified and initiated a sequence of systems development projects to construct this architecture. By insisting on a corporate architecture - composed of shared databases and shared application systems - IS had redefined its role in the firm. Instead of responding to the business units' requests for systems, the IS division now dictated (on the basis of the strategic plan and information architecture) which systems would be built, when, and how, as well as what data would be collected, stored, and accessed, and by whom. It further insisted on cross-functional development projects and required common funding of shared databases and applications.

Consequences of adopting and using CASE tools

The consequences of adopting and using CASE tools can be categorized in terms of the reactions of clients, IS managers, and system developers.

Client reactions to CASE changes
Despite the fact that one of the documented objectives of adopting the IE methodology and CASE tools was to 'transform the business and business practices', little business change had occurred. The business units had not implemented any modifications in structure, work practices, or norms as a result of the corporate-wide information architecture and IE business analyses completed by IS. Instead, PCC business managers reacted to the IS initiatives by ignoring or resisting them. An IS manager noted:

> The company is not ready for this architecture. It is not willing to change business procedures, organization procedures, organization structures, and practices as a result of the architecture approach...A key aspect of the architecture approach is changing the business, and there is a problem because people do not want to change old, familiar ways of doing things. People are uncomfortable with radical change, which is disruptive, expensive, and time-consuming.

The clients' opposition stemmed from their perception that the changes instituted by the IS division threatened established organizational norms, practices, and privileges. For example, the notion of a corporate information architecture with shared access to data ran counter to PCC's long-standing policy on information sharing, which restricted access to data to only those people with a clearly defined and authorized 'need to know'. The shared data policy inherent in the information architecture reversed this policy by allowing access to anyone who was interested. A senior business manager explained:

> We used to have a closed information environment; that is, all doors are closed unless you prove otherwise. Now [with IE] our policy is the reverse. All doors are open unless you justify otherwise. I think this strategy will probably fail because people don't want to share data. There is no tradition of open information in this company...People were successful in the past by building boxes and walls around their data and not sharing it.

Because sharing data is a basic premise of the information architecture, the reluctance of business units to accept it has been a serious stumbling block in IS's attempt to change the kind of systems delivered. Two senior IS managers commented:

> This sort of paradigm shift is difficult to implement as people are reluctant to force searchlights into dark corners. It's very political.

It's at the business unit levels where we have met the most resistance. Our reward systems are a problem. They don't reward sharing.

Reinforcing this resistance was the business units' focus on their own short-term needs and goals. An IS manager explained the impact of this on IS:

Implementing a shared architecture in a decentralized environment is a real challenge. The problem is that not many pieces of the architecture have value to the business people, and so they don't want to sponsor them. Middle-level people tend to take a short-term and narrow functional view, and it is hard to focus them on the corporate view...they want immediate results and immediate returns on their investment.

IS manager reactions to CASE changes

Most IS managers were very frustrated with the resistance of the business to the development of the architecture and the attempt to make data accessible across the corporation. They endeavoured to overcome the business units' resistance by outlawing the concept of data ownership. A manager explained that the word 'ownership' had been dropped from their vocabulary, because 'it is too possessive, too explosive, and too functional'. While helpful, these proactive steps were not entirely successful because they too were bound up in expectations about the appropriate role of the IS division. While IS had redefined its role and received approval for it from PCC's senior management, such a shift had not been clearly communicated to or accepted by the business unit managers and their users. A senior technical specialist observed that the change in IS's role was counter-cultural and hence difficult for the business units to accept:

Here at PCC, IS tends to do as we're told. In the past, users have tended to get what they want. It's unusual for us to be pushing stuff. Our culture is such that on every IS person's office are the words: 'Systems do not drive the Business'. Unless business people are forced to conform to the architecture, they won't. They've had it their own way for so long they don't want to change, as it is more work and more cost to them.

An IS manager confirmed this perspective noting:

Right now, IEF is driven by the systems community...All the [planning] was done by systems people - some with good business background - but not many business people were involved. It was probably driven too much by the systems community, which may be why there is so much consternation about the architecture.

Not having substantial political clout in the organization, the IS managers felt somewhat immobilized by the unexpected and hostile reaction of their clients. Some considered involving PCC's senior management in an attempt to get top-down enforcement of the IS plan. A project leader commented:

The nature of the bureaucracy here at PCC is that the customer comes first, and so we will slap in something quick and dirty. It will take us a long time to get an architected solution because you can't stop people doing this if they can rationalize it for the customer...we've sold IEF and the shared data concept to senior business management, but we have not filtered the message down to the masses. It is just as important to get buy-in from business users as it is to get senior management commitment. I see this all the time. We say, 'This is the way the corporate level wants to do it', and the user on our team says, 'I'm the one using the system, and I'm still going to do it the way I want to'...Senior management has to talk to their own people as we have to get real users involved and committed if this is ever going to work.

Systems developer reactions to CASE changes

In contrast to SCC, PCC developers' reactions to CASE tools did not differ by technical or business orientation. Most PCC developers welcomed the IE methodology and the CASE tools, despite having experienced significant changes in work practices, norms, skills, and responsibilities. More than three quarters (77 per cent) of the 26 system developers interviewed indicated that the introduction of tools was a positive move, both for PCC and for their individual careers. In attempting to understand this unexpected reaction, the researcher searched for clues in the data that might account for such enthusiasm and identified five potential explanations. The first three - frustration with the status quo, believing the CASE strategy, and valuing CASE skills - reflect developers' perceptions, interpretations, and experiences. The fourth - willingness to change - involves an individual attribute of the developers, and the fifth - human resource policies - is a property of the firm. While treated separately here for analytical reasons, these explanations are clearly interdependent and may even overlap. An examination of such interactions and overlap cannot be attempted here, but the issue warrants further research. The five explanations are elaborated on below.

Frustration with the status quo: Many of the developers had experienced first-hand the problems of PCC's 'systems mess' and believed that IEM and IEF could bring much-needed order to a chaotic situation. One project leader expressed his frustration this way: 'We were trying to compete in the Indy 500 in 1989 with a 1962 motor car'. Yet another noted, 'Because of the lack of integration among our systems, when you built a new system you often had to build 10 or 12 different interfaces. So the pain, agony, and cost of building a new system in our environment, and to maintain it, were enormous.'

Believing the CASE strategy: Many of the developers believed that the strategy behind the standardized methodology and CASE tools - to build high-quality, integrated systems and to share data throughout the firm - would enhance PCC's competitive advantage. In contrast to the system developers at SCC, who perceived their firm's strategy around CASE tools as attempting to decrease costs, reduce dependence on developers' expertise, and improve senior managers' incomes, PCC's system developers believed that CASE tools would yield better systems for PCC. One senior analyst remarked, 'I know [PCC] is trying to use CASE tools to build an architecture, and so we have to enforce rigor and consistency in systems development so we can share data across the corporation. We see tools as a means to do this.'

Valuing CASE skills: PCC system developers believed that their new skills in business analysis and CASE tools were valuable and enhanced rather than diminished their future marketability. This perception was helped by the fact that the IEF CASE tools had high market penetration relative to other CASE tools, in marked contrast to the limited diffusion of SCC's in-house tools. A senior analyst commented:

> IEF provides a core set of skills that are highly marketable. There will be a lot of demand for experienced users of IEF and people who know how to use them intelligently...PCC analysts see IEF as a new skill, on the leading edge, that makes them more marketable.

Many of the PCC system developers also believed that their work had improved as a result of CASE tools. One analyst indicated that his job was more pleasant now, noting, 'The tool has automated the drudgery of my job'. Another remarked:

> I enjoy my job more now as I feel more like an analyst...in the past, new hires would be the grunt programmers, and a senior person would be the business analyst. Now new hires can deal with users, and this provides a better sense of accomplishment for people who are not technical hackers.

Viewing CASE tools as enhancing skills and expanding jobs was related to the perception by some of the junior developers that tools had augmented their status vis-à-vis their seniors. A junior analyst stated, '[The tools] are an equalizing force. Everyone is thrown back to zero. This is good for me just coming into the firm. I can come out looking better than people my senior.'

Willingness to change: The shared applications development group - the group in the front line of CASE tools use - was populated by system developers without long, technical IS careers to their name. Because the IS group hires at entry level, its developers had accumulated less experience and technical skills than comparably sized IS departments in other organizations. Two senior IS managers observed:

> Most of our people are younger, so they don't have much invested in the old traditional ways of doing systems development.

> As they're younger, they don't carry much baggage and so have accepted IEF/IEM quicker, easier, and more enthusiastically.

The manager of the shared applications development group echoed this view, suggesting that the experience of his group members critically influenced their attitude toward the tools: 'Learning IEF is like learning a second language. A person with 15 years experience will have a harder time adapting to it than a younger person...I got lucky - my shop is younger, thirtyish, and my most senior project leader is only 27 years old.'

To confirm this claim, the age distribution of the shared applications group was obtained. The average age in this group of 44 members (including managers) was 33 years (standard deviation of 5.98; range of 20 to 46), with two-thirds of the group being less than 35 years old. That this somewhat youthful group was more willing to change is likely influenced by the fact that they have spent less time in systems development and hence have a lower investment in the status quo - in either their personal skill portfolios or traditional systems development practices - than would developers who have spent more years building up a set of skills and establishing cognitive and behavioural habits around systems development. It is interesting to note that SCC also hires at the entry level, so willingness to change is not a function of experience alone but likely interacts with other factors, such as career orientation and human resource policies.

Human resource policies: PCC had a well-respected set of human resource strategies that mitigated much potential anxiety around organizational change. Like SCC, PCC hires its system developers straight after graduation from college, but unlike SCC, PCC claims to hire people 'for a career' and to treat them as 'life-time employees'. Under such conditions, PCC system developers - even those who may opt for the technical specialist career track - are less likely to interpret the tools as a threat to their job security or career advancement. Two analysts commented:

> This company is progressive. They promote career development, encourage new things, and rotate you a lot, every two to three years.

> PCC is excellent at promoting its people's self-development. There's a belief here that people are a number one resource, so you need to invest money in your people. We have an extensive human resources system to check on your development. We have a lower turnover than the norm - 2 percent for our systems group, 25 percent in other companies. We hire a lot of outside contractors to do grunt work. We have better working conditions as well, reasonably good salaries, and less working hours.

An IS manager concurred, noting that, 'At PCC, we're committed to our people' observing that the firm has a policy not to lay off people and that the IS division makes a practice of hiring contractors to provide a float when more or fewer systems people are needed.

In the following discussion, the organizational changes experienced by PCC around CASE tools are contrasted with those of SCC. Table 11.3 includes a summary of both companies' experiences with CASE tools.

Discussion

While SCC and PCC both implemented CASE tools within their systems development practices, their experiences differ significantly. The comparative analysis method of grounded theory, which allows contrasting SCC with PCC on a common set of concepts (see Table 11.3), suggests that these differences can be attributed to variations in the change process, the organizational context, and the intentions and actions of key players around the adoption and use of the CASE tools (see Figure 11.1). While these two sites have yielded a grounded theoretical framework of organizational changes associated with the adoption and use of CASE tools it is possible to try and generalize the patterns discerned. By attempting to connect the grounded theory with aspects of existing formal theory, a more general substantive theory can result (Glaser and Strauss, 1967). Eisenhardt (1989) also advocates this approach, noting: 'Overall, tying the emergent theory to existing literature enhances the internal validity, generalizability, and theoretical level of theory building from case study research' (p.545).

A useful classification in the innovation literature is that of incremental and radical types of innovation (Dewar and Dutton, 1986; Ettlie et al., 1993; Pennings, 1988; Tushman and Romanelli, 1985). These concepts can be applied here to characterize the different intentions and actions around CASE tools in the two organizations. Incremental change represents an extension of the status quo, that is, adjustments or refinements in current products, practices, relationships, skills, and norms. Such changes represent 'minor improvements or simple adjustments in current technology' (Dewar and Dutton, 1986, p.1423). They serve to tacitly reinforce present understandings as well as the established configuration of interests and interest groups. Radical change goes beyond augmenting the status quo, requiring a shift to fundamentally different products, practices, relationships, skills, and norms. It involves adopting a different paradigm, a step that typically disrupts the established pattern of understandings and interests.

To illustrate the difference between incremental and radical changes, consider the comment made by an IS manager at PCC describing the new IS world his group was attempting to usher in:

> Let me give you an analog as to how we were building systems before the architecture. We had this jigsaw of systems in the company – a jigsaw of molten steel. And when you took out a piece of the jigsaw, redesigned it, and then tried to put it back in its place in the jigsaw, lo and behold, you found that the jigsaw looked exactly the same as before. So what opportunity do you have to change the business when you have a jigsaw of molten steel? To change the jigsaw we need jigsaw pieces with flexible edges, which would allow us to change the way we do business.

An incremental change amounts to improving individual jigsaw pieces that nonetheless leave the existing jigsaw picture intact. A radical change requires reconfiguring the entire jigsaw and its pieces so that a totally different jigsaw picture emerges.

Using these concepts of incremental and radical change, we can characterize SCC and PCC's different experiences with CASE tools. Within SCC, the senior managers did not intend CASE tools to fundamentally change their practice of producing and delivering information systems to external clients. Indeed, they had specifically designed their CASE tools to embody existing practices and knowledge. They intended merely to improve the productivity and decrease the costs of their existing way of doing systems development. As a result, no major changes to IS policies, practices, structures, or client relations were instituted, and the firm experienced increased efficiencies and leveraging of technical knowledge without radically transforming its systems development practice or the products delivered to clients. Thus, in terms of both the process and product of systems development, SCC intended and enacted incremental change with CASE tools. Within PCC, on the other hand, the senior managers intended to transform not only their own systems development practice but also the business processes and role of IS in the firm. They enacted a series of changes that fundamentally changed PCC's systems development process to reflect the IE methodology and IE-based CASE tools, and they transformed the IS product from stand-alone functional systems to a corporate-wide information architecture. PCC, thus, intended and had begun to use CASE tools to enact radical change in both the process and product of systems development.

These specific findings can now be represented more generally by expressing them in terms of two dimensions: (1) the nature of change (incremental and radical), and (2) the locus of change (process and product of systems development). These dimensions yield a four-fold classification of changes associated with CASE tools (depicted in Figure 11.2). Normann's (1971) labels for incremental change ('variations') and radical change ('reorientations') can be used to conveniently characterize each of the quadrants.

		LOCUS OF	CHANGE
		Process of Systems Development	**Product of Systems Development**
	Incremental Change	Process Variation (SCC)	Product Variation (SCC)
NATURE OF CHANGE	Radical Change	Process Re-orientation (PCC)	Product Re-orientation (PCC)

Figure 11.2 Nature and locus of change associated with CASE tools

Such a classification, along with the process model of CASE changes presented in Figure 11.1, can be used - either ex ante or ex post - to explain, anticipate, or evaluate the organizational changes associated with CASE tools. Where IS managers introduce CASE tools to improve the existing process of systems development through increasing productivity or cutting costs, organizations will likely experience process variations. Where the CASE tools are used to improve the product delivered to clients, without significantly altering its nature, ownership, or delivery arrangements, organizations will likely experience product variations. The change process enacted (expressed in terms of context, initiating conditions, strategic conduct, and resultant consequences) will likely resemble that experienced by SCC (represented in Figure 11.3).

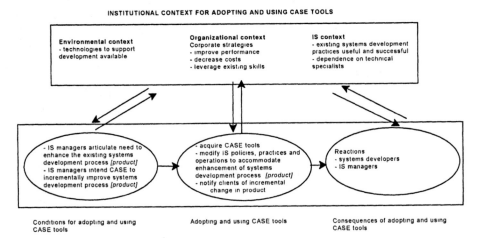

Figure 11.3 Process of organizational change around CASE tools:
an illustration of incremental change

On the other hand, where managers implement CASE tools to substantially change how systems are developed through radically changing the process of systems development, organizations will likely experience process reorientations. Where managers use CASE tools to significantly change the nature of the product delivered to clients, including ownership and delivery arrangements, organizations will likely experience product reorientations. The change process enacted will likely resemble that experienced by PCC (represented in Figure 11.4).

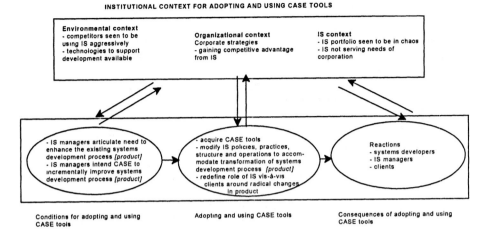

Figure 11.4 Process of organizational change around CASE tools:
an illustration of radical change

While Figures 11.2, 11.3, and 11.4 depict the content and process of organizational change that may be experienced by organizations adopting and using CASE tools in difference situations, it is important to keep in mind that the relationships depicted are not deterministic. The organizational changes occasioned by the adoption and use of CASE tools are not always those intended by key players. First, process and product variations/reorientations may be the result of unintended consequences. For example, key players may intend an incremental change, but due to unforeseen factors, such as more complex software or a poorly conceived implementation plan, these may become more fundamental than anyone anticipated and be experienced as radical, not incremental, change. Second, unintended changes may occur that go well beyond the specific process and product variations/reorientations intended. For example, in conditions such as those at PCC, the tension between the IS division and the business units may, over time, become so unsatisfactory that users seek IS services outside of the organization. Alternatively, in conditions such as those at SCC, the system developers' technical knowledge may eventually become so depleted that they become significantly less productive in non-standard, non-tooled environments.

Implications for research and practice

This chapter has presented the findings of a grounded theory study into the adoption and use of CASE tools and has developed a theoretical framework for conceptualizing this as a process of organizational change. The process represented in Figure 11.1 and the framework of CASE intentions given in Figure 11.2 provide one way of examining these organizational changes around CASE tools. By taking into account the existing institutional context and IS managers' intentions for and actions around CASE tools, the nature and locus of changes associated with CASE tools (as well as the consequences of these changes) can be anticipated, explained, and evaluated. The framework developed here does not imply that CASE tools per se cause process and product variations (as in SCC's case) or process and product reorientations (as in PCC's case). Rather, as shown in Figures 11.3 and 11.4, it indicates that such changes emerge from particular interactions of institutional context, key players' intentions and actions, and the CASE technology. The findings and framework articulated here have implications for both the research and practice of systems development.

Implications for systems development research

The framework and findings discussed in this chapter suggest that the contradictory results evident in the CASE literature likely reflect the fact that differences in intentions, processes, and contexts around the adoption and use of CASE tools are largely overlooked by research that seeks invariant outcomes from CASE tools. In this, the framework proposed here is different from existing frameworks on technology adoption and implementation. These frameworks tend to share three characteristics: (1) they consist of causal models based on the deterministic assumptions of either a technological or organizational imperative (Markus and Robey, 1988) and therefore discount the importance of human intentions and action in shaping the adoption and use of technology; (2) they are variance models (Markus and Robey, 1988) and thus do not adequately capture the contextual and processual issues that are fundamental to examining organizational change (Dutton and Dukerich, 1991; Pettigrew, 1990); and (3) they focus primarily on activities of development and implementation and hence do not examine the use or consequences of a new technology.

While more empirical work is necessary to elaborate and verify the framework, it is believed that a useful starting point has been made. Understanding the process of change around CASE tools (as depicted in Figure 11.1) and distinguishing between the nature of change and its locus of influence (as depicted in Figure 11.2) allow us to explain why two companies - on the surface introducing similar technology (integrated CASE tools) - should experience such different organizational changes. The framework suggests that to understand the adoption and use of CASE tools and their influence on systems development, it is necessary to examine the intentions and actions of key players, the social context into which the CASE tools are being implemented, and the change processes enacted as a result. Figure 11.1 details the kind of concepts that usefully capture these elements and their interaction over time. Further, the distinctions drawn between the locus of the technological change and its nature focus attention on where the influence of the CASE tools is being experienced and what challenges are being posed to the existing process and product of systems development.

Empirical validation and elaboration of these concepts in other settings are clearly needed. The theoretical framework was generated by only examining two sites, albeit in depth. More empirical grounding and comparisons will sharpen and enrich the concepts developed here and yield more complex understanding of the phenomenon. Three initial strategies for further research can be proposed.

First, it is necessary to investigate different contexts where CASE tools have been introduced. While the two companies studied here differed significantly on environment, strategy, size, structure, and culture, they still only represent two oganizational types. More organizations need to be examined to see whether the proposed concepts and framework are relevant in other situations. In this way, the analytic generalization posited here - that other organizations' experiences with CASE tools will resemble the patterns detailed above - will be tested and elaborated.

Second, some of the dimensions in the Figure 11.2 grid may need to be elaborated or refined. While a dichotomous distinction in change intentions was adequate for this study, it is possible that future empirical work will require extending the dimensions. For example, some researchers have proposed finer-grained distinctions in types of innovation (Bartunek and Moch, 1987; Henderson and Clark, 1990; Meyerson and Martin, 1987), recognizing three or four rather than two types of change. Likewise, the distinctions between the process and product of systems development may not always be clear-cut, and a more finely calibrated classification of the systems development domain may be needed, for example, to distinguish between development and maintenance activities or between the development of mainframe applications and client-server applications.

Third, other combinations of positions on the Figure 11.2 grid should also be studied to find out the organizational consequences of hybrid changes. Both SCC and PCC adopted systems development changes that were consistent across process and product. It is conceivable, however, to think of organizations picking diagonal positions on the grid. Consider the following:

- An organization implements CASE tools to achieve process reorientations and product variations. This might occur, for example, when the IS unit continues to deliver stand-alone products to separate functional areas but transforms its process from one based on structured systems design to one using the object-oriented paradigm.
- An organization implements CASE tools to achieve process variations and product reorientations. This might occur, for example, when an existing process based on IE methodology is supplemented by the acquisition of IE-based CASE tools, and the IS unit decides to use the automated aids to implement a strategic IS plan and build a corporate information architecture with shared applications.

Empirical research into such experiences will help to establish the particular conditions, intentions, actions, and consequences associated with hybrid change strategies.

Implications for systems development practice

The theoretical framework developed here meets the criteria of practical applicability proposed by Glaser and Strauss (1967). First, it fits the substantive area of study. The concepts and relations posited as central are intimately related to (because they are derived from) the arena of actual CASE tools adoption and use. Second, the theoretical framework is sufficiently general to be applicable to a range of situations around the adoption and use of CASE tools. It covers not only the process of change but also the location and type of change intended and experienced. Third, it is readily understandable by practitioners and should consequently provide some useful guidance in the actual change management plans of organizations introducing CASE tools. By providing practitioners with some insight into the context, structure, and process of CASE tools implementations, the framework serves as a basis from which the IS practitioner can assess and manage what is typically a poorly understood, complex, and dynamic situation.

The framework developed and presented here has important implications for IS practitioners. It suggests that before the implementation of a technology such as CASE tools, key players in the organization should articulate their intentions with respect to the tools and assess the context of systems development. Doing so will significantly influence the change process and resultant organizational consequences. Having examined and articulated these issues, key players can more effectively plan the implementation of CASE tools and facilitate the action required to enact the intended changes. The ensuing process will further shape the reactions, appropriations, and consequences of the CASE tools.

With respect to the impact of CASE tools on system developers, the findings suggest that it is not CASE tools alone that determine the reaction of the system developers. Rather, three types of attributes - individual, organizational, and technological - appear to significantly influence system developers' response to CASE tools (see Table 11.4). While these findings are from only two organizational sites and require further investigation, they do have considerable face validity because many anecdotal reports have hinted at one or other such influence. In general, where system developers are not committed to a long-term career in IS, the implementation of CASE tools is unlikely to be seriously troubling to them. They may even welcome the tools' hiding of technical details and facilitation of business analysis. System developers who seek IS careers and value their technical skills may be distressed by the implementation of CASE tools. They may fear the obsolescence of their skills and object to the decreased involvement in the details of their work. This concern appears to be particularly acute when the tools are implemented as cost-cutting or productivity-improving measures. As we saw in the case of PCC, however, such concerns may be addressed by supportive human resource policies that provide adequate training and incentives to encourage sceptical or uncertain developers to learn and use the tools (for example, by reassuring them that their jobs are not at risk or by not punishing initial poor performance) and that endorse alternative career paths (for example, allowing technically-oriented developers to move into more technical areas, such as systems programming, database management, or CASE tool support).

Table 11.4 Individual, organizational, and technological influences on system developers' reactions to CASE tools

Category	Facilitating Characteristics	Constraining Characteristics
Attributes of Individuals		
Systems experience	Low investments in traditional systems development knowledge and practices	Heavy investment in traditional systems development knowledge and practices
Time in Systems Development	Less	More
Career Orientation	Business	Technical
Attributes of Organization		
Strategy Behind CASE Tools	Improve systems and data quality	Decrease costs
	Enhance skills and practices	Increase productivity
		Decrease reliance on system developers
Human Resource Policies	Supportive of individual growth and development	Not supportive of individual growth and development
	Job security	Limited job security
	Use of contract workers	
Career Paths	Multiple, alternative career paths	Single, competitive career path
Attributes of Technology		
Market Penetration	High	Low (for example, built in-house)

The training and incentives given to system developers should be tailored to the type of change attempted. Incremental change, which builds on existing skills, work practices, and norms, requires programs and policies that reinforce the existing cognitive and social processes. Radical change, which departs from existing skills, work practices, and norms, requires programs and policies that foster the acquisition of new cognitive and social processes. While radical change offers the opportunity to implement a new vision and create fundamental change, it also invites greater risk and difficulty. Because it can be quite disruptive, radical change is often associated with ambiguity and chaos (Bartunek, 1984; Gash and Orlikowski, 1991; Hedberg, 1981; Tushman and

Romanelli, 1985) and usually is only attempted when managers perceive a rare opportunity or a crisis (as occurred in PCC).

Reorientations in systems development require IS managers to engender significant structural, procedural, and cultural change in their own unit and, in the case of product reorientations, throughout the organization. Radical change implies a paradigm shift, which requires a reframing and renegotiation of the IS mission, role, and relationships in the organization. With process reorientations, it is the system developers and IS managers - primarily involved in the IS work practices, structures, and skills - who are most directly affected. In such cases, senior IS managers need to champion and implement the radical changes in IS structure, knowledge, and work practices. Because there was no established, standardized systems development process in PCC prior to the adoption of CASE tools, the reorientation did not have to challenge longstanding norms or overcome deeply entrenched systems development practices.

When the IS product is changed, it is not only the IS unit but also the clients who will be affected. Product reorientations, thus, require senior and middle managers of the business units to champion and motivate the organizational changes required around fundamentally different IS products. As primary users of such products, business units may need to change their business processes, policies, and norms to take advantage of radically different information systems. To the extent that business managers do not recognize or accept the paradigm shift implicit in a product reorientation, as was evident in the case of PCC, the influence of CASE tools will be limited to the IS unit. Because PCC's practice of developing stand-alone IS products for separate business units was firmly institutionalized in PCC's decentralized culture, the shift to a corporate information architecture with shared data and applications proved to be a significant challenge. The business units' refusal to change as a result of the attempted IS product reorientation prevented any fundamental changes in the business. While these findings do not show that structural, procedural, and cultural changes by business units will lead to the successful adoption of IS product reorientations, they do suggest that where such changes are absent there will be significant problems of inertia, territorialism, and resistance.

This chapter has argued that the implementation of CASE tools within systems development creates organizational change and that much can be gained by researching and managing it accordingly. While all research methodologies have strengths and weaknesses, the use of the grounded theory approach here was particularly appropriate, generating a set of insights, concepts, and interactions that address the critical organizational elements involved in adopting and using CASE tools, elements that to date have been largely overlooked in the CASE literature. The theoretical framework generated from the empirical findings suggests that the intentions and actions of key players, the change process they enact, as well as the social context into which tools are implemented, critically influence what changes are associated with CASE tools. This proposes a different approach to doing CASE tools research, one that takes into account the interaction over time of intentions, context, process, and action around the technology. Both researchers and practitioners alike should find the framework useful as they examine the implementation and use of this important but still poorly understood technology.

Acknowledgements

The support of MIT's Center for Information Systems Research is gratefully acknowledged. Thanks are also due to Debra Hofman for many helpful discussions, to Jack Baroudi, Chris Kemerer, and Marcie Tyre for comments on an earlier draft of this chapter, and to the associate editor and anonymous reviewers for their suggestions.

Part IV

Modes of Analysing and Interpreting Qualitative Data

12 Information System Use as a Hermeneutic Process

Richard J. Boland, Jr

This chapter argues for an interpretive approach to understanding the way users of an information system make its outputs meaningful. Several themes important to the hermeneutic tradition for studying the process of interpretation are presented. These themes are then drawn upon in making an interpretive reading of the way four experienced managers analyse and give meaning to the output of a personnel evaluation information system. Some unique features of the user as an active reader of the information system text are identified, and some reorientations for our research on information requirements and use are suggested.

Hermeneutics is the study of interpretation, especially the process of coming to understand a text. Hermeneutics emerged in response to the problem of interpreting ancient religious texts and has evolved to address the general problem of how we give meaning to what is unfamiliar and alien. Information systems research, to the extent that it is concerned with the value and usefulness of its output, can profitably draw upon the hermeneutic tradition to guide its inquiries. The output from an information system would then be viewed as a text being read and interpreted by the information system user. Viewing information system use as a hermeneutic process can help us understand how a reader makes system outputs meaningful and how they (IS outputs) become incorporated in decision and action.

A hermeneutic approach was proposed during the 1984 IFIP WG8.2 conference on research methods (Boland, 1985) and defended by using Gadamer (1976b) as the major theoretical source. This chapter will extend that position by exploring some central hermeneutic ideas and arguing that they open up possibilities for novel and interesting types of information systems research. An example of hermeneutically inspired research on information systems will be presented and some implications for future research directions will be proposed.

This chapter does not survey the hermeneutic tradition, but simply focuses on a few ideas that are helpful in guiding hermeneutic studies, especially studies of information systems use. The ideas I will highlight are found in the work of three individuals who, taken together, pose a new agenda for research in the social sciences.

Firstly, I will take seriously the idea of world hypotheses as articulated by S. C. Pepper. Although Pepper is not normally associated with hermeneutic studies, his historical review of the root metaphors underlying western metaphysics provides a preliminary guide to the possibilities for declaring an interpretation as being well founded.

Secondly, I will take seriously the anti-foundationalist position of Richard Rorty, and his ideas on the contingency of our vocabularies for doing social science. His focus on the evolving metaphors of our practice-based conversations broadens the possibilities for justifying our interpretations to include the full range of our practical concerns.

Thirdly, I will take seriously the phenomenological hermeneutics of Paul Ricoeur, and his ideas on how we might use 'text' as a metaphor in our study of action. Ricoeur helps us see that the problem of interpretation is always an open one, and that in the readings we make of the texts of our day to day life we bring both the world and ourselves into being.

The point of weaving ideas from these three philosophers together is to argue that our research in information systems can profitably be seen as the study of how texts are produced and read in modern organizations. This position is put forward as part of a dialectic confrontation with the modern conception of standard science. The output of an information system is not simply a representation of some aspect of the world being transmitted in as clear and unbiased a way as possible to its user. Instead, the output of an information system is an unfamiliar text to be read, interpreted and made meaningful by those who use it in ways that will always surpass any particular understanding the system's creators had in mind. In making their interpretation, the readers bring the world into being in a certain way, and bring themselves into being differently as well. Studying that process of interpretation is the hermeneutic task for information systems research. In this chapter, I will use hermeneutics to redescribe this aspect of information systems research in the hopes of stimulating new and hopefully more interesting ways of talking about it and doing it.

Three hermeneutic voices

Stephen Pepper

Stephen Pepper in *World Hypotheses* (1942) proposed that the metaphysical longings of humanity for a single, consistent and coherent 'theory of the world' was doomed not by impossibility but by indecideability. The type of world theory that we long for is one that could take any specific observation of an event or feature in the world and subsume it under (explain it within) that theory. Pepper argued that far from being impossible to construct such a theory, there were several equally plausible or as he put it 'relatively adequate' ways of doing so. He explored a number of organizing themes that have been used throughout history to try and develop such a theory. Pepper discarded several of these themes as being inadequate in the scope or precision of analysis that they could provide, but four of those organizing themes were found suitable for developing such a universally encompassing theory. He called these four his 'world hypotheses' and the underlying images each was based upon were called their 'root metaphors'. His world hypotheses and their root metaphors are shown in Table 12.1:

Table 12.1 World hypotheses and root metaphors

World Hypotheses	Root Metaphors	Principal Exponents
FORMISM	SIMILARITY	Plato; Aristotle
MECHANISM	MACHINE	Hobbes; Locke; Hume
CONTEXTUALISM	HISTORIC EVENT	James; Bergson; Peirce
ORGANICISM	HARMONIC UNITY	Hegel; Royce

He identified these four as relatively adequate by characterizing western metaphysics on two dimensions. On the first dimension, theories that purported to explain any and all 'raw facts' were either analytic (explaining facts by breaking them into their component parts) or synthetic (explaining facts by relating them to their place within greater wholes). On the second dimension, such theories were either dispersive or integrative. Dispersive theories take facts as they appear in whatever sequence they become known and deal with them separately. Each fact need not stand in a fixed and determinate relation to every other. For integrative theories, in contrast, each fact is expected to have a determinate place and fit into a totalized, law-like system. On these two dimensions, Pepper locates the four world hypotheses and their root metaphors as shown in Table 12.2:

Table 12.2 Location of world hypotheses and root metaphors

	Analytical Theories	Synthetic Theories
Dispersive Theories	FORMISM (SIMILARITY)	CONTEXTUALISM (HISTORIC EVENT)
Integrative Theories	MECHANISM (MACHINE)	ORGANICISM (HARMONIC UNITY)

It is beyond the scope of this chapter to dwell more deeply into Pepper's analysis of these world hypotheses. Instead, I will merely highlight the significance of Pepper's argument and identify some of its implications for a hermeneutic study of information system use. To begin, consider that a theory is a vocabulary - a way of talking about the world that takes some parts as focal elements and leaves others as subsidiary issues. Within the vocabulary of a world hypothesis, it is productive to engage in a dialogue: questions can be posed and answered, and arguments can be resolved. Between two different world hypotheses, however, arguments will often prove irresolveable. What is significant and compelling to one vocabulary will be beside the point to another. Each vocabulary, with its distinctive root metaphor and world hypothesis, is capable of denying the validity of any other's claims and guaranties.

Pepper went on to propose that inquiry constrained within any one world hypothesis could only support its claims to universality and 'Truth' by denying a voice to any other world hypothesis. Since any one-world hypothesis could not demonstrate superiority in argument with another, it could survive as a sole world hypothesis only by becoming dogmatic and imposing silence on its rivals. Pepper argued against any form of dogmaticism and encouraged an eclecticism in the use of world hypotheses as an antidote to the indecideability among them. But Pepper was left open to charges that he was himself being dogmatic (against dogmaticism) and that his eclecticism led to a relativism where 'anything goes'. If any world hypothesis is as good as any other, if there is no apparent basis for preferring one over another, then there are no solid grounds for the beliefs we settle upon.

Richard Rorty

Richard Rorty provides a stimulating voice that we might propose as a kind of answer to these problems that some have raised against Pepper, even though Rorty is working on his own agenda and never refers to Pepper or his work. Rorty is a pragmatist and an antifoundationalist, who questions the whole metaphysical enterprise and debunks the role of philosophy as the 'Queen' of the natural or the human sciences. In a series of beautifully argued books (Rorty, 1979; 1982; 1989), he attacks the pretensions of a philosophical search for foundations to guarantee our beliefs. Like Pepper, he characterizes our traditions for making claims to truth as being cast within vocabularies and he argues that such claims are only defensible within a particular vocabulary: we cannot argue coherently across two vocabularies, we can only pit them against each other in a kind of dialectic.

Rorty begins by questioning the entire tradition that Pepper had taken for granted: the tradition of seeing philosophy (and epistemology in particular) as a search for an underlying essence, a ground or a foundation within reality upon which we could build our knowledge of the world. He likens it to a search for nature's own vocabulary - a search for a way to 'mirror' nature the way it really is - the way nature itself would speak to us, if it could. An important theme for Rorty is the absence of a privileged access to nature's own vocabulary. Our theories, be they world hypotheses or more local affairs, are vocabularies which please us - which we find useful for certain purposes - and we should value them as such, not try to burden them and ourselves with arguments about their closeness to some underlying essence in the world. New theories or vocabularies emerge as a new metaphor is coined to describe some aspects of the world. New metaphors emerge from our practical concerns with making things work and with keeping things interesting. Different vocabularies describe and redescribe the world in different ways - some redescriptions are good for some purposes; some are good for other purposes. Given our context of practice, some descriptions are seen as interesting, some are not. But none are good for all purposes, and none can claim to be the way nature itself prefers to be described.

Rorty draws on Davidson to question the way we traditionally think about language as a process of representation. There is usually a two directional process of representation being assumed - one in which language is used to represent the world and another in which language is used to represent our ideas. In each case, we tend to presume that there is a pre-existing, underlying essence, a foundation or ultimate ground to either the world or our ideas, and that language represents it with some greater or lesser degree of accuracy. In contrast to this representation metaphor used to describe our language practice, Rorty proposes a creation metaphor through which we might come to see our language practice as a way of making the world and ourselves in a particular way - bringing the world and ourselves into being through our particular kind of language practices.

The vocabulary and language practice we currently use is profoundly contingent in the sense that it is the result of a long, complicated chain of historical accidents, unanticipated events and strange juxtapositions of people, places, and metaphors. Our vocabularies and our practices, and the way they bring ourselves and our world into being, are forever changing in response to contingencies, but we seem to believe that our current vocabulary (especially as practised in the tradition of modern science) is our final one - the best method of accurately representing reality and our thoughts about it. We realize that our current vocabulary is in need of some marginal improvements and refinements but we believe that it is essentially 'in touch' with reality in a way that can serve as a universal foundation for further developing our knowledge of the world. This essentialist and foundationalist ideal for our knowledge of the world is one that a hermeneutic approach tries to dispel. It tries to replace it with Rorty's sense of contingency and creation of justified beliefs through language and practical action.

Paul Ricoeur

The third author I would like to consider is Paul Ricoeur. Ricoeur (1981) is important because he gives us a new metaphor for structuring a vocabulary with which we might think about the human sciences. In the course of developing his phenomenological hermeneutics, he uses the central metaphor of 'the situation as text' and the associated metaphors of 'producing the text' (through speaking, writing or acting) and 'reading the text'. Ricoeur helps us break from the traditional notion that a text is a written document by arguing that action and situations also be understood and read as texts. He further helps us break the traditional notion that a text represents some well-formed idea of its author and that we should try to recover this original meaning through interpretation. He does this by highlighting the dialectic of distanciation and appropriation in the production and reading of texts.

Distanciation refers to the way that any single and intended meaning that speakers or writers may have is separated from them in the acting, speaking or writing of a text. Distanciation is evident in a primary way even in the intimate dialogue of two individuals, and becomes more pronounced and easily recognized as we move from the moment of two people speaking together, to a speech before a large audience that is later transcribed, to a text written by an author for a general and unknown audience, and finally to the transaction collection and reporting structures created by an information system.

Beginning with the moment of two persons speaking together and extending out to the computer-based information system, we see that the production of a text exteriorizes its meaning from the speaker in a way that surpasses the original moment of action, as well as any clear and singular meaning that might have been intended by it. The text is distanced from its author, decontextualized from the moment of its production and from any intended audience, and is made available for reading and interpretation by anyone who can read (now and in the future). As the text is distanced from its author, the idea of a single meaning that may or may not have been associated with its production is less and less relevant. The distanciated text becomes open to the interpretations that can be made of it by its readers. The text opens new possible worlds to the reader in the sense that it makes available to the reader an unfolding set of possibilities for understanding the text and thereby the kinds of worlds and selves that can be appropriated from it:

> '...to understand a text, we shall say, is not to find a lifeless sense which is contained in it, but to unfold the possibility of being indicated by the text'. (Ricoeur, 1981, p.501)

Distanciation of the text from an author thus sets the conditions for the reader's appropriation of its meaning. By appropriation. Ricoeur emphasizes that interpretation is 'to make one's own what was initially alien' as it 'actualizes' the meaning of the text for the present reader. Appropriation also emphasizes that a personal achievement is involved in the interpretation of a text and that a new understanding of both self and world is opened up as we appropriate the text 'to unfold the possibility of being' that it opens up to us about the world and ourselves.

Implications of these three voices

My position, simply put, is that viewing information systems as a hermeneutic process will open up interesting ways of talking about how users read information systems and make meaning with them. It will include a new respect for the individual readers as appropriators of meaning. We should not expect this meaning to be justified as a recapturing of an original essence, but as a metaphorically framed dialogue with the text. The dialogue will be guided by metaphors from practical concerns. In this dialogue, the readers of the information system text are open to the possibilities it affords for discovering meaning both about the world and about themselves. In the next section, as an example of this point, I will make an interpretive reading of the way four experienced managers appropriate meaning from an information system report.

The Milne experiment: reading the information system as text

The dissertation of Ronald Milne (1981) provides us an instance of the reading of reports from a personnel evaluation information system that I will use as my empirical example. Milne created a set of reports about the performance of two divisional personnel managers as part of an experiment on budget slack. In the experiment, 67 experienced managers enrolled in an Executive MBA programme, analysed personnel evaluation reports and decided which of two Divisional Managers should be promoted to the position of Corporate Director of Personnel.

The reports contained task performance measures along with expense summaries covering a four-year period. Milne had two conditions in his experiment. In one, the reports contained expense summaries that showed only actual expenses for the period. In the other condition, the reports showed the same actual expenses along with budgeted expenses, side by side. I will be looking only at the no-budget condition in which nothing but the actual expenses appeared in the reports. A copy of the case instrument and the reports from the no-budget condition of the Milne experiment are shown in the Appendix.

The case instrument states that the two managers have no qualitative differences in personalities or managerial styles, and that their two departments 'are remarkably comparable in terms of number of employees serviced, employee turnover, training requirements, complexity of recruiting, and general workload'. On 57 activities determined to be 'necessary and sufficient for the support of both the individual divisions and the achievement of the corporate goals', each performed satisfactorily, although one candidate, called East, had more Satisfactory Plus ratings. East also is shown as having performed more unspecified 'Additional' activities that were neither required nor necessary. On the other hand, the financial performance data shows the other candidate, called West, spending less money than East ($450,000 for West, $754,000 for East in 1980).

Milne was interested in budget slack and motivation theory but I am not going to discuss the purpose or findings of his study. Instead, I want to use his experimental data as an instance in the reading of an information system as text. Fortunately for my purposes, Milne asked his subjects to give the reasons for their decisions to promote either East or West, but did not analyse those responses. I will take advantage of Milne's data by interpreting four of his subjects' readings of the reports, as examples of the hermeneutic process involved in the creation of meaning from an information system text. I will first present the reason provided by a subject for her choice, and will then present an interpretation of the argument she makes.

Subject 61: Choosing East

> My preference was for the East manager because he appeared to be more outgoing. Company wise, he performed a lot more than the 57 required activities. Also, those activities were scored on the average more 'satisfactory plus' than the West manager. Although the West manager is doing good, he's only so-so. It seems he should become more active and try harder. Maybe he had the satisfactory ratings because of the people who work for him. It seems the East manager does a better job.

This subject opens with an assertion about East's personality and the way it manifests itself in the context of this company. East's general capacity for outgoing behaviour is identified as the reason for his performing more activities than were strictly required by his position in the company. The subject follows this qualitative, personal assessment of East's character and its consequences for the company by citing quantitative evidence from the reports, using both raw number of activities and a calculated 'average' of activity scores.

The subject then returns to a qualitative interpretation of the motivations and personalities of the managers behind these numbers. The subject allows that although West 'is doing good' by achieving consistent satisfactory ratings, West as a person is 'only so-so'. She reads him as not trying hard enough and being too passive. She proposes as a remedy to become 'more active' and to 'try harder' to overcome this personal failing. As with East, the reader alternates from a qualitative interpretation of West's psyche to a quantitative justification. The report scores (being highly satisfactory) do not on their face justify her negative attributions toward West, so the reader calls the numbers themselves into question. She does this by recontextualizing the situation and portraying West's staff as achieving these good ratings on their own, in spite of West's passivity and lack of leadership. The numbers, she suggests, are not true indicators of his performance and are more reflective of the talent, energy and self-management of the workers themselves.

This subject has thus read the rather cold and objective categories and numbers of the text in a way that brings the two managers, East and West, alive before her. She invests them with personal characteristics, which manifest themselves in the specific context of this company. Their personal qualities are reflected in the numbers of the reports. For East the reflection is like a mirror, for West the reflection is badly distorted, and requires a subtle reading that invokes a rich contextual interpretation of the setting that lies behind the numbers.

For East, she reads the situation as one in which his outgoing quality manifests itself through a motivation in his workforce and a higher than required level of performance. For West, she reads the situation as one in which his personal failings and his ineffectiveness as a manager are masked by the numbers. In each case, the reader makes an interpretation that not only brings the two managers to life as human beings with enduring personal characteristics used to explain what is happening, but also brings the company to life as well. The types of workers in the departments, their relations with their managers, and their history of performing as a group are all brought into being in the act of making this reading.

Notice, too, that the reading proceeds with an alternation of qualitative and quantitative assessments. The qualitative assessments of personal characteristics are the lead, causal factors, with quantitative factors used to give evidence for the qualitative interpretations. If the quantitative data in the text do not seem to fully support the qualitative reading, as is the case with West, then further qualitative readings are made to recontextualize the situation and reframe the meaning and significance of the quantitative factors.

Subject 67: Choosing West

> I picked the West manager because he ran a tighter ship as far as budget was concerned and seemed to be more time organized. If he used the amount of money East did, he would definitely have better results. Both had approximately the same number of employees but salaries were very different. West didn't spend an inordinate amount of time on activities other than the required since it is wasteful given the fact there is little direction as to what is important.

The reader names her choice for promotion using a captain-and-the-sea metaphor. West is seen as a strong captain with a disciplined crew and tight, lean expenses. Use of this metaphor recontextualizes the financial issue in West's favour with a dramatic flourish. It frames the larger budget expense level of East as bloated and less seaworthy. Instead of indicating that East is outgoing and highly motivated, his higher expenses are seen by this reader as a sign of weakness. Against the sudden storms of the sea, East is not as prepared and West is positioned as the one who will survive.

The reader then leaves the ship-and-the-sea metaphor, and gives an example of how a text can open new possible worlds to a reader. She asserts that other system outputs, reflecting other histories, could have been written, and she tells us what those other reports would have shown. This gives an opportunity for the reader to bring West to life and simulate his behaviour in another possible world and to claim a knowledge of the outcome based on a knowledge of West's inner qualities.

The reader then returns to the interpretive themes of 'time', 'time efficiency' and 'tightness', as she penetrates deeper into West's psyche and replays how West as ship captain had appropriately economized his attention and energy on those things he knows, ignoring what was vague and potentially irrelevant to the running of his tight ship.

Like the previous subject, this reader also alternates between qualitative and quantitative analyses with a qualitative understanding in a lead, causal role. The metaphor of the captain-and-the-sea invests both East and West with personal as well as managerial qualities. The activity scores and departmental expenses are dramatically and uniquely given meaning in the context of this metaphorical framing. Also like the previous subject, this reader is exploring her own possibilities for being as she engages in dialogue with the text. She is exploring personal qualities, making value judgments about them and simulating behaviours in alternative futures.

Subject 46: Choosing East

> Although they do not have any obvious differences, I would select East...His Division had a higher number of satisfactory plus ratings on the 57 required activities. Although he did have two marginal ratings in 1977, this problem did not recur again. This indicates a 'cracking down' on his staff....East also had more extra activities which, I feel, demonstrates initiative and ambition....Although East's expenses were higher, I feel this is partly due to the fact that he had no budget. I feel if he were promoted, and given a budget to stick to, that he would do very well.

The reader opens by declaring the difficulty of her decision between the two candidates. There is no obvious difference, yet she still will make a decision. She begins by recognizing the larger number of satisfactory plus ratings for East, but then goes beyond this simple tale of higher scores and proposes to penetrate behind the numbers and to retell the history of how East has managed his department. The reader relives East's response to some early marginal ratings and dramatizes his 'cracking down' on the staff to bring them back in line. The reader has brought East to life as a strong manager whose iron will shapes the behaviour of his workers. East is painted as both a forceful human being and as the responsible author of the department's performance. He is not an average individual who just happens to be in charge of an energetic group of workers, but is the causal agent who created its abilities and success.

The reader then proceeds to fill out East's character. The strength and boldness attributed to him earlier is now complemented with further attributions of 'initiative and ambition'. She reads the report as a reflection of his will to succeed and advance through the corporation. None the less, the reader recognizes that other readings could be made of this report. In particular, she recognizes that the higher expenses of East could be read as a negative element in East's character or managerial record. She forestalls this possibility by constructing a pre-emptive counter argument. The reason that East has higher expenses, she explains, is that he was not operating under a budget. Ignoring the conflict between this claim and the strong level of wilful control that had previously been attributed to East, the reader assures us that once he is elevated to the new position and given budget guidelines, East will be more frugal and cost-conscious.

So we see the reader moving from a difficult moment of choice between two very similar candidates, to an inference about the managerial history of East, to an insight into his character and deep felt motivations, to a defence of his future managerial behaviour in response to a hypothesized criticism of him. The reader has progressively moved from a calculated assessment to a psychological analysis to an assertion of deep human knowledge of East as a person. This subject provides another example of how the people behind the numbers are brought to life and animated in hypothetical worlds, allowing the reader to explore her own possibilities for being through dialogue with the text.

This subject also displays the strategy of alternating between qualitative and quantitative modes of analysis. The initial qualitative statements about the managers are justified by a quantitative analysis of the reports. Later, the subject shifts back to a qualitative mode as she retells the organization's history, and proposes how the managers would behave in different circumstances.

Subject 53: Choosing West

The manager in the West had consistently higher satisfactory ratings than the East, but the East had higher satisfactory plus ratings....It seems that the East manager tried harder to get the satisfactory plus ratings and achieved it, but in addition they had twice as many additional activities which might imply they tried too hard for the satisfactory plus ratings and had to go back...Financially the West operated at a lower cost and accomplished more satisfactorily without having to go back and do things over.

The subject first acknowledges that East had more satisfactory plus ratings, but notes that West had a consistently higher percentage of satisfactory ratings. In one sense, this is a way of asserting the difficulty of making a choice between them and the subjects frequently make this assertion of difficulty. But in another sense, this is a unique reframing of the setting and the meaning to be found in the data. By asserting the value of consistent satisfactory ratings by West, the subject opens the possibility of questioning the value of so many satisfactory plus ratings achieved by East. The assertion of a quantitative balance of rating category frequencies between the two managers opens the possibility for this reader to make her own interpretation of the numbers and to reveal their deeper significance.

In the next section the reader continues to reframe the data and the setting it implies by interpreting East's satisfactory plus ratings as the result of his having tried too hard. The additional activities are thus reframed and read not as an extra accomplishment, but as a kind of rework - a going back and redoing in order to compulsively achieve the consistent string of satisfactory plus ratings.

The reader then switches from a qualitative to a quantitative assessment by presenting a calculation of efficiency showing West operating at a lower cost. The reader completes the reframing of the data by praising West for operating 'more satisfactorily'. Here, the reader has managed to turn West's merely satisfactory ratings into a strongly positive assessment and to belittle the value of satisfactory plus as a rating. Finally, by asserting that West did not have 'to go back and do things over', the reader reinforces the negative connotation of additional activities.

This subject demonstrates the power of the reader to appropriate the text for her own purposes. What others might see on the surface as unquestionably meritorious (satisfactory plus and additional activities) she sees as negative indicators. She does this by bringing East to life as compulsive and overly motivated, trying too hard and having to repeat himself in a questionable search for ever higher ratings. In reframing the data and its meaning she recontextualizes the organizational setting, and uses its newly implied reward systems, review processes and histories of accomplishment in order to dramatize the motivations and behaviours of East and West.

Implications of a hermeneutic approach

In Ricoeur's terms, the information system report from Milne's experiment is quite easily seen as a text, and its users as involved and serious readers of that text. As Pepper argues, there are multiple world hypotheses or organizing images for making a coherent sense of the information system text, and the four subjects presented above display a diverse set of root metaphors used to guide their interpretive readings. We do not see them using a world hypothesis in Pepper's metaphysical sense, but in Rorty's pragmatist sense we do see them using practical, action-based images to create a unique vocabulary for the situation and the meaning behind the text.

Using the captain and his ship as a way of framing the situation as subject 67 did is an obvious example of metaphor. But each subject proposes metaphorical images of humans in practical action in order to give meaning to the text. Subject 61 contrasts images of the outgoing, active personality type with the passive, retiring personality type; subject 46 draws on the image of a stern disciplinarian, cracking down on workers; and subject 53 poses the image of a compulsive over-achiever. Each of these are metaphors of character types in practical action settings. Each of them frames the setting and its problems in a rich and thoroughgoing way (Schön, 1979). As root metaphors for interpreting these settings, they provide a specific context of personalities, motivations, relations with workers, departmental dynamics, organizational histories, and organizational futures.

Each subject has, in effect, brought a different world into being in reading the seemingly straightforward text of this report. There is no simple way to blend these interpretations together into one shared vocabulary and arrive at a consensus. They might, as Rorty suggests, be pitted against each other in a dialectic, but they cannot be defeated in terms of their own unique definition of the situation and its associated vocabulary. What is passive and weak for one reader is prudent and disciplined for another. What is a grand level of accomplishment for one reader is compulsive and wasteful for another.

Most evident, though, is the way the readers 'appropriate' meaning from the text by, in Ricoeur's sense, being receptive to the possibilities of being it opens up to them. The readers are not simply passive receivers of the message that the information system carries. Instead, they actively inject themselves into the readings and create characters, settings and contexts, which they then use to understand both the text and themselves. They take the data and weave back and forth from calculation to emotion, and from quantity to quality as they fill out the possibilities for being found in the conjunction of their root metaphor and the information system text. This alternation of qualitative and quantitative modes of interpretation is similar to the decision behaviour observed in a budget setting by Boland and Pondy (1986) although the lead role played by qualitative reading is more clearly pronounced here.

Even though the reports contain only numbers - dollars of expense and simple performance category counts - the readers do not let the cold, dead numbers just lie there. Rather, they bring the people and situations behind the numbers to life. They appropriate a warm, human reality from the cold numbers. They take the hard, objective data and create a subjective reality of people with vibrant personalities, strong motivations, deeply-felt intentions and complex histories. First they create a primary context in order to bring the actors and the situation to life, and then they proceed to invent alternative contexts and hypothetical histories in order to engage in dialogue with other, possible readings of the text. From subject 67 we hear what would happen if West had had as much money as East. From subject 46 we hear what would have happened if East had had a budget. They not only create but also play with the reality they appropriate from the text.

Conclusion

This brief example of viewing information system use as a hermeneutic process opens new ways of seeing and talking about information systems. It puts forward an image of the user as an autonomous, inventive force. The user does not have 'information needs' in any foundational, pre-existing sense. The basis for determining such needs is only to be found in the action of reading the text itself. Reading is a process of constructing a context for interpreting not only the data immediately at hand, but also the personalities of those being reported upon, and the hypothetical histories and futures used to engage the text in dialogue.

Viewing information system use as a hermeneutic process would open a new set of research concerns. Taking a hermeneutic view, attention would shift from how well an information system represented a situation to how well it enabled a reader to appropriate possibilities for being, both in the situation and in their own lives. Attention would shift from identifying the user's essential, foundational and enduring set of information needs to identifying how different information availability enabled the juxtaposition of quantity and quality, the shifting back and forth from numbers and calculation to persons and values. Attention would shift from the information system as a device for data output to the information system as an environment for acting out interpretations - a space for actively appropriating meaning about our situations and ourselves.

I do not argue that a hermeneutic view supplants all other views, or that it should silence all others. I argue only that it opens an interesting and potentially valuable way of talking about information systems and that talking about them differently opens the possibility for making them and ourselves differently.

Appendix: Case instrument from Milne experiment

Promotion selection
1. This case situation asks you to do three things:
(a) Use the information provided in the case to select one of two managers being considered for promotion.
(b) Rate each of the managers on a scale of zero to one hundred.
(c) Provide the reasons for your decisions.

Overview
2. You are in a corporate home office that is physically separated from its two decentralized operating divisions. Each operating division, call them East and West, has a personnel department and the home office has a personnel department as well. The Director of Personnel position at the home office is vacant. You are required to select a person to fill this vacant position. You have narrowed your search down to the personnel department managers at the two operating divisions. You are now faced with making the final selection. The following information is available to you.

Individual characteristics
3. The personnel records of both managers have been reviewed and, though differences exist in specific background information, little significance can be attached to these differences. Both managers have excellent performance ratings which were prepared, over several years, by several different divisions managers. Both managers have been interviewed and observed in a social situation. Although they exhibit different personalities and have different 'styles', no qualitative differences can rationally be assigned to these differences. The home office staff appears to have divided preferences, but both managers appear to have about equal support from their own staff.

Financial
4. The home office maintains financial performance data on the two personnel departments. Although the two divisions are physically separated by approximately 12 miles, their personnel departments are remarkably comparable in terms of number of employees serviced, employee turnover, training requirements, complexity of recruiting, and general workload. It is normal procedure for home office executives who visit the divisions to report on activities observed. One area of concern is if managers fully utilize their physical

resources (space, equipment, people, etc.). A review of several past reports on file indicates that both managers fully utilize their physical capacity and there are no reports of idle resources. The division personnel department managers do not prepare or submit budgets. Budgets were attempted in prior years but were discontinued by the home office. Expense data for the past four years is on an attached page.

Performance data
5. The home office personnel department routinely collects and records data on the performance of the two division personnel departments. The home office has identified 57 activities which have been determined to be necessary and sufficient for the support of both the individual divisions and the achievement of the corporate goals. The company has developed a set of performance criteria relating to quality which results in each activity receiving one of four performance ratings. The ratings and their meanings are as follows:

Unsatisfactory:	Performance which clearly fails to meet the objective of the specified goal.
Marginal:	Performance which fails to meet the objective, but does make a contribution.
Satisfactory:	Performance which meets all of the requirements of the specified goal.
Satisfactory Plus:	Performance which significantly exceeds the level necessary to meet all of the requirements of the specified goal.

6. The home office supplements the ratings of the 57 required items by recording activities performed by the division personnel departments that are in addition to the 57 required activities. Because this optional category of activities is diverse and unspecified, the home office simply records the number of such activities and the number of man-hours the divisions devote to such activities.

7. Both sets of performance data are on an attached page.

Ratings on 57 required activities

| Ratings By Year | Number of Activities Receiving Each Rating | |
	East Division	West Division
1977		
Unsatisfactory	0	0
Marginal	2	2
Satisfactory	45	50
Satisfactory Plus	10	5
1978		
Unsatisfactory	0	0
Marginal	0	0
Satisfactory	40	49
Satisfactory Plus	17	8

1979
Unsatisfactory	0	0
Marginal	0	0
Satisfactory	30	48
Satisfactory Plus	27	9

1980
Unsatisfactory	0	0
Marginal	0	0
Satisfactory	27	45
Satisfactory Plus	30	12

Activities performed in addition to the 57 required activities

	East Division		West Division	
Year	Number of Activities	Total Man-hours Used	Number of Activities	Total Man-hours Used
1977	8	1160	3	309
1978	12	1740	5	420
1979	17	2280	7	605
1980	21	2740	9	790

Expense data

(Thousands of Dollars)

	EAST DIVISION	WEST DIVISION
1977		
Salaries	$417	$267
Equipment	68	33
Other	21	31
Total	506	331
1978		
Salaries	$595	$290
Equipment	69	39
Other	11	31
Total	675	360
1979		
Salaries	$564	$329
Equipment	31	51
Other	31	36
Total	626	416
1980		
Salaries	$611	$371
Equipment	107	47
Other	36	41
Total	754	459

13 Symbolism and Information Systems Development: Myth, Metaphor and Magic

Rudy Hirschheim and Mike Newman

It is our intention to challenge the commonly-held assumption that information systems development (ISD) can be conceived of as a normative process reflecting conventional economic rationality. We ask: is systems development the rational process so eloquently described in the 'classic' works of DeMarco (1978), Gane and Sarson (1979), Weinberg (1980), Yourdon (1982), Jackson (1983), and Martin (1985)? Or does this orthodox view fail to explain the actual practice of systems development? It is our view that even the basic assumptions about the rationality of the actors and the social processes they engage in need to be critically appraised. We suggest that if the assumptions about economic rationality are closely analysed, it can be seen that they do not reflect the reality of systems development. ISD tends to defy rational explanations. As an alternative to basing our understanding of systems development on economic rationality, we contend that symbolism holds more promise. Instead of focusing on data flow diagrams, structured walkthroughs, requirements specifications, and the like, we concentrate on the role of myth, metaphor, and magic. These concepts offer considerable scope in interpreting the social actions that are embodied within ISD. We feel they facilitate a much richer understanding of systems development.

Over the years, a great deal has been written about information systems development. It is a topic of growing interest as organizations increasingly recognize the role computer-based information systems (IS) are likely to play in their survivability. Indeed, the strategic use of new information technology and systems is seen as the key to the future (Beath and Ives, 1986; Ives and Learmonth, 1984; McFarlan, 1984b; Parsons, 1983; Porter and Millar, 1985). Yet the history of ISD does not paint a bright picture. The past decades have seen numerous failed systems - some of the monumental variety, others more mundane (Lucas, 1974; Lyytinen and Hirschheim, 1987). According to Mowshowitz (1976) many, if not most, information systems are failures in one sense or another. More worrisome, perhaps, is the survey done by Gladden (1982) who reports that in 75% of all the cases of systems development he surveyed, either the development is never completed or the product of completed development is not used. Subsequently, some commentators have gone so far as to refer to a 'crisis in systems development' (Bubenko, 1986; Martin, 1985; Sibley, 1986).

Given the strategic importance of information systems for both now and the future, it is imperative that we understand why so many ISD efforts have not been successful and why ISD has been so problematic. In the literature one can, of course, find as many reasons for ISD failures as the numbers of failures themselves (Lyytinen and Hirschheim, 1987). It is our contention that there is one underlying reason systems development is as problematic as it is, and why there have been so many failures: ISD has been too narrowly conceived. A major part of the problem has been the inadequate recognition that ISD is largely a social process (Checkland, 1981; Hirschheim et al., 1987; Keen, 1981; Kling and Iacono, 1984; Lyytinen, 1986b; Markus, 1984; Mumford, 1983; Newman and Rosenberg, 1985; Robey and Markus, 1984). Treating systems development as largely a technical process is now seen by many designers - although not all - as a recipe for disaster.

It comes as no surprise to systems developers that social interaction is important: obtaining requirements, discussing design options, performing structured walkthroughs, prototyping, and the like, are all intensely social in nature. But while it might be recognized that ISD is essentially a social process, this in and of itself is not sufficient to guarantee success. For quite some time, conventional systems development approaches have acknowledged the importance of the social element of ISD. Nevertheless, they concentrate on the technical process of systems development. They equip the developer with neither the tools nor the knowledge for dealing with the social processes intrinsic to ISD. Simple platitudes such as 'get the support of senior management' or 'involve the end user' are hardly sufficient to guide systems development. They tend to mask the social nature of ISD or portray it in simplistic ways. They do not allow developers to understand, let alone fully appreciate, the social nature of systems development.

Developing an understanding of the social nature of ISD is, however, by no means a simple matter. It is first necessary to conceive of systems development as largely a social process which relies to an increasing extent on new information technology for its effective operation (Goldkuhl and Lyytinen, 1982; Land and Hirschheim, 1983). Systems development proceeds through the social interplay of multiple actors who attempt to interpret or 'make sense' of their and others' actions, largely through the medium of language (Boland, 1985). Attempts to construct 'theories' of ISD which account for its social nature are beginning to emerge (Boland and Day, 1982; Ciborra, 1985; Hirschheim et al., 1987; Kling and Scacchi, 1982; Lyytinen, 1986b; Markus, 1984). They are all, unfortunately, at an elementary stage of development. Further work must be done to see how well they (a) represent or explain systems development and (b) aid developers in their tasks of designing, building and implementing information systems. In this context, we propose to make sense of the social nature of ISD by relying on the use of symbolism, that is, the practice of representing ISD situations in terms of symbols. (Symbolism has a subtly different meaning for ISD participants and ISD researchers. For the former, symbolism connotes the expression of a set of attitudes and beliefs (including the creation of symbols themselves) in order to make sense of their ISD situations. For the latter, symbolism is an analytical approach for understanding the behaviours of ISD participants.) We feel such an approach permits a richer understanding of ISD, as we will proceed to show in the remainder of this chapter.

The value of a symbolic approach lies in its ability to interpret seemingly irrational events as symbols, which serve one or more actors' rational functions. Indeed, symbolism has been widely used in anthropology and sociology to help interpret the actions of social actors. It has more recently found its way into the organizational theory literature to explain the role and function of management (Feldman and March, 1981; Gowler and Legge, 1983; Kets de Vries and Miller, 1984; Morgan, 1986; Pondy et al., 1983; Trice and Beyer, 1984; Westerlund and Sjostrand, 1979); into the accounting literature to explain budgeting (Boland, 1985; Covaleski and Dirsmith, 1988) and other phenomena (Gambling, 1977); and even, to some degree, into the information systems literature (Boland, 1987; Lanzara, 1983; Robey and Markus, 1984). Here, we draw on the work of those who have applied the symbolic approach to other domains to provide a new way of conceiving of and thinking about ISD. In order to do so, we adopt a phenomenological position from which we see the world as a 'script.' The approach allows us to interpret the world - in this case, ISD - in terms of symbols. We define a symbol as an image used for, or regarded as, representing something else. Symbols give meaning to what is perceived; they act as the filter through which the script 'is read.' This is a hermeneutic exercise and has a rich historical tradition, particularly in theology, where the 'script' to be interpreted is the scriptures (see Gadamer, 1976b; Habermas, 1984).

The chapter proceeds as follows. In the next section we outline the notion of symbolism, which we use as the mechanism for interpreting systems development. We specifically focus on three key symbols: myth, metaphor and magic. We also look at their role in helping us understand ISD, and explore examples of these three symbols in the literature. The third section provides some empirical evidence from case studies of myth, metaphor and magic. These examples show how symbolism manifests itself in practice. In particular, we show evidence to lend further support to some of the examples from the literature discussed previously; for each of these three kinds of symbols, we also show evidence for examples not discussed. Then we discuss why a symbolic interpretation of ISD might lead to better systems development in the future, specifically in terms of the movement toward multi-perspective approaches in development methodologies. We conclude by pointing out the value of symbolism, particularly as a vehicle for actors to simplify their world, as well as the potential dangers of ignoring symbolism - inappropriate designs, conflict, and dysfunctional behaviours.

Symbolism and information systems development

Symbolism is not a new notion; anthropologists and other social scientists have recognized its importance for centuries. Philosophers such as Aristotle also recognized the value of symbolism, and were intrigued by the use of metaphors (Ortony, 1979). Whitehead (1927) may have captured the essence of symbolism best when he wrote: 'Symbolism is no mere idle fancy or corrupt degeneration: it is inherent in the very texture of human life' (quoted in Morgan, 1983, p.3).

More recently, organizational theorists have been concerned with the role of symbolism in organizations, and specifically, the relationship between symbolism and organizational culture (Frost et al., 1985; Pondy et al., 1983). Organizational culture is often perceived as the reason that organizations (and more specifically, organizational behaviour) are not generalizable (Van Maanen, 1985). And it is precisely here that symbolism is thought to be helpful. Staw (1985) for example argues that symbolism may have greater 'predictive power over more conventional observations of variables' (p.117). His example of an organizational argument, which on the surface may be interpreted as a hostile action, but symbolically is a form of supreme compliment because the combatant acknowledges the value of his opponent's argument by contesting it, suggests how symbolism provides a richer understanding of organizational behaviour. Of course there are those such as Alvesson (1984) who question whether symbolism is relevant in studying organizations, because they are not like the well-integrated units of nations or tribes where symbolism is most prevalent. But according to Turner (1986), such a view is misguided: symbolism is an important weapon in the arsenal of the organizational scientist.

Organizational researchers such as Wexler (1983), Smircich (1983b), Feldman (1989) and Dandridge (1983) see the value of symbolism in its fundamental ability to permit people to act. Astley (1984) writes:

> Symbols...do not just fulfil expressive, sense-making functions for managers...By fixating individual perception on common beliefs and values that de-emphasize differences between organizational participants they bridge across idiosyncratic cognitions to produce a basis for coherence that justifies and facilitates the mobilization of collective action. In this respect, theories, worldviews, goals, visions, expectations, plans, myths, stories, rituals and terminology affect practice not directly, but indirectly, through ideologies which fuse organizations into a unitary body and thereby lubricate the process of change (p.270).

Mitroff (1983) echoes this thought when he states that symbolic meaning 'provides the emotional comfort that is needed in coping with a precarious and often terrifying world' (p.388).

Thus, symbols play a critical role in organizational life. They are an important means for simplifying and understanding a complex world. They help reduce uncertainty, facilitate interaction and communication, clarify relationships, and generally, make people feel more comfortable with their surroundings. Managers use symbolism all the time; it helps them to interpret the significance of their actions and the actions of others.

According to Dandridge (1983), symbols - particularly ceremonies - are concerned with social maintenance; they offer actors the opportunity to practise organizationally useful behaviour in the arena of the social community. Eoyang (1983) sees the value of symbolism in its ability to facilitate the communication of meanings between individuals. Symbols are a powerful vehicle for conveying deep-rooted meanings. They are critical for organizational sense-making. Indeed, if symbols are stripped away from the societies in which they are embedded, 'all sorts of psychological and social confusion occurs. When the 'life supporting illusions are destroyed, communities go to pieces' (Bowles, 1989, p.410).

Traditionally, symbols evoke a negative connotation - that myths, for example, are opposed to reality, that they are antithetical to fact - but they need not. As Boland and Hoffman's (1983) analysis of symbols in a machine shop has shown, symbols do have a positive value. The specific symbol they analysed, humour, was shown to convey important patterns of meanings which helped the workers to frame and control their jobs while allowing them to reaffirm their identities within the work group. Similarly, Smircich (1983b), in her case study of an insurance company, showed how symbols such as rituals provided a common ground for organized action. It must be noted, however, that such positive interpretations of symbols are in the minority. In an analysis of the management literature, Ingersoll and Adams (1986) report that symbolism is treated as a negative phenomenon in 80 out of the 85 papers they looked at. So while symbolism can be seen in a positive light, in the management literature it traditionally is not.

Morgan (1983) defines a symbol as a sign which 'denotes something greater than itself' (p.4). The key feature of symbols is that they are 'created subjectively and are invested with a particular kind of subjective meaning' (p.4). They are a means of expressing and sustaining valued patterns of beliefs. According to Morgan (1983), symbolism is the practice of symbolic representation. In this chapter, we define symbolism as the practice of representing ISD situations in terms of symbols. It is the expression of a set of attitudes and beliefs. Here, we view our role as one of documenting the behaviour of ISD participants who are trying to make sense of their ISD situations, and classifying the symbols they use for sense making. We classify these into three types: myths, metaphors and magic. There is no set of universally accepted categories of symbols in organizations. The 'myth, metaphor, and magic' triad accounts for most of the phenomena we observed in our case studies. Also, many of the notions in the literature can be accommodated. For example, ceremonies or rituals can often be seen as 'magic.' We do not enter into the debate on the construction and propagation of symbols - how people learn to use symbols, how they are formed, how they are communicated and perpetuated (Tinker, 1986). Neither do we consciously attempt to privilege some symbols over others. It is clear that the researcher and the research process are themselves influenced by a symbolic interpretation of the world. We are in a real sense 'trapped' in our mental models which form an 'iron cage' around us, permitting us to observe certain artifacts while denying us access to others.

Symbolism is, of course, largely unobservable directly. It is by observing the behaviours of systems designers that we infer the attitudes and beliefs they hold. The process of attitude and belief formation (socialization processes, word-of-mouth anecdotes, training, etc.) is highly important and has received some consideration in the IS literature (Dagwell and Weber, 1983; Hedberg and

Mumford, 1975; Kumar and Welke, 1984; Mumford, 1972; Vitalari and Dickson, 1983). For the purpose of this chapter, however, we will consider only the actual behaviours themselves when observing the people involved in ISD. The evidence for the behaviours comes from case studies which are described below. The relationship between behaviours and symbolism is complex, involving an understanding of attitude/belief formation in communities, and the adoption of those beliefs/attitudes by individuals. Symbolism first and foremost revolves around shared meanings: patterns of beliefs, rituals and myths, which evolve through time and function as social glue, binding communities together (Smircich, 1983b). By observing the behaviours of subjects, and by a careful interpretation of the records of their behaviours gathered through the case studies, we believe it is possible to infer features of the subjects' attitudes and beliefs (that is, the symbols they use). Consequently, we believe that the filters or symbols used by the subjects to 'read' the world can be explicated.

Here we concentrate on interpreting ISD in terms of three key symbols: myths, metaphors, and magic. These symbols are usually inextricably linked during the processes of ISD, but we shall try to deal with them individually.

Myth

Myth can be defined as 'a dramatic narrative of imagined events, usually used to explain origins or transformations of something. Also, an unquestioned belief about the practical benefits of certain techniques and behaviours that is not supported by demonstrated facts' (Trice and Beyer, 1984, p.655).

Myths are important for a number of reasons. According to Bolman and Deal (1984) they provide explanations, reconcile contradictions, and help resolve dilemmas. Myths can serve a number of functions: (1) myths explain, (2) myths express, (3) myths maintain solidarity and cohesion, (4) myths legitimize, (5) myths communicate unconscious wishes and conflicts, (6) myths mediate contradictions, and (7) myths provide narrative to anchor the present to the past (Cohen, 1969). But myths are also ambiguous. According to Bolman and Deal (1984) they can distort our images and misdirect attention, but 'despite their negative traits myths are necessary to create meaning, solidarity and certainty - myths keep us sane.' Myths transcend ordinary rules and logic. Pondy, Frost et al. (1983) state 'anomaly and contradictions can be resolved with mythical explanations' (p.163).

Myths tend to be communicated to insiders and outsiders via the medium of the story. 'A good story provides a pleasant way of responding to unpleasant facts, they help to address problems of morale, security and legitimacy' (Bolman and Deal, 1984, p.158).

Bowles (1989) sees myth as an important tool in the analysis of organizational practices. We have identified six myths that systems developers use as guides to design, the first five of which have been investigated by Newman (1989). They will be explored below in turn, using evidence from the literature, and later using empirical evidence produced by Newman (1989) to show the dangers of following them slavishly.

1. User involvement is beneficial and should be encouraged

This myth stems from the widely-held belief that users should be encouraged to participate in designing systems which will affect them personally. Manifestation of this myth may vary from the traditional rationality where the designer extracts facts from the users and prepares the design independently, to an alternative rationality in which the user heads the design team and involvement is continual. However, regardless of the approach, the designer may still interpret involvement very narrowly, not allowing users to radically challenge the proposed design.

That user involvement is beneficial is a widely-held belief, and almost every analyst will advocate its practice in ISD. Its benefits are extensively discussed in the literature (for example, Bjørn-Andersen and Hedberg, 1978; Mumford, 1983). For example, in order to obtain user requirements for the new system, the key users must be involved. User involvement is also supposed to defuse resistance. Furthermore, it is promoted because users should have the right to influence the system they are going to use. Building and allowing users to experiment with mock-up systems to test out designs (prototyping) is the latest variation of this issue. While user involvement can be beneficial, a number of writers suggest that its practice may raise more problems than it solves (see Ives and Olson, 1984; Keen et al., 1982; Opperman, 1986; Robey and Markus, 1984). For example, user involvement can be subject to manipulation by the designer, making it more of a weapon than an aid; furthermore, it can easily precipitate conflict among the user groups.

2. Resistance to systems development is dysfunctional and should be eradicated ·

This myth starts with the belief that resistance to ISD is almost inevitable in large-scale systems development. Markus (1983) studied a divisionalized organization where the corporate accountants attempted to wrest control over financial information from their divisional counterparts. When the divisional accountants realized what was happening, they resisted any further erosion of their control. The new system was centralized, a design that was contrary to the decentralized structure in the organization. In other words the system and the organization did not, and indeed could not, fit together. As Markus concludes:

> The analyst should recognize that the goal of the exercise is not to 'overcome' resistance, but to avoid it, if possible, and to confront it constructively if not. In some cases, this indicates that the implementer may have to lose the battle and sacrifice a pet system project in order to win the war. Resistance is not a problem to be solved so a system can be installed as intended: it is a useful clue to what went wrong and how the situation can be righted (p.441).

3. Information systems should be integrated wherever possible

This myth is based on the belief that organizations are full of dysfunctions and that management information systems (MIS) can eliminate them by integrating functions from the different units. By doing so, managers can apply more rational approaches to management (Argyris, 1970b). This belief goes back to the time in the 1960's and early 1970's when the total systems concept was debated in the literature (for example, Dearden, 1966). The same utopianism now finds expression in applying technologies such as database management systems, and the concept of Information Resource Management (Synnott and Gruber, 1981).

The integration motive offers many advantages, but it is also a source of much conflict within organizations, as it undermines the existing commitments and power structures:

> MIS undercuts the existing 'rules of the game' as these are tied to the variety of weak or strong political systems in organizations which unify the various layers of management. Such a supposedly neutral act as one manager supplying data from his division to a common database...finds...that the data becomes the property of all units in the organization, increasing the potential of senior managers to control middle level managers directly (Newman and Rosenberg, 1985, p.403).

4. *The systems developer is generally the best person for making decisions about the system*

Despite the many failures and unfulfilled promises reported in the ISD literature, the zeal of many systems analysts remains surprisingly strong. The culture of systems staff inculcates a belief in its own mission to civilize organizations, producing a 'we know best' attitude (Franz and Robey, 1984; Rose, 1969). Armed with an arsenal of technical wonders, the analyst is often only too willing to make policy decisions when managers abdicate their responsibility:

> What tended to happen in the absence of definition was that the people responsible for systems analysis made policy decisions about the various controlling factors almost without being aware of doing so. There was therefore the danger of long-term decisions being made in terms of their appropriateness to systems design rather than in relation to more fundamental criteria. Thus real control tended to shift to the systems designers (Hedley, 1970).

The literature on ISD is replete with evidence about the differences between users and systems staff, and the misunderstanding these differences cause (Hedberg and Mumford, 1975; Hirschheim et al., 1987; Newman and Rosenberg, 1985; Rose, 1969). Rose, for example, contrasts the position and goals of the systems personnel with those of the users:

> Conflict is structured into their relationships...Resentment of the innovation is aggravated by resentment of the innovator, resentment of his rewards, his values, his manner, his vocabulary, his prestige as change-maker, his apparent freedom from 'normal company discipline,' his promotability, his dress, his fickle loyalty to the firm, and, not least, his youth (Rose, 1969, pp.169-170).

This is echoed by the findings of Mumford (1972) who also found a wide gulf between the designers and the clerical staff in attitude and behaviour: 'They [the systems designers] don't give us much information. They don't tell us what is going to happen. It just happens and we are told about it'...'They just give you a book to read. There is little explanation of the new things that are happening.'... 'The user cannot resist, he can only be reluctant.'

The belief or myth of 'we know best,' while more muted than in the late 60's and 70's, still, we believe, remains a powerful force which shapes ISD.

5.   Politics should not be the concern of the system developer
This commonly-believed myth is also related to the view that introducing well-designed systems can eliminate organizational dysfunctions. Many designers often view politics as part of the problem of organizations, as if it were an irrational aberration which needs to be eliminated or curtailed. While designers can to a large extent insulate themselves from politics when developing small systems in single departments, no such protection is available when major systems which cross-organizational boundaries are introduced. If designers disdain politics or see their role as separate from it, they will never be able to play an effective part in the negotiation process vital to introducing such systems. In these circumstances, ISD and politics are inextricably entwined.

For her case study, Markus (1983) specifically acknowledged the role of power and politics in the design of the Financial Information System (FIS). Her view is that the FIS was a deliberate strategy of the corporate accountants to wrest more control from the divisional accountants:

> The way in which FIS was designed implied a major gain of power for corporate accountants relative to their prior position vis-à-vis the divisional accountants. Prior to FIS, divisional accountants summarized raw data on the transactions in their divisions and sent the summaries to the corporate accountants for consolidations...After FIS, however, all financial transactions were collected into a single database under the control of corporate accountants (p.438).

Whereas the users in these cases seemed only too aware of the political society in organizations, it was rationality that was constantly stressed by the systems analysts. Mumford (1972) contrasts the approach of systems staff in designing the technical features with the non-technical, human element:

> Human relations and the ability to manage the human part of change are skill areas which are dealt with intuitively and unsystematically and this is in striking contrast to the technical side of computer systems where the programmers and systems analysts continually stress the need for a logical approach.

6.   The key to successful design is the use of a top-down approach
A sixth myth not often heralded in the literature anymore but nonetheless visible is the belief in the 'top-down approach.' To some systems staff, the top-down approach to systems development offers a mythical quality to the design of systems. This has a history dating back to the 1960's, when the 'Total Systems'

approach was extensively debated in the literature (see Dearden, 1966; Young, 1968). While the 'total systems' approach has fallen into disrepute because of its failure to produce workable systems, many systems people still cling to the top-down approach as a kind of touchstone or ideal form.

There are other well-known (and not so well-known) myths which can be found in the IS literature; for example, 'the mythical man-month' (Brooks, 1975), 'the total systems concept' (Dearden, 1966), the 'seven mortal sins of systems work' (Lyytinen and Lehtinen, 1987), the myth of the 'true and complete specification of requirements' (McMenamin and Palmer, 1984), the myth that structured analysis mitigates the disruption of organizational politics because it 'makes analysis procedures more formal' (DeMarco, 1978), the myth that 'system integration is a virtue' (Kraemer and King, 1979), the myth that software accounts for the major (and growing) proportion of an organization's IS budget (Ein-Dor, 1988), and the myth that we can find a process that allows software to be designed in a perfectly rational way (Pamas and Clements, 1989).

Metaphor

Metaphors are commonly-used vehicles for understanding. The use of metaphor is 'a way of thinking and a way of seeing that pervade how we understand our world generally' (Morgan, 1986, p.12). A metaphor is essentially a way of understanding and experiencing one kind of thing in terms of another. According to Lakoff and Johnson (1980):

> Metaphor is pervasive in everyday life, not just ordinary language but in thought and action. Our ordinary conceptual system, in terms of which we both think and act, is fundamentally metaphorical in nature...The way we think, what we experience, and what we do every day is very much a matter of metaphor (p.3).

Morgan (1980) concurs. He states:

> Metaphors are not to be seen as representations of a reality 'out there,' but as tools for capturing and dealing with what is perceived to be 'out there'...The process of metaphorical conception is a basic mode of symbolism, central to the way in which humans forge their experience and knowledge of the world they live in...More fundamentally it is a creative form which produces its effect through a crossing of images (p.610).

According to Pondy, metaphors have a dual-purpose - that of facilitating change while maintaining stability: 'In organizing, the use of metaphor simultaneously facilitates change and reinforces traditional values...metaphor can fulfil the dual function of enabling change and preserving continuity' (Pondy et al., 1983, p.164).

However, although metaphors are pervasive and sometimes helpful, they can also mislead. Boland (1987) identifies five metaphors which he feels guide systems development, but which are really dangerous fantasies 'and not suited for guiding serious thought' (p.367). They reify the human actor in ISD, and inevitably lead to dysfunctional consequences.

1. Information is structured data

This most basic metaphor sees information as an object or entity. This metaphor is embraced in order to get around the hermeneutic problem of interpreting information. Instead of being concerned with the meaning of information to a free, intentional human actor, this metaphor treats information as some publicly observable, immutable object. The metaphor imposes a stereotypical, rationalistic version of meaning, values, and significance on the actors (Boland, 1979).

2. Organization is information

This metaphor permits an image of organizational control as the differential distribution of information and decision parameters. Organizations can be guided and controlled by the manipulation of structured data. This metaphor emphasizes a highly 'rationalistic way of characterizing organizational life as goal-driven and purposive which further legitimates ignoring the individual actor's need to interpret and make sense of organizational situations' (Boland, 1987, p.369).

3. Information is power

This metaphor creates the image that information is power, in that it permits control over an individual. Power is conceived of as a one-way relationship. This metaphor transforms information and power into entities which are manipulated. The role of the human actor is further removed. The metaphor inflates the role of system developer to that of one who, through system design, creates and reallocates power. Yet it neglects the duality of power relationships. As Boland (1987) notes, power follows from the dialogue of organizational actors who attempt to interpret and understand their organizational world.

4. Information is intelligence

This metaphor links information to human intelligence. Information is seen as that which allows us to move through a problem space, and it is seen as equal to intelligence. Here, intelligence is reified; it is transformed into an object which is contained and localized in a computer. Boland (1987) suggests that the 'result is the complete removal of human beings and their problems of action and sense making from the domain of information systems discourse' (p.370).

5. Information is perfectible

This last metaphor is the culmination of the other four. Here, information is fantasized as capable of being perfect and 'true.' Systems can be developed to supply the decision maker with 'perfect information.' This metaphor removes the concrete historical moment of the situation from consideration, and discusses systems design in terms of a timeless, context-free, ideal future. But for this to be possible, we need 'complete and error-free knowledge.' This is something which Boland (1987) argues is impossible. Citing the examples of John Kennedy's assassination and the oil crisis of 1973, he contends that situations 'will always be open to interpretation and reinterpretation....The world has no single, immutable meaning, which the possibility of perfect information requires' (Boland, 1987, p.375).

Hirschheim (1986) uses the notion of metaphor to describe the relationship between technology and its users (man). (In the context of ISD, technology can be interpreted as an information system.) Hirschheim uses two dual metaphors to discuss optimistic and pessimistic scenarios for the man-technology relationship.

1.   Technology as tool and man as craftsman
In an optimistic scenario, the metaphors 'technology as a tool' and 'man as craftsman' are used. Technology is thought to be a tool in the hands of the workers. It is used when and where appropriate, to make their work more efficient and to raise the quality of life in general. The tool is of itself neutral, and can be used in many ways. Man is looked upon as a craftsman who scans his surroundings, choosing the most appropriate tools for the task at hand. The craftsman is skilled and can apply the tools to advantage. Should the tools be unsatisfactory, the craftsman can modify them or choose not to use them. Through time, the tasks that the craftsman performs are likely to become more sophisticated; he then comes to rely on new and better tools for help. The development of new tools often drives the development of new skills and crafts. The relationship between craftsman and tool is that of master and slave.

2.   Technology as governor and man as machine
In a pessimistic scenario, the metaphors 'technology as governor, man as machine' are used. Here, technology is used to govern or control the operation of some task(s). For the governor to work properly, the tasks have to be highly structured so that all possible variances can be responded to. The governor is applied to a machine which performs activities in a structured and routinized way. Machines are built (trained) to engage in certain tasks and are provided with the appropriate raw materials. When machines wear out, they are discarded and usually replaced by more modern and better ones. Machines are capable of only action, not thought. They cannot suggest improvements in the types of activities to be performed or how they are carried out. They are under the control of the governor which regulates what they can and cannot do. The governor is not neutral, in that those who are ultimately in control set it. The relationship between machine and governor is also master-slave, except that in this case it is technology which is the master while man is relegated to the slave.

The battle metaphor
The military metaphor of 'battle' is particularly powerful, and is frequently evoked by both users and developers in systems development. Keen (1981), for example, portrayed systems implementation in terms of battles played out between users and developers. Each would adopt particular offensive and defensive strategies to overcome the other party. This was predicted by Lakoff and Johnson (1980) who noted the pervasiveness of this metaphor in everyday life. They showed the importance of 'battle' in a wide variety of interactions between both individuals and groups. Raspa (1984) calls this 'a stunning

metaphor for evoking an atmosphere where one's survival is constantly at stake' (p.10).

Other examples of metaphors can be found in the IS literature: for example, 'information systems as competitive weapons' (Ives and Learmonth, 1984; Parsons, 1983; Wiseman, 1985), and 'information systems development as engineering' (Buckingham and Land, 1987; Land, 1989). See also Madsen (1989) who used the metaphors 'warehouse,' 'store,' and 'meeting place' to describe a library for which a system was being developed. As will be seen, our case study data provides further support for the 'man as machine' metaphor, as well as for one additional metaphor, namely 'organizations as fiefdoms.'

Magic

Magic has played, and continues to play, an important organizational function. Like rituals, it binds people together; it is a mechanism for group solidarity. Earl (1983) defines magic as 'the superstitious or religious, as opposed to the scientific method used to control nature for a definite practical end, particularly to aid the functioning, binding, and survival of a society' (p.128).

Of course scientism, a belief in the infallibility of the scientific method to reveal knowledge, is itself a form of magic. Cleverly (1971) defines magic as 'Beliefs that cannot be destroyed by the presentation of contrary evidence, and the practices whose continuance is independent of their efficacy' (p.9).

Although magic may be 'unscientific' and 'irrational,' Cleverly (1971) makes the following point:

> I am not advocating any attempt to root out all magical and religious behaviour from management. To do so would be to disorient the entire [management] culture and invite disaster. Moreover, it would be impossible...To disturb that would be dangerous. To understand it is essential. For if we wish to understand the people we deal with, to influence them and control them - to manage them - the worst mistake we can make is to assume that the manager, even in the twentieth century, is a rational being (p.12).

However, because management is expected to be objective and rational, these myths and rituals become taboo - they cannot be discussed openly (Cleverly, 1971 p.150).

Cleverly (1971), in describing magic in more detail, identifies two dimensions associated with human behaviour; both are dichotomous. The first dimension reflects the purpose of human behaviour - the 'ends.' Behaviour is either 'instrumental' in that it is directed at controlling or influencing the environment, including other actors; or it is 'expressive' in that it is directed at the releasing of inner conflict or emotion. The second dimension reflects the nature of how beliefs are held. Cleverly distinguishes between the 'sceptics' and the 'believers.' The former do not believe in, or adopt, any theories or practices unless they can see them working and producing positive (and better) results. For the sceptic, truth is a transient phenomenon. 'Believers', on the other hand, are those who have steady faith in what they believe in. They stick firmly to their beliefs even when confronted with disconfirmatory evidence, often to the extent of denying their own sense perceptions because truth is construed as eternal and unquestionable.

In this chapter, we distinguish magic from myth. Whereas the image created by myth has some basis and anchor in our collective experience ('reality'), the image created by magic, while appearing to be 'real,' is but a facade (like a hologram). Magic manifests itself in ISD in many areas.

1. The systems developer as high priest

The image of the systems developer is not uncommonly portrayed as that of the 'high priest of technology,' the individual (or group of individuals) who can harness the power of computer technology to the benefit of the organization. The developer in such a role uses a variety of rituals and ceremonies which add to the imagery of the 'high priest.' Good examples of these rituals are the 'structured walkthrough,' the 'sign-off,' and the 'system test' (DeMarco, 1978; Gane and Sarson, 1979; Yourdon, 1982). Such rituals are important to the perpetuation of the image. Rituals are also equally important to the developer as part of the IS profession, as they provide order and structure to what, without them, may appear random; moreover, they are a key ingredient in the expression of professional solidarity (Trice and Beyer, 1984).

As the high priest of technology, the developer possesses the apparent magical quality of making the computer productive, transforming a highly unintelligible piece of technology (to the layperson) into a key organizational tool. The magic is further enhanced by the separation of the high priest from the laity (the users). This separation involves a disparity in both knowledge and authority. Because of this disparity, the laity perceives the priests to possess magical qualities. They also therefore look to the priests for guidance and leadership (Boguslaw, 1965; Mowshowitz, 1976).

2. Expert systems as the embodiment of the human expert

Expert systems have been portrayed as vehicles for substituting a computer for a human expert; they can reproduce the knowledge possessed by experts or professionals. For example, one of the stated reasons for building medical expert systems is to provide advice to lower level medical staff where the use of full time physicians would be impractical (as might be the case in submarines - Rogers et al., 1979). Expert systems have been shown to work well in domains which are well structured and where the knowledge base is reasonably clear (Barnett, 1982; Blois, 1980; Hayes-Roth et al., 1983; Jackson, 1986; Leonard-Barton and Sviokla, 1988). While computer professionals generally recognize the limitations of expert systems, to the layperson they give the impression of intelligent behaviour. This 'intelligence' has a particular magical quality about it because an inanimate object possesses it. (Stevenson 1987 provides an excellent case of how expert systems in the U.K. financial services sector have taken on such a magical quality.) The system to mimic a therapeutic encounter between a patient and a psychotherapist developed by Weizenbaum (1966) called ELIZA was plausible enough to suggest intelligent behaviour to several lay subjects.

Although the system was not originally developed as an expert system (it predated the advent of expert systems by almost a decade), it was viewed by the subjects as embodying a human expert. The magical quality of a computer program (the expert system) mimicking a human expert such that it is perceived as possessing human characteristics is viewed with disquiet by a number of commentators (Dreyfus, 1972; Mumford, 1987; Weizenbaum, 1966).

Other examples of magic within the context of information systems can be found in Stamper's (1985) notion of 'information as mystical fluid,' Scarrott's (1985) contention that 'information is the life blood of organizations,' Shallis' (1984) image of the 'computer as idol,' Brooks' (1987) contention of 'no silver bullet' for software development, and Hoare's (1984) classic concern 'programming as sorcery or science.'

Evidence of symbolism in information systems development

In order to illustrate symbolism in ISD, we present a series of excerpts from six case studies conducted over the last decade (Newman, 1989). Here, no attempt is made to demonstrate all aspects of symbolism in ISD. But through an interpretation of the records from the case study interviews, we see numerous instances of myth, metaphor and magic indicating the richness of using symbolism for understanding ISD.

These cases involved private and public organizations, some of which were commercial and some non-profit. The sites included banking, insurance, financial services, utilities, and universities and were drawn from the U.S., Canada and the U.K. The organizations were chosen on the basis of the following criteria:

1. The organization was introducing (or had recently introduced) a major information system which crossed traditional organizational boundaries. The scale of the project would thereby ensure that if ISD issues are important they will be highlighted in such projects.
2. Sufficiently high-level access could be obtained to enable the researchers to observe and interview subjects in several locations or departments.

Once access had been negotiated, the researchers attempted to identify key subjects at different levels in the development process, including systems staff, user personnel, user managers, and non-user decision-makers. This enabled the researchers to obtain multiple perspectives of the same process. As research progressed, existing personnel suggested further subjects. A non-directive interviewing technique was used, as this allowed the respondents to express their own views in their own words rather than force their experience into predetermined categories. However, the interviews focused on certain topics which are important in the literature (user involvement, top management support, power, politics, etc.). Subjects were also encouraged to illustrate the development process through critical incidents, episodes which subjects believed were crucial to the success (or failure) of the system. The interviews were tape-recorded, and verbatim transcripts were produced from the recordings. The evidence here is presented mainly from four of the most representative cases. (A detailed description of the cases and the research methodology is contained in Hirschheim and Klein, 1989.)

Evidence of myth in information systems development
The six myths noted previously, where we provided evidence from the literature, are now revisited using extracts from the case studies.

1.   User involvement is beneficial and is to be encouraged
While there is an apparent, strong belief that user involvement can bring benefits, we present some evidence which suggests that its practice may raise as many problems as it solves. Not only can it be subject to manipulation by analysts or designers, making it more of a weapon than an aid, but it can also precipitate conflict among the user groups which must then be carefully dealt with. Both these phenomena were illustrated in the case studies.

Manipulation
In the course of involving users in design, some analysts cannot resist the temptation to manipulate. Here an analyst at a wholesale company candidly describes his approach to user involvement with one user in particular. Firstly, he acknowledges the user's importance:

> Analyst: The best designed system in the world will bomb completely if they don't want it and even with these 'little people', and that is not meant derogatively...Oh yes, I had one person, one female, who had been with the company 10 years at that time, and she was the top person. Boy did she resist! Took a long time to win her over...I kept asking her advice...I had already figured it out but I wanted her to do it...You have to work on these people, butter them up...You are actually sometimes designing it yourself but let them think they did it.

This extract shows how such a commonly advocated technique like user involvement can easily dissolve into manipulation. Although he believes the users to be a homogeneous group ('little people') he skillfully identifies one of the employees as key to ISD success. He then manipulates the relationship to achieve what is a preconceived design ('butter them up...let them think they did it').

Conflict generated by user involvement
One of the unintended consequences of user involvement is the conflict it sometimes generates or precipitates (Robey et al., 1989). Forcing hostile people to cooperate in designing an information system can reveal conflicts which have lain dormant for years. In the case of a large state university which was trying to implement an on-line, university-wide admissions system, the process of user involvement brought sharply into focus some of the differences between departments. These departments had, up to that point, acted in a largely independent fashion and had each developed unique procedures for dealing with admissions. Over two decades, these loosely-coupled departments (Weick, 1976)

had developed their own batch processing systems. They were now being requested to cooperate in a corporate, uniform design which would bring many benefits to the university if only a few to the departments. There were many examples of where the new system required that the users across several departments sit down with each other and debate policy issues. This was often a painful experience for the participants because it forced the department administrators to make explicit their policies on admissions. These often-vague procedures, which had co-existed comfortably for many years, were largely irreconcilable. For example, the issue of students' addresses forced the different units to sit down with each other and define a student's address. There turned out to be 13 possible unique addresses a student could use. However, the issue that precipitated the most conflict was who should have the authority to change addresses. In the following extract one of the directors of admissions describes the process vividly:

> Director: If you want to see a fight or you want to ask a question that will give you an example of the tenderness, ask 'Who can change somebody's address?' I have never seen so much argument over addresses...There have been knock-down graveyard fights over who can change an address.

Clearly, from the users' viewpoint the issue over addresses (and this was only one of several issues raised) had generated considerable friction among the user groups. This is indicated by the terms reported - 'fight,' 'tenderness,' 'argument,' 'knockdown,' and 'anger.' The new system was acting as a catalyst for this conflict.

> User Liaison: It is forcing them to interact with each other in ways they have never thought about before, and that has been fraught with frustrations up to this point, and I suspect that we'll have much more frustration as time goes on. And whether or not it will even wind up being worth it is not clear.

User involvement may bring many benefits but, as can be seen from the examples presented, it can also be accompanied by significant 'costs.' Much of the conflict generated may be unavoidable, especially if an organization seeks to impose a corporate approach to information processing. Nonetheless, the consequent resistance and entrenchment need to be managed by the project leader before it proliferates.

2.   Resistance to ISD is dysfunctional and should be eradicated

The strength of the myth that resistance to ISD is dysfunctional was apparent in several of the case study records. We have already noted that the response of the analyst at the wholesale company to user resistance was to manipulate the relationship, giving the impression that he was involving the user. Although resistance to ISD may be inevitable in any medium to large-scale project, the methods of dealing with it vary. In certain instances, resistance is active and takes place during development. We term this type 'preventive' resistance. In other situations, resistance occurs after implementation of the system. This we call 'post facto' resistance. Both are described below.

Preventive resistance

As an example of preventive resistance, at the state university the admissions staff was increasingly frustrating the project leader. The users were being asked to accept a multi-screen design which was to be general enough to be used by all admissions units. This meant that for each student processed, admissions would need to flip between eight to 10 screens. Moreover, each screen change was taking around 60 seconds. This was unacceptable to the users who knew operationally that they would be in severe difficulties if the design went ahead:

> Technical Coordinator. We rebelled against that. The reaction of the systems people was 'Oh, it's going to go like this. It's going to go really quickly once you get used to it, but you are just nervous about it'...The screen change was so slow. We would sit for over 60 seconds and wait for the screen to change, and we were hysterical. We were hysterical because all you had to do was...multiply this by eight screens by 2000 applications and we would be dead in the water.

When this elementary attempt at consensus building failed (as quoted above by the user), the project leader moved quickly to more coercive techniques:

> Project Leader...In Undergraduate Admissions, one of the people there said 'We don't really want it. We've talked it over and we don't really want this new system...We resist the change. We don't want to spend the time working at this pace with you. We don't want to give.' And basically the computer centre says 'Well, look, you have no choice.' I guess this is not the computer centre. I guess maybe the mandate comes from higher level: 'The old system will be turned off and Thruway will be here to stay and you're not going to have that choice.'

Although the users resist, they are delivered an ultimatum by the computer centre ('you have no choice' and 'the system will be turned off'). When breakdowns in communications such as this occur between systems and user personnel, it is a small step to use raw power to 'clear the path' (Keen, 1981; Markus, 1983; Newman and Rosenberg, 1985).

In this case, the issue over screen design did not turn out as the project leader had hoped. It was clear that neither systems nor admissions could resolve this issue at the ground level. Neither the project leader nor the technical coordinator had the authority to insist on their way. So the problem was pushed up to the admissions director who issued an ultimatum. The users got their single customized screen (although it was not on-line). Once the reasons for confrontation were resolved, the possibility of genuine cooperation emerged. However, the result could have been quite different if the systems staff had coerced the users and forced them to proceed with the original multi-screen design. If the system had gone ahead, the 'victory' for systems would have been short-lived. Admissions' staff, with their 'private,' inside knowledge knew the system was not operationally feasible. Although they could have entered each applicant's details into the system, the volume of applications and the time to process each one (30 minutes) would have overwhelmed them. This was obvious to the users but not to the systems staff, who failed to grasp the magnitude of admission's task - hence the users' resistant stance. If the design had gone ahead as originally proposed (that is, unworkable), the subsequent problems could have easily brought the whole project to a messy end.

Post facto resistance

In other cases, the resistance may be far more muted and may occur after the system is implemented, and thus not be addressed at all by the technicians. For one medium-sized insurance company, the computerization of personal lines insurance had been largely successful. When it came time for the commercial underwriters to begin using their system, the result was far less successful with many underwriters either ignoring the system or using it minimally for documentation.

> Underwriter: A lot of things were getting jammed and that's where some of the unresolved frictions emerged. And now you are not only being controlled by the home office...you've got administration controlling you, because they are shipping out the policies for you without you requesting them. We used to try every chance we could not to put it on the computer. We would say, 'sorry, this can't go on the computer'.

The underwriting system was cumbersome and awkward to operate. Because the underwriters felt unable to change the system they simply stopped using it. Although the resistance in this case was passive, it was nonetheless a sign of problems with the system.

It is our belief, therefore, that users' resistance is not always a behaviour that must be eradicated, as is often supposed in the management literature, and observed in the university case cited above. Moreover, even where the resistance arises after the system is implemented as in the insurance underwriting case, the developer needs to be aware of passive (post facto) resistance. In these cases, as Markus (1983) also noted, the signs of resistance signal the designer that further investigation is warranted.

In conclusion, the analyst on a project can choose to focus on techniques and technologies to overcome resistance, as if resistance were behaviour to be suppressed or eradicated. On the other hand, the analyst can try to understand the reasons for the resistance and treat such signals as signs of the organizational stresses induced by the system changes. Indeed, the signs of resistance might show that the proposed system would be unworkable if pursued, as in the university example.

3. Information systems should be integrated wherever possible

The integrative motive among systems designers forms a strong influence in ISD. Like many of the myths of design, it offers enormous potential in rationalizing organizations, but the delivered product can fall well short of the ideal. In the university, each of the admissions units had developed their own independent systems. These were batch-processing systems where admissions data is accumulated over a pre-defined period (day, week, etc.). The processes would vary from one unit to another because each had developed its own system to meet its own needs.

The drawbacks of such systems are well documented (for example, Everest, 1974). Apart from poor timeliness, the information produced by different systems would inevitably be incompatible, making it extremely difficult to compare admissions data between units as would be required in a corporate approach to admissions and recruiting. In contrast, the new system would be on-line and integrated with the rest of the student information system: as admissions data are entered into the database, the files would be instantaneously updated. Access to the database would, therefore, provide the latest information on students and, because data would be stored in a standard format, reports could be readily extracted. The project leader here compares the two approaches:

> Project Leader: You want to get an integrated system, so that all of the systems have one database, a biographical database, and have an integrated system for financial aid, billing, Thruway (admissions) and eventually student records. We do not have that. That will never happen on their old way. Right now they're able to process their applicants fine. But if it's in the best interests of the university to have an integrated system, that won't work, not with their old batch systems, isolated systems.

The admissions function at this university was previously a collection of independent data entry and processing systems (undergraduate, graduate, law, etc.). The new design was a corporate approach to admissions, a radical change from the status quo. But in order for the corporate approach to work, the different groups had to cooperate. Users, on the other hand, did not generally have an integrated view of systems and organizations. They largely viewed systems bottom-up and did not appreciate the corporate advantages continually stressed by the project leader.

Similarly, in the insurance company, the 18 branch offices had been run largely autonomously. The type of business each office wrote was a matter for them to determine. Under the manual system, the commercial underwriters enjoyed a considerable flexibility in work procedures. Documentation, a key task in underwriting, was a good example. When an underwriting decision is made, it is not always possible to document the process because of the pressures of other work:

> Underwriter: If you have an account that you know you've not done proper or you haven't had time to fully document though you know your decision is good, they hide those.
> Interviewer: So there are ways of hiding the problems.
> Underwriter: I wouldn't even call it a lot of times the problems. It was just if you were working on a couple of large accounts at once and your underwriters really

didn't have time to do a terrific job actually hand-documenting the decisions say that you and he or you and she came up with, you put that off and do it later, just to keep the paper moving.

When the head office auditors came to verify that procedures were correctly followed, the underwriting staff could offer up accounts, together with any explanations in an accompanying report as a way of 'embellishing' them. With the new system, head office had control of the underwriting database. Instead of offering up accounts for auditing purposes, the head office auditors could select the ones they wanted with no chance for the underwriter to offer written or verbal explanations:

Underwriter: Now what was happening was that they were pulling this stuff up on the computer with no explanation.

Interviewer: No way of you interpreting.

Underwriter: And calling down, 'What the hell is going on here? I see your increase. You just had a production of 20%. You know we've kind of asked you to stay at 15.' Whereas having been able to write a report, you could say, 'Well, gee. One account just went on the books from the last quarter,' and such and such...And it always seemed to work well. But now we were being put in a defensive position instead of offensive in that way. The other thing they used to do a lot was they'd come down and audit...The manager used to send them a list of our larger accounts or whatever mix they wanted. Now they just pulled it off the computer.

It was clear that the new system, designed as a centralized strategy to underwriting, did not 'fit' the organization's decentralized structure. Using a head office database afforded a degree of integration of procedures unknown before in the company. However, the system, as we have already seen, was rejected by some of the underwriters who refused to use it or used it only minimally.

In summary, organizations may desire the advantages that greater integration apparently offers. However, this strategy needs to be weighed against the dysfunctional consequences of pursuing greater rationalization and integration. The cases cited above indicate that the solution can sometimes become the problem.

4. *The systems developer is generally the best person for making decisions about the system*

The myth of 'we know best' is particularly well illustrated in the gulf in attitude between systems personnel and users. Users at the university had misgivings about working with the systems people. In the following extract from an interview, the technical coordinator from admissions shows the depth of her feelings:

Interviewer. How did you react to people who were trying to get the specifications from you? What kind of relationship did you enjoy with the systems people?

Technical Coordinator. We were very defensive, because we felt they were trying to have us fit the system and we wanted to have the system fit us...We were convinced they weren't after our best interests and they were convinced we weren't after theirs. So that we were just against anything new. We had quite a time of it...We felt that they didn't have our best interests in mind, they had their best interests in mind. We literally didn't believe a word they said.

The analyst at the telephone company was an exceptional person by most standards and enjoyed excellent relationships with users. Nonetheless, he summarily dismissed any suggestion that human behaviour was complex: he held a very simple model of human behaviour.

Analyst: I have very little time for all this psychological stuff, as I call it. [A person] is a leader or a follower. To me there are two categories that make sense...That's the way everything has worked for two million years.

The project leader on the Materials Management System at the telephone company was even more dismissive than the systems analyst concerning the importance of users, some of whom were left uninformed about impending changes:

Project Leader...To me this... [is] just another tool. Using the tube is very simple. And this thing is just another tool.
Interviewer. Are they [the clerical staff] at the moment fully aware of what's going to happen and how the change is going to affect them?
Project Leader: No they're not.

The attitude of systems staff has been consistently cited as one of the causes of bad relations with users whose frequent response is to resist the system's development. In the case of the university, the differences were clearly seen in the interests of each group. The systems group was perceived to be only concerned with implementing the system as originally designed. In contrast, the users' interest was to get their task done. The result was poor communication and distrust ('We literally didn't believe a word they said').

5.   Politics should not be the concern of the systems developer
The myth that 'politics should not be the concern of the developer' had wide credence in our case examples. At the university, the central arguments of the users were about resources and what affects the proposed system was going to have on their domain. The project leader constantly stressed the corporate benefits of the new admissions system:

Project Leader. Right now they're able to process their applicants fine. But if it's in the best interests of the university to have an integrated system, that won't work, not with their old batch systems, isolated systems.

She seemed perplexed by the reactionary stance of the users, clinging to their 'old batch systems, isolated systems' like ancients clinging to their idols. An appeal to university goals seemed to fall on deaf ears. But from the users' perspective, this was entirely reasonable. Indeed the analyst herself acknowledged the effectiveness of their existing systems ('They're able to process their applicants fine'). In contrast, the director of undergraduate admissions demonstrated her political acumen in dealing with the systems group. She realized that the new system would require her staff to perform much more data entry work. In negotiating with the systems people, she was able to campaign effectively for additional staff:

> Director. I said to them, 'we'll try, but if we can't do this, we're going to batch it over.' And they say, 'Oh no, you can't. What's the point of an on-line system if you're going to batch the data?' This was after the Director had said to me that he didn't see why I would need additional staff people; that existing staff wouldn't have to code things now, they could just input directly. So I said, 'That's fine. We'll try that and we'll do our best, but if we can't handle the volume, then we'll be batching over.' So the next thing was that we'd be needing additional people to help.

Here the director of admissions, faced with a system which she considered to be unworkable, does not reject it out of hand ('We'll try that and we'll do our best'). Instead she offers what she knows to be an unacceptable solution to systems staff ('We're going to batch it over'). As we have noted in previous comments, this would have meant abandoning the on-line philosophy and a return to 1960's batch technology. The director's final comment is spoken as if she is reporting a remark by the systems staff. The additional staff which admissions would need for data entry would now be forthcoming.

For the insurance company, the politics were concerned not so much with conflict resolution but with conflict avoidance. The new system was an accepted fact, but nonetheless, the job of underwriting needed to have priority. The branch realized they were not strong enough to fight the systems group:

> Underwriter. And you became good at circumventing [the system]. Because it becomes a political ball game. You can't undermine what the computer department is trying to do, yet you know that you are in for short-term, long-term strategies - you've got to survive. And you can't really be subversive to their efforts, because it comes back to haunt you anyway, but you have to do what you have to do to get your work out. You can't complain. It's one of those things you do quietly. Everybody found different ways. Maybe they won't find out. Maybe they won't ever see it.

Even their manager was a party to circumventing the power of the computer department:

Underwriter. You know, it was one of those situations where you really could not bring it up in your department meeting that you were having these problems...I really think [her manager] must have known that we were not using it to its capabilities. I mean he had to have known. Politically, he could not come out in the meeting and say, 'Yeah, I support you'. I think he more or less let it go, and then if a problem arose he would deal with it. Again, all crisis management.

In the illustrations above, we see both the ineffectiveness of avoiding politics on the part of the systems developer and the willingness of the users to participate in the political process which they saw as a natural part of organizational life.

6. The key to successful design is the use of a top-down approach

To some systems staff, the top-down approach to systems development offers a mythical quality to the design of systems. In the telephone company, the project leader outlines the approach used for the materials management system, noting the normative nature of the top-down approach.

Project Leader. We're following a certain approach, a top-down approach, and what we've done is define all the logical functions of the system first so we haven't cluttered our minds up with how it's currently being done, or who is doing it, or where it necessarily is happening. That is, the approach we're taking is the totally top-down approach. That's how you have to design and work on management information systems.

Note how the ideal approach leads him to ignore the current organizational realities which 'cluttered our minds up.' But he notes the approach is not without its problems for the users.

Project Leader. Top-down is a troublesome approach for the users because the user is used to his function and so that means his view of looking at it is bottom-up really. Now when we look at it top-down, especially in the initial stages, he's busy saying 'that's a function but where does my thing fit into this?' He's trying to fit his bottom-up view into this top-down and it doesn't fit very well because he isn't going to get his bottom-up [view] until we get through the methods and procedures. While we're at the stage of designing the logical system, it's a very troublesome thing for him to relate to.

Nonetheless, the project leader returns to the 'advantages' of the approach for those who will use it even if reality (for example, conflict of interests) occasionally creeps in:

Project Leader. I think their concern is the current people that are here and if we're going to give a system that is going to give job enrichment to those people, its going to free them of the number crunching that they currently do, it will give them more tools to be effective in their jobs. And it's going to increase their productivity in a painless way. Why the hell should they be concerned, they should be happy, they should want to be part of this thing and endorse it. Naturally, things don't work out like that in reality. You get a conflict of interests, perverse things creeping in, little rules and regulations, glitches, and all the rest.

Like many projects which employed this approach, the project was never completed and cost the organization over $2 million. While it is rare to observe this myth in its pure form, it appears to be widely held among developers. And as this case shows, it will often manifest itself in a series of organizational contradictions.

Evidence of metaphor in information systems development

In the case studies, various ISD participants used a number of powerful metaphors. The following are three such metaphors, only one of which has not been discussed in our literature review.

1. Information systems development as a battle

As previously discussed, military metaphors are particularly common not only in everyday experience but also in systems development. For example, a senior systems analyst at the telephone company likened systems development to a battle between the analysts and the users. He found that in dealing with some resistant managers, the only way to handle them was to get rid of them. If this wasn't possible, he found it necessary to bring in the 'heavy artillery' of a higher authority:

> Systems Analyst. A prime requirement of this type of project is to have a very high level, naturally-respected [manager]...You have got to have a lot of weight to fling about unfortunately, in a lot of these cases, to try things out. You can't just force them on the users. Obviously it has got to be done with agreement, but at the same time, where you run into these problems, you have got to be able to rely on somebody to clear the path.

Note how the concept 'clear the path' can be interpreted in its military connotation just as a general may call on firepower to flush out the enemy. The context of this example was a succession of conflicts between the systems analyst and various user managers which resulted in top management removing several resistant managers from their posts. The analyst clearly saw the organization as a battlefield. Similarly, in the university context we observed the clear drawing up of battle lines. The systems coordinator demonstrates this in the following extract:

> Systems Coordinator. So questions on screen design were resolved by the users getting their way...There was an issue on how many data entry screens were too many. And they won the battle. We simply redesigned data entry screens.

Although we have only shown two instances of this metaphor, its occurrence was widespread in our data indicating that 'battle' needs to be given serious consideration in further studies in this area. This is a point also emphasized by Lakoff and Johnson (1980).

2. *Organizations as fiefdoms*

It is possible to conceive of organizations in terms of many different metaphors (see for example Morgan's (1986) eight organizational metaphors). For example, in the university case, one particular user manager interpreted his own organization in feudalistic terms:

> User Manager. In terms of fiefdoms...there are different barons responsible for the different parts of the university. And they tend to be very much like many feudal systems. They tend to be very protective of their domain.

In this example, the user manager saw the university as a collection of fiefdoms. He resorted to this metaphor in order to understand the departmentalism and consequent friction that he observed. This territorialism is particularly important for systems which cross traditional organizational boundaries (Newman and Rosenberg, 1985).

3. *Man as machine*

This metaphor is a common one, used in many contexts ranging from the 'engineering' of organizations to treating individuals simply as units of production. Here, the project leader at the telephone company assumes that the clerical staff will simply adapt their work patterns to accommodate the new information processing system. The workers are seen as passive components of the designer's new system, and hence, there is no contradiction in keeping them uninformed:

> Interviewer. What about at the shop floor level? I noticed there are manual files kept up there; rotary type of files, will all that disappear?
> Project Leader. Yes.
> Interviewer. And how are you going to handle that kind of changeover?
> Project Leader. The rotary file you speak of is a work order file of materials for plan requirements. That will all be contained in the computer...That rotary will be replaced by a different kind of rotary, a dual density disk with all the data stored on it, and then instead of accessing the paper, they'll have a 'tube'...To me this was just another tool. Using the 'tube' is very simple. And this thing is just another tool. The information systems give then the same capabilities of a pencil. The computer enables them to add, delete, or change information within it.
> Interviewer. Are they at the moment fully aware of what's going to happen and how the change is going to affect them?
> Project Leader. No, they're not.

In this example, workers are treated as largely irrelevant, and hence, there is no need to involve them - only use them. The 'man as machine' metaphor is particularly powerful here because it allows the project leader to simplify a messy world by treating users homogeneously, that is, as machines (Burns, 1981).

Evidence of magic in information systems development

In the case studies, we often observed the rituals inherent in magic rather than magic itself. In each case the rituals had form but no substance - they were facades. The participants, however, were believers - they saw no contradiction between form and substance. The following are three representative examples of magic within ISD, which complement the two examples commonly discussed in the literature and previously reviewed.

1.   User involvement as magic
We have already seen some of the mythical dimensions of user involvement. In the following extract, we see evidence of associated rituals. In this example, the analyst from the wholesale company goes through an elaborate ritual in order to convince a key user that her views are significant for the design of the system:

> Analyst. I'd say, 'So-and-so, I can't quite figure this out. Now, you have more experience than anyone else, what would you do? We want to be able to put into the computer such-and-such piece of information and we are going to use it to produce other reports, and so on, but what is the best way of getting it to the computer?' And let her work out the problem. I had already figured it out but I wanted her to do it.

The ritual hides the fact that the analyst has already designed the system. This type of user involvement has form but no substance; the user has no genuine opportunity to influence the design of the system. In this sense, user involvement is but a facade.

2.   Sign-off as magic
Sign-offs are typically discussed as a procedure for letting the user know in advance what the final system design will be. Not only does it allow the systems developer to maintain control of development, but also control of user expectations. His belief is that the sign-off is the manifestation of the users' understanding of the system. The user signs-off only when he understands and approves the system on paper. In the following extracts, however, we see the user neither understands the system nor the implications of her signing-off (a situation which we suspect is not unusual). In the university case, the analyst quoted had spent a long time with the users obtaining requirements (the scope document):

Analyst. The user has been involved right from the scope document...and they agreed. So they basically read it and approved it...It took months and months to get approval.

The user saw the process very differently, not realizing the implications for signing-off the system:

User. They introduced us to the system and we created things like scope documents, what we wanted out of the system, what we felt we needed, what it should do for us, staffing issues. Really we were operating blindly because we had very little to no experience with it.

This ritualistic exercise resulted in a compound failure. It did not live up to its purported objective of securing the users' understanding of the system-to-be. But more importantly, it was in fact counter-productive: it helped create, nurture and seal a deep misunderstanding which eventually led to the users' rejection of the implemented system.

3. Ownership of data as magic

The ritual surrounding the ownership of data is a strong one and can be vividly seen in the university case where one of the user groups was reluctant to pool student data despite having no experience with data sharing on a computer in the past. Here one of the user managers bemoans their attitude:

User Manager. But what I see is that people are very proprietary about the information that they have. 'It's not the university's, this is our information'... A asked 'If we ever had the capability, could we access that data in an on-line environment?' and immediately alarm bells went off...the law school got extremely nervous about the idea that somebody else possibly might be able to have access to any type of information on law students.

As this example suggests, it can often be noted that there is a mystical value attached to the ownership of data. The sharing of data is thus to be avoided. There is a strongly-held belief that harm will come from others accessing 'our' data, often without any basis in experience.

Table 13.1 summarizes where the empirical evidence for the various myths, metaphors and magic came from, that is, from which case studies. It can be seen that each of the 12 symbols presented in this chapter were represented in at least one case study, and six of the instances were represented in two case studies. It should be noted that the university case was the source of nine of the symbols. This apparent imbalance is due to the in-depth nature of that particular case study material. Furthermore, because of the loosely-coupled nature of the organizational departments at the university, conflicts were more overt.

Discussion

It might be argued that many IS professionals realize that information systems development is not the highly rationalistic exercise portrayed in IS texts and trade publications, and that successful developers have always been conscious of the importance social interaction plays in systems development. However, the large number of IS failures acts as a constant reminder that such professionals are likely to be in the minority. While many would agree that a considerable part of ISD is based on myth, metaphor and magic, there is less agreement on what to do about it. Symbolism may play an important role in systems development, but just noting it does not necessarily lead to better or more successful systems. There is a need to translate such knowledge into practical application - to suggest how traditional systems development might be modified to take symbolism into account.

Table 13.1 Case study/symbol mapping

CASE STUDY	MYTHS						METAPHORS			MAGIC			TOT
	USER INVOLVEMENT	RESISTANCE TO SYSTEMS DEVELOMENT	INTEGRATED INFORMATION SYSTEMS	SYSTEMS DEVELOPER-BEST PERSON	NON -CONCERN FOR POLITICS	TOP-DOWN APPROACH	ISD AS A BATTLE	ORGANIZATIONS AS FIEFDOMS	MAN AS MACHINE	USER INVOLVEMENT	SIGN-OFF	OWNERSHIP OF DATA	
University	X	X	X	X	X	X	X	X			X	X	10
Insurance		X	X		X								3
Telephone				X		X	X		X				4
Wholesale	X									X			2

In the case of myths, we can see some dangers if system developers cling blindly to these without considering the particular situation they face. For example, if resistance to information systems is always seen as a negative feature of development which must be contained or eliminated, the designer will never then see the opportunities for 'reading' the signals from the users. In the examples cited above, the users were not blindly resisting the systems; they were, in their different ways, showing that the designed product was flawed in some significant way. In the university case, if the developer had taken these signals of resistance seriously, she would have avoided a great deal of unnecessary conflict and stress, and at the same time, produced a better system, one which would have been acceptable to the users. As another example, developers often see politics as an organizational problem, and thus not the concern of systems staff. In contrast, we have shown that for large projects the systems developer needs to be able to enter meaningfully into the negotiations required to implement systems. These negotiations will be both between systems personnel and users and between the different user groups. Far from disdaining politics and political behaviour, such circumstances require developers to become politicians themselves.

While there are many metaphors used in ISD by both users and developers, the one that surfaces frequently is the military one of 'battle' (Lakoff and Johnson, 1980). This is significant because it indicates how often development of information systems is conceived of in confrontational terms. Thus expressions such as 'battle,' 'winners,' 'losers,' 'clearing the path' are found, and appeals to formal authority structures are often resorted to. It appears that developers, and users to a lesser extent, often enter the design process with the expectation that conflict will occur, and thereby enact such behaviour. While some conflict can be constructive and result in improved design, the win/lose situations typically benefit only a small number of groups of 'winners' in organizations. As in the case of the insurance underwriters, the 'losers,' if from the user community, will be reluctant users of the system and may never fully cooperate as they retire to 'tend their wounds.' Such destructive conflict has great financial consequences for the organization in both time and cost overruns and in unproductive systems (Markus, 1983). Moreover, in the long term, reinforcing patterns of 'us vs. them' conflict leads to behaviour which is difficult to change.

We also observe many magic rituals in ISD. These are rituals which have an outward form but no substance: they are magic. Although the analyst at the wholesale company believed he was practising 'user involvement,' he went through a ritual which involved tricking the user into believing she was participating in the design. This may be an effective way of proceeding with the design, but it involves distorting communications. From the users' perspective, she believed that she was contributing from her skills and experience to the new design. This, however, was a facade. She was given no way of influencing the design outcome, as that was preconceived. This appears to be one characteristic of such rituals: they involve distorted communication between analyst and user. If this distortion were allowed to proliferate, we would expect designs which do not match the user's requirements. Moreover, if the facade is ever destroyed, the users will lose confidence in the developers, resulting in an atmosphere of distrust.

While the above discussion and examples illustrate some of the 'constraining' influences of symbolism in ISD (for example, myopia, reification, prejudice, territorialism), there is also another side. Symbolism can be seen in its 'enabling' form (for example, solidarity building, sharing of meanings, value-reinforcing, continuity preserving). For example, previously we showed sign-off as a constraining symbol - a ritual having form but no substance. In contrast, it could be seen as an enabling symbol of consensual agreement, building solidarity between systems designers and users.

In order to develop these ideas more fully, consider the issue of user resistance both non-symbolically and symbolically. User resistance has traditionally been interpreted non-symbolically (Hirschheim and Newman, 1988). However, an interpretation of how actors use symbols can, we claim, provide new insights about their constraining as well as their enabling influences.

Non-symbolic interpretation
When viewed non-symbolically, user resistance is perceived as the normal reaction to change. This is a consequence of a person's inherent fear of change, innate conservatism, inertia and general uncertainty (Ginzberg and Reilley, 1957). Typically, strategies to overcome resistance are designed to mitigate the negative effects of change for the users. For example, the use of a change agent is recommended together with planned change models (such as the Lewin-Schein or Kolb-Frohman models). In such scenarios, the object is to 'unfreeze' current practices. This approach recognizes the reality of resistance which is seen as inertia in the user community. However, users must be educated and structures altered before changes can be introduced, and a variety of techniques have been recommended in the literature. After the change, the new practices can be reinforced as they become established ('refreeze').

Symbolic interpretation
When viewed symbolically, user resistance is seen as an integral part of a metaphorical 'battle' - the conflict between the two opposing sides, the designers and the users. Such an interpretation frequently reveals the constraining influence of symbols. However, we also want to suggest that the same symbol can be seen in its more enabling form.

ISD as 'battle' - a constraining metaphor
We choose the metaphor of ISD as battle because of its pervasiveness and the powerful images that it conveys (as vividly portrayed in Lakoff and Johnson, 1980). The metaphor of 'battle' as used by systems designers acts as a powerful constraint on behaviour. As with all symbols, it shapes the perspective of the designers as they react to their mental images of relationships with users. Thus, the practitioners 'enact' their mental models producing all manner of constraining and prejudicial influences and behaviours (Morgan, 1986; Weick, 1979). This perspective helps us to understand that systems designers expect users to resist systems development. There will also be 'winners and losers' in the ensuing conflict. The focus has shifted from organizational development to strategies and tactics designed so that one party can prevail over the other. Therefore, we observe game-playing, manipulation, threats, coercion, and finally, pleas to authority when all else fails (Bardach, 1977; Keen, 1981). In this

scenario, users are seen as territorial - defending their turf, protecting their fiefdoms, etc., and many of these issues have been illustrated in some detail.

ISD as 'constructive conflict' - an enabling metaphor
If we still accept that there are deeply-held differences in attitudes and beliefs between designers and users, that is, that there is conflict between the opposing sides, we want to suggest a modification to the traditional military metaphor of ISD as 'battle.' Instead of the destructive conflict that researchers frequently report, where stakeholder groups struggle until one prevails, we suggest a metaphor shift to constructive conflict. Using this metaphor sheds new light on user resistance. While constructive conflict may involve some simplification of the ISD process, it does transform many of the issues noted above. For example, when designers meet users there may be conflict (Robey et al., 1989) but the aim could be to reach a consensus on the design, and efforts toward this end could be promoted. In such circumstances, participation would be genuine and not manipulative, and designers and users would be open to learn from each other. This is in contrast to destructive conflict where such genuine participation is precluded. Moreover, instead of reacting to the conflicts which occur, designers could choose to create encounters which both reveal and resolve conflicts, for example, through the use of hermeneutic role-playing (Klein and Hirschheim, 1983). In contrast to designers dominating ISD, we would see a greater role for user-led designs. Instead of resolving conflicts by threats, coercion, and pleas to authority, a designer might seek ways of building a consensus with users. In the place of territorialism we would not see a submergence of ideologies, but a mutual respect for differing traditions and customs.

The issue of constraining vs. enabling influences of symbols derives from the inevitability of symbolism in human interaction. When one adopts a particular symbolic view of the world, one inevitably commits to seeing some things and not to seeing others. Thus, whatever symbols systems developers commit to will enable certain actions as they will inevitably constrain others. In the cases cited previously, certain symbols emerged from the evidence, while others did not (Glaser and Strauss, 1967). In the case of the 'battle' metaphor, one that we found in several instances, we do not know how it came to be held by the subjects or how they would discard it in favour of enabling metaphors.

While we did not specifically find empirical support for enabling metaphors such as 'constructive conflict' in our case studies, some of these enabling symbols are supported by new systems development methods which seek to manifest and articulate differences in the beliefs and attitudes of systems designers and users. The methods attempt in their differing ways to provide an appropriate vehicle for eliciting and resolving the multiple and often conflicting perceptions of the problem domain addressed by ISD. There is a need not only to have more and better user participation within ISD, but also to have meaningful dialogue about the nature and type of organizational change which systems development brings about. Development methods such as ETHICS (Mumford, 1983), PORGI (Kolf and Oppelland, 1979) and other socio-technical approaches (Bostrom and Heinen, 1977a; Bostrom and Heinen, 1977b; Pava, 1983) move some way toward this, but they are generally weak on specific tools and techniques for attitude and belief elicitation. (Nevertheless, as reported in Hirschheim (1985b), participative systems development methods such as ETHICS have been favourably received by the user community.)

Other approaches such as Strategic Assumption Surfacing (Mason and Mitroff, 1981) and Soft Systems Methodology (Checkland, 1981) offer specific guidelines and tools for facilitating such elicitation. The Functional Analysis of Office Requirements (FAOR) project (Schafer et al., 1988) provides an example of one systems development approach - based on Checkland's Soft Systems Methodology - which focuses on the multi-faceted and multi-perspective nature of requirements. Through the use of tools and techniques such as 'rich pictures,' 'root definitions,' and 'conceptual models,' the attitudes and beliefs of the various parties involved with systems development are more likely to be brought out into the open. Once these attitudes and beliefs are out in the open, the prospect of resolution increases, although the possibility of conflict due to differences in attitudes and beliefs may increase as well (Robey et al., 1989).

Another systems development approach which accommodates multiple perspectives is the MARS project (Lanzara and Mathiassen, 1985; Mathiassen and Bogh-Andersen, 1987). Here the focus of attention is on working practices. The starting point is an explicit recognition of the chronic deficiencies of working practices in any group. Various tools such as diagnostic, ecological, virtual and historical 'maps' are used to help record and reflect upon the practices (Lanzara and Mathiassen, 1985). Maps provide different interpretations of a situation, which help to identify possible ways of acting in this or related situations.

We see approaches such as ETHICS, FAOR and MARS to be better suited for dealing with the symbolic nature of ISD. While such approaches are not panaceas, they nevertheless provide practical vehicles for dealing with the symbolism inherent in ISD. While we do not wish to claim that a symbolic interpretation of ISD is the 'right' way to conceive of ISD, and the orthodox or rational approach is wrong, it does nevertheless provide an interesting alternative perspective. Such an interpretation is strictly routed in social anthropology - an area that has been largely ignored by the IS community. It provides a fresh way to think about the problems facing systems development, and may lead to models of social interaction within ISD which would not be possible with our more orthodox conceptions. By adopting a symbolic perspective, we suggest that a better understanding of the nature of the ISD task is allowed.

Conclusions

In this chapter, we have tried to present evidence from the literature and case studies to demonstrate that symbolism is important in the development of IS. Whether myth, metaphor or magic, we have shown the power of symbolism in *describing* and *explaining* the behaviour of developers and users in the ISD process when faced with design tasks that are complex and full of uncertainty. We have shown that symbolism offers simplification, allowing actors to cope better with their world. By patterning behaviour and responses to others' behaviour, symbolism reduces a messy, complicated world to a simpler one. It also facilitates cohesion, permitting individuals to become accepted members of a group.

Our analysis does, however, point to a number of *dangers* of symbolism in constraining the systems development process. As pointed out in our examples, the myths, metaphors and magic (rituals) employed by developers can lead to inappropriate responses to specific or unique situations. Because it tends to make the developer insensitive to individuals and organizational-specific situations, symbolism can lead developers to make design choices and interact with users in ways which can precipitate dysfunctional (although avoidable) responses from users. They enact the mental images that they use. If 'battle,' for example, is a frequently evoked metaphor in organizations, systems designers will tend to 'see' and expect to see conflict everywhere. While this may be a helpful insight, we also suggest that symbols may be the subject of transformation in organizations leading to alternative approaches to ISD. Thus, for example, instead of accepting *constraining* metaphors such as 'battle,' design groups could promote and facilitate more *enabling* symbols; for example, as an instance of counterpart to the 'battle' metaphor, we explored 'ISD as constructive conflict' as a potentially enabling metaphor. We compared the effects such a shift in symbolism might have upon the ISD process, indicating some of the ways of codifying this into systems development methods. It must be said, however, that symbols have an enduring and robust quality which makes them less prone to overt manipulation. Nonetheless, the prospect of mitigating dysfunctional behaviour in ISD may appeal to some management coalitions. Consequently, they may attempt to recast symbols into their more enabling form in the hope of building more effective systems. But if managers wish to encourage transformations in symbolism they must be ready to put in place vehicles, such as the emerging systems development methodologies discussed above, to facilitate this process (Smircich, 1983b). In addition to more general case studies exploring the role of symbolism, we also need detailed case studies of how these transformations might be worked out in practice.

Bibliography

Ackoff, R. (1979) 'The future of operational research is past', *Journal of the Operational Research Society*, 30, 2, 93-104.

Agar, M. H. (1980) *The professional stranger*, Academic Press, New York.

Alavi, M. and Carlson, P. (1992) 'A review of MIS research and disciplinary development', *Journal of Management Information Systems*, 8, 4, 45-62.

Alavi, M., Carlson, P. and Brook, G. (1989) 'The ecology of MIS research: A twenty-year status review', in *Proceedings of the tenth international conference on information systems*, ACM Press, Baltimore, 363-371.

Alavi, M. and Henderson, J. C. (1981) 'Evolutionary strategy for implementing a decision support system', *Management Science*, 27, 11, 1309-1323.

Allison, G. T. (1971) *Essence of decision: Explaining the Cuban missile crisis*, Little, Brown, Boston, MA.

Alter, S. L. (1975) *A study of computer aided decision-making in organizations*, Massachusetts Institute of Technology, Doctoral dissertation, Cambridge, MA.

Alvesson, M. (1984) 'On the idea of organizational culture', in *First international conference on organizational symbolism and corporate culture*, Lund, Sweden, Quoted in Turner, B. (1986).

Ancona, D. (1990) 'Outward bound: Strategies for team survival in an organization', *Academy of Management Journal*, 33, 2, 334-365.

Archer, S. (1988) '"Qualitative" research and the epistemological problems of the management disciplines', in Pettigrew, A. (Ed.), *Competitiveness and the management process*, Basil Blackwell, Oxford, 265-302.

Argyris, C. (1970a) *Intervention theory and method*, Addison-Wesley, Cambridge, MA.

Argyris, C. (1970b) 'Resistance to rational management systems', *Innovation*, 10.

Argyris, C., Putnam, R. and Smith, D. (1985) *Action science*, Jossey-Bass, San Francisco, CA.

Argyris, C. and Schön, D. (1974) *Theory in practice: Increasing professional effectiveness*, Jossey-Bass, San Francisco, CA.

Argyris, C. and Schön, D. (1978) *Organizational learning: A theory of action perspective*, Addison-Wesley, Reading, MA.

Astley, W. G. (1984) 'Subjectivity, sophistry and symbolism in management science', *Journal of Management Studies*, 21, 3, 259-272.

Astley, W. G. (1985) 'Administrative science as socially constructed truth', *Administrative Science Quarterly*, 30, 4, 497-513.

Astley, W. G. and Van de Ven, A. (1983) 'Central perspectives and debates in organization theory', *Administrative Science Quarterly*, 28, 2, 245-273.

Attewell, P. and Rule, J. (1984) 'Computing and organizations: What we know and what we don't know', *Communications of the ACM*, 27, 12, 1184-1192.

Avison, D. E., Lau, F., Myers, M. D. and Nielsen, P. A. (1999) 'Action research', *Communications of the ACM*, 42, 1, 94-97.

Bakos, J. Y. and Treacy, M. E. (1986) 'Information technology and corporate strategy: A research perspective', *MIS Quarterly*, 10, 2, 107-119.

Banker, R. D. and Kauffman, R. A. (1991) 'Reuse and productivity in integrated computer-aided software engineering: An empirical study', *MIS Quarterly*, 15, 3, 375-401.

Banville, C. and Landry, M. (1989) 'Can the field of MIS be disciplined?', *Communications of the ACM*, 32, 1, 48-61.

Bardach, E. (1977) *The implementation game*, MIT Press, Cambridge, MA.

Barley, S. R. (1986) 'Technology as an occasion for structuring: Evidence from observations of CT scanners and the social order of radiology departments', *Administrative Science Quarterly*, 31, 1, 78-108.

Barnett, G. (1982) 'The computer and clinical judgement', *New England Journal of Medicine*, 308, 8, 494-495.

Baroudi, J. J. (1985) 'The impact of role variables on information systems personnel work attitudes and intentions', *MIS Quarterly*, 9, 4, 341-365.

Baroudi, J. J., Olson, M. H. and Ives, B. (1986) 'An empirical study of the impact of user involvement on system usage and information satisfaction', *Communications of the ACM*, 29, 3, 232-238.

Baroudi, J. J. and Orlikowski, W. (1989) 'The problem of statistical power in MIS research', *MIS Quarterly*, 13, 1, 87-106.

Bartol, K. M. (1983) 'Turnover among DP personnel: A causal analysis', *Communications of the ACM*, 26, 10, 807-811.

Bartunek, J. (1984) 'Changing interpretive schemes and organizational restructuring: The example of a religious order', *Administrative Science Quarterly*, 29, 3, 355-372.

Bartunek, J. and Moch, M. (1987) 'First order, second order, and third order change and organization development interventions: A cognitive approach', *Journal of Applied Behavioral Science*, 23, 4, 483-500.

Baskerville, R. (1991) 'Philosophical bias of methods and tools', in Nissen, Klein et al. (1991).

Beath, C. and Ives, B. (1986) 'Competitive information systems in support of pricing', *MIS Quarterly*, 10, 1, 85-93.

Behling, O. (1980) 'The case for the natural science model for research in organizational behavior and organization theory', *Academy of Management Review*, 5, 4, 483-490.

Benbasat, I. (1984) 'An analysis of research methodologies', in McFarlan (1984a), 47-85.

Benbasat, I., Goldstein, D. K. and Mead, M. (1987) 'The case research strategy in studies of information systems', *MIS Quarterly*, 11, 3, 369-386.

Benson, J. K. (1973) 'The analysis of bureaucratic-professional conflict: Functional versus dialectical approaches', *Sociological Quarterly*, 14, 376-394.

Benson, J. K. (1983) 'Paradigm and praxis in organizational analysis', in Cummings, L. L. and Staw, B. M. (Eds), *Research in organizational behavior*, JAI Press, Greenwich, CT, 33-56.

Bentley, R., Rodden, T., Sawyer, P., Sommerville, I., Hughes, J., Randall, R. and Shapiro, D. (1992) 'Ethnographically-informed systems design for air traffic control', in *CSCW '92. ACM 1992 conference on computer-supported cooperative work: Sharing perspectives*, ACM Press, New York, 123-129.

Berger, P. and Luckman, T. (1967) *The social construction of reality: A treatise in the sociology of knowledge*, Penguin, London.

Bernstein, R. (1978) *The restructuring of social and political theory*, University of Pennsylvania Press, Philadelphia, PA.

Bernstein, R. (1983) *Beyond objectivism and relativism: Science, hermeneutics, and praxis*, University of Pennsylvania Press, Philadelphia, PA.

Bernstein, R. J. (1985) *Beyond objectivism and relativism*, University of Pennsylvania Press, Pennsylvania.

Bhaskar, R. (1978) *A realist theory of science*, Harvester Press, Brighton.

Bhaskar, R. (1979) *The possibility of naturalism*, Harvester Press, Brighton.

Bjørn-Andersen, N. (1986) 'Action research on the impact of IS on clerical workers', in *Seventh international conference on information systems*, San Diego, CA, 338.

Bjørn-Andersen, N. and Hedberg, B. (1978) 'Designing information systems in organizational perspective', in Nystrom, P. and Starbuck, W. (Eds), *Prescriptive models of organizations*, North-Holland, Amsterdam, 171-181.

Bjørn-Andersen, N. and Pederson, P. H. (1980) 'Computer facilitated changes in the management power structure', *Accounting, Organizations and Society*, 5, 2, 203-216.

Blackler, F. (1988) 'Information technologies and organizations: Lessons from the 1980s and issues for the 1990s', *Journal of Occupational Psychology*, 61, 2, 113-127.

Bleicher, J. (1980) *Contemporary hermeneutics: Hermeneutics as method, philosophy and critique*, Routledge & Kegan Paul, London.

Bleicher, J. (1982) *The hermeneutic imagination - outline of a positive critique of scientism and sociology*, Routledge & Kegan Paul, London.

Blois, M. (1980) 'Clinical judgment and computers', *New England Journal of Medicine*, 303, 4, 192-197.

Blum, F. (1955) 'Action research - a scientific approach?', *Philosophy of Science*, 22, January, 1-7.

Boguslaw, R. (1965) *The new Utopians*, Prentice-Hall, Englewood Cliffs, NJ.

Boland, R. (1979) 'Control, causality and information system requirements', *Accounting, Organizations and Society*, 4, 4, 259-272.

Boland, R. (1985) 'Phenomenology: A preferred approach to research in information systems', in Mumford, Hirschheim et al. (1985), 193-201.

Boland, R. and Hoffman, R. (1983) 'Humour in a machine shop: An interpretation of symbolic actions', in Pondy, Frost et al. (1983), 187-198.

Boland, R. J. (1991) 'Information system use as a hermeneutic process', in Nissen, Klein et al. (1991), 439-464.

Boland, R. J. and Day, W. F. (1989) 'The experience of system design: A hermeneutic of organizational action', *Scandinavian Journal of Management*, 5, 2, 87-104.

Boland, R. J. and Pondy, L. R. (1986) 'The micro-dynamics of a budget-cutting process: Modes, models and structure', *Accounting, Organizations and Society*, 11, 4/5, 403-422.

Boland, R. J., Jr (1987) 'The in-formation of information systems', in Boland, R. J. and Hirschheim, R. A. (Eds), *Critical issues in information systems research*, Wiley, Chichester, 363-379.

Boland, R. J., Jr and Day, W. (1982) 'The phenomenology of systems design', in Ginzberg, M. and Ross, C. (Eds), *Proceedings of the third international conference on information systems*, Ann Arbor, MI, 31-36.

Bolman, L. and Deal, T. (1984) *Modern approaches to understanding and managing organizations*, Jossey-Bass, San Francisco, CA.

Bonoma, T. V. (1985) 'Case research in marketing: Opportunities, problems, and a process', *Journal of Marketing Research*, 22.

Bostrom, R. P. and Heinen, J. S. (1977a) 'MIS problems and failures: A socio-technical perspective. Part 1: The causes', *MIS Quarterly*, 1, 3, 17-32.

Bostrom, R. P. and Heinen, J. S. (1977b) 'MIS problems and failures: A socio-technical perspective; part 2: The application of socio-technical theory', *MIS Quarterly*, 1, 4, 11-28.

Bouchard, T. J., Jr (1976) 'Field research methods: Interviewing, questionnaires, participant observation, systematic observation, unobtrusive measures', in Dunnette, M. D. (Ed.), *Handbook of industrial and organizational psychology*, Rand McNally, Chicago, IL, 363-413.

Bowles, M. (1989) 'Myth, meaning and work organization', *Organizational Studies*, 10, 3, 405-421.

Braverman, H. (1974) *Labor and monopoly capital*, Monthly Review Press, New York.

Brooks, F. (1975) *The mythical man-month*, Addison-Wesley, Reading, MA.

Brooks, F. (1987) 'No silver bullet: Essence and accidents of software engineering', *Computer*, 10-19.

Bryman, A. (1989) *Research methods and organization studies*, Unwin Hyman, London.

Bubenko, J. (1986) *Information systems methodologies - a research view*, University of Stockholm, SYSLAB Report No. 40, Sweden.

Buckingham, R. and Land, F. (1987) 'Education for ISE: What does it mean?', *Computer Bulletin*, 3, 2, 33-35.

Burawoy, M. (1985) *The politics of production*, Verso Press, London.

Burns, A. (1981) *The microchip: Appropriate or inappropriate technology*, Ellis Horwood, Chichester.

Burrell, G. and Morgan, G. (1979) *Sociological paradigms and organizational analysis*, Heinemann, London.

Campbell, D. T. (1975) '"Degrees of freedom" and the case study', *Comparative Political Studies*, 8, 2, 178-193.

Campbell, D. T. and Stanley, J. C. (1963) *Experimental and quasi-experimental designs for research*, Houghton Mifflin, Boston, MA.

Card, D. N., McGarry, F. E. and Page, G. T. (1987) 'Evaluating software engineering technologies', *IEEE Transactions on Software Engineering*, 13, 7, 845-851.

Carr, W. and Kemmis, S. (1986) *Becoming critical: Education, knowledge and action research*, Falmer Press, London.

Cash, J. I. and Lawrence, P. R. (Eds) (1989) *The information systems research challenge: Qualitative research methods*, Harvard Business School Press, Boston, MA.

Chandler, A. D., Jr (1962) *Strategy and structure: Chapters in the history of the American industrial enterprise*, MIT Press, Cambridge, MA.

Checkland, P. (1985) 'From optimizing to learning: A development of systems thinking for the 1990s', *Journal of the Operational Research Society*, 36, 9, 757-767.

Checkland, P. (1991) 'From framework through experience to learning: The essential nature of action research', in Nissen, Klein et al. (1991), 397-403.

Checkland, P. and Scholes, J. (1990) *Soft systems methodology in practice*, Wiley, Chichester.

Checkland, P. B. (1981) *Systems thinking, systems practice*, Wiley, New York.

Christenson, C. (1976) 'Proposals for a program of empirical research into the properties of triangles', *Decision Sciences*, 7, 3, 631-648.

Chua, W. F. (1986) 'Radical developments in accounting thought', *The Accounting Review*, 61, 4, 601-632.

Ciborra, C. (1985) 'Reframing the role of computers in organizations', in Gallegos, L., Welke, R. and Wetherbe, J. (Eds), *Proceedings of the sixth international conference on information systems*, Indianapolis, IN, 57-69.

Clark, P. A. (1972) *Action research and organizational change*, Harper and Row, London.

Cleverly, G. (1971) *Managers and magic*, Longman, London.

Clifford, J. (1988) *The predicament of culture: Twentieth-century ethnography, literature and art*, Harvard University Press, Cambridge, MA.

Clifford, J. and Marcus, G. E. (1986) *Writing culture: The poetics and politics of ethnography*, University of California Press, Berkeley, CA.

Cohen, A. P. (1985) *The symbolic construction of community*, Ellis Horwood, London.

Cohen, P. (1969) 'Theories of myth', *Man*, 4.

Cook, T. D. and Campbell, D. T. (1979) *Quasi-experimentation: Design and analysis issues for field settings*, Rand McNally, Chicago, IL.

Cooper, R. (1988) 'Review of management information systems research: A management support emphasis', *Information Processing & Management*, 24, 1, 73-102.

Copi, I. (1986) *Introduction to logic*, Macmillan, New York.

Covaleski, M. and Dirsmith, M. (1988) 'Budgeting as a means for control and loose coupling', *Accounting, Organizations and Society*, 8, 4, 323-340.

Crozier, M. (1964) *The bureaucratic phenomenon*, University of Chicago Press, Chicago, IL.

Culnan, M. J. (1986) 'The intellectual development of management information systems, 1972-1982: A co-citation analysis', *Management Science*, 32.

Culnan, M. J. (1987) 'Mapping the intellectual structure of MIS, 1980-1985: A co-citation analysis', *MIS Quarterly*, 11.

Culnan, M. J. and Markus, M. L. (1987) 'Information technologies', in Jablin, F. M., et al. (Eds.), *Handbook of organizational communication*, Sage, Newbury Park, CA, 420-443.

Culnan, M. J. and Swanson, E. B. (1986) 'Research in management information systems, 1980-1984: Points of work and reference', in *MIS Quarterly*, 10.

Daft, R. (1983) 'Learning the craft of organizational research', *Academy of Management Review*, 8, 4, 539-546.

Daft, R. L. and Wiginton, J. C. (1979) 'Language and organization', *Academy of Management Review*, 4, 2, 179-191.

Dagwell, R. and Weber, R. (1983) 'System designers' user models: A comparative study and methodological critique', *Communications of the ACM*, 26, 11, 987-997.

Dalton, M. (1959) *Men who manage*, Wiley, New York.

Dandridge, T. (1983) 'Symbols' function and use', in Pondy, Frost et al. (1983), 69-79.

Danziger, J. N., Dutton, W. H., Kling, R. and Kraemer, K. L. (1982) *Computers and politics - high technology in American local government*, Columbia University Press, New York.

Darnell, R. (1974) *Readings in the history of anthropology*, Harper & Row, New York.

Datta, L. (1982) 'The politics of qualitative methods', *American Behavioral Scientist*, 26, 11, 133-144.

Davies, L. J. (1991) 'Researching the organisational culture contexts of information systems strategy: A case study of the British army', in Nissen, Klein et al. (1991), 145-167.

Davies, L. J. and Nielsen, S. (1992) 'An ethnographic study of configuration management and documentation practices in an information technology centre', in Kendall, K. E., Lyytinen, K. and De Gross, J. I. (Eds), *The impact of computer supported technology on information systems development*, Elsevier/North-Holland, Amsterdam, 179-182.

Dearden, J. (1966) 'The myth of real-time management information', *Harvard Business Review*, May-June.

DeMarco, T. (1978) *Structured analysis and system specification*, Yourdon, New York.

Denzin, N. K. and Lincoln, Y. S. (Eds) (1994) *Handbook of qualitative research*, Sage, Thousand Oaks, CA.

DeSanctis, G. and Poole, M. S. (1994) 'Capturing the complexity in advanced technology use: Adaptive structuration theory', *Organization Science*, 5, 2, 121-147.

Dewar, R. D. and Dutton, J. E. (1986) 'The adoption of radical and incremental changes: An empirical analysis', *Management Science*, 32, 11, 1422-1433.

Dickson, G. W. and Janson, M. (1984) 'The failure of a DSS for energy conservation: A technical perspective', *Systems, Objectives, Solutions*, 4, 2, 69-79.

Dreyfus, H. (1972) *What computers can't do*, Harper & Row, New York.

Dukes, W. (1965) 'N = 1', *Psychological Bulletin*, 64, 11, 74-79.

Dutton, J. E. and Dukerich, J. M. (1991) 'Keeping an eye on the mirror: Image and identity in organizational adaptation', *Academy of Management Journal*, 34, 3, 517-554.

Dutton, W. H. (1981) 'The rejection of an innovation: The political environment of a computer-based model', *Systems, Objectives, Solutions*, 1, 4, 179-201.

Earl, M. (Ed.) (1983) *Perspectives on management*, Oxford University Press, Oxford.

Edwards, R. (1979) *Contested terrain*, Basic Books, New York.

Ein-Dor, P. (1986) 'An epistemological approach to the theory of information systems', in *Proceedings of the 1986 annual meeting of the Decision Sciences Institute*, Honolulu, HI, 563-565.

Ein-Dor, P. (1988) 'Hardware vs. software costs: The composition of data processing budgets', in Jeffery, J. R. (Ed.), *Proceedings of the joint international symposium on information systems*, Sydney, 107-125.

Ein-Dor, P. and Segev, E. (1984) 'Perceived importance, investment and success of MIS, or the MIS zoo', *Systems, Objectives, Solutions*, 4, 2, 61-67.

Eisbach, K. D. and Sutton, R. I. (1992) 'Acquiring organizational legitimacy through illegitimate actions: A marriage of institutional and impression management theories', *Academy of Management Journal*, 35, 4, 699-738.

Eisenhardt, K. M. (1989) 'Building theories from case study research', *Academy of Management Review*, 14, 4, 532-550.

Elden, M. and Chisholm, R. F. (1993) 'Emerging varieties of action research: Introduction to the special issue', *Human Relations*, 46, 2, 121-142.

Eoyang, C. (1983) 'Symbolic interpretation of belief systems', in Pondy, Frost et al. (1983), 109-121.

Ettlie, J., Bridges, W. and O'Keefe, R. (1993) 'Organization strategy and structural differences for radical versus incremental innovation', *Management Science*, 30, 6, 682-695.

Evans-Pritchard, E. E. (1950) *Witchcraft, oracles and magic among the Azande*, The Clarendon Press, Oxford.

Evered, R. and Louis, M. R. (1981) 'Alternative perspectives in the organizational sciences: "Inquiry from the inside" and "inquiry from the outside"', *Academy of Management Review*, 6, 3, 385-395.

Everest, G. (1974) 'Database management systems tutorial', in Chervany, N. (Ed.), *Proceedings of the fifth annual Midwest AIDS conference*, Minneapolis, MN.

Fay, B. (1987) 'An alternative view: Interpretive social science', in Gibbons, M. T. (Ed.), *Interpreting politics*, New York University Press, New York, 82-100.

Feldman, M. (1989) *Order without design: Information production and policy making*, Stanford University Press, Stanford, CA.

Feldman, M. and March, J. (1981) 'Information in organizations as signal and symbol', *Administrative Science Quarterly*, 26, 2, 171-186.

Filstead, W. (1970) *Qualitative methodology*, Markham, Chicago, IL.

Forester, J. (1992) 'Critical ethnography: On field work in an Habermasian way', in Alvesson, M. and Willmott, H. (Eds), *Critical management studies*, Sage, London, 46-65.

Foucault, M. (1970) *The order of things*, Tavistock, London.

Foucault, M. (1972) *The archaeology of knowledge*, Tavistock, London.

Franz, C. R. and Robey, D. (1984) 'An investigation of user-led systems design: Rational and political perspectives', *Communications of the ACM*, 27, 12, 1202-1209.

Frazer, J. G. (1890) *The golden bough*, Macmillan, London.

Frisby, D. (1972) 'The Popper-Adorno controversy: The methodological dispute in German sociology', *Philosophy of the Social Sciences*, 2, 105-119.

Frost, P. J., Moore, L. F., Louis, M. R., Lundberg, C. C. and Martin, J. (Eds) (1985) *Organizational culture*, Sage, Beverly Hills, CA.

Fulk, J. and Dutton, W. (1984) 'Videoconferencing as an organizational information system: Assessing the role of electronic meetings', *Systems, Objectives, Solutions*, 4, 2, 105-118.

Gable, G. (1994) 'Integrating case study and survey research methods: An example in information systems', *European Journal of Information Systems*, 2, 3, 112-126.

Gadamer, H.-G. (1976a) 'The historicity of understanding', in Connerton, P. (Ed.), *Critical sociology, selected readings*, Penguin Books, Harmondsworth, 117-133.

Gadamer, H.-G. (1976b) *Philosophical hermeneutics*, University of California Press, Berkeley, CA.

Galliers, R. (Ed.) (1992) *Information systems research: Issues, methods, and practical guidelines*, Blackwell Scientific, Oxford.

Galliers, R. and Land, F. (1988) 'Authors' response', *Communications of the ACM*, 31, 12, 1504-1505.

Galliers, R. D. (1985) 'In search of a paradigm for information systems research', in Mumford, Hirschheim et al. (1985), 281-291.

Galliers, R. D. and Land, F. F. (1987) 'Choosing appropriate information systems research methodologies', *Communications of the ACM*, 30, 11, 900-902.

Gambling, T. (1977) 'Magic, accounting and morale', *Accounting, Organizations and Society*, 2, 141-153.

Gane, C. and Sarson, T. (1979) *Structured systems analysis: Tools and techniques*, Prentice-Hall, Englewood Cliffs, NJ.

Garfinkel, H. (1967) *Studies in ethnomethodology*, Prentice-Hall, Englewood Cliffs, NJ.

Gash, D. C. and Orlikowski, W. J. (1991) 'Changing frames: Towards an understanding of information technology and organizational change', in Wall, J. L. and Jauch, L. R. (Eds), *Academy of management best papers proceedings*, Ada, OH, 189-193.

Geertz, C. (1973) *The interpretation of cultures*, Basic Books, New York.

Geertz, C. (1983) *Local knowledge: Further essays in interpretive anthropology*, Basic Books, New York.

Geertz, C. (1988) *Works and lives: The anthropologist as author*, Polity Press, Cambridge.

George, A. and McKeown, T. (1985) 'Case studies and theories of organizational decision making', in Sproull, L. and Larkey, P. (Eds), *Advances in information processing in organizations*, JAI Press, Greenwich, CT, 21-58.

George, J. F. and King, J. L. (1991) 'Examining the computing and centralization debate', *Communications of the ACM*, 34, 7, 63-72.

Gibbons, M. T. (1987) 'Introduction: The politics of interpretation', in Gibbons, M. T. (Ed.), *Interpreting politics*, New York University Press, New York, 1-31.

Gibson, C. F. (1975) 'A methodology for implementation research', in Schultz, R. L. and Slevin, D. P. (Eds), *Implementing operations research/management science*, American Elsevier, New York.

Giddens, A. (1979) *Central problems in social theory: Action, structure and contradiction in social analysis*, University of California Press, Berkeley, CA.

Giddens, A. (1981) *A critique of contemporary historical materialism*, University of California Press, Berkeley, CA.

Giddens, A. (1984) *The constitution of society: Outline of the theory of structuration*, University of California Press, Berkeley, CA.

Giddens, A. (1987) *Social theory and modern sociology*, Stanford University Press, Stanford, CA.

Ginzberg, E. and Reilley, E. (1957) *Effecting change in large organizations*, Columbia University Press, New York.

Ginzberg, M. (1981a) 'A prescriptive model for system implementation', *Systems, Objectives, Solutions*, 1, 1, 33-46.

Ginzberg, M. J. (1981b) 'Early diagnosis of MIS implementation failure: Promising results and unanswered questions', *Management Science*, 27, 4, 459-478.

Ginzberg, M. J. (1974) *A detailed look at implementation research*, Massachusetts Institute of Technology, Report CISR-4, Cambridge, MA.

Ginzberg, M. J. (1975) *Implementation as a process of change: A framework and empirical study*, Massachusetts Institute of Technology, Report CISR-13, Cambridge, MA.

Gladden, G. (1982) 'Stop the life-cycle, I want to get off', *Software Engineering Notes*, 7, 2, 35-39.

Glaser, B. and Strauss, A. (1967) *The discovery of grounded theory: Strategies for qualitative research*, Aldine, Chicago.

Godel, K. (1962) *On formally undecidable propositions*, Basic Books, New York.

Goldkuhl, G. and Lyytinen, K. (1982) 'A language action view of information systems', in Ginzberg, M. and Ross, C. (Eds), *Proceedings of the third international conference on information systems*, Ann Arbor, MI, 13-30.

Goldstein, D. (1986) 'The use of qualitative methods in MIS research', in *Proceedings of the seventh international conference on information systems*, San Diego, CA, 338.

Gowler, D. and Legge, K. (1983) 'The meaning of management and the management of meaning: A view from social anthropology', in Earl, M. (Ed.), *Perspectives on management*, Oxford University Press, Oxford.

Gronn, P. C. (1983) 'Talk as they work: The accomplishment of school administration', *Administrative Science Quarterly*, 23, 1, 1-21.

Gummesson, E. (1988) *Qualitative methods in management research*, Chartwell-Bratt, Bromley.

Habermas, J. (1963) *Theory and practice*, Heinemann, London.

Habermas, J. (1968) *Knowledge and human interest*, Beacon Press, Boston, MA.

Habermas, J. (1979) *Communication and the evolution of society*, Heinemann, London.

Habermas, J. (1981) *Theorie des kommunikativen Handelns: Zur Kritik der funktionalistishcen Vernunft band 2*, Suhrkamp Verlag, Frankfurt am Main.

Habermas, J. (1984) *The theory of communicative action: Reason and the rationalization of society*, Beacon Press, Boston, MA.

Hamilton, S. and Ives, B. (1982) 'MIS research strategies', *Information & Management*, 5, 6, 339-347.

Hayes-Roth, F., Waterman, D. and Lenat, D. (Eds) (1983) *Building expert systems*, Addison-Wesley, Reading, MA.

Hedberg, B. (1981) 'How organizations learn and unlearn', in Nystrom, P. and Starbuck, W. (Eds), *Handbook of organizational design*, Oxford University Press, New York, 1-27.

Hedberg, B. and Mumford, E. (1975) 'The design of computer systems: Man's vision of man as an integral part of the systems design process', in Mumford, E. and Sackman, H. (Eds), *Human choice and computers*, North-Holland, Amsterdam, 31-59.

Hedley, A. (1970) 'Organizational objectives and managerial controls', in Woodward, J. (Ed.), *Industrial organization - behaviour and control*, Oxford University Press, Oxford.

Henderson, R. M. and Clark, K. (1990) 'Architectural innovation: The reconfiguration of existing product technologies and the failure of established firms', *Administrative Science Quarterly*, 35, 1, 9-30.

Herriot, R. (1982) 'Tension in research design and implementation: The rural experimental schools study', *American Behavioral Scientist*, 26, 11, 23-44.

Hersen, M. and Barlow, D. H. (1976) *Single-case experimental designs: Strategies for studying behavior*, Pergamon, New York.

Heydebrand, W. V. (1980) 'Organizational contradictions in public bureaucracies: Towards a Marxian theory of organizations', in Etzioni, A. and Lehman, E. (Eds), *A sociological reader on complex organizations*, Holt, Rinehart and Winston, New York, 56-73.

Heydebrand, W. V. (1983) 'Organization and praxis', in Morgan (1983), 306-320.

Heydebrand, W. V. (1985) 'What is a critical theory of organizations?', in *Conference on critical perspectives in organizational analysis*, New York.

Hirschheim, R. (1985a) 'Information systems epistemology: An historical perspective', in Mumford, Hirschheim et al. (1985), 13-38.

Hirschheim, R. (1992) 'Information systems epistemology: An historical perspective', in Galliers, R. (Ed.), *Information systems research: Issues, methods and practical guidelines*, Blackwell Scientific, Oxford, 28-60.

Hirschheim, R. and Klein, H. (1994) 'Realizing emancipatory principles in information systems development: The case for ETHICS', *MIS Quarterly*, 18, 1, 83-109.

Hirschheim, R., Klein, H. and Newman, M. (1987) 'A social action perspective of information system development', in DeGross, J. and Kriebel, C. (Eds), *Proceedings of the eighth international conference on information systems*, Pittsburgh, PA, 45-56.

Hirschheim, R. and Klein, H. K. (1989) 'Four paradigms of information systems development', *Communications of the ACM*, 32, 10, 1199-1216.

Hirschheim, R. and Newman, M. (1988) 'Information systems and user resistance: Theory and practice', *The Computer Journal*, 31, 6, 398-408.

Hirschheim, R. and Newman, M. (1991) 'Symbolism and information systems development: Myth, metaphor and magic', *Information Systems Research*, 2, 1, 29-62.

Hirschheim, R. A. (1985b) 'User experience with and assessment of participative systems design', *MIS Quarterly*, 9, 4, 295-304.

Hirschheim, R. A. (1986) 'The effect of a priori views of the social implications of computing: The case of office automation', *Computing Surveys*, 18, 2, 165-195.

Hoare, C. A. (1984) 'Programming: Sorcery or science', *IEEE Software*, April, 5-16.

Holzblatt, K. and Beyer, H. (1993) 'Making customer-centered design work for teams', *Communications of the ACM*, 36, 10, 93-103.

Huberman, A. and Crandall, D. (1982) 'Fitting words to numbers: Multisite/multi-method research in educational dissemination', *American Behavioral Scientist*, 26, 1, 62-83.

Hughes, J. A., Randall, D. and Shapiro, D. (1992) 'Faltering from ethnography to design', in *CSCW '92. ACM 1992 conference on computer-supported cooperative work: Sharing perspectives*, ACM Press, New York, 115-123.

Hult, M. and Lennung, S.-Å. (1980) 'Towards a definition of action research: A note and bibliography', *Journal of Management Studies*, 17, May, 241-250.

Ingersoll, V. and Adams, G. (1986) 'Beyond organizational boundaries: Explaining the management myth', *Administration and Society*, 18, 3, 360-381.

Isabella, L. A. (1990) 'Evolving interpretations as a change unfolds: How managers construe key organizational events', *Academy of Management Journal*, 33, 1, 7-41.

Israel, B., Schurman, S. and House, J. (1989) 'Action research on occupational stress: Involving workers as researchers', *International Journal of Health Services*, 19, 1, 135-155.

Ivancevich, J., Napier, A. and Wetherbe, J. (1983) 'Occupational stress, attitudes, and health problems in the information systems professional', *Communications of the ACM*, 26, 10, 800-806.

Ives, B. and Learmonth, G. P. (1984) 'The information system as a competitive weapon', *Communications of the ACM*, 27, 12, 1193-1201.

Ives, B. and Olson, M. (1984) 'User involvement and MIS success: A review of research', *Management Science*, 30, 5, 586-603.

Ives, B. and Olson, M. H. (1981) 'Manager or technician? The nature of the information systems manager's job', *MIS Quarterly*, 5, 4, 49-63.

Jackson, M. (1983) *System development*, Prentice-Hall, Englewood Cliffs, NJ.

Jackson, P. (1986) *Introduction to expert systems*, Addison-Wesley, Reading, MA.

Jarvenpaa, S., Dickson, G. and DeSanctis, G. (1985) 'Methodological issues in experimental IS research: Experiences and recommendations', *MIS Quarterly*, 9, 2, 141-156.

Jarvenpaa, S. L. (1988) 'The importance of laboratory experimentation in IS research', *Communications of the ACM*, 31, 12, 1502-1504.

Jenkins, A. M. (1986) 'Management information systems researcher's workshop', in *Proceedings of the 1986 annual meeting of the Decision Sciences Institute*, Honolulu, HI, 559-562.

Jenkins, M. (1985) 'Research methodologies and MIS research', in Mumford, Hirschheim et al. (1985), 103-117.

Jepsen, L., Mathiassen, L. and Nielsen, P. (1989) 'Back to the thinking mode: Diaries for the management of information systems development projects', *Behaviour and Information Technology*, 8, 3, 207-217.

Jick, T. D. (1979) 'Mixing qualitative and quantitative methods: Triangulation in action', *Administrative Science Quarterly*, 24, 4, 602-611.

Jones, M. and Nandhakumar, J. (1993) 'Structured development? A structurational analysis of the development of an executive information system', in Avison, D., Kendall, J. E. and DeGross, J. I. (Eds), *Human, organizational, and social dimensions of information systems development*, North-Holland, Amsterdam, 475-496.

Jönsson, S. (1991) 'Action research', in Nissen, Klein et al. (1991), 371-396.

Jowett, S. (1988) 'Hospital and community liaison links in nursing: The role of the liaison nurse', *Journal of Advanced Nursing*, 13, 5, 579-587.

Kahn, J. S. (1989) 'Culture: Demise or resurrection?', *Critique of Anthropology*, 9, 2, 5-25.

Kahn, W. A. (1990) 'Psychological conditions of personal engagement and disengagement at work', *Academy of Management Journal*, 33, 4, 692-724.

Kaplan, A. (1964) *The conduct of inquiry*, Chandler, New York.

Kaplan, B. and Duchon, D. (1988) 'Combining qualitative and quantitative methods in information systems research: A case study', *MIS Quarterly*, 12, 4, 571-587.

Kaplan, R. S. (1985) *The role of empirical research in management accounting*, Harvard Business School, Working Paper 9-785-001, Boston, MA.

Kauber, P. (1986) 'What's wrong with a science of MIS?', in *Proceedings of the 1986 annual meeting of the Decision Sciences Institute*, Honolulu, HI, 572-574.

Keen, P. (1991) 'Relevance and rigor in information systems research: Improving quality, confidence cohesion and impact', in Nissen, Klein et al. (1991), 27-49.

Keen, P. G. W. (1980) 'MIS research: Reference disciplines and a cumulative tradition', in McLean, E. R. (Ed.), *International conference on information systems*, 9-18.

Keen, P. G. W. (1981) 'Information systems and organizational change', *Communications of the ACM*, 24, 1, 24-33.

Keen, P. W., Bronsema, G. and Zuboff, S. (1982) 'Implementing common systems: One organization's experience', *Systems, Objectives, Solutions*, 2, 3, 125-142.

Kets de Vries, M. and Miller, D. (1984) *The neurotic organization*, Jossey-Bass, San Francisco, CA.

King, J. (1983) 'Successful implementation of large-scale DSS', *Systems, Objectives, Solutions*, 3, 4, 183-205.

Kirk, J. and Miller, M. L. (1986) *Reliability and validity in qualitative research*, Sage, Newbury Park, CA.

Klein, H., Hirschheim, R. and Nissen, H.-E. (1991) 'A pluralist perspective of the information systems research arena', in Nissen, Klein et al. (1991), 1-20.

Klein, H. K. (1984) 'Which epistemologies for future information systems research', in Saaksjarvi, M. (Ed.), *Report of the 7th Scandinavian research seminar on systemeering (part I)*, Helsinki Business School, 60-90.

Klein, H. K. (1986a) 'The critical social theory perspective on information systems development', in *Proceedings of the 18th annual meeting of the Decision Sciences Institute*, 575-577.

Klein, H. K. (1986b) 'Organizational implications of office systems: Toward a critical social action perspective', in Verrijn-Stuart, A. A. and Hirschheim, R. A. (Eds), *Office systems*, North-Holland, Amsterdam.

Klein, H. K. and Hirschheim, R. (1983) 'Issues and approaches to appraising technological change in the office: A consequentialist perspective', *Office Technology & People*, 2, 1, 15-42.

Klein, H. K. and Hirschheim, R. (1985) 'Fundamental issues of decision support systems: A consequentialist perspective', *Decision Support Systems*, 1, 1, 5-24.

Klein, H. K. and Hirschheim, R. (1988) 'Rationality concepts in information systems development methodologies', in *Symposium on system analysis and design*, Atlanta, GA.

Klein, H. K. and Lyytinen, K. (1985) 'The poverty of scientism in information systems', in Mumford, Hirschheim et al. (1985), 131-162.

Klein, H. K. and Myers, M. D. (1999) 'A set of principles for conducting and evaluating interpretive field studies in information systems', *MIS Quarterly*, 23, 1, 67-93.

Klein, H. K. and Truex III, D. P. (1995) 'Discourse analysis: A semiotic approach to the investigation of organizational emergence', in Andersen, P. B. and Holmqvist, B. (Eds), *The semiotics of the workplace*, Walter De Gruyter, Berlin.

Klein, H. K. and Welke, R. J. (1982) 'Information systems as a scientific discipline', in *Proceedings of the Administrative Services Association conference*, University of Ottawa, 106-116.

Kling, R. (1978a) 'Automated information systems as social resources in policy making', in *Proceedings of the Association for Computing Machinery*, 666-674.

Kling, R. (1978b) 'Automated welfare client tracking and service integration: The political economy of computing', *Communications of the ACM*, 21, 6, 484-493.

Kling, R. (1980) 'Social analyses of computing theoretical perspectives in recent empirical research', *Computing Surveys*, 12, 1, 61-110.

Kling, R. (1982) *Defining the boundaries of computing in complex organizations: A behavioral approach*, University of California, Working Paper, Irvine, CA.

Kling, R. and Iacono, S. (1984) 'The control of information systems developments after implementation', *Communications of the ACM*, 27, 12, 1218-1226.

Kling, R. and Scacchi, W. (1982) 'The web of computing: Computer technology as social organization', in *Advances in computing*, Academic Press, New York, 1-90.

Kolf, F. and Oppelland, H. (1979) 'A design oriented approach in implementation research: The project PORGL', in Szyperski, N. and Groschla, E. (Eds), *Design and implementation of computer-based information systems*, Sijthoff and Noordhoff, Amsterdam.

Kraemer, K., Dickhoven, S., Tierney, S. and King, J. D. (1987) *Datawars: The politics of modeling in federal policymaking*, Columbia University Press, New York.

Kraemer, K. and King, J. (1979) 'Requirements for USAC', *Policy Analysis*, 5, 3, 313-349.

Kraemer, K. I. and King, J. L. (1988) 'Computer-based systems for cooperative work', *Computing Surveys*, 20, 2, 115-146.

Kraemer, K. L. (1981) 'The politics of model implementation', *Systems, Objectives, Solutions*, 1, 4, 161-178.

Kuhn, T. (1970a) 'Reflections on my critics', in Lakatos, I. and Musgrave, A. (Eds), *Criticism and the growth of knowledge*, Cambridge University Press, New York, 231-278.

Kuhn, T. S. (1970b) *The structure of scientific revolutions*, The University of Chicago Press, Chicago, IL.

Kumar, K. and Welke, R. (1984) 'Implementation failure and system developer values', in Maggi, L., King, J. and Kraemer, K. (Eds), *Proceedings of the fifth international conference of information systems*, Tucson, AZ, 1-17.

Kuper, A. (1973) *Anthropologists and anthropology*, Pica Press, New York.

Lakoff, G. and Johnson, M. (1980) *Metaphors we live by*, The University of Chicago Press, Chicago, IL.

Land, F. (1989) 'From software engineering to information systems engineering', in Knight, K. (Ed.), *Participation in systems development*, Kogan Page, London, 9-33.

Land, F., Detjejarvwat, N. and Smith, C. (1983) 'Factors affecting social controls: The reasons and values - part 2', *Systems, Objectives, Solutions*, 3, 4, 207-226.

Land, F. and Hirschheim, R. (1983) 'Participative systems design: Rationale, tools and techniques', *Journal of Applied Systems Analysis*, 10.

Land, F. F. (1986) 'Social aspects of information systems', in Piercy, N. (Ed.), *Management information systems: The technology challenge*, Croom Heim, London.

Lanzara, G. and Mathiassen, L. (1985) 'Mapping situations within a systems development project', *Information and Management*, 8, 1, 3-11.

Lanzara, G. F. (1983) 'The design process: Frames, metaphors, and games', in Briefs, U., Ciborra, C. and Schneider, L. (Eds), *Systems design for, with and by the users*, North-Holland, Amsterdam, 29-40.

Laudon, K. C. (1974) *Computers and bureaucratic reform*, Wiley, New York.

Lawler, E. and Rhode, I. G. (1976) *Information and control in organizations*, Goodyear, Palisades, CA.

Layder, D. (1993) *New strategies in social research*, Polity Press, Cambridge.

Lee, A. (1985) 'The scientific basis for conducting case studies of organizations', in Robinson, R. and Pearce, J. (Eds), *Academy of Management proceedings*, San Diego, CA, 320-323.

Lee, A. (1986) *The case study of an organization as a scientific research strategy*, Working Paper 86-25, Northeastern University, Boston, MA.

Lee, A. (1987a) *Integrating positivist and interpretive approaches to organizational research. Southern Management Association*, New Orleans, LA.

Lee, A. (1987b) 'Quixotic communication: The case of expert witness testimony', *Knowledge*, 8, 4, 549-585.

Lee, A. S. (1989) 'Case studies as natural experiments', *Human Relations*, 42, 2, 117-137.

Lee, A. S. (1991) 'Integrating positivist and interpretive approaches to organizational research', *Organizational Science*, 2, 4, 342-365.

Lee, A. S. (1994) 'Electronic mail as a medium for rich communication: An empirical investigation using hermeneutic interpretation', *MIS Quarterly*, 18, 2, 143-157.

Lee, A. S., Liebenau, J. and DeGross, J. I. (Eds) (1997) *Information systems and qualitative research*, Chapman and Hall, London.

Leonard-Barton, D. (1987) 'Implementing structured software methodologies: A case of innovation in process technology', *Interfaces*, 17, 3, 6-17.

Leonard-Barton, D. and Sviokla, J. (1988) 'Putting expert systems to work', *Harvard Business Review*, 66, 2, 91-98.

Leonard-Barton, D. A. (1990) 'A dual methodology for case studies: Synergistic use of a longitudinal single site with replicated multiple sites', *Organization Science*, 1, 3, 248-266.

Lewin, K. (1951) *Field theory in social science*, Harper, New York.

Lewis, I. M. (1985) *Social anthropology in perspective*, Cambridge University Press, Cambridge.

Lincoln, Y. S. and Guba, E. G. (1985) *Naturalistic inquiry*, Sage, Beverly Hills, CA.

Lippit, G. and Lippit, R. (1978) *The consulting process in action*, University Associates, San Diego, CA.

Louis, K. (1982) 'Multisite/multimethod studies: An introduction', *American Behavioral Scientist*, 26, 1, 6-22.

Lucas, H. (1974) *Why information systems fail*, Columbia University Press, New York.

Lucas, H. (1978) 'Empirical evidence for a descriptive model of implementation', *MIS Quarterly*, 2, 2, 27-42.

Lucas, H. C., Jr (1981) *Implementation: The key to successful information systems*, Columbia University Press, New York.

Lucas, H. C., Jr (1984) 'Organizational power and the information services department: A re-examination', *Communications of the ACM*, 27, 1, 58-65.

Lukka, K. (1987) 'Budgetary biasing in organizations: Theoretical framework and empirical evidence', *Accounting Organizations and Society*, 13, 3, 281-301.

Luthans, F. and Davis, T. R. V. (1982) 'An idiographic approach to organizational behavior research: The use of single case experimental designs and direct measures', *Academy of Management Review*, 7, 3, 380-391.

Lyotard, J.-F. (1984) *The postmodern condition: A report on knowledge*, Manchester University Press, Manchester.

Lyotard, J.-F. (1988) *The differend: Phrases in dispute*, Manchester University Press, Manchester.

Lyotard, J.-F. and Thebaud, J.-L. (1985) *Just gaming*, Manchester University Press, Manchester.

Lyytinen, K. (1986a) 'Implications of theories of language for information systems', *MIS Quarterly*, 9, 1, 61-76.

Lyytinen, K. (1986b) *Information systems development as social action: Framework and critical implications,*, PhD Dissertation, Department of Computer Science, University of Jyvaskyla, Finland.

Lyytinen, K. (1987) 'Different perspectives on information systems: Problems and solutions', *Computing Surveys*, 19, 1, 5-46.

Lyytinen, K. and Hirschheim, R. (1987) 'Information systems failures: A survey and classification of the empirical literature', *Oxford Surveys in Information Technology*, 4.

Lyytinen, K. and Klein, H. K. (1985) 'The critical theory of Jurgen Habermas as a basis for a theory of information systems', in Mumford, Hirschheim et al. (1985).

Lyytinen, K. and Lehtinen, E. (1987) 'Seven mortal sins of systems work', in Docherty, P., Fuchs-Kinowski, K., Kolm, P. and Mathiassen, L. (Eds), *System design for human development and productivity: Participation; and beyond*, North-Holland, Amsterdam, 63-79.

Madsen, K. H. (1989) 'Breakthough by breakdown: Metaphors and structured domains', in Klein, H. K. and Kumar, K. (Eds), *Systems development for human progress*, North-Holland, Amsterdam, 41-53.

Malone, T. W., Yates, J. and Benjamin, R. I. (1987) 'Electronic markets and electronic hierarchies: Effects of information technology on market structure and corporate strategies', *Communications of the ACM*, 30, 6, 484-497.

Mann, R. I. and Watson, H. J. (1984) 'A contingency model for user involvement in DSS development', *MIS Quarterly*, 8, 1, 27-38.

Marcus, G. E. (1992) *Rereading cultural anthropology*, Duke University Press, Durham, NC.

Marcus, G. E. and Fischer, M. M. (1986) *Anthropology as cultural critique*, Chicago University Press, Chicago, IL.

Marcuse, H. (1968) *Negations: Essays in critical theory*, Heinemann, London.

Markus, M. L. (1979) *Understanding information systems use in organizations: A theoretical explanation*, Case Western Reserve University, Doctoral Dissertation, Cleveland, OH.

Markus, M. L. (1981) 'Implementation politics - top management support and user involvement', *Systems, Objectives, Solutions*, 1, 4, 203-215.

Markus, M. L. (1983) 'Power, politics, and MIS implementation', *Communications of the ACM*, 26, 6, 430-444.

Markus, M. L. (1984) *Systems in organizations: Bugs and features*, Pitman, Boston, MA.

Markus, M. L. (1986) 'Case study research and the use of communication systems in organizations', in *Proceedings of the seventh international conference on information systems*, San Diego, CA, 339.

Markus, M. L. and Bjørn-Andersen, N. (1987) 'Power over users: Its exercise by system professionals', *Communications of the ACM*, 30, 6, 498-504.

Markus, M. L. and Pfeffer, J. "Power and the design and implementation of accounting and control systems," *Accounting, Organizations and Society* (8:2/3), 1981, pp. 205-218.

Markus, M. L. and Robey, D. (1988) 'Information technology and organizational change: Causal structure in theory and research', *Management Science*, 34, 5, 583-598.

Martin, J. (1985) *Information systems manifesto*, Prentice-Hall, Englewood Cliffs, NJ.

Martin, J. (1990a) *Information engineering: Book I introduction*, Prentice-Hall, Englewood Cliffs, NJ.

Martin, J. (1990b) *Information engineering: Book II planning and analysis*, Prentice-Hall, Englewood Cliffs, NJ.

Martin, J. (1990c) *Information engineering: Book III design and construction*, Prentice-Hall, Englewood Cliffs, NJ.

Martin, P. Y. and Turner, B. A. (1986) 'Grounded theory and organizational research', *The Journal of Applied Behavioral Science*, 22, 2, 141-157.

Mason, R. and Mitroff, I. (1981) *Challenging strategic planning assumptions*, Wiley, New York.

Mathiassen, L. and Bogh-Andersen, P. (1987) 'Systems development and use: A science of the truth or a theory of lies', in Bjerknes, G., Elm, P. and Kyng, M. (Eds), *Computers and democracy - a Scandinavian challenge*, Avebury, Aldershot, 395-417.

McCarthy, T. (1978) *The critical theory of Jurgen Habermas*, Polity Press, Cambridge.

McFarlan, F. W. (1984a) *The information systems research challenge*, Harvard Business School Press, Boston, MA.

McFarlan, F. W. (1984b) 'Information technology changes the way you compete', *Harvard Business Review*, 62, 3, 98-103.

McMenamin, S. and Palmer, J. (1984) *Essential systems analysis*, Yourdon, New York.

Mechanic, D. (1962) 'Sources of power of lower participants in complex organization', *Administrative Science Quarterly*, 7, 349-364.

Meyerson, D. and Martin, J. (1987) 'Cultural change: An integration of three different views', *Journal of Management Studies*, 24, 6, 623-647.

Miles, M. (1979) 'Qualitative analysis as an attractive nuisance: The problem of analysis', *Administrative Science Quarterly*, 24, 4, 590-601.

Miles, M. (1982) 'A mini-cross-site analysis', *American Behavioral Scientist*, 26, 1, 121-131.

Miles, M. B. and Huberman, A. M. (1984) *Qualitative data analysis: A sourcebook of new methods*, Sage, Newbury Park, CA.

Milne, R. (1981) *Budget slack*, University of Illinois at Urbana, Doctoral Dissertation, Champaign, IL.

Mingers, J. (1984) 'Subjectivism and soft systems methodology - a critique', *Journal of Applied Systems Analysis*, 11, 85-103.

Mingers, J. C. (1981) 'Towards an appropriate social theory for applied systems thinking: Critical social theory and soft systems methodology', *Journal of Applied Systems Analysis*, 7, 41-49.

Mingers, J. C. and Stowell, F. (Eds) (1997) *Information systems: An emerging discipline?*, McGraw-Hill, London.

Mintzberg, H., Raisinghard, D. and Theoret, A. (1976) 'The structure of "unstructured" decision processes', *Administrative Science Quarterly*, 21, 246-275.

Mitroff, I. L. (1983) 'Archetypal social systems analysis: On the deeper structure of human systems', *Academy of Management Review*, 8, 387-397.

Mohr, L. B. (1982) *Explaining organizational behavior*, Jossey Bass, San Francisco, CA.

Morey, N. C. and Luthans, F. (1984) 'An emic perspective and ethnoscience methods for organizational research', *Academy of Management Review*, 9, 1, 27-36.

Morgan, G. (1980) 'Paradigms, metaphors and puzzle-solving in organization theory', *Administrative Science Quarterly*, 25, 4, 605-622.

Morgan, G. (Ed.) (1983) *Beyond method: Strategies for social research*, Sage, Beverly Hills, CA.

Morgan, G. (1986) *Images of organization*, Sage, Newbury Park, CA.

Morgan, G. and Smircich, L. (1980) 'The case for qualitative research', *Academy of Management Review*, 5, 4, 491-500.

Mowshowitz, A. (1976) *Information processing in human affairs*, Addison-Wesley, Reading, MA.

Mumford, E. (1972) *Job satisfaction: A study of computer specialists*, Longman, London.

Mumford, E. (1981) 'Participative systems design: Structure and method', *Systems, Objectives, Solutions*, 1, 1, 5-19.

Mumford, E. (1983) *Designing human systems - the ETHICS method*, Manchester Business School Press, Manchester.

Mumford, E. (1985) 'Researching people problems: Some advice to a student', in Mumford, Hirschheim et al. (1985), 315-320.

Mumford, E. (1987) 'Managerial expert systems and organizational change: Some critical research issues', in Boland, R. and Hirschheim, R. (Eds), *Critical issues in information systems research*, Wiley, Chichester, 135-155.

Mumford, E., Hirschheim, R. A., Fitzgerald, G. and Wood-Harper, T. (Eds) (1985) *Research methods in information systems*, North-Holland, Amsterdam.

Mumford, E. and Weir, M. (1979) *Computer systems in work design: The ETHICS method*, Halstead Press, New York.

Myers, M. D. (1987) *Independens long Vanuatu: The churches and politics in a Melanesian nation*, University of Auckland, Doctoral Dissertation, Auckland.

Myers, M. D. (1994) 'A disaster for everyone to see: An interpretive analysis of a failed IS project', *Accounting, Management and Information Technologies*, 4, 4, 185-201.

Myers, M. D. (1995) 'Dialectical hermeneutics: A theoretical framework for the implementation of information systems', *Information Systems Journal*, 5, 1, 51-70.

Myers, M. D. (1997a) 'Qualitative research in information systems', *MISQ Discovery*, http://www.misq.org/misqd961/isworld/.

Myers, M. D. (1997b) 'Qualitative research in information systems', *MIS Quarterly*, 21, 2, 241-242.

Myers, M. D. (living) 'Qualitative research in information systems: Living version', *MISQ Discovery*, http://www.auckland.ac.nz/msis/isworld.

Nagel, E. (1979) *The structure of science*, Hacket, Indianapolis, IN.

Nandhakumar, J. (1993) *The practice of executive information systems development: An in-depth case study*, University of Cambridge, PhD Thesis, Cambridge.

Naumann, J. D. (1986) 'The role of frameworks in MIS research', in *Proceedings of the 1986 annual meeting of the Decision Sciences Institute*, Honolulu, HI, 569- 571.

Naur, P. (1983) 'Program development studies based on diaries', in Green, T. (Ed.), *Psychology of computer use*, Academic Press, London, 159-170.

Necco, C., Tsai, N. W. and Holgeson, K. W. (1989) 'Current usage of case software', *Journal of Systems Management*, 40, 5, 6-11.

Newman, M. (1989) 'Some fallacies in information systems development', *International Journal of Information Management*, 9, 2, 127-143.

Newman, M. and Robey, D. (1992) 'A social process model of user-analyst relationships', *MIS Quarterly*, 16, 2, 249-266.

Newman, M. and Rosenberg, D. (1985) 'Systems analysts and the politics of organizational control', *Omega*, 13, 3, 393-406.

Ngwenyama, O. K. (1987) *Fundamental issues of knowledge acquisition: Towards a human action perspective of knowledge systems*, PhD Thesis, State University of New York, Binghamton, NY.

Ngwenyama, O. K. and Lee, A. S. (1997) 'Communication richness in electronic mail: Critical social theory and the contextuality of meaning', *MIS Quarterly*, 21, 2, 145-167.

Nissen, H.-E., Klein, H. K. and Hirschheim, R. A. (Eds) (1991) *Information systems research: Contemporary approaches and emergent traditions*, North-Holland, Amsterdam.

Noble, D. F. (1979) 'Social choice in machine design: The case of automatically controlled machine tools, and a challenge for labor', in *Case studies in the labor process*, Monthly Review Press, New York, 15-50.

Norman, R., Corbitt, G., Butler, M. and McEiroy, D. (1989) 'Case technology transfer: A case study of unsuccessful change', *Journal of Systems Management*, 40, 5, 33-37.

Norman, R. and Nunamaker, J. F. (1988) 'An empirical study of information systems professionals' productivity perceptions of case technology', in *Proceedings of the ninth international conference on information systems*, Association for Computing Machinery, New York, 111-118.

Normann, R. (1971) 'Organizational innovativeness: Product variation and reorientations', *Administrative Science Quarterly*, 16, 2, 203-215.

Ollman, B. (1976) *Alienation*, Cambridge University Press, New York.

Olson, M. (1981) 'User involvement and decentralization of the development function: A comparison of two case studies', *Systems, Objectives, Solutions*, 1, 2, 59-69.

Olson, M. H. and Primps, S. B. (1984) 'Working at home with computers: Work and nonwork issues', *Journal of Social Issues*, 40, 3, 97-112.

Opperman, R. (1986) 'User participation: Some experiences and recommendations', *Systems, Objectives, Solutions*, 6.

Orlikowski, W. J. (1988a) 'CASE tools and the IS workplace: Some findings from empirical research', in Awad, E. M. (Ed.), *Proceedings of the ACM SIGCPR conference*, ACM Press, Baltimore, MD, 88-97.

Orlikowski, W. J. (1988b) *Information technology in post-industrial organizations: An examination of the computer-mediation of production work*, Stern School of Business, New York University, unpublished PhD thesis, New York.

Orlikowski, W. J. (1989) 'Division among the ranks: The social implications of CASE tools for system developers', *Proceedings of the tenth international conference on information systems*, 199-210.

Orlikowski, W. J. (1991) 'Integrated information environment or matrix of control? The contradictory implications of information technology', *Accounting, Management and Information Technologies*, 1, 1, 9-42.

Orlikowski, W. J. (1992) 'The duality of technology - rethinking the concept of technology in organizations', *Organization Science*, 3, 3, 398-427.

Orlikowski, W. J. (1993) 'CASE tools as organizational change: Investigating incremental and radical changes in systems development', *MIS Quarterly*, 17, 3, 309-340.

Orlikowski, W. J. and Baroudi, J. J. (1991) 'Studying information technology in organizations: Research approaches and assumptions', *Information Systems Research*, 2, 1, 1-28.

Orlikowski, W. J. and Gash, D. C. (1994) 'Technological frames: Making sense of information technology in organizations', *ACM Transactions on Information Systems*, 12, 2, 174-207.

Orlikowski, W. J. and Robey, D. (1991) 'Information technology and the structuring of organizations', *Information Systems Research*, 2, 1, 143-169.

Ortony, A. (1979) 'Metaphor: A multidimensional problem', in Ortony, A. (Ed.), *Metaphor and thought*, Cambridge University Press, New York.

Palmer, R. (1969) *Hermeneutics: Interpretation theory in Schleiermacher, Dilthey, Heidegger, and Gadamer*, Northwestern University Press, Evanston, IL.

Pamas, D. and Clements, P. (1989) 'A rational design process: How and why to fake it', in Ehrigg, H., Floyd, C., Nivat, M. and Thatcher, J. (Eds), *Formal methods and software development (TAPSOFT proceedings)*, Springer-Verlag, Berlin.

Parsons, G. L. (1983) 'Information technology: A new competitive weapon', *Sloan Management Review*, 25, 1, 3-14.

Pava, C. (1983) *Managing new office technology: An organizational strategy*, Free Press, New York.

Pennings, J. (1988) 'Information technology in production organizations', *International Studies of Management and Organization*, 17, 4, 68-89.

Pepper, S. C. (1942) *World hypotheses*, University of California Press, Berkeley, CA.

Pettigrew, A. (1985) 'Contextualist research and the study of organizational change processes', in Mumford, Hirschheim et al. (1985), 53-78.

Pettigrew, A. (1987) 'Context and action in the transformation of the firm', *Journal of Management Studies*, 24, 6, 649-670.

Pettigrew, A. (1990) 'Longitudinal field research on change: Theory and practice', *Organizational Science*, 1, 3, 267-292.

Pettigrew, A. M. (1972) 'Information control as a power resource', *Sociology*, 6, 2, 187-204.

Pettigrew, A. M. (1989) 'Issues of time and site selection in longitudinal research on change', in Cash and Lawrence (1989), 13-19.

Pfeffer, J. (1978) *Organizational design*, AHM, Arlington Heights, IL.

Pfeffer, J. (1981) *Power in organization*, Pitman, Marshfield, MA.

Pfeffer, J. (1982) *Organizations and organization theory*, Pitnam, Boston, MA.

Podsakoff, P. M. and Dalton, D. R. (1987) 'Research methodology in organizational studies', *Journal of Management*, 13, 2, 419-441.

Polkinghorne, D. E. (1988) *Narrative knowing and the human sciences*, State of New York University Press, Albany, NY.

Pondy, L., Frost, P., Morgan, G. and Dandridge, T. (Eds) (1983) *Organizational symbolism*, JAI Press, Greenwich, CT.

Poole, M. S. and DeSanctis, G. (1989) 'Use of GDSS as an appropriation process', in *Proceedings of the Hawaii international conference on information systems*, 149-157.

Popper, K. (1968) *The logic of scientific discovery*, Harper Torchbooks, New York.

Porter, M. E. and Millar, V. E. (1985) 'How information gives you competitive advantage', *Harvard Business Review*, 64, 4, 149-160.

Preston, A. M. (1991) 'The "problem" in and of management information systems', *Accounting, Management and Information Technologies*, 1, 1, 43-69.

Putnam, L. L. (1983) 'The interpretive perspective: An alternative to functionalism', in Putnam, L. L. and Pacanowsky, M. E. (Eds), *Communication and organization*, Sage, Beverly Hills, CA, 31-54.

Pyburn, P. (1983) 'Linking the MIS plan with corporate strategy: An exploratory study', *MIS Quarterly*, 7, 2, 1-14.

Radnitzky, G. (1970) *Contemporary schools of metascience*, Scandinavian University Books, Goteborg.

Rapoport, R. N. (1970) 'Three dilemmas in action research', *Human Relations*, 23, 4, 499-513.

Raspa, R. (1984) 'The refocussing of folkloric expression under stress in the automobile industry', in *First international conference on organizational symbolism and corporate culture*, Lund.

Ricoeur, P. (1974) *The conflict of interpretations: Essays in hermeneutics*, Northwestern University Press, Evanston, IL.

Ricoeur, P. (1976) *Interpretation theory, discourse and the surplus of meaning*, Texas Christian University Press, Fort Worth, TX.

Ricoeur, P. (1981) *Hermeneutics and the human sciences*, Cambridge University Press, Cambridge.

Rivard, S. and Huff, S. L. (1984) 'User developed applications: Evaluation of success from the DP department perspective', *MIS Quarterly*, 8, 1, 39-50.

Robey, D. (1981) 'Computer information systems and organization structure', *Communications of the ACM*, 24, 10, 679-686.

Robey, D. (1983) 'Information systems and organizational change: A comparative case study', *Systems, Objectives, Solutions*, 3, 3, 143-154.

Robey, D., Farrow, D. L. and Franz, C. R. (1989) 'Group process and conflict in system development', *Management Science*, 35, 10, 1172-1191.

Robey, D. and Markus, M. L. (1984) 'Rituals in information system design', *MIS Quarterly*, 8, 1, 5-15.

Robey, D. and Taggart, W. (1981) 'Measuring managers' minds: The assessment style in human information processing', *Academy of Management Review*, 6, 3.

Rockart, J. F. and Flannery, L. S. (1983) 'The management of end-user computing', *Communications of the ACM*, 26, 10, 776-784.

Roethlisberger, F. J. (1977) *The elusive phenomena*, Harvard Business School, Boston, MA.

Rogers, E. M. (1983) *The diffusion of innovation*, The Free Press, New York.

Rogers, W., Ryack, B. and Moeller, G. (1979) 'Computer-aided medical diagnosis: A literature review', *International Journal of Biomedical Computing*, 10, 267-289.

Rorty, R. (1979) *Philosophy and the mirror of nature*, Princeton University Press, Princeton, NJ.

Rorty, R. (1982) *Consequences of pragmatism*, University of Minnesota Press, Minneapolis.

Rorty, R. (1989) *Contingency, irony and solidarity*, Cambridge University Press, Cambridge.

Rose, M. (1969) *Computers, managers, and society*, Penguin, Harmondsworth.

Rosen, M. (1986) 'Ethnographic study of the role of information technology in organizational control systems', in *Proceedings of the seventh international conference on information systems*, San Diego, CA, 339.

Rosen, M. (1991) 'Coming to terms with the field: Understanding and doing organizational ethnography', *Journal of Management Studies*, 28, 1, 1-24.

Rosenau, P. (1992) *Post-modernism and the social sciences: Insights, inroads, and intrusions*, Princeton University Press, Princeton, NJ.

Rowan, J. (1973) *The social individual*, Davis-Poynter, London.

Rubin, H. and Rubin, I. (1995) *Qualitative interviewing: The art of hearing data*, Sage, Thousand Oaks, CA.

Sanday, P. R. (1979) 'The ethnographic paradigm(s)', *Administrative Science Quarterly*, 24, 4, 527-538.

Sanford, N. (1976) 'Whatever happened to action research?', in Clark, A. (Ed.), *Experimenting with organizational life: The action research approach*, Plenum, New York.

Saunders, C. S. and Scamell, R. W. (1986) 'Organizational power and the information services department: A re-examination', *Communications of the ACM*, 29, 2, 142-147.

Scarrott, G. (1985) 'Information, the life blood of organization', *Computer Journal*, 28, 3, 203-205.

Schafer, G., Hirschheim, R., Harper, M., HansJee, R., Domke, M. and Bjørn-Andersen, N. (1988) *Functional analysis of office requirements: A multiperspective approach*, Wiley, Chichester.

Schein, E. (1969) *Process consultation: Its role in organizational development*, Addison-Wesley, Reading, MA.

Schein, E. (1987) *The clinical perspective in fieldwork*, Sage, Newbury Park, CA.

Scholte, B. (1972) 'Toward a reflexive and critical anthropology', in Hymes, D. (Ed.), *Reinventing anthropology*, Random House, New York.

Schön, D. (1979) 'Generative metaphor: A perspective on problem setting in public policy', in Ortony, A. (Ed.), *Metaphor and thought*, Cambridge University Press, Cambridge, 254-282.

Schön, D., Drake, W. and Miller, R. (1984) 'Social experimentation as reflection-in-action', *Knowledge*, 6, 1, 5-36.

Schön, D. A. (1983) *The reflective practitioner: How professionals think in action*, Basic Books, New York.

Schonberger, R. J. (1981) 'Strategy and structure: A tale of two information systems departments', *Systems, Objectives, Solutions*, 1, 2, 71-77.

Scott Morton, M. (1971) *Management decision systems: Computer-based support for decision making*, Harvard Business School, Boston, MA.

Seashore, S. (1976) 'The design of action research', in Clarke, A. (Ed.), *Experimenting with organizational life: The action research approach*, Plenum, New York, 103-117.

Shallis, M. (1984) *The silicon idol*, Oxford University Press, London.

Sibley, E. (1986) 'The evolution of approaches to information systems design methodologies', in Olle, T. W., Sol, H. and Verrijn-Stuart, A. (Eds), *Information systems design methodologies: Improving the practice*, North-Holland, Amsterdam, 1-17.

Silverman, D. (1993) *Interpreting qualitative data*, Sage, London.

Smircich, L. (1983a) 'Concepts of culture and organizational analysis', *Administrative Science Quarterly*, 28, 3, 339-358.

Smircich, L. (1983b) 'Organizations as shared meanings', in Pondy, Frost et al. (1983), 55-65.

Smith, S. (1988) 'How much change at the store? The impact of new technologies and labour processes on managers and staffs in retail distribution', in Knights, D. and Willmott, H. (Eds), *New technology and the labour process*, Macmillan, London, 143-162.

Sproull, L. and Kiesler, S. (1986) 'Reducing social context cues: Electronic mail in organizational communication', *Management Science*, 32, 11, 1492-1512.

Stamper, R. (1985) 'Towards a theory of information: Mystical fluid or a subject for scientific enquiry?', *Computer Journal*, 28, 3, 195-199.

Staw, B. (1985) 'Spinning on symbolism: A brief note on the future of symbolism in organizational research', *Journal of Management*, 11, 2, 117-118.

Steffy, B. D. and Grimes, A. J. (1996) 'A critical theory of organization science', *Academy of Management Review*, 322-336.

Stevenson, H. (1987) *Expert systems in the UK financial services sector: Accounting for the discrepancies - the relevance of a symbolic approach*, Oxford University, MSc Dissertation, Oxford.

Stone, E. F. (1978) *Research methods in organizational behavior*, Scott, Foresman, Glenview, IL.

Straub, D. (1991) 'Rigor in information systems research', Nissen, Klein et al. (1991), 103-106.

Strauss, A. and Corbin, J. (1990) *Basics of qualitative research: Grounded theory procedures and techniques*, Sage, Newbury Park, CA.

Strauss, G. (1974) 'Tactics of lateral relationship: The purchasing agent', in Kolb, D. et al. (Eds), *Organizational psychology: A book of readings*, Prentice-Hall, Englewood Cliffs, NJ.

Suchman, L. (1987) *Plans and situated actions: The problem of human-machine communication*, Cambridge University Press, Cambridge.

Suchman, L. and Wynn, E. (1984) 'Procedures and problems in the office', *Office, Technology and People*, 2.

Susman, G. I. (1983) 'Action research: A sociotechnical systems perspective', in Morgan (1983), 95-113.

Susman, G. I. and Evered, R. D. (1978) 'An assessment of the scientific merits of action research', *Administrative Science Quarterly*, 23, 4, 582-603.

Sutton, R. I. (1987) 'The process of organizational death: Disbanding and reconnecting', *Administrative Science Quarterly*, 32, 4, 542-569.

Sviokla, J. S. (1986) *Planpower, XCON, and Mudman: An in-depth analysis into three commercial expert systems in use*, Harvard Business School, Doctoral Dissertation, Boston, MA.

Swanson, K., McComb, D., Smith, J. and McCubbrey, D. (1991) 'The application software factory: Applying total quality techniques to systems development', *MIS Quarterly*, 15, 4, 567-579.

Synnott, W. and Gruber, W. (1981) *Information resource management: Opportunities and strategies for the 1980's*, Wiley, New York.

Taylor, C. (1976) 'Hermeneutics and politics', in Connerton, P. (Ed.), *Critical sociology, selected readings*, Penguin Books, Harmondsworth, 153-193.

Taylor, C. (1979) 'Interpretation and the sciences of man', in Rabinow, P. and Sullivan, W. (Eds), *Interpretive social science*, University of California Press, Berkeley, CA, 25-71.

Thompson, J. B. (1981) *Critical hermeneutics: A study in the thought of Paul Ricoeur and Jurgen Habermas*, Cambridge University Press, Cambridge.

Tice, T. N. and Slavens, T. P. (1983) *Research guide to philosophy*, American Library Association, Chicago, IL.

Tinker, T. (1986) 'Metaphor or reification: Are radical humanists really libertarian anarchists?', *Journal of Management Studies*, 9, 4, 363-384.

Todd, P. and Benbasat, I. (1987) 'Process tracing methods in decision support research: Exploring the black box', *MIS Quarterly*, 11, 4, 493-512.

Towl, A. R. (1969) *To study administrations by cases*, Harvard Business School, Boston, MA.

Trice, H. and Beyer, J. (1984) 'Studying organizational cultures through rites and ceremonials', *Academy of Management Review*, 9, 4, 653-669.

Trist, E. (1976) 'Engaging with large-scale systems', in Clark, A. (Ed.), *Experimenting with organizational life: The action research approach*, Plenum, New York, 43-75.

Turner, B. (1986) 'Sociological aspects of organizational symbolism', *Organization Studies*, 7, 2, 101-115.

Turner, B. A. (1983) 'The use of grounded theory for the qualitative analysis of organizational behaviour', *Journal of Management Studies*, 20, 3, 333-348.

Turner, J. and Kraut, R. (Eds) (1992) *Proceedings of the conference on computer-supported co-operative work: Sharing perspectives (CSCW '92)*, ACM Press, New York.

Turner, J. A. (1984) 'Computer-mediated work: The interplay between technology and structured jobs', *Communications of the ACM*, 27, 12, 1210-1217.

Tushman, M. L. and Romanelli, E. (1985) 'Organizational evolution: A metamorphosis model of convergence and reorientation', in Cummings, L. L. and Staw, B. M. (Eds), *Research in organizational behavior*, JAI Press, Greenwich, CT, 171-222.

Van Eynde, D. and Bledsoe, J. (1990) 'The changing practice of organization development', *Leadership & Organization Development Journal*, 11, 2, 25-30.

Van Maanen, J. (1979) 'The fact of fiction in organizational ethnography', *Administrative Science Quarterly*, 24, 4, 530-550.

Van Maanen, J. (1982) 'Introduction', in Van Maanen, J. (Ed.), *Varieties of qualitative research*, Sage, Beverly Hills, CA, 11-29.

Van Maanen, J. (1988) *Tales from the field: On writing ethnography*, Chicago University Press, Chicago, IL.

Van Maanen, J. (1989) 'Some notes on the importance of writing in organization studies', in Cash and Lawrence (1989), 27-33.

Van Maanen, T. (1985) 'Spinning on symbolism: Disquisition', *Journal of Management*, 11, 2, 119-120.

Vattimo, G. (1988) 'Hermeneutics as koine', *Theory, Culture and Society*, 5, 2-3.

Vessey, L., Jarvenpaa, S. L. and Tractinsky, N. (1992) 'Evaluation of vendor products: CASE tools as methodology companions', *Communications of the ACM*, 35, 4, 90-105.

Vitalari, N. and Dickson, G. (1983) 'Problem solving for effective systems analysis: An exploration', *Communications of the ACM*, 26, 11, 948-956.

Vogel, D. and Wetherbe, J. C. (1984) MIS research: A profile of leading journals and universities, in *Data Base*, 16, 3-14.

Von Schelling, F. W. J. (1958) 'Werke', in Schroter, M. (Ed.), *Schellings Werke*, Beck, Munich, 299.

Walsham, G. (1993) *Interpreting information systems in organizations*, Wiley, Chichester.

Walsham, G. and Waema, T. (1994) 'Information systems strategy and implementation: A case study of a building society', *ACM Transactions on Information Systems*, 12, 2, 150-173.

Wand, Y. and Weber, R. (1986) 'On paradigms in the IS discipline: The problem of the problem', in *Proceedings of the annual meeting of the Decision Sciences Institute*, 566~568.

Warmington, A. (1980) 'Action research: Its methods and its implications', *Journal of Applied Systems Analysis*, 7, 23-39.

Webb, C. (1989) 'Action research: Philosophy, methods and personal experiences', *Journal of Advanced Nursing*, 14, 5, 403-410.

Webb, E., Campbell, D., Schwartz, R. and Sechrest, L. (1966) *Unobtrusive measures: Nonreactive research in the social sciences*, Rand McNally, Chicago, IL.

Weber, M. (1947) *The theory of social and economic organization*, Free Press, Glencoe IL.

Weber, R. (1987) 'Toward a theory of artifacts: A paradigmatic base for information systems research', *Journal of Information Systems*, 1, 2, 3-19.

Webster, J. and Starbuck, W. H. (1988) 'Theory building in industrial and organizational psychology', in *International review of industrial and organizational psychology*, Wiley, London, 93-138.

Weick, K. E. (1976) 'Educational establishments as loosely-coupled systems', *Administrative Science Quarterly*, 21, 1, 11-19.

Weick, K. E. (1979) *The social psychology of organizing*, Addison-Wesley, Reading, MA.

Weick, K. E. (1984) 'Theoretical assumptions and research methodology selection', in McFarlan (1984a), 111-132.

Weinberg, V. (1980) *Structured analysis*, Prentice-Hall, Englewood Cliffs, NJ.

Weiss, M. (1983) 'Effects of work stress and social support on information systems managers', *MIS Quarterly*, 7, 1, 29-44.

Weizenbaum, J. (1966) 'ELIZA - a computer program for the study of natural language communications between man and machine', *Communications of the ACM*, 9, 1, 36-45.

Westerlund, G. and Sjostrand, S. (1979) *Organizational myths*, Harper & Row, London.

Wexler, M. (1983) 'Pragmatism, interactionism and dramatism: Interpreting the symbols in organizations', in Pondy, Frost et al. (1983), 237-253.

White, K. B. (1984) 'MIS project teams: An investigation of cognitive style implications', *MIS Quarterly*, 8, 2, 95-101.

Whitehead, A. N. (1927) *Symbolism: Its meaning and effect*, Macmillan, New York.

Winograd, T. and Flores, F. (1987) *Understanding computers and cognition: A new foundation for design*, Addison-Wesley, New York.

Wiseman, C. (1985) *Strategy and computers: Information systems as competitive weapons*, Irwin, IL.

Wood-Harper, A. T. (1989) *Comparison of information systems definition methodologies: An action research multiview perspective*, University of East Anglia, Doctoral Dissertation, Norwich.

Wynn, E. (1979) *Office conversation as an information medium*, University of California, Doctoral Dissertation, Berkeley, CA.

Wynn, E. (1991) 'Taking practice seriously', in Greenbaum, J. and Kyng, M. (Eds), *Design at work*, Lawrence Erlbaum, Hillsdale, NJ.

Yates, J. and Orlikowski, W. J. (1992) 'Genres of organizational communication: A structurational approach to studying communication and media', *Academy of Management Review*, 17, 2, 299-326.

Yellen, R. (1990) 'Systems analysts performance using CASE versus manual methods', in *Proceedings of the twenty-third annual Hawaii international conference on system sciences*, IEEE Computer Society Press, Los Alamitos, CA, 497-501.

Yin, R. (1981a) 'The case study as a serious research strategy', *Knowledge*, 3, 1, 97-114.

Yin, R. (1981b) 'The case study crisis: Some answers', *Administrative Science Quarterly*, 26, 1, 58-65.

Yin, R. (1982a) *The case study strategy: An annotated bibliography*, Case Study Institute, Washington, DC.

Yin, R. (1982b) 'Studying phenomenon and context across sites', *American Behavioral Scientist*, 26, 1, 84-100.

Yin, R. (1989) 'Research design issues in using the case study method to study management information systems', in Cash and Lawrence (1989), 1-6.

Yin, R. (1994) *Case study research: Design and methods*, Sage, Newbury Park, CA.

Young, S. (1968) 'Organization as a total system', *California Management Review*, 10, 3, 21-32.

Yourdon, E. (1982) *Managing the systems life cycle*, Yourdon Press, New York.

Yourdon, E. and Constantine, L. L. (1978) *Structured design*, Yourdon Press, New York.

Zuboff, S. (1988) *In the age of the smart machine*, Basic Books, New York.

Author Index

Ackoff, R. 166, 275
Adams, G. 245, 284
Agar, M. H. 68, 188, 275
Alavi, M. 8, 56, 140, 275
Allison, G. T. 83, 160, 275
Alter, S. L. 19, 21, 275
Alvesson, M. 244, 275, 281
Ancona, D. 183, 275
Andersen, P. B. 57, 285
Archer, S. 103, 275
Argyris, C. 122, 123, 124, 135, 142, 247, 275
Aristotle, 227, 243
Astley, W. G. 51, 66, 244, 275
Attewell, P. 57, 275
Avison, D. E. vii, viii, 3, 8, 276, 284
Awad, E. M. 291

Bakos, J. Y. 97, 276
Banker, R. D. 181, 276
Banville, C. 52, 129, 137, 276
Bardach, E. 271, 276
Barley, S. R. 176, 276
Barlow, D. H. 85, 147, 283
Barnett, G. 254, 276
Baroudi, J. J. 5, 6, 8, 51, 57, 61, 62, 63, 101, 129, 130, 139, 171, 172, 177, 182, 184, 221, 276, 291
Bartol, K. M. 57, 276
Bartunek, J. 217, 219, 276
Baskerville, R. 8, 129, 139, 276
Beath, C. 241, 276
Behling, O. 148, 276
Benbasat, I. 6, 8, 52, 67, 79, 80, 81, 97, 98, 101, 130, 147, 149, 276, 295
Benjamin, R. I. 288
Benson, J. K. 71, 72, 73, 276
Bentley, R. 172, 276
Berger, P. 175, 276

Bernstein, R. 62, 70, 148, 276, 277
Beyer, H. 9, 173, 283
Beyer, J. 243, 246, 254, 295
Bhaskar, R. 62, 110, 277
Bjerknes, G. 289
Bjørn-Andersen, N. 57, 165, 247, 277, 288, 293
Blackler, F. 130, 277
Bledsoe, J. 129, 295
Bleicher, J. 10, 11, 14, 277
Blois, M. 254, 277
Blum, F. 133, 277
Bogh-Andersen, P. 273, 289
Boguslaw, R. 254, 277
Boland, R. 6, 11, 15, 66, 77, 101, 103, 104, 175, 184, 225, 237, 242, 243, 245, 250, 251, 277, 290
Bolman, L. 246, 277
Bonoma, T. V. 81, 83, 84, 93, 277
Bostrom, R. P. 56, 272, 277, 278
Bouchard, T. J. Jr. 86, 278
Bowles, M. 245, 246, 278
Braverman, H. 24, 278
Bridges, W. 280
Briefs, U. 286
Bronsema, G. 93, 95, 285
Brook, G. 275
Brooks, F. 250, 255, 278
Bryman, A. 175, 278
Bubenko, J. 242, 278
Buckingham, R. 253, 278
Burawoy, M. 72, 73, 278
Burns, A. 267, 278
Burrell, G. 51, 63, 64, 70, 148, 166, 278
Butler, M. 290

Campbell, D. 296
Campbell, D. T. 86, 152, 161, 278, 279

Card, D. N. 181, 278
Carlson, P. 8, 275
Carnap, R. 148
Carr, W. 6, 278
Cash, J. I. 278, 292, 295, 297
Chandler, A. D. Jr. 93, 278, 284
Checkland, P. 15, 82, 104, 129, 132, 136, 137, 138, 242, 273, 278
Chervany, N. 280
Chisholm, R. F. 6, 280
Christenson, C. 80, 278
Chua, W. F. 5, 52, 55, 57, 58, 60, 63, 64, 71, 72, 73, 76, 184, 278
Ciborra, C. 242, 278, 286
Clark, A. 293, 295
Clark, K. 217, 283
Clark, P. A. 6, 8, 132, 133, 278
Clarke, A. 294
Clements, P. 250, 291
Cleverly, G. 253, 279
Clifford, J. 174, 279
Cohen, A. P. 174, 279
Cohen, P. 246, 279
Connerton, P. 281, 295
Constantine, L. L. 185, 297
Cook, T. D. 86, 279
Cooper, R. 130, 279
Copi, I. 151, 152, 153, 279
Corbin, J. 188, 294
Corbitt, G. 290
Covaleski, M. 243, 279
Crandall, D. 147, 283
Crozier, M. 24, 279
Culnan, M. J. 52, 53, 54, 57, 279
Cummings, L. L. 276, 295

Daft, R. L. 67, 148, 279
Dagwell, R. 245, 279
Dalton, D. R. 76, 292
Dalton, M. 24, 279
Dandridge, T. 244, 279, 292
Danziger, J. N. 57, 279
Darnell, R. 173, 279
Datta, L. 147, 279
Davies, L. J. 9, 173, 279
Davis, T. R. V. 147, 166, 287
Day, W. F. 101, 103, 104, 242, 277
Deal, T. 246, 277
Dearden, J. 248, 250, 279
DeGross, J. I. 283, 284, 287
DeMarco, T. 241, 250, 254, 279

Denzin, N. K. 4, 279
DeSanctis, G. 57, 182, 280, 284, 292
Detjejarvwat, N. 286
Dewar, R. D. 212, 280
Dickhoven, S. 161, 163, 286
Dickson, G. W. 92, 130, 246, 280, 284, 296
Dirsmith, M. 243, 279
Docherty, P. 288
Domke, M. 293
Drake, W. 293
Dreyfus, H. 255, 280
Duchon, D. 67, 284
Dukerich, J. M. 182, 216, 280
Dukes, W. 147, 280
Dunnette, M. D. 278
Dutton, J. E. 182, 212, 216, 280
Dutton, W. H. 88, 89, 90, 91, 92, 94, 95, 96, 99, 147, 161, 163, 279, 280, 281

Earl, M. 253, 280, 282
Edwards, R. 71, 280
Ehrigg, H. 291
Ein-Dor, P. 93, 165, 250, 280
Eisbach, K. D. 183, 184, 280
Eisenhardt, K. M. 104, 105, 182, 183, 185, 186, 188, 191, 192, 212, 280
Elden, M. 6, 280
Elm, P. 289
Eoyang, C. 244, 280
Ettlie, J. 212, 280
Etzioni, A. 283
Evans-Pritchard, E. E. 174, 280
Evered, R. D. 8, 59, 82, 132, 133, 148, 166, 280, 294
Everest, G. 260, 280

Farrow, D. L. 292
Fay, B. 64, 66, 70, 280
Feldman, M. 243, 244, 280
Filstead, W. 149, 166, 280
Fischer, M. M. 175, 288
Fitzgerald, G. 290
Flannery, L. S. 80, 293
Flores, F. 175, 296
Floyd, C. 291
Forester, J. 175, 281
Foucault, M. 171, 281
Franz, C. R. 56, 80, 92, 95, 99, 248, 281, 292

Frazer, J. G. 174, 281
Frisby, D. 116, 281
Frost, P. J. 175, 244, 246, 277, 279, 280, 281, 292, 294, 296
Fuchs-Kinowski, K. 288
Fulk, J. 92, 94, 95, 99, 147, 161, 163, 281

Gable, G. 101, 281
Gadamer, H-G. 10, 175, 176, 225, 243, 281, 291
Gallegos, L. 278
Galliers, R. D. 4, 5, 13, 15, 59, 137, 173, 281, 283
Gambling, T. 243, 281
Gane, C. 241, 254, 281
Garfinkel, H. 149, 281
Gash, D. C. 102, 219, 281, 291
Geertz, C. 102, 103, 149, 174, 281
George, A. 147, 182, 281
George, J. F. 147, 182, 281
Gibbons, M. T. 61, 64, 70, 280, 281
Gibson, C. F. 82, 282
Giddens, A. 62, 70, 76, 105, 107, 282
Ginzberg, E. 21, 22, 44, 56, 82, 182, 184, 271, 277, 282
Gladden, G. 241, 282
Glaser, B. 66, 105, 106, 130, 182, 183, 184, 185, 186, 188, 192, 212, 218, 272, 282
Godel, K. 77, 282
Goldkuhl, G. 242, 282
Goldstein, D. K. 6, 79, 101, 130, 165, 276, 282
Gowler, D. 243, 282
Green, T. 290
Greenbaum, J. 297
Grimes, A. J. 73, 294
Gronn, P. C. 123, 282
Groschla, E. 286
Gruber, W. 248, 295
Guba, E. G. 59, 63, 287
Gummesson, E. 139, 144, 282

Habermas, J. 73, 115, 116, 117, 118, 123, 175, 176, 243, 282, 288, 289, 295
Hamilton, S. 52, 87, 282
HansJee, R. 293
Harper, M. 278, 279, 280, 287, 292, 293, 296

Harvey, L. 9, 169
Hayes-Roth, F. 254, 282
Hedberg, B. 219, 245, 247, 248, 277, 283
Hedley, A. 248, 283
Heinen, J. S. 56, 272, 277, 278
Henderson, J. C. 56, 275
Henderson, R. M. 217, 283
Herriot, R. 147, 283
Hersen, M. 85, 147, 283
Heydebrand, W. V. 71, 73, 76, 283
Hirschheim, R. A. vii, 5, 7, 11, 15, 52, 92, 95, 96, 99, 115, 121, 131, 172, 175, 241, 242, 248, 252, 256, 271, 272, 273, 277, 281, 283, 284, 285, 286, 288, 289, 290, 291, 293
Hoare, C. A. 255, 283
Hoffman, R. 245, 277
Holgeson, K. W. 290
Holmqvist, B. 285
Holzblatt, K. 9, 173, 283
House, J. 284, 293
Huberman, A. M. 4, 147, 188, 192, 283, 289
Huff, S. L. 92, 292
Hughes, J. A. 9, 172, 173, 178, 276, 283
Hult, M. 135, 284
Hymes, D. 293

Iacono, S. 57, 92, 147, 160, 161, 163, 242, 286
Ingersoll, V. 245, 284
Isabella, L. A. 183, 284
Israel, B. 94, 132, 284
Ivancevich, J. 57, 284
Ives, B. 52, 87, 92, 99, 130, 241, 247, 253, 276, 282, 284

Jablin, F. M. 279
Jackson, M. 241, 284
Jackson, P. 254, 284
Janson, M. 92, 280
Jarvenpaa, S. L. 5, 62, 130, 284, 296
Jauch, L. R. 281
Jeffery, J. R. 280
Jenkins, A. M. 137, 165, 284
Jepsen, L. 142, 284
Jick, T. D. 96, 284
Johnson, M. 250, 252, 266, 270, 271, 286

Jones, M. 111, 284
Jönsson, S. 132, 140, 284
Jowett, S. 132, 284

Kahn, J. S. 177, 284
Kahn, W. A. 184, 185, 284
Kant, E. 118
Kaplan, A. 157, 167, 284
Kaplan, B. 67, 284
Kaplan, R. S. 81, 284
Kauber, P. 165, 285
Kauffman, R. A. 181, 276
Keen, P. G. W. 22, 44, 52, 93, 95, 99, 129, 143, 242, 247, 252, 258, 271, 285
Kemmis, S. 6, 278
Kendall, J. E. 284
Kendall, K. E. 279
Kets de Vries, M. 243, 285
Kiesler, S. 57, 294
King, J. D. 286
King, J. L. 57, 95, 182, 250, 281, 285, 286
Kirk, J. 144, 149, 166, 285
Klein, H. K. vii, 5, 6, 7, 8, 10, 52, 115, 116, 121, 130, 165, 256, 272, 276, 277, 278, 279, 283, 284, 285, 288, 290, 294
Kling, R. 20, 22, 23, 44, 45, 48, 57, 92, 147, 160, 161, 163, 242, 279, 285, 286
Knight, K. 286
Knights, D. 294
Kolf, F. 272, 286
Kolm, P. 288
Kraemer, K. L. 57, 92, 95, 147, 161, 163, 250, 279, 286
Kraut, R. 172, 295
Kriebel, C. 283
Kuhn, T. S. 62, 148, 151, 286
Kumar, K. 246, 286, 288
Kuper, A. 173, 286
Kyng, M. 289, 297

Lakatos, I. 148, 286
Lakoff, G. 250, 252, 266, 270, 271, 286
Land, F. 4, 13, 59, 94, 137, 242, 253, 278, 281, 286
Landry, M. 52, 129, 137, 276
Lanzara, G. F. 243, 273, 286
Larkey, P. 281

Lau, F. 276
Laudon, K. C. 45, 57, 147, 161, 163, 286
Lawler, E. 46, 286
Lawrence, P. R. 278, 292, 295, 297
Layder, D. 106, 111, 286
Learmonth, G. P. 241, 253, 284
Lee, A. S. vii, 5, 7, 8, 11, 67, 101, 104, 147, 148, 149, 157, 167, 172, 175, 286, 287, 290
Legge, K. 243, 282
Lehman, E. 283
Lehtinen, E. 250, 288
Lenat, D. 282
Lennung, S-Å. 135, 284
Leonard-Barton, D. A. 147, 161, 163, 166, 182, 188, 254, 287
Lewin, K. 93, 131, 132, 271, 287
Lewis, I. M. 9, 287
Liebenau, J. vii, 5, 287
Lincoln, Y. S. 4, 59, 63, 279, 287
Lippit, G. 132, 287
Lippit, R. 132, 287
Louis, K. 147, 149, 287
Louis, M. R. 59, 166, 280, 281
Lucas, H. C. Jr. 19, 56, 184, 241, 287
Luckman, T. 175, 276
Lukka, K. 132, 287
Lundberg, C. C. 281
Luthans, F. 147, 166, 287, 289
Lyotard, J-F. 169, 287
Lyytinen, K. 52, 116, 121, 241, 242, 250, 279, 282, 285, 287, 288

Madsen, K. H. 253, 288
Maggi, L. 286
Malone, T. W. 57, 288
Mann, R. I. 92, 94, 288
March, J. 35, 40, 243, 280
Marcus, G. E. 174, 175, 279, 288
Marcuse, H. 116, 117, 288
Markus, M. L. 5, 8, 19, 23, 26, 41, 56, 63, 88, 90, 92, 93, 99, 101, 147, 152, 153, 154, 155, 156, 157, 158, 160, 161, 163, 165, 182, 184, 216, 242, 243, 247, 249, 258, 259, 270, 279, 288, 292
Martin, J. 9, 183, 184, 185, 205, 217, 241, 242, 281, 288, 289
Martin, P. Y. 9, 183, 184, 185, 205, 217, 241, 242, 281, 288, 289

Mason, R. 273, 288
Mathiassen, L. 273, 284, 286, 288, 289
McCarthy, T. 61, 73, 289
McComb, D. 295
McCubbrey, D. 295
McEiroy, D. 290
McFarlan, F. W. 13, 115, 241, 276, 289, 296
McGarry, F. E. 278
McKeown, T. 147, 281
McLean, E. R. 285
McMenamin, S. 250, 289
Mead, M. 6, 79, 276
Mechanic, D. 46, 289
Meyerson, D. 217, 289
Miles, M. B. 4, 147, 150, 188, 192, 289
Millar, V. E. 241, 292
Miller, D. 243, 285
Miller, M. L. 144, 149, 285
Miller, R. 293
Milne, R. 231, 236, 238, 289
Mingers, J. C. 5, 103, 115, 289
Mintzberg, H. 47, 289
Mitroff, I. L. 244, 273, 288, 289
Moch, M. 217, 276
Moeller, G. 293
Mohr, L. B. 184, 289
Moore, L. F. 281
Morey, N. C. 166, 289
Morgan, G. 11, 51, 59, 63, 64, 70, 77, 126, 148, 166, 243, 244, 245, 250, 266, 271, 278, 283, 289, 292, 294
Mowshowitz, A. 241, 254, 289
Mumford, E. vii, 5, 13, 15, 52, 56, 63, 82, 96, 106, 107, 115, 242, 246, 247, 248, 249, 255, 272, 277, 281, 283, 284, 285, 288, 289, 290, 291
Myers, M. D. vii, viii, 3, 4, 6, 8, 9, 11, 169, 175, 176, 276, 285, 290

Nagel, E. 156, 290
Nandhakumar, J. 107, 111, 284, 290
Napier, A. 284
Naumann, J. D. 165, 290
Naur, P. 142, 290
Necco, C. 181, 290
Newman, M. 11, 172, 175, 241, 242, 246, 248, 255, 258, 266, 271, 283, 290
Ngwenyama, O. K. 7, 115, 121, 290
Nielsen, P. A. 276, 284

Nielsen, S. 9, 173, 279
Nissen, H-E. vii, 5, 276, 277, 278, 279, 284, 285, 290, 294
Nivat, M. 291
Noble, D. F. 23, 46, 290
Norman, R. 181, 290
Normann, R. 213, 291
Nunamaker, J. F. 181, 290
Nystrom, P. 277, 283

Olle, T. W. 294
Ollman, B. 71, 291
Olson, M. H. 57, 63, 91, 94, 96, 99, 130, 247, 276, 284, 291
Oppelland, H. 272, 286
Opperman, R. 247, 291
Orlikowski, W. J. 5, 6, 8, 9, 51, 68, 69, 101, 102, 104, 105, 109, 111, 129, 130, 139, 171, 172, 173, 177, 178, 181, 182, 184, 186, 192, 194, 219, 276, 281, 291, 297
Ortony, A. 244, 291, 293

Pacanowsky, M. E. 292
Page, G. T. 278, 286
Palmer, J. 250, 289
Palmer, R. 11, 291
Pamas, D. 250, 291
Parsons, G. L. 96, 241, 253, 291
Pava, C. 272, 291
Pearce, J. 286
Pederson, P. H. 57, 277
Pennings, J. 212, 291
Pepper, S. C. 226, 227, 228, 236, 291
Pettigrew, A. M. 45, 104, 105, 173, 184, 185, 186, 188, 216, 275, 291, 292
Pfeffer, J. 23, 44, 45, 47, 48, 51, 288, 292
Piercy, N. 286
Podsakoff, P. M. 76, 292
Polkinghorne, D. E. 11, 292
Pondy, L. R. 237, 243, 244, 246, 250, 277, 279, 280, 292, 294, 296
Poole, M. S. 57, 182, 280, 292
Popper, K. 117, 131, 148, 151, 152, 153, 155, 281, 292
Porter, M. E. 241, 292
Preston, A. M. 9, 173, 292
Primps, S. B. 57, 291
Putnam, L. L. 60, 63, 65, 292

Putnam, R. 122, 142, 275
Pyburn, P. 89, 90, 91, 92, 94, 99, 292

Rabinow, P. 295
Radnitzky, G. 10, 175, 176, 292
Raisinghard, D. 47, 289
Randall, D. 9, 178, 276, 283
Rapoport, R. N. 7, 132, 139, 140, 292
Raspa, R. 252, 292
Reilley, E. 271, 282
Rhode, I. G. 46, 286
Ricoeur, P. 10, 175, 176, 226, 229, 230, 236, 237, 292, 295
Rivard, S. 92, 292
Robey, D. 31, 56, 63, 80, 92, 94, 95, 99, 104, 105, 111, 172, 173, 182, 184, 192, 194, 216, 242, 243, 247, 248, 256, 272, 273, 281, 288, 290, 291, 292, 293
Robinson, R. 286
Rockart, J. F. 80, 293
Rodden, T. 276
Roethlisberger, F. J. 80, 293
Rogers, E. M. 182, 293
Rogers, W. 254, 293
Romanelli, E. 212, 220, 295
Rorty, R. 226, 228, 229, 236, 293
Rose, M. 248, 293
Rosen, M. 65, 165, 293
Rosenau, P. 130, 131, 293
Rosenberg, D. 242, 248, 258, 266, 290
Ross, C. 277, 282
Rowan, J. 63, 66, 293
Rubin, H. 4, 293
Rubin, I. 4, 293
Rule, J. 57, 275
Ryack, B. 293

Saaksjarvi, M. 285
Sackman, H. 283
Sanday, P. R. 149, 174, 293
Sanford, N. 132, 293
Sarson, T. 241, 254, 281
Saunders, C. S. 57, 293
Sawyer, P. 276
Scacchi, W. 57, 147, 161, 163, 242, 286
Scamell, R. W. 57, 293
Scarrott, G. 255, 293
Schafer, G. 273, 293
Schein, E. 93, 129, 132, 293

Schneider, L. 286
Scholes, J. 129, 278
Scholte, B. 177, 293
Schön, D. A. 124, 135, 148, 236, 275, 293
Schonberger, R. J. 92, 93, 94, 294
Schultz, R. L. 282
Schurman, S. 284
Schwartz, R. 296
Scott Morton, M. 82, 294
Seashore, S. 140, 294
Sechrest, L. 296
Segev, E. 93, 280
Shallis, M. 255, 294
Shapiro, D. 276, 283
Sibley, E. 242, 294
Silverman, D. 4, 294
Sjostrand, S. 243, 296
Slavens, T. P. 148, 295
Slevin, D. P. 282
Smircich, L. 59, 102, 244, 245, 246, 274, 289, 294
Smith, C. 286
Smith, D. 275
Smith, J. 295
Smith, S. 73, 74, 75, 294
Sol, H. 294
Sommerville, I. 276
Sproull, L. 57, 281, 294
Stamper, R. 255, 294
Stanley, J. C. 152, 278
Starbuck, W. H. 52, 277, 283, 296
Staw, B. M. 244, 276, 294, 295
Steffy, B. D. 73, 294
Stevenson, H. 254, 294
Stone, E. F. 81, 294
Stowell, F. 5, 289
Straub, D. 139, 294
Strauss, A. 66, 105, 106, 130, 182, 183, 184, 185, 186, 188, 192, 212, 218, 272, 282, 294
Strauss, G. 46, 294
Suchman, L. 9, 101, 104, 111, 112, 173, 178, 294
Sullivan, W. 295
Susman, G. I. 8, 82, 132, 133, 134, 135, 148, 294
Sviokla, J. S. 96, 254, 287, 295
Swanson, E. B. 52, 279
Swanson, K. 181, 295
Synnott, W. 248, 295

Szyperski, N. 286

Taggart, W. 31, 293
Taylor, C. 10, 149, 175, 176, 295
Thatcher, J. 291
Thebaud, J.-L. 169, 287
Theoret, A. 289
Thompson, J. B. 11, 176, 295
Tice, T. N. 148, 295
Tierney, S. 286
Tinker, T. 245, 295
Todd, P. 97, 295
Towl, A. R. 83, 295
Tractinsky, N. 296
Treacy, M. E. 97, 276
Trice, H. 243, 246, 254, 295
Trist, E. 131, 295
Truex III, D. P. 10, 285
Tsai, N. W. 290
Turner, B. A. 9, 183, 184, 244, 275, 288
Turner, J. A. 57, 172, 295
Tushman, M. L. 212, 219, 295

Van de Ven, A. 51, 275
Van Eynde, D. 129, 295
Van Maanen, J. 68, 79, 102, 109, 149, 166, 174, 179, 244, 295
Vattimo, G. 175, 296
Verrijn-Stuart, A. A. 285, 294
Vessey, L. 181, 296
Vitalari, N. 246, 296
Vogel, D. 13, 14, 15, 87, 296
Von Schelling, W. J. 125, 296

Waema, T. 8, 111, 296
Wall, J. L. 281
Walsham, G. 6, 7, 8, 101, 104, 105, 111, 172, 179, 296
Wand, Y. 165, 296
Warmington, A. 132, 136, 296

Waterman, D. 282
Watson, H. J. 92, 94, 288
Webb, C. 132, 296
Webb, E. 86, 296
Weber, M. 62, 296
Weber, R. 52, 165, 245, 279, 296
Webster, J. 52, 296
Weick, K. E. 59, 63, 66, 68, 80, 256, 271, 296
Weinberg, V. 241, 296
Weir, M. 56, 290
Weiss, M. 57, 296
Weizenbaum, J. 254, 296
Welke, R. J. 52, 246, 278, 285, 286
Westerlund, G. 243, 296
Wetherbe, J. C. 13, 14, 15, 87, 278, 284, 296
Wexler, M. 244, 296
White, K. B. 92, 93, 99, 296
Whitehead, A. N. 244, 296
Wiginton, J. C. 67, 279
Willmott, H. 281, 294
Winograd, T. 175, 296
Wiseman, C. 253, 296
Wood-Harper, A. T. 8, 129, 137, 290, 297
Woodward, J. 283
Wynn, E. 9, 123, 173, 178, 294, 297

Yates, J. 173, 288, 297
Yellen, R. 181, 297
Yin, R. 5, 8, 81, 83, 84, 85, 86, 94, 95, 97, 101, 108, 110, 147, 149, 166, 179, 182, 188, 192, 297
Young, S. 250, 297
Yourdon, E. 185, 195, 241, 254, 279, 289, 297

Zuboff, S. 9, 57, 101, 102, 104, 109, 110, 111, 112, 173, 176, 178, 285, 297

Subject Index

Action learning, 123
Action research, 4, 6, 7, 8, 15, 81, 82, 87, 96, 107, 108, **129ff**, 278, 280, 284, **292ff**
Action science, **121ff**
Administrative science, 51, 79
Agriculture, 3
Anthropology, 9, 51, 102, **173ff**, 177, 243, 273, 279, 281, 282, **286ff**, 293
Architecture, 175, 190, 191, **204ff**
Argumentative, 15
Artificial intelligence, 112
Assumptions, **5ff**, 19, 20, 22, **24ff**, 33, 34, **51ff** 87, 105, **115ff**, 120, 122, 125, 130, 134, 135, 142, 178, 216, 241, 288, 291, 296
Astronomy, 156
Attitudes, 41, 61, 242, 245, 272, 273, 276, 284
Axial coding, 188

Behavioral, 286
Behavioural, 13, 35, 118, 124, 211, 286
Beliefs, 22, 24, 52, **57ff**, 61, 64, 66, 67, 70, 73, 135, 170, 174, 228, 229, 242, 244, 245, 253, 254, 272, 273
Bias, 15, 76, 77, 90, 95, 183, 276
Biology, 156, 157
Business, 3, 15, 39, 41, 68, 79, 85, **89ff**, 105, 111, 177, 185, **189ff**, 260

Case study, **4ff**, 25, 26, **80ff**, **101ff**, 130, 138, **147ff**, 179, 212, 245, 249, 253, 255, 257, 268, **278ff**, 284, 286, 290, 292, 296, 297
Causality, 65, 137, 184, 277
Change, *vii*, 7, **19ff**, 62, 65, **68ff**, **80ff**, 92, 93, 105, 117, 121, 122, 125, **132ff**, 154, 156, 169, **181ff**, 198, 199, **206ff**, 244, **248ff**, **257ff**, 276, 278, **281ff**
Citation analysis, 52, 279
Class politics, 24
Coding, 185, 186, 188, 201, 204
Cognitive maps, 124
Communication, 3, 11, 21, 23, 57, 71, 99, 112, 118, 244, 262, 270, 279, 287, 288, 294, 297
Complexity, 13, 15, 67, 79, 81, 82, 86, 90, 93, 172, 191, 201, 231, 238, 280
Computer science, 3, 131, 196, 203
Computer-aided software engineering (CASE), 68, 69, 105, **181ff**, 276, 291, 296
Confidentiality, 85, 106
Conflict, 25, 26, **60ff**, 65, 69, 70, 72, 74, 95, 143, 171, 206, 234, 243, 247, 248, 253, 256, 257, **263ff**, **270ff**, 292
Consensus, 148, 170, 236, 258, 272
Consistency, 19, 124, 144, 151, 152, 155, 160, 162, 198, 210
Constructionist, 66, 67
Consulting, 68, 132, 139, 141, 142, 144, 185, 186, 195, 287
Content analysis, 188
Context, 6, **8ff**, 21, 25, 26, **32ff**, 47, 59, 63, **69ff**, 80, 81, 84, 89, 92, 94, 97, 104, 105, 119, 123, 124, 129, 136, 140, 142, 144, 153, 155, 166, **171ff**, 179, **181ff**, 193, 194, 201, 212, 214, 216, 218, 220, 229, 232, 234, 236, 237, 242, 251, 252, 255, 265, 294, 297
Contingent, 19, 71, 89, 136, 229
Contradiction, 7, 56, 60, 65, **70ff**, 75, 246, **265ff**, 282, 283

Control, 21, 23, 36, 37, 44, 45, **59ff**, 63, 74, 76, 81, 83, 97, 118, 119, 130, 149, 155, 156, 164, 170, 178, 184, 185, 195, 196, 234, 245, **247ff**, **251ff**, 261, 267, 276, 279, 283, 286, 288, **290ff**

Critical, 5, 7, 8, 11, 24, 34, 55, 56, 59, 62, 64, 65, **70ff**, 80, 81, 83, 84, 86, 90, 93, 95, 98, 109, 110, **115ff**, 125, 130, **142ff**, 149, 169, 171, **173ff**, 180, 182, 201, 202, 220, 244, 245, 255, 278, 283, 285, **287ff**, 293, 294

Culture, 22, 26, 63, 69, 174, 175, 177, 185, 186, 189, 195, 202, 208, 217, 220, 244, 248, 253, 275, 279, 281, 292, 294

Cybernetics, 118

Data analysis, 9, 61, 86, 109, 123, 124, 142, 186, 192, 289

Data collection, 4, 7, 9, 53, 59, 61, 66, 72, 81, 82, 86, **88ff**, **95ff**, 104, 105, 123, 124, 132, 139, 142, 145, 170, 186, 188, 192

Data entry, 31, 34, 35, 260, 263, 265

Database, 28, 29, 31, 36, 81, 95, 155, 164, 170, 196, 201, 219, 248, 249, 260, 261

Decision support systems, 48, 97, 172, 285

Deconstruction, 130

Deductions, 65, 150, 152, 157

Determinate, 63, 227

Deterministic, 55, 63, 67, 76, 215, 216

Dialectic, 10, 118, 120, 125, **175ff**, 226, 228, 230, 236

Diaries, 139, 142, 290

Discipline, 3, 8, 9, 15, 52, 58, 115, 116, 129, 139, 144, 169, 170, 171, 174, 198, 248, 285, 289, 296

Distanciation, 230

Doctoral program, 77

Documentation, 68, 86, **186ff**, 192, 259, 279

Double hermeneutic, 107

Double loop learning, 122

Econometrics, 4

Economics, 58

Education, 3, 8, 51, 64, 165, 175, 182, 198

Electronic commerce, 3

Emancipatory, 7, 73, 118, 120, 283

Emergence, 192, 285

Empirical, 5, 8, 9, 13, 14, 16, 24, 53, **58ff**, 68, 69, 73, 101, 102, 105, 106, 110, 111, 119, 122, 130, 131, 139, 140, 142, 151, 152, 156, 158, 160, 161, 164, **181ff**, 216, 217, 220, 231, 243, 246, 268, 272, 276, 278, 280, 282, 284, 285, 287, 288, 290, 291

Empirical observations, 9, 184

EndNote, 4

Engineering, 3, 44, 68, 119, 131, 181, 185, 190, 196, 203, 205, 253, 266, 276, 278, 286, 288

Epistemology, 5, 53, 55, 56, 103, 165, 228, 283

Ethics, 140, 141

ETHICS, 140, 141, 272, 273, 283, 289, 290

Ethnocentrism, 174

Ethnography, 4, 7, 9, 102, 169, 171, **173ff**, **177ff**, 279, 281, 283, 293, 295

Evaluation, 6, 8, 22, 25, 42, 76, 79, 92, 132, 135, 139, 225, 231

Executive information systems, 290

Experiment, 14, 16, 54, 83, 91, 96, 98, 142, **157ff**, 231, 236, 238, 247

Expert system, 96, 254, 282, 284, 287, 290, 295

Explanations, 9, 10, **19ff**, 41, 62, 63, 65, 91, 93, 110, 139, 160, 175, 192, 209, 241, 246, 261

Exploration, 51, **82ff**, 93, 96, 105, 176, 296

Falsifiability, 122, 131, 151, 152, 155, **160ff**

FAOR, 273

Field notes, 68, 69, 74

Fieldwork, 4, 109, 125, 173, 174, 293

Formal methods, 4

Frameworks, 97, 165, 169, 177, 179, 216, 290

Functionalism, 292

Future research, 15, 135, 167, 183, 225

Gender, 75

Generalisation, 72, **110ff**, 143, 144, 182, 217

Geology, 156
Goals, 7, 23, 24, 26, 47, 80, 86, 93, 101, 116, 136, 140, 144, 184, 200, 201, 208, 231, 239, 244, 248, 263
Goodness of fit, 93
Grounded theory, 7, 9, 10, **104ff**, 130, **181ff**, 188, 191, 212, 216, 220, 282, 295

Health, 132, 284
Hermeneutic circle, 10, 175
Hermeneutics, 10, 11, 104, 173, **175ff**, 180, 226, 229, 277, 281, 290, 292, 295
Heuristics, 20, 44
Historical studies, 72
Historiography, 177
Human factors, 21, 26, 30, 31, 33, 35, 37, 42
Hypothesis, 6, 31, 61, 82, 83, 92, 93, 96, 134, 227, 228, 236

Ideal types, 5, 124
Ideals, 59
Ideology, 69, 117
Idiographic, 80, 140, 143, 145, 150, 166, 287
Impact, *viii*, 3, 8, 13, 23, 40, 46, 61, 62, 74, 88, 92, **94ff**, 163, 164, 208, 218, 276, 277, 279, 285, 294
Impartiality, 139, 144
Implementation, 5, 13, **19ff**, 24, 26, 34, 37, **40ff**, 47, 56, 75, 82, 88, 89, **92ff**, 99, 105, 132, 152, 153, 155, 161, 163, 178, 181, 182, 184, 186, 187, 198, 206, 215, 216, 218, 220, 252, 258, 276, 282, 283, **285ff**, 290, 296
Independence, 62, 66, 175
Inferences, 6, 55, 124
Informate, 102, 110, 111, 112
Information, *vii*, 3, 6, 8, 9, 11, 13, 14, **19ff**, **29ff**, 33, 36, 39, 40, 43, **44ff**, **51ff**, **56ff**, 64, **68ff**, 73, 74, 76, **79ff**, **90ff**, 96, 97, 101, 103, 105, 107, **110ff**, 115, 116, 118, 120, 125, 129, 136, 147, **152ff**, 158, 164, 165, **170ff**, 177, 178, **180ff**, **184ff**, 189, 190, 192, **194ff**, 199, **201ff**, 213, 217, 220, **225ff**, 230, 231, **236ff**, 241, 242, 243, 247, 249, **251ff**, **255ff**, 260, **264ff**, **275ff**, 296, 297

Information Engineering, 185, 205
Information systems, *vii*, 3, 8, 9, 11, 13, **19ff**, 31, **44ff**, **51ff**, 56, 59, 62, 64, 70, 76, 79, 80, 81, 101, 111, 112, 115, 116, 118, 120, 125, 129, 147, 153, 165, **170ff**, 177, 178, 180, 181, 185, 190, 195, 196, 197, 199, **202ff**, 206, 213, 220, 225, 226, 230, 237, 238, **241ff**, 247, 251, 253, 255, 256, **264ff**, 269, 270, **275ff**, 296, 297
Information systems development, 11, 115, 177, 179, 241, 243, 253, 255, 256, 265, 267, 269, 279, **283ff**, 290
Information technology, 3, 9, 11, 51, 56, 60, 61, 63, 68, 69, 71, 73, 74, 96, 97, 105, 110, 111, 173, 178, 182, 184, 189, 201, 202, 204, 241, 242, 279, 281, 288, 291, 293
Innovation, 80, 89, 182, 183, 212, 217, 248, 280, 283, 287, 293
Institutions, 3, 13, 71, 75, 77, 130, 144, 174, 175, 179
Intentions, 23, 24, 25, 39, 46, 55, 58, 59, 61, 64, 69, 70, 181, 182, 190, 192, 193, 196, 197, 203, 204, 212, **216ff**, 220, 237, 276
Interactionist, 182
International Conference on Information Systems, 275, 277, 278, 282, 283, 288, **290ff**
Internet, *vii*, 3
Inter-organisational systems, 3
Interpretive, 5, 6, 8, 11, 15, 16, 55, 59, 62, **64ff**, 72, **75ff**, **101ff**, **108ff**, 122, 131, 141, 142, 172, 176, 179, 184, 225, 231, 233, 236, 276, 281, 285, 287, 290, 292
Intervention, 23, 82, 92, 119, 120, 122, 134, 135, 137, 138, 142, 143
Interviews, *vii*, 4, 26, 38, 68, 74, 86, 88, 90, 91, 95, 108, 109, 124, 142, 152, 187, 188, 192, 255
Iterations, 142, 143

Job satisfaction, 57, 61

Knowledge, *vii*, 5, 8, 13, 14, **58ff**, 72, 76, 77, **80ff**, 88, 93, 95, 96, 98, **103ff**, 115, **117ff**, 122, 124, 125, 130, 132, 133, 135, 136, 139, 140, 143, 145, 166, **169ff**, 178, 180, 183,

186, 190, **196ff**, 200, 203, 213, 215, 219, 220, 228, 229, 233, 235, 242, 250, 251, 253, 254, 258, 269, 276, 278, 281, 286, 287, 290

Laboratory, 4, 14, 15, 53, 56, 59, 81, 137, 149, 152, 156, 158, 159, 284
Language, 6, 11, 61, 65, 67, 72, 104, 115, 171, 174, 184, 211, 229, 242, 250, 282, 287, 296
Logic, 20, 59, 110, **122ff**, 142, 151, 155, 157, 159, 167, 246, 279, 292
Logical positivist, 148

Magic, 241, 243, 245, 246, **253ff**, **267ff**, 273, 274, 279, 280, 283
Management, 3, 9, 19, 20, 26, 28, 31, 32, 38, 39, 43, 44, 46, 48, 53, 54, 62, 74, 75, 80, 81, 90, 96, 118, 132, 142, **147ff**, 165, 173, 183, 196, 201, 208, 209, 218, 219, 232, 242, 243, 245, 247, 248, 253, 255, 259, 264, 265, 274, 275, 277, **279ff**, 284, 288, 292, 293, 295, 297
Management Science, 275, 282
Manufacturing, 3, 26, 32, 44, 88, 111, 186
Marketing, 32, 64, 85, 119, 202, 277
MARS, 273
Mathematics, 131, 157, 159
Meaning, 10, 11, 64, 66, 67, 71, 119, 122, 147, 152, 161, **173ff**, 179, 225, 229, 230, 231, 233, 234, **235ff**, **242ff**, 251, 252, 278, 282, 290, 292, 296
Measurement, 14, 60, 61, 81, 97, 130, 142, 199
Medicine, 3, 11, 175
Memoranda, 86, 95
Mental models, 19, 20, 245, 271
Metaphor, 10, 11, 57, 105, 161, 163, 164, 226, 228, 229, 233, 234, 236, 237, 241, 243, 245, **250ff**, 255, **265ff**, 269, **271ff**, 283, 293
Metaphysics, 226, 227
Modeling, 286
Modes of analysis, 9, 10, 235
Motivation, 36, 105, 231, 232
Multivariate, 79, 131, 137, 138, 140, 143, 149

Myth, 241, 243, **245ff**, 249, 250, **254ff**, 261, 262, 265, 269, 273, 279, 284

Narrative, 10, 11, 124, 246
Natural science, 4, 13, 15, 57, 62, 110, 130, 144, **148ff**, 155, 156, 158, 159, 166, 167, 276
Natural setting, 25, 55, **81ff**, 88, 152
Nomothetic, 80, 131, 150, 166
Normative, 97, 122, 124, 241, 264

Object of study, 10, 165, 175
Objectives, 24, 25, 42, 43, 47, 65, 79, 82, 83, 87, 89, 90, **92ff**, 97, 130, 135, 159, 169, 207, 283
Objectivity, 62, 82, 95, 150, 176
Ontology, 103
Open coding, 188
Operations research, 42, 166, 282
Opportunism, 191
Organisation, *viii*, 4, 8, 10, 11, 13, 23, 24, 32, 38, 44, 46, 60, 69, 72, 73, 80, 82, 83, 85, 88, **90ff**, 102, 103, 107, 116, **133ff**, 141, 148, 152, 156, 158, 164, 178, 179, 181, 183, 184, 188, 190, 191, 204, 207, 208, 215, 217, 218, 220, 235, 247, 248, 250, 254, 255, 257, 261, 265, 266, 270, 275, 276, 278, 279, 283, 285, 286, 289, **292ff**
Organisation studies, 278, 295
Organisational learning, 44, 48
Organisational politics, 32, 164, 250
Organisational structure, 32, 41, 60, 64, 85, 119
Organisational theory, 11, 118, 243

Paradigms, 5, 93, 115, 131, 165, 278, 283, 296
Participant, *vii*, 4, 69, 82, 107, 108, 120, 124, 136, 142, 278
Participant observation, *vii*, 4, 69, 107, 108, 120, 124, 278
Participation, 30, 41, 42, 63, 64, 85, 88, 91, 119, **121ff**, 272, 291
Phenomenology, 15, 104, 277
Philosophy, *viii*, **4ff**, 10, 46, 51, 52, 57, **59ff**, **67ff**, 73, **75ff**, 101, 102, 104, 112, 118, 121, 125, 130, 131, 139, 141, 144, 148, 228, 263, 277, 295

Physics, 131, 155
Political science, 64
Politics, 5, 24, 32, 35, 44, 47, 63, 161, 163, 164, 182, 249, 250, 255, **262ff**, 270, **278ff**, 286, 288, 290, 295
PORGI, 272
Positivist, 5, 6, 8, 55, 56, **58ff**, **64ff**, 70, 72, **75ff**, **101ff**, 105, 116, **129ff**, 141, 143, 144, 172, 184, 287
Post positivist, **129ff**, 144
Power, 5, **21ff**, 26, 32, **36ff**, 40, **43ff**, 57, 70, 88, 93, 116, 117, 130, 152, 153, 160, 162, 164, 165, 191, 236, 244, 248, 249, 251, 254, 255, 258, 263, 273, 276, 277, 287, 289, 292, 293
Practice, 5, 11, 14, 46, **57ff**, 61, 62, 65, 66, 72, 73, 77, 80, 81, 112, **115ff**, **120ff**, 129, 133, **135ff**, 145, 150, 154, 157, **169ff**, 173, **180ff**, 195, 197, 206, 211, 213, 216, 218, 220, 226, 229, **241ff**, 247, 256, 274, 275, 278, 282, 283, 290, 292, 294, 295, 297
Practices, 7, 56, 61, 63, 65, **69ff**, 90, 120, **170ff**, 177, 178, 190, 193, 195, 197, 198, **203ff**, 207, 209, **211ff**, 219, 220, 229, 246, 253, 271, 273, 279
Practitioners, 13, 19, 80, 81, 123, 130, **133ff**, 165, 166, **169ff**, 177, 178, 180, 181, 183, 218, 220, 271
Pragmatic, 135
Private, 3, 65, 72, 85, 167, 255, 258
Probability, 106, 116, 148
Professionalism, 132
Protocol analysis, 53, 97
Psychology, 51, 64, 131, 132, 144, 278, 294, 296
Public, 3, 36, 39, 85, 92, 94, 95, 99, 117, **122ff**, 132, 141, 167, 255, 283, 293

Qualitative, *vii*, *viii*, **3ff**, 12, **79ff**, 83, 96, 132, 144, 150, 157, 165, 166, **171ff**, **231ff**, 235, **237ff**, 282, 284, 285, 287, 289, 294, 295
Quantitative, **3ff**, 9, 79, 94, 96, 97, 132, 150, 165, 166, 172, 173, 182, 232, 233, 235, 237, 284
Questionnaires, 4, 79, 91, 95, 278

Race, 75
Rational, 60, 136, 137, 241, 243, 247, 250, 253, 273, 275, 291
Reality, 6, 7, 33, 58, 60, **62ff**, 65, 66, 70, 71, 73, 75, 103, 104, 116, 119, 135, 140, 170, 173, 228, 229, 237, 241, 245, 250, 254, 264, 265, 271, 276
Reasoning, 87, 91, 92, 151
Reflexive, 62, 73, 76, 117, 177, 293
Relevance, 14, 101, 115, 129, 138, 139, 143, 165, 166, 173, 180, 185, 294
Repeatability, 143
Replicability, 62, 150, 152, 157, 162
Reporting, 27, 30, 31, 38, 40, 41, 68, **106ff**, 112, 230, 263
Requisite variety, 67
Research method, *vii*, *viii*, **3ff**, **7ff**, 15, 17, 51, 53, 58, 61, 65, 67, 72, 79, 96, 97, **129ff**, 133, **135ff**, 141, 144, 148, 165, 169, **171ff**, **177ff**, 183, 188, 220, 225, 256, 276, 278, 281, 296
Research plan, 95, 97
Research techniques, 63
Resistance, **19ff**, **30ff**, **37ff**, 92, **152ff**, 158, 161, 163, 164, 181, 191, 208, 220, 247, **257ff**, 269, 271, 272, 283
Results, **13ff**, 22, 39, 43, 51, 62, 69, 79, 82, **84ff**, **89ff**, 102, 105, **108ff**, 112, 125, 139, 144, 156, 164, 179, 182, 184, 192, 208, 216, 233, 239, 253, 282
Rigour, 62, 133, 139, 140, 141, 143, 144, 160, 161, 162, 166, 180, 210, 285
Rituals, 244, 245, 246, 253, 254, 267, 268, 270, 271, 274
Role playing, 15, 16
Roles, 21, 70, 71, 107, 129

Sample, 6, **53ff**, 58, 79, 80, 87, **91ff**, 97, 99, 182
Science, 3, 7, 8, 14, 15, 51, **57ff**, 61, 62, 64, 73, 111, **115ff**, **120ff**, 125, **130ff**, **139ff**, 144, 145, **147ff**, 155, **157ff**, 166, 173, 175, 196, 203, 226, 229, 255, **275ff**, 280, 282, 283, 285, 287, 289, 290, 294, 295
Scientific method, 8, 117, 118, 132, 133, 140, 147, 149, 150, 152, 153, 155, 156, 159, 160, 165, 166, 253

Self reflection, 52, 73, 77, 122
Semiotics, 10, 285
Shared meanings, 6, 70, 246, 294
Simulation, 15
Site selection, 82, 84, 85, 89, 90, 93, 94, 292
Social context, 21, 32, 63, 119, 172, 181, 182, 216, 220, 294
Social reality, 7, 58, 60, **62ff, 69ff**, 73, 75, 119, 170
Social science, 4, 7, 8, 11, 15, 52, **57ff**, 62, 64, 110, 111, **116ff, 130ff**, 133, **139ff**, 144, 145, 148, 151, 173, 225, 226, 280, 287, 293, 295, 296
Social systems, 56, 65, 70, 132, 135, 289
Socialisation, 64, 75, 245
Socially constructed, 6, 65, 117, 173, 175, 275
Sociology, 51, 64, 175, 243, 276, 277, 281, 282, 295
Socio-technical, 21, 82, 175, 272, 277, 278
Soft systems methodology, 15, 104, 129, 132, 289
Stakeholders, 11, 169, 178
Statistical analysis, 14
Stochastic, 67
Structural, 38, 56, 68, 70, 72, 76, 133, 198, 205, 206, 220, 280
Structural contradiction, 56, 76
Structuration theory, 105, 280
Structured systems analysis, 42
Subjective, 15, 55, 58, 61, 64, 65, 67, 91, 95, 103, 104, 119, 120, 166, 237, 245
Surveys, 14, 53, 58, 61
Symbolism, 11, 22, 153, **241ff**, 250, 255, 269, 270, **272ff**, 275, 292, 294, 295
System designers, 23, 24, 41, 200
System purpose, 23
Systems analysts, 19, 20, 42, 43, 177, 248, 249, 290, 297
Systems theory, 115, 132

Tape recordings, 95, 108
Technical aspects, 130
Technological frames, 102
Testing, 6, 55, 68, 74, 80, 83, 84, 92, 93, 96, 122, 123, 124, 140, 149, 151, 153, 154, 155, 159, 160, 161, 164, 165, 181, 185, 187
Textual analysis, 10
Theorem, 77
Theory, 6, 7, **9ff, 21ff**, 25, 26, **31ff**, 37, 38, **40ff**, 47, **55ff**, 61, 66, 67, 72, 73, 76, 80, 83, 84, **91ff**, 102, **104ff**, **109ff, 115ff, 130ff, 135ff, 139ff**, 148, **151ff**, 175, 179, **181ff**, 188, 192, 212, 216, 220, 226, 227, 231, 243, **275ff**, 280, 282, 283, 285, **287ff, 294ff**
Theory-in-use, 124
Thick description, 102, 174
Training, 24, 26, 41, 42, 138, 140, 181, 186, 196, 198, 199, 203, 205, 206, 219, 231, 238, 245
Triangulation, 67, 86, 88, 90, 95, 97, 99, 140, 186

Uncertainty, 44, 47, 244, 271, 273
Users, 19, 22, 23, 25, 26, 30, 31, 41, 42, 46, 47, 57, 63, 91, 95, 103, 152, 153, 169, 177, **186ff**, 194, **198ff**, 203, 204, 206, **208ff**, 215, 220, 225, 230, 236, **247ff**, 252, 254, 256, **257ff, 261ff**, 267, 268, **270ff**, 286, 288

Validation, 88, 217
Values, 14, 23, 24, 47, 52, 59, 66, 67, 103, 104, 122, 174, 237, 244, 248, 250, 251, 286
Variables, 6, 14, 55, 62, 81, 82, 94, 97, 124, 149, 156, 163, 164, 173, 184, 244, 276
Voices, 226, 230

Web model, 165

Printed in the United States
1284100001B/153-154